Encyclopaedia of Art, Archaeology and Literature in Central India

Encyclopaedia of Art, Archaeology and Literature in Central India

R.K. SHARMA

Vol. II

Aryan Books International
New Delhi

Encyclopaedia of Art, Archaeology and Literature in Central India

ISBN: 978-81-7305-126-5 (Vol. II)
978-81-7305-127-2 (Set)

First Published: 1998

Reprinted: **2026**

Published by:
Aryan Books International
Pooja Apartments, 4B, Ansari Road
New Delhi - 110 002 (INDIA)
Tel: 011- 23255799/41099562
Email: aryanbooks@gmail.com
www.aryanbooks.com

Printed in India

Contents

List of Illustrations

List of Abbreviations

ABIA	:	Annual Bibliography of Indian Archaeology, Leiden.
ABORI	:	Annals of the Bhandarkar Oriental Research Institute, Pune.
ACSP	:	Archaeological Congress and Seminar Proceedings, Kurukshetra, 1976.
AG	:	Garde, M.B., *Archaeology in Gwalior*, 2nd. ed., Gwalior, 1934.
AI	:	Ancient India—The Bulletin of the Archaeological Survey of India, New Delhi.
AIOC	:	All India Oriental Conference.
AR	:	Asiatic Researches.
ARIE	:	Annual Report of Indian Epigraphy.
ASIAR	:	Archaeological Survey of India, Annual Report.
BC	:	Brown, C., *Catalogue of Prehistoric Antiquities in the Indian Museum*, 1917.
BDCRI	:	Bulletin of the Deccan College Research Institute, Pune.
BDG	:	Bilaspur District Gazetteer (1910).
Bhandarkar	:	Bhandarkar, D.R., *A List of the Inscriptions of Northern India in Brahmi and its derivative scripts from about 200 AD. Appendix to Epigraphia Indica*, Vols. XIX-XXIII.
BMC, AI	:	*Catalogue of Indian Coins in the British Museum—Ancient India.*
BPWM	:	Bulletin of the Prince of Wales Museum, Bombay.
BT	:	*Bhilsa Topes.*
CAI	:	Cunningham's *Coins of Ancient India.*
CASIR	:	Cunningham's Archaeological Survey of India Reports, Vols. I-XXIII.
CCIMC	:	*Catalogue of Coins, Indian Museum*, Calcutta.

CCNP	:	Trivedi, H.V., *Catalogue of Coins of the Naga Kings of Padmavati.*
CIGS	:	Central Indian State Gazetteer Series, Vols. I, V, pt. A., 1908.
CII	:	*Corpus Inscriptum Indicarum.*
CJT	:	Dikshit, R.K., *The Candellas of Jejakabhukti*, New Delhi, 1977.
CLAR	:	Cousens' *List of Antiquarian Remains in C.P. and Berar*, Calcutta, 1897.
CMI	:	Cunningham's *Coins of Medieval India.*
CN	:	*Chalcolithic Navdatoli.*
CPMC	:	*Chronology of Punch Marked Coins*, Varanasi, 1966.
CPR	:	Cousens, H., *Progress Report of Archaeological Survey of India.*
DD	:	Hiralal, R.B., *Damoh Dipak.*
DDG	:	Durg District Gazetteer, Bhopal, 1972.
DER	:	Chakravarty, K.K., *Dandwada Excavation Report*, Bhopal, 1989.
DFGS	:	Garde, M.B., *Directory of Forts in Gwalior State.*
DMDG	:	Damoh District Gazetteer.
EAK	:	Ansari, Z.A. and Dhavalikar, M.K., *Excavation at Kayatha*, Pune, 1975.
EAT	:	Bajpai, K.D. and Pandey, S.K., *Excavation at Tumain.*
EI	:	Epigraphia Indica.
EK	:	Sharma, R.K., *Excavation at Kakrehta*, Delhi, 1992.
EMN	:	Sankalia, H.D., Subbarao and Deo, *The Excavations at Maheshwar and Navdatoli.*
GAR	:	Annual Administration Reports, Archaeology Department, Gwalior State.
GC	:	Garde, M.P., *Guide to Chanderi.*
GDG	:	Gwalior District Gazetteer, Bhopal, 1965.
GGS	:	Garde, M.P., *Guide to Survaya.*
GSMD	:	Dikshit, S.K., *A Guide to the State Museum, Dhubela*, Nowgong.
GSP	:	Trivedi, H.V., *Gandhisagar ka Puratattva.*
HC	:	*History of Chhattisgarh*, Vol. I (1986).

HI	:	Mishra, P.K. and Sullerey, S.K., *Heritage of India—Past and Present* (Prof. R.K. Sharma Fel. Vol.), Delhi, 1994.
Hiralal List	:	Hiralal, R.B., *Inscriptions in C.P.* and *Berar,* Nagpur, 1932.
HK	:	Anand, Mulk Raj, *Homage to Khajuraho, Marg,* X, No. 3, 1957.
HMIM	:	Handlist of Monuments, Indore Museum.
HMM	:	Handlist of Monuments, Mandu.
HTM	:	Banerji, R.D., *The Haihayas of Tripuri and their Monuments,* Calcutta, 1931.
IA	:	Indian Antiquary.
IAL	:	Indian Art and Letters.
IANP	:	Sharma, R. K. (ed.), *Indian Archaeology — New Perspectives.*
IAR	:	Indian Archaeology — A Review.
IC	:	Indian Culture.
IHQ	:	Indian Historical Quarterly.
IK	:	Kawarlal, *Immortal Khajuraho,* 1965.
ILN	:	Illustrated London News.
INC	:	Indian Numismatic Chronicle.
INHAC	:	*Indian Numismatics, History and Culture* (Dr. P.L. Gupta Fel. Vol.), Delhi, 1992.
IO	:	Rajguru, S.N., *Inscriptions of Orissa,* Vol. IV.
ISPS	:	Shastri, A.M. (ed.), *Inscriptions of the Sarabhapuriyas, Panduvamsis and Somavamsis,* pt. I-II, Delhi, 1995.
JA	:	Journal Asiatique.
JAHRS	:	Journal of the Andhra Historical Research Society.
JASB	:	Journal of the Asiatic Society of Bengal.
JBBRAS	:	Journal of the Bombay Branch of the Royal Asiatic Society.
JBHU	:	Journal of the Banaras Hindu University.
JBORS	:	Journal of the Bihar Orissa Research Society.
JESI	:	Journal of the Epigraphical Society of India.
JIH	:	Journal of Indian History.

JIM	:	Journal of Indian Museum.
JKHRS	:	Journal of the Kalinga Historical Research Society.
JMPIP	:	Journal of Madhya Pradesh Itihasa Parishad.
JMSUB	:	Journal of the M.S. University of Baroda.
JNSI	:	Journal of the Numismatic Society of India.
JOI	:	Journal of Oriental Institute, Baroda.
JOHRS	:	Journal of the Orissa Historical Research Society.
JOR	:	Journal of Oriental Research, Madras.
JRAS, GB	:	Journal of the Royal Asiatic Society, Great Britain and Ireland.
JUPHS	:	Journal of the U.P. Historical Society.
JVU	:	Journal of Vikram University, Ujjain.
KD	:	Dhama, B.L., *Khajuraho* (Guide Book), 1953.
KDI	:	Khajuraho Album by Directorate of Information, M.P. Govt., Bhopal.
KDP	:	Awasthi, R.A., *Khajuraho ki Deva Pratimayen*, Agra, 1967.
KE	:	Kalachuri Era.
KKC	:	Chakravarty, K.K., *Khajuraho*.
KKD	:	*Khajuraho* (Guide Book) by Krishna Deva, 1965.
KSS	:	Agrawal, Urmila, *Khajuraho Sculptures and their Significance*, Delhi, 1964.
KV	:	Sagar, Muni Kanti, *Khandharon Ke Vaibhav,* Kashi, 1953.
KVJ	:	*Khajuraho* (Guide Book) by J. Vijayatunga.
KVP	:	Vidya Prakash, *Khajuraho*, 1967.
KZ	:	Zennas, E. and Auboyer, *Khajuraho*, 1960.
MAR	:	Annual Administration Report, Department of Archaeology, Madhya Bharat.
MASI	:	Memoirs of the Archaeological Survey of India.
MB	:	Madhya Bharati, Research Journal of Sagar University.
MBI	:	Dwivedi, H.N., *Madhya Bharat Ka Itihas*, Gwalior, 1956.
MDG	:	Mandla District Gazetteer, 1912.

ME	:	Man and Environment, Pune.
MER	:	Bajpai, K.D., and Pandey, S.K., *Malhar* : 1975-78.
MHSP	:	Mahakoshal Historical Research Society's Papers, Bilaspur.
MP	:	Bajpai, K.D., *Madhya Pradesh Ka Puratattva,* Bhopal, 1970.
MPR	:	Dikshit, M.G., *Madhya Pradesh Ke Puratattva Ki Ruprekha.*
MPS	:	Madhya Pradesh Sandesh, Special No. on Archaeology, June 13, 1970.
MPSG	:	Sharma, R.K., *Madhya Pradesh Ke Puratattva Ka Sandarbha Grantha*, Bhopal, 1974.
MS	:	Marshall and Foucher, *Monuments of Sanchi*, 3 Vols., Delhi, 1940.
MUH	:	Patil, D.R., *Monuments of Udayagiri Hills.*
ND	:	Numismatic Digest.
NDG	:	Narasimhapur District Gazetteer, Bhopal, 1971.
NIA	:	New Indian Antiquary, Bombay.
NMAR	:	Nagpur Museum Acquisition Report.
NMB	:	Nagpur Museum Bulletin.
NMC	:	*Catalogue of Existing Coins in the Central Museum*, Nagpur, 1908.
NNM	:	Numismatic Notes and Monographs.
NPP	:	Nagri Pracharini Patrika, Varanasi.
NUJ	:	Nagpur University Journal.
NS	:	Numismatic Supplement.
PAI	:	Sharma, R.K. and Tripathi, K.K. (eds.), *Recent Perspectives on Prehistoric Art in India and Allied Subjects*, Delhi, 1996.
PASB	:	Proceedings of the Asiatic Society of Bengal.
PIHC	:	Proceedings of Indian History Congress.
PP	:	Prachya Pratibha.
PPIP	:	Sankalia, H.D., *Prehistory & Protohistory of India and Pakistan,* Pune, 1974.

PRASIWC	:	Progress Report of the Archaeological Survey, Western Circle.
PRS	:	Khare, M.D., *Painted Rock Shelters,* Bhopal, 1981.
QJMS	:	Quarterly Journal of the Mythic Society.
RAHS	:	Reports of the Administration of the Holkar State.
RAI	:	Chakraverty, K.K., *et al.* (eds.), *Rock-Art of India.*
RDG	:	Raipur District Gazetteer, Bhopal, 1973.
RGSI	:	Reports of the Geological Survey of India.
SAG	:	*Shukla Abhinandan Granth.*
SAPI	:	Wakankar and Brooks, *Stone Age Paintings in India*, 1976.
SC	:	Science and Culture.
SDG	:	Sagar District Gazetteer, Bhopal, 1967.
SE	:	Saka Era.
SI	:	Solomon, R., *Shell Inscriptions*, Calcutta, 1980.
SIA	:	De Terra and Paterson, *Studies on the Ice Age in India and Associated Human Cultures*, Washington, 1939.
SIS	:	Saraswati, S.K., *Survey of Indian Sculptures,* Calcutta, 1957.
SPCPC	:	Seminar of Papers on the Chronology of Punch Marked Coins, Varanasi.
SPLC	:	Seminar of Papers on the Local Coins of North India (300 BC-200 AD).
SSS	:	Sharma, R.K. (ed.), *Studies in Shell Script.*
TCYB	:	Sharma, R.K., The *Temple of Chaunsatha Yogini* at Bheraghat.
TTR	:	Treasure Trove Reports of M.P.
UDJ	:	Ujjain District Gazetteer, Bhopal, 1982.
VE	:	Vikram Era.
VRIA	:	Mirashi, V.V., *Vakataka Rajvansh Ka Itihas Tatha Abhilekh,* Nagpur.
VS	:	Vikram Samvat.
WNDG	:	West Nimar District Gazetteer, Bhopal, 1970.

V
Numismatics

Numismatics has played an important role in reconstructing the past history and culture of Central India. This may be evidenced by the following account.

(A) Punch-Marked Coins

Silver and copper punch-marked coins of imperial and non-imperial series have been found in a large number from all over M.P. The sites are: Akaltara, Arang, Avra, Balpur, Bar or Bayar, Badagaon, Barwani, Besnagar, Bhilsa, Bhopal, Bilaspur, Bilawali, Dangwada, Dhapewara, Eran, Hoshangabad, Indore, Jharda, Kakrehta, Karchulha, Kasrawad, Kayatha, Kesur, Maheshwar, Mamdar, Nagda, Raipur, Runija, Sambhalpur, Sarangpur, Tarapur, Thathari, Tripuri, Tumain, Udela, Ujjain and Vidisha.

These coins are of different shapes and denominations and have been assigned to Pre-Mauryan, Mauryan and Post-Mauryan periods.

(B) Uninscribed, Die-struck and Cast Coins

A large number of uninscribed die-struck and cast coins in a variety of shapes and mostly of copper have been found in explorations and excavations in various parts of M.P. The recorded sites are: Avra, Dangwada, Ujjain, Eran, Kasrawad, Kayatha, Runija, Jamunia, Pawaya, Kakrehta, Maheshwar, Vidisha, Tripuri and Tumain. These are assigned to c. 200 BC-100 AD.

(C) Tribal Coins and Coins of the Janapadas and Local Rulers

Recent explorations in the Narmada and Betwa valleys have led to discovery of inscribed coins of the city-states of Tripurī, Ujjayinī, Vidiśā, Erakiṇa, Māhiṣmatī, Bhāgila and Kurara. The sites of discovery are: Tripuri, Ujjain, Vidisha, Eran, Maheshwar, Nandaur, Nandner, Jamunia, Khidia and Pawaya. Some of these exist in musuems and personal collections at Indore, Raipur, Jabalpur, Bhopal, Hoshangabad, Gwalior, Nagpur and Vidisha. Several local coins of the city of Padmāvatī have been found at Pawaya. All these city-issues are made of copper or some alloy of it of both round and square shapes. The coins are either die-struck or cast and are multi-variety issues.

Inscribed coins of local rulers of eastern Malwa region datable between c. 200 BC-100 BC have also been recently found in a large number in explorations and excavations conducted in the Betwa and Narmada valleys. These coins of copper and in various shapes are punch marked in technique. These have been issued by Mitra and non-Mitra rulers, whose names revealed from the coins are: Mitra rulers: Nārāyaṇamitra, Bhānumitra, Vasu (or Vajra)mitra and Ravimitra. Non-Mitra rulers are: Rāmabhadra, Dāmabhadra, Hastideva, Ravibhūti, Bhūmidatta, Madāvika. One die-struck coin from Ujjain, now in British Museum, reads Rajño Dharmapālasa. Local coins of South Kosala have been found in Malhar excavations.

Tripuri has yielded lead coins of Bhavadatta, Ajadatta and Abhayadatta datable to c. late 2nd or early 1st century BC before the penetration of Sātavāhana rule in this region. A Mitra coin has also been reported from Tripuri.

In addition to these, unscribed, die-struck or cast copper or lead Janapada coins of Eran, Ujjain, Vidisha and Taxila type are in collection or have been found at Indore, Ujjain, Eran, Vidisha, Kasrawad, Khidia, Jamunia, Tewar, Kakrehta, Pawaya, Besnagar, Balpur, Balaghat, Raipur and Maheshwar.

(D) Indo-Greek Coins

A few silver and copper coins of Indo-Greek rulers collected from different places are in Advani collection at Indore. A coin of Menander was also found from Balaghat. The concerned rulers are: Plato, Heliocles, Strato, Epander, Archebois, Pheloxenos, Nicias, Appolophanes, Amintas, Hermaeos, Eucratides, Menander and Zoilus. How far these coins help in reconstructing the early history of M.P. is difficult to say.

(E) Coins of the Sātavāhanas

The penetration of the rule of the Sātavāhanas of the Deccan in M.P. is amply confirmed by a large number of their coins found in its territorial jurisdiction. Coins of Sātakarṇī I found at Ujjain, Dewas, Vidisha, Jamunia, Tewar, Bheraghat and Tripuri prove extension of Sātavahana empire over Malwa and Ḍāhala. Āpilaka coins have been found at Balpur in Raigarh district and Malhar in Bilaspur district. Coins of Gautamiputra Sātakarṇī have been located at Ujjain and one preserved at Indore. From Bhilsa and Dewas coins of Vāsiṣṭhīputra Pulumāvi have been found and these are indicative of the rule of the Sātavāhanas over a large part of Madhya Pradesh. Coins of Yajñaśrī Sātakarṇī, the last powerful ruler, have been located at Besnagar, Tripuri and Dewas. Another ruler, Kumbha Sātakarṇī is known from his coins found at Dewas. A hoard of two hundred

Sātavahana coins has been located at Indore.

During the Sātavāhana rule India had established flourishing trade contacts with Rome. Some of the Roman coins found in M.P. at Avra, Chakarbera, Bilaspur, Tripuri and Mamda-khedi are indicative of this.

(F) Coins of the Śaka-Kṣatrapas

The Śaka-Kṣatrapas succeeded the Indo-Greek rulers over vast portions of north and western India. Coins of the early Śaka rulers viz. Maus, Azes, Azilises and Azes II have been located in the Indore collection of late Shri Advani. The Muniraj collection of Shivpuri has copper coins of Western Kṣatrapa ruler Bhūmaka of Kṣaharāta lineage. Shivpuri has also yielded silver coins of Nahapāna, the most powerful Western Kṣatrapa ruler. These coins are found re-struck by Gautamiputra Sātakarṇī — the Sātavahana ruler who had defeated him. Coins of Mahu, Dāsa and Sauma have been collected from Ujjain. Similarly a coin of Kṣaharāta Arta is preserved in the Muniraj collection at Shivpuri.

Coins of the rulers of Kārdamarka lineage of the Western Kṣatrapas have also been found in M.P. Coins of Chaṣṭana, the founder of this branch have been located at Ujjain and Shivpuri. Ujjain was capital of Chaṣṭana and his successors. A large number of coins of the successors of Chaṣṭana, viz. Mahākṣatrapa Rudrasiṁha, Rudrasena I, Daṃajādaśrī, Dāmasena, Viśvasiṁha, Bhartridāman, Viśvasena, Rudrasena III, Rudrasiṁha II and III, Īsvaradatta and Śrīdaman have been found from all over Malwa and this proves their continued hold over this region for a long period. A hoard of 670 coins of the Western Kṣatrapas found at Sonepur in Chhindwara district throws important light on their activities over Mahakoshal.

(G) Kuṣāṇa Coins

The Kuṣāṇas had also extended their sway over some parts of M.P. Two coins of Wema Kadphises, the early ruler of this dynasty have been found at Vidisha and Shahdol. However, on the basis of these two coins, extension of his territory over Madhya Pradesh cannot be surmised. A hoard of 757 coins has been discovered at Shahdol and this hoard contains practically all the rulers of the Kalachuri dynasty including 324 coins of Kaniṣka I. Jhajhapuri in Bilaspur district has yielded 15 coins of Kaniṣka I and Huviṣka. At Sanchi has been found an inscription of the reign of Vāsiṣka, the successor of Kaniṣka I. At Raigarh a Boddo-type of gold coin of Kaniṣka I has been acquired. Huviṣka was the next ruler and his coins in large number have been found at Jhajhapuri, Shahdol and Harda. Harda has also yielded coins of Kaniṣka II or Kaniṣka III. Vāsudeva I succeeded Huviṣka and a copper coin of his period has been found at Tewar. Inscriptions of Kuṣāṇa period found at Bheraghat also confirm the rule of the Kuṣāṇas over Jabalpur region. No coin of the successors of Vāsudeva has been found from M.P.

(H) Coins of the Nāgas

A branch of the Nāgas ruled in Vidisha around 2nd century AD. A coin of the founder of the dynasty, Vṛṣanāga, has been found at Vidisha. Bhīmanāga was the next ruler and during his reign the capital of this branch of the Nāgas was shifted to Padmāvatī. Coins of three successive rulers viz. Skandanāga, Vasunāga and Bṛhaspatināga have been located at Pawaya (ancient Padmāvatī). The last six rulers of the Nāgas of Padmāvatī were respectively Ravināga, Vibhunāga, Bhavanāga, Prabhākaranāga, Devanāga and Gaṇapatināga. Pawaya has yielded coins of all these rulers. Nāga coins have also been located at Akoda, Indore, Ujjain, Eran, Kutwar, Gohad, Narwar and Besnagar.

(I) Coins of the Bodhis

The Bodhis were ruling at Tripurī in Jabalpur district around 2nd-3rd century AD. Coins and sealings of the rulers of this dynasty viz. Śrī Bodhi, Vasu Bodhi, Chandra Bodhi and Śiva Bodhi have been found in Tripurī excavations. Coins of eight rulers of this dynasty are in collection of Dr. M.C. Choube at Jabalpur. These are Śrī Bodhi, Chandra Bodhi, Śiva Bodhi, Vasu Bodhi, Vīra Bodhi, Vīra Bodhi Datta, Sirivasaka and Siriśiva. A clay sealing from Tripurī has revealed the name of another ruler viz. Dharma Bodhi.

(J) Coins of the Senas

Tripurī has also yielded terracotta seal and coins of Mahāsena, Sujeṣṭhyasena and Sundarasena who seem to have been ruling over the region around 350 AD. Ten coins of Sudarsanasena or Sundarasena are in collection of Dr. M.C. Choubey of Jabalpur. From lead and potin coins and terracota seals found from Tripurī names of seven rulers of Sena dynasty are known. These are : Yaśasena, Sundarsena, Mahāsena I, Sujeṣṭhasena, Siṁhasena, Vitilaya Skanda and Mahāsena II. These rulers ruled at Tripurī after the Bodhis and before the Guptas.

(K) Magha Coins

The contemporaries of the Bodhis were the rulers of the Magha dynasty which ruled over Baghelkhand region of M.P. Bhadramagha and Sivamagha were important rulers of this dynasty. Their coins and seals have been found at Kausambi, Bhita and Bandhavgarh, Malhar and Tripuri. They resisted Kuṣāṇa rule over Mahakoshal region of M.P.

(L) Coins of the Guptas and their Contemporaries

The earliest Gupta ruler whose coins have been found in M.P. is Samudragupta. These have been located at Bamnala, Sakaur and Runija. Coins of Kācha are known from Vidisha, Sakaur and Pagara. Vidisha has yielded copper coins of Rāmagupta. Gold coins of Chandragupta II have been located at Pattan, Bamnala, Sakaur, Runija, Seoni, Sihora, Harda, Pagara and Anuppur. His copper and bronze coins have been found at Sanchi, Vidisha and Ujjain. Coins of Kumāragupta have been discovered at Bamnala, Pagara, Indore and Arang. Similarly Skandagupta's gold coins have been explored at Sakaur in the Damoh district of M.P. His silver coin bearing the date 141 has been reported from Vidisha.

A good number of copper coins of Jiṣṇu, a contemporary of the Guptas, who was ruling over Malwa have been found from Ujjain-Vidisha region.

The Hūṇas, who were contemporary of the Guptas had penetrated up to Central India. This is confirmed by their inscriptions as well as the copper coins of Toramāṇa found in the excavations conducted at Eran.

An unusual repoussé type of coins in gold and silver issued in South Kosala during the Gupta and post-Gupta period is a special feature of the numismatic history of M.P. Such coins of Parasannamātra (of Śarabhapurīya dynasty), Mahendrāditya and Kramāditya have been located at Behrampur, Salhepali, Khairatal, Malhar, Madanpur, Bhandara, Pitaiband, Sirpur, Shahabad, Mahasamund, Riva, Nahna, Kulia, Tala, Riawan, Raipur and Madaguda as well as in musuem collections at Lucknow, Calcutta, Nagpur and Raipur. The Nala rulers of Bastar-Koraput region also issued similar coins. These coins of Nala rulers viz. Varāharaja, Bhānudatta, Arthapati, Nandanrāja and Stambha have been found in hoards located at Edenga and Kulia.

Four copper coins of Later Gupta rulers — one of Satyagupta, a new ruler, and three of Mahārāja Harigupta — two from Mandsaur and one from Vidisha have been found.

(M) Ādivarāha Dramma

A hoard of 513 Ādivarāha drammas was discovered at Umaria in Sihora tahsil of Jabalpur district. Also from Bastar three such coins were located. These are in the collection of Nagpur Museum.

(N) Indo-Sassanian Coins

In the territorial jurisdiction of M.P. hoards and isolated finds of Indo-Sassanian coins of silver and copper have been discovered from time to time. The sites of discoveries and dispositions are : Avra, Indore, Ujjain, Eran, Kherua, Guida, Ghatauda, Chanderi, Chhindwara, Devatpur, Patan, Bardia, Balaghat, Bhat-Pachlana, Maharajpur, Mandhata, Murwara, Multai, Mohaniakhurd, Raipur, Sirsa, Bahoriband, Seoni, Harsud, Hoshangabad and Tumain.

(O) Coins of the Chandellas

Some Chandella rulers are known to have issued coins. Kīrtivarman was the first ruler to isssue coins which were in gold. One is in collection of Indian Museum, Calcutta and the other was in the collection of Cunningham. His successor Sallakṣaṇavarman issued coins in gold and copper and these have been found in the excavation at Tulapar in Raisen district. Cunningham also had a few of these coins in his collections. The next ruler Jayavarman issued coins in silver and copper. His coins are in the collection of the British Museum. His half dramma coins have recently been found from Khajuraho. His successor Prthvīvarman too issued coins in copper during his short rule. These were in Cunningham's collection. A hoard of silver coins of Madanavarman, the next ruler, has been found at Rewa. His gold and copper coins are also known from different collections. These are in different denominations. The next ruler Paramardi's gold and copper coins have been reported from Tripuri. One of his gold coins found from Khajuraho is in the collectiion of Indian Museum, Calcutta. Copper and gold coins in different denominations of Trailokyavarman, the next ruler are known from Ajaigarh and Banda. His successor was Vīravarman. Only a few of his coins in gold and silver are known from Tripuri and Khajuraho. A few existed in Cunningham's collection and Indian Museum, Calcutta.

(P) Coins of the Paramāras

Some rulers of the Paramāra dynasty of Malwa also issued coins. Thus gold coins of Udayāditya have been located at Ujjain and Peepaliya Nagar. In the Central Museums of Nagpur and Assam gold coins of Jagaddeva exist in collection. Similarly from Indore, gold and copper coins of Naravarman have been found. Gold coins of Jayavarman, Udayāditya and Naravarman have been found in excavation conducted at Tulapar, district Raisen. Tulsipur has also yielded some gold coins of the Paramāras.

(Q) Coins of the Kalachuris of Māhiṣmatī, Tripurī and Ratanpur

The earliest coins of the Kalachuris are those issued by Kṛṣṇarāja of Māhiṣmatī branch, found in M.P. from Tewar, Pattan and Besnagar. His coins were in wide circulation over Maharashtra, Konkan and Rajasthan from where a number of sites yielding hoards of his coins have been reported. No other ruler of the Māhiṣmatī branch of the Kalachuris is known to have issued coins.

Of the Tripurī branch of the Kalachuris, only Gāṅgeyadeva is known to have issued coins. His coins have also been from sites located in Uttar Pradesh, Bihar, Bengal, Orissa, Assam, and Maharashtra in addition to M.P. From M.P. the known sites are: Isurpur, Baretha, Barela, Mandu, Sagar, Sonsari, Tripuri, Jargawan, Dungaria and Tingamali. His coins are in gold, silver and copper in different denominations. His Laxmi type of coins had deep impact on the coinage of the contemporary dynasties of North and Central India. No other ruler of the Tripurī branch of the Kalachuris is known to have issued coins.

Most of the rulers of the Ratanpur branch of the Kalachuris, however, issued coins in gold, silver and copper in different denominations. The rulers known from the coins are: Ratnadeva, Pṛthvīdeva, Jājalladeva, Jagaddeva and Pratāpamalla. In the genealogy of kings of this dynasty, since three rulers named Ratnadeva, two named Pṛthvīdeva and two named Jājalladeva exist, the attribution of these coins has become a problem for the scholars. Since no dates exist on these coins, their identification is a matter of controversy among scholars. The different sites yielding the coins are : gold coins from Sonsari, Khairagarh, Sarangarh, Bhagaund, Dalal Seoni, Bachhauda and Ratanpur in M.P., Sonepur in Orissa, Aṅga in Bihar and British Museum collection. Silver coins are from Balpur, copper coins are from hoards located at Dhanpur, Raigarh, Khairagarh, Balpur, Bhagaund, Sirpur. Dr. A.S. Altekar had also a copper coin of Ratnadeva in his personal collection.

(R) Coins of the Chhindaka Nāgas of Chakrakoṭa (Bastar)

A Nāga dynasty known as the Chhindaka Nāgas established their rule over Chakrakotya (now known as Bastar) in M.P. Many of their inscriptions have been found from the region. That Someśvara of this dynasty issued coins is testified by the fact that four coins of him were located in Sonasari hoard found in 1921.

(S) Coins of the Yādavas of Devagiri

The Yādavas of Devagiri ruling in 11th-12th century AD had also extended their sway over parts of M.P. In addition to their inscriptions found at Balaghat and Lanji, their coins have been located at Kotha, Dewas, and Parsadih.

(T) Coins of the Kachchhapaghātas

Only two rulers of this dynasty are known to have issued coins. The first was Mahipāla of the Gwalior branch and the other was Vīrasiṁha of the Narwar branch of this dynasty. Hoards of coins of Mahipāla in gold and silver have been found from Gwalior and Jhansi. Horseman type of gold coins of Vīrasiṁha, only three in number, have been located, one each at Gwalior in M.P. and Lucknow and Gorakhpur districts in Uttar Pradesh.

(U) Coins of the Yajvapālas of Narwar

Some rulers of the Yajvapāla dynasty ruling at Narwar also issued coins. The founder of this dynasty, Chāhaḍa issued coins which have been found at Gwalior. These are datable between 1237 and 1254 AD. His successor Āsalladeva also issued coins, which were located at Gwalior. These are datable between 1254 and 1279 AD. Coins of his successor Gopāladeva have also been found in the hoard of 791 coins of this dynasty found at Gwalior.

(V) Miscellaneous Coins

In addition to these, M.P. has yielded the following miscellaneous inscribed coins:

One copper coin of Dāmasena (Advani collection), one copper coin of Jayāśraya from Ujjain, four copper coins of Paśupati, one copper coin of Śrī Guhilapati from Gwalior, three Chinese coins of gold from Balpur, two of copper (from Balpur and Sirpur excavations), one gold coin of Kesari from Balpur, 32 gold Fanams of Anantavarman Choḍaganga from Raipur, one coin each of Śivagupta and Sakhadeva from Vidisha, one silver coin of Raṇahastin in Muniraj collection at Indore, one lead coin of Chandra from Tripuri, two silver coins of Siṁhendrapāla from Bhopal, four copper coins of Vijayaka from Ujjain and two coins of king Śeṣadatta from Gwalior.

(W) Seals, Sealings and Impressions

Explorations and excavations conducted in different parts of M.P have yielded a good number of seals, sealings and impressions related to different periods. An account of the same is provided in the following pages.

List of Coins, Seals and Sealings

(A) Punch - Marked Coins

Akaltara (Bilaspur) :

A hoard of two hundred and fifty-three silver punch-marked coins (of them 85 were minute coins of the *māśaka* series) and two copper minute coins of *māśaka* series, probably silver-plated, discovered from this place. Only 233 coins of this hoard were acquired and they were distributed to various museums. *TTR* of 1925-26; *NNM*, No. 2, p. 13; *Ibid.*, No. 5, pp. 1-2.

Arang (Raipur) :

Six punch-marked coins found and preserved in MGM Museum. *HC*, 38.

Avra (Mandsaur) :

Punch-marked coins discovered in the excavation of 1960-61 and in surface exploration. *JMPIP*, No. 4 (1962), p. 33.

Balpur (Bilaspur) :

(a) Four - symbol punch-marked coins collected by the Mahakoshal Historical Society from Sonepur, Sambalpur, Tarapur and other sites. *JNSI*, XIX, pp. 107-10.

(b) Silver (?) punch-marked coins discovered and preserved in the L.P. Pandeya collection, Raigarh. *NNM*, No. 2, p. 22.

Bar or Bayar (Raigarh) :

A hoard of silver punch-marked coins discovered and deposited in treasury of Sarangarh. Whereabouts of the hoard and its actual number are presently not known. *EI*, XXVII, p. 319; *NNM*, No. 5, p. 1.

Badagaon (Shajapur) :

Punch-marked and cast copper coins found. *IAR*, 1969-70, p. 17.

Barwani (West Nimar) :

A hoard of 3,450 silver punch-marked coins discovered in 1942 and preserved in the CAA Museum, New Delhi. *JNSI*, V, p. 172; *Ibid.*, p. 95; *NNM*, No. 2, p. 4; *ND*, XVI (1992), pp. 6-23.

Besnagar (Vidisha) :

(a) Copper punch-marked coins found in the excavations of Khambaba and near the temple of Ganeśa during 1913-14 and 1914-15. Most of the coins are of oblong shape and bear the common symbols. *ASIR*, 1913-14, pp. 186-226 and 1914-15, pp. 66-68.

(b) Six punch-marked coins found. *CASIR*, X, p. 37; *NNM*, No. 2, p. 20.

(c) Punch-marked coins found in excavations during 1963-64 and 1964-65. *IAR*, 1963-64, pp. 16-17; 1964-65, p. 19.

Bhilsa (Vidisha) :

Punch-marked coins collected at and preserved in Bharat Kala Bhavan, Varanasi. *JNSI*, X, p. 80; *NNM*, No. 2, p. 20.

Bhopal (Bhopal) :

Ten silver punch-marked coins of Imperial Series I in personal collection of Prof. Shankar Tiwari. *JNSI*, L (1988), pt. I-II, pp. 10-13.

Bilaspur (Bilaspur) :

Nine silver punch-marked coins preserved in the Nagpur Museum. *NNM*, No. 5, p. 4; *NMC*.

Bilawali (Dewas) :

Punch-marked coins found. *IAR*, 1956-57, 1962-63; Wakankar, *ACSP*.

Dangawada (Ujjain) :

Six punch-marked coins discovered in stratified layers during excavations. Eight were collected from surface. *DER*, pp. 107-10.

Dhapewara (Balaghat) :

Ninety-two silver punch-marked coins discovered in 1893 at and deposited in Nagpur Museum. *NNM*, No. 2, p. 12; No. 5, p. 1; *Balaghat District Gazetteer* (1907), p. 68.

Eran (Sagar) :

(a) A hoard of 3,268 copper and silver punch-marked coins discovered. *IAR*, 1961-62, p. 94; *CPMC*, pp. 46-47.

(b) A big hoard of punch-marked coins preserved in the British Museum, London. *CASIR*, X, p. 77; *CAI*, pp. 99-102; *BMC, AI*, pp. 140-44.

Hoshangabad (Hoshangabad) :

Two silver punch-marked coins in collection of Shri K.B. Tiwari. *JNSI*, XXXIX (1977), pt. I-II, p. 154.

Indore (Indore) :

(a) Eleven copper and silver punch-marked coins in the Advani collection, collected from Ujjain, Bhopal and Bhilsa. *JNSI*, XIV, pp. 41-44.

(b) Some peculiar punch-marked coins examined in the Advani collection. *JNSI*, XIII, pp. 207-08.

(c) Copper punch-marked coin in the collection of late Mr. Tikekar. *JNSI*, X, pp. 26-42.

Jharda (Mandsaur) :

Punch-marked and cast copper coins found. *IAR*, 1969-70.

Kakrehta (Jabalpur) :

(a) A silver punch-marked coin found in exploration of the mound. *JNSI*, XXXIX (1977), pt. I-II, p. 153.

(b) Two silver punch-marked coins found in excavation. *EK*, pp. 183-85.

Karchulha (Jabalpur) :

A hoard of ninety-eight punch-marked coins (silver 80, copper 15, brass 3) found in 1908. *NNM*, No. 2, p. 12; No. 5, p. 3; *TTR*, No. 16 of 1908.

Kasrawad (West Nimar) :

(a) Ten punch-marked copper coins found in the excavation of 1939-40. *JNSI*, VIII, pp. 99ff.

(b) Thirty-six silver punch-marked coins found in the excavations. *JNSI*, X, pp. 146ff; XIV, pp. 93-98.

(c) Thirty-nine punch-marked coins found in the excavations during 1936-39. Of these 29 were of silver and 10 of gold. *IHQ*, XXV, No. 1 (1949), pp. 1-18.

Kayatha (Ujjain) :

Punch-marked coins found in Kayatha excavations. *JVU* pp. 18-20; *EAK*, p. 151.

Kesur (Dhar) :

A copper punch-marked coin found. *JNSI*, XV, p. 125.

Maheshwar (West Nimar) :

Punch-marked silver and copper coins discovered during exploration and excavation. *EMN*, pp. 68-70; *JNSI*, XVI, pp. 36-39; XV, pp. 197-201.

Mamdar (Rewa) :

A hoard of fifty-four silver punch-marked coins found and deposited with the

Director General, Archaeological Survey of India, New Delhi. *NNM*, No. 2, p. 12.

Nagda (Dewas) :

Four silver punch-marked coins from village Nagda near Dewas have a few unidentified symbols. Similar coins were also found in Ujjain excavations conducted by N.R. Banerjee. *JNSI*, L (1988), pt. I-II, p. 9.

Raipur (Raipur) :

Twenty-eight silver and other copper punch-marked coins in the collection of M.G.M. Museum. *JNSI*, XXIII, p. 505.

Runija (Ujjain) :

Two punch-marked coins found in the excavations of 1981. *JNSI*, XLVII (1985), pt. I-II, pp. 22-24.

Sambhalpur (Raigarh) :

Punch-marked coins found at and deposited in the L.P. Pandey collection at Raigarh. *NNM*, No. 2, p. 225.

Sarangpur (Rajgarh) :

Punch-marked coins found. *NNM*, No. 2, p. 21; *CASIR*, II, p. 288; *CIGS*, p. 67.

Tarapur (Raipur) :

Nine silver punch-marked coins found. *JAHRS*, III, p. 81; *NNM*, No. 2, p. 22; *ibid.*, No. 5, p. 1.

Thathari (Bilaspur) :

A hoard of 253 silver punch-marked coins of māśaka and kārṣāpaṇa series found. *JNSI*, XIX, pp. 110-12.

Tripuri (Jabalpur) :

(a) Thirteen copper punch-marked coins found in the excavations of 1951-52. *JNSI*, XVI, pp. 66-68; *Tripuri*-1952, pp. 121-24; *NNM*, No. 2; No. 5, p. 4.

(b) Nine punch-marked coins, one of silver, two of alloy and six of copper found. *JNSI*, XVI, pp. 55-58.

(c) Punch-marked coins from Tripuri discovered between 1966 and 1971 classified and discussed. *PP*, VIII, No. 1-2, Jan-July, 1980, pp. 93-105.

Tumain (Guna) :

Punch-marked coins found in excavation. *EAT*, p. 38.

Udela (Raipur) :

Punch-marked coins found. *HC*, 38.

Ujjain (Ujjain) :

(a) Thirteen punch-marked coins — one of silver, one of copper coated with silver and eleven of copper—found at and preserved in Wakankar collection. *JNSI*, XVI, pp. 177-78.

(b) Different types of punch-marked coins in collection of Wakankar. *Ujjayini Darshan*, pp. 46-49.

(c) Thirty-four punch-marked coins in personal collection of N. Kothari and M. Morrison. *ND*, XI (Dec. 1987), pp. 13-19.

Vidisha (Vidisha) :

Silver and copper punch-marked coins acquired from Vidisha in the collection of MGM Museum, Raipur. *JNSI*, XXIII, pp. 303-05.

(B) Uninscribed, Cast and Die-Struck Coins

Avra (Mandsaur):

(a) Copper cast coins found in the excavation of 1960-61. *JMPIP*, No. 4 (1962), p. 33.

(b) Copper die-struck coins with Ujjain symbol. *JMPIP*, No. 4 (1962), p. 33.

Dangawada (Ujjain) :

Nineteen uninscribed cast coins found in excavation. Twenty-seven coins collected from surface. *DER*, pp. 111-25.

Eran (Sagar) :

(a) Five copper die-struck coins found. *JNSI*, XIV, pp. 60-61.

(b) Some Kārṣāpaṇa coins found. *Sagar Through the Ages*, p. 8.

Jamunia (Hoshangabad) :

Seven interesting copper cast and die-struck coins found. *JNSI*, XIV, pp. 56-58.

Kakrehta (Jabalpur) :

One inscribed cast copper coin found in the excavation. *EK*, pp. 185-87.

Kasrawad (West Nimar) :

(a) Five cast copper coins found in the excavations of 1939-40. *JNSI*, VIII, pp. 99ff.

(b) Sixteen copper cast and one hundred copper coins bearing Ujjayini symbols found. *IHQ*, XXV, pt. I (1949), pp. 1-18.

Kayatha (Ujjain) :

Copper cast and die-struck coins found in the excavation. *JVU*, pp. 18-20; *EAK*, p. 151.

Maheshwar (West Nimar) :

Uninscribed cast copper coins found during exploration and excavations. *EMN*, pp. 70-72; *JNSI*, XVII, pp. 42-44.

Padam-Pawaya (Gwalior) :

(a) Twenty-two early single type, cast and die-struck coins found. *JNSI*, XVIII, pp. 163-68.

(b) Two uninscribed cast coins found. *JNSI*, XVIII, pp. 67-68.

(c) Three early single type silver coins found at and preserved in the Gwalior Museum. *JNSI*, XVII, pp. 38-39.

Runija (Ujjain) :

Eight cast coins found in the excavations of 1981. *JNSI*, XLVII (1985), pt. I-II, pp. 22-24.

Tripuri (Jabalpur) :

(a) One copper uninscribed coin with elephant and hill device found in the excavation of 1951-52. *JNSI*, XVI, p. 69; *Tripuri-1952*, p. 125.

(b) A new variety of uninscribed brass coin found in the mound of Karanbel. *JNSI*, XVI, p. 70.

(c) A copper die-struck coin of Eran-Ujjain type found. *JNSI*, XVI, pp. 61-62.

(d) Twenty-eight and four die-struck coins found in excavations from 1967 to 1971, classified into fifteen different varieties and critically discussed. *PAI*, pp. 236-41.

Tumain (Guna) :

Cast coins found in the excavation. *EAT*, p. 38.

Ujjain (Ujjain) :

(a) Uninscribed cast coins found at and preserved in Wakankar collection. *JNSI*, XVI, pp. 178-79.

(b) An uninscribed copper coin found in the hoard of coins discovered at.

JNSI, XIII, p. 25.

(c) Four varieties of thirteen copper coins of Ujjayini discovered from Garhkalika locality in personal collection of K.G. Verma. All the coins are uninscribed and datable between c. 300 BC-300 AD. *JNSI*, XLIX (1987), pt. I-II, pp. 19-21.

Vidisha (Vidisha) :

Uninscribed cast coins found at and preserved in Raipur Museum. *JNSI*, XXIII, pp. 305-06.

(C) Tribal Coins and Coins of the Janapadas and Local Rulers

Balaghat (Balaghat) :

Forty-seven copper tribal coins found at and deposited in Nagpur Museum. *Balaghat District Gazetteer* (1907), p. 69; *NNM*, No. 5, p. 7.

Balpur (Bilaspur) :

Four square uninscribed copper coins found in the Mahanadi. *JNSI*, IX, pp. 31-33; Vol. XII, pp. 8-10.

Besnagar (Vidisha) :

Fifty uninscribed coins of Ujjain and Eran types found. *CASIR*, X, p. 37.

Bhilsa (Vidisha) :

A unique Eran type of copper coin found. *JNSI*, XVII, p. 46.

Eran (Sagar) :

(a) Punch-marked, die-struck and inscribed cast coins found and deposited in British Museum, London. One of the coins had the legend *Rajño Dharmapālasa* and two had the legend *Erakiṇa*. A broken bronze die was also found for casting punch-marked coins. *CASIR*, X, p. 77ff; *CAI*, pp. 99-102; *BMC, AI*, pp. 140-44.

(b) Thirty-eight copper and brass coins of Eran, mostly purchased from Burhanpur and Indore. *JNSI*, L-III (1991), pt. I-II, pp. 27-29.

Indore (Indore) :

(a) Two bronze coins of Jyeṣṭhapura, capital of the Śibis (?) found and preserved in the Advani collection. *JNSI*, XIV, pp. 5-8.

(b) Seven interesting Ujjayini coins examined in the Advani collection. *JNSI*, XIII, pp. 211-14.

(c) Seven coins of Ujjain type in the collection of Late Shri Tikekar. *JNSI*, X, pp. 26-42.

(d) A collection of 546 pieces of copper and 2 of lead coins of Ujjayini examined in the Advani collection. *JNSI*, XIII, pp. 206-07.

(e) Two coins of probably of the Taxila type in the collection of Late Shri Tikekar. *JNSI*, X, pp. 26-42.

Jamunia (Hoshangabad) :

(a) Three copper die-struck Eran coins belonging to two new varieties found. *JNSI*, XVI, pp. 63-64.

(b) Five copper coins of the city of Bhāgila found. *JNSI*, XIV, pp. 9-14; XLIV (1982), pt. I-II, pp. 29-38.

(c) A copper die-struck coin of Eran-Ujjain type found. *JNSI*, XVI, p. 61.

Kasrawad (West Nimar) :

A hoard of Ujjain coins discovered in course of excavation of 1939-40. *JNSI*, VIII, pp. 99ff.

Khidia (Hoshangabad) :

One bronze coin of Tripurī city state discovered. *JNSI*, XIII, pp. 40-45; *NNM*, No. 5, p. 5.

Maheshwar (West Nimar) :

(a) Eighteen tribal Ujjayini copper coins found during excavation at Maheshwar and Navadatoli. *EMN*, pp. 72-79 (1952-53).

(b) Coins of the city-state of Māhiṣmatī found during explorations and excavations at Maheshwar and Navdatoli (1952-53). *EMN*, pp. 77-79, *JNSI*, XVII, pp.94-96.

(c) Six tribal copper Taxila coins found during excavations at Maheshwar and Navdatoli (1952-53). *EMN*, pp. 72-73.

Malhar (Bilaspur) :

Local coins of South Kosala found in excavations. *MER*, p. 34.

Nandner (Sehore) :

(a) Inscribed punch-marked coins from Nandner in personal collection of Shri K.B. Tiwari of Hoshangabad have been assigned to the local rulers viz. Dāmabhadra, Ravibhūti, Hastideva, Bhūmidatta and Nārāyaṇamitra. *JNSI*, XLIII (1981), pt. II, pp. 38-44.

(b) Inscribed punch-marked coin of a new ruler Bhānumitra in personal collection of Shri K.B. Tiwari of Hoshangabad. *JNSI*, XLIII (1981), pt. II, p. 45.

(c) Inscribed punch-marked coins of Madāvike found in exploration and preserved in personal collection of Prof. Shankar Prasad Tiwari of Bhopal. *JNSI*, XLV (1983), pt. I-II, pp. 112-16.

(d) Five varieties of coins of the Bhāgila city-state (Bhāgilāya) found and preserved in the personal collection of Prof. Shankar Prasad Tiwari of Bhopal. *JNSI*, XLV (1983), pts. I-II, pp. 112-16.

(e) Coins of the city state of Bhāgila and coins of Dāmabhadasa and Nārāyaṇamitra found and preserved in personal collection of K.B. Tiwari of Hoshangabad. *ND*, IV, pt. I (June 1980), pp. 1-8.

(f) Coins of the ancient city state of Kurara (three varieties) and Tripurī (two varieties) found. *ND*, IV, pt. II (Dec. 1980), pp. 1-5.

Pawaya (Gwalior) :

(a) Seven local coins of the city of Padmāvatī of about 1st-2nd century AD found. *JNSI*, XVIII, pp. 69-70.

(b) Five coins bearing lotus design, probably local coins of Padmāvatī, found. *JNSI*, XVIII, p. 68.

(c) Mālava coins found. *CCNP*, pp. 57-58.

(d) Ten copper and die-struck tribal or local (?) coins found and preserved in the Gwalior Museum. *JNSI*, XVII, pp. 40-42.

Raipur (Raipur) :

(a) Five hundred seventy-five cast and local coins of Eran and Ujjain in the collection of MGM Museum. *JNSI*, XXIII, p. 505.

(b) Eighteen Eran coins in the collection of MGM Museum. *JNSI*, XXIV, pp. 168-72.

(c) Twenty-one coins of the city-state of Vidisha in the collection of MGM Museum. *JNSI*, XXIII, p. 505.

(d) Twenty local coins of South Kosala in MGM Museum. *JNSI*, XIX, pp. 72-73.

Tewar (Jabalpur) :

(a) Two copper coins of the city-state of Tripurī preserved in the Hiralal

Archaeological Society at Jabalpur. *NNM*, No. 5, p. 6.

(b) A copper die-struck coin of Eran-Ujjain type found. *JNSI*, XVI, pp. 61-62.

(c) Ten copper coins of the city-state of Tripurī found in the excavations of 1951-52 and 1952-53. *JNSI*, XVI, pp. 68-69; *Tripuri-1952*, p. 125.

(d) Three copper coins of the Tripurī city-state deposited in the British Museum. *BMC, AI*, p. 239; *JRAS*, 1894, p. 553.

(e) A bronze Tripurī city coin with a new symbol found. *JNSI*, XXI, pp. 186-87.

(f) A new bronze Tripurī coin with elephant on the obverse discovered. *PP*, VI, No. 1, January 1978, pp. 71-72.

(g) A new fourth variety of Tripurī coin of bronze with elephant, triangle-headed standard and legend in Brāhmī mentioning *'Tipuri'* found. *ND*, V, pt. I (June 1981), pp. 6-7; VIII, pt. I-II (1984), pp. 20-21.

(h) Two unknown ancient coins datable to c. 1st-2nd century BC found. *ND*, VIII, pt. I-II, pp. 22-23.

(i) A coin very close to (b) above has the legend of '---- *Yamatasa*'. He was ruler of 'Mitra' dynasty which was ruling over Tripurī in about 1st-2nd century BC/AD before the Sātavāhanas had any hold there. *ND*, IX, pt. I-II (1985), pp. 31-33.

(j) One uninscribed lead coin of an unknown dynasty and of unknown date with prominent figure of a frog on the obverse and a triangle placed over a four compartmental railing with a human figure holding spear in hand to right found. *ND*, XII-XIII (1989), pp. 6-8.

(k) One round lead coin of Abhayadatta found. It is datable to c. 1st-cent. BC. *ND*, XII-XII (1989), pp. 6-8.

(l) One lead coin of Bhavadatta with legend '*(Ra) no Bhavada (tasa)*' on the reverse found. *ND*, XVI (1992), pp. 29-46.

(m) Four lead coins of Ajadatta with legend *'Rajo Ajadatasa'* on the reverse found. *ND*, XVI (1992), pp. 29-46.

Ujjain (Ujjain) :

(a) About thirty coins belonging to the Ujjain series found. On one of them the word *Ujayina* is quite legible. *JASB*, VII, p. 1052.

(b) Coins of Ujjain series found. *CASIR*, XIV, p. 138; *JASB*, VIII, p. 1052; *IHQ*, X, p. 723; *JNSI*, II, p. 81; VIII, p. 90; X, p. 38; XIII, p. 73, 206, 209.

(c) Some rare varieties of the coins of Ujjayinī found at and preserved in the Wakankar collection. *JNSI*, XVI, pp. 179-81.

(d) Seven rare Ujjain type of copper coins found. *JNSI*, XVII, pp. 44-46.

(e) Coins of Ujjayinī found in the hoard of coins discovered. *JNSI*, XIII, p. 75.

(f) A copper cast or die-struck coin of Ujjayinī, bearing Ujjayinī symbol found in the hoard of coins discovered. *JNSI*, XIII, p. 74.

(g) A copper cast coin, die-struck only on one side, with legend *'Māhisa'* on obverse in Brāhmī script of 3rd century BC found in the hoard discovered. *JNSI*, XIII, p. 74.

(h) A new type of copper tribal coins, with Lakṣmī holding a stalked lotus on the obverse and tree-in-railing and other symbols on the reverse found. *IAR*, 1961-62, p. 94.

(i) Four rare copper coins of Vijayaka, probably a local ruler of c. 1st century BC in collection of Wakankar. *JNSI*, XLVI (1984), pt. I-II, pp. 34-36.

Vidisha (Vidisha) :

(a) Coins of the city-State of Vidisha with Brāhmī legend *'Vedisa'* or *'Veddasa'* found and preserved in MGM Museum, Raipur. *JNSI*, XXIII, pp. 307-308.

(b) Copper coin of Śivagupta found. *JNSI*, XXV, pp. 104-05.

(c) A cast copper coin of about 1st century BC with legend *'Śivamitasa'* found. *IAR*, 1967-68, p. 63.

(d) A unique coin with legend '. . . *Kanam*' in Brāhmī, probably issued by a guild of merchants at Vidisha found. *IAR*, 1962-63, p. 63.

(e) Two copper coins of Śivagupta and Sakhadeva, probably rulers of Padmāvatī found. *JNSI*, XXII, pp. 132-33; *IAR*, 1960-61, p. 55.

(f) Four coins of the city issue of Vidisha found. *JNSI*, LI (1989), pt. I-II, p. 15.

For a critical review of the city issues of M.P., see Bela Lahiri, *JNSI*, XXXVIII (1976), pt. II, pp. 35-54.

(D) Indo-Greek and Indo-Bactrian Coins

Balaghat (Balaghat) :

Six copper coins found at; two of them belonging to Menander and the rest difficult to identify. *Balaghat District Gazetteer* (1907), p. 69.

Indore (Indore) :

(a) Interesting Indo-Bactrian coins found in the late N.R. Advani collection. The coins noticed are:

(1) A Tetradrachm of Plato.

(2) A copper coin of Heliokles.

(3) A Hemidrachm of Strato.

(4) Two Hemidrachms of Strato I and one of Strato I with Strato II.

(5) A Hemidrachm of Strato with Agathokleia.

(6) A Hemidrachm of Epander.

(7) A square copper coin of Archebois.

(8) Two silver coins of Philoxenos.

(9) A Hemidrachm of Nikias.

(10) Two Hemidrachms of Apollophanes.

(11) A Didrachm of Amyntas.

(12) A Hemidrachm of Hermaios and Kalliope. *JNSI*, XIII, pt. I, pp. 78-91.

(b) Indo-Bactrian coins noticed in the Advani collection. The coins are as follows :

(1) Two Tetradrachms of Eukratides.

(2) Two silver Hemidrachms of Menander with owl on reverse.

(3) Another silver Hemidrachm of Menander.

(4) A square copper coin of Zoilos.

(5) A Hemidrachm of Zoilos. *JNSI*, XIII, pt. II, pp. 215-18.

(E) Satavahana Coins

Avra (Mandsaur) :

Three lead coins of the Sātavahanas found in surface collection during excavations of 1960-61. *JMPIP*, No. 4 (1962), p. 34.

Balpur (Bilaspur) :

(a) Two coins of the Sātavahanas found. *IAR*, 1958-59, p. 66.

(b) A copper coin of Śivaśrī Āpilaka of Āndhra family, datable to about 3rd century AD found in the sands of Mahanadi river. *NS*, XLVII, (344), 1937-38; *JAHRS*, X, p. 225; *JNSI*, XLIII (1981), pt. II, pp. 134-36.

(c) A new Sātavāhana portrait coin found. *JNSI*, XXI, pp. 107-09.

Besnagar (Vidisha) :

One lead coin of Gautamīputra Yajñaśrī Sātakarṇī found in the excavations of 1913-14. *ASIR*, 1913-14, pp. 186-226.

Bheraghat (Jabalpur) :

A new bronze coin of Siri Sāta of Sātavāhana dynasty found. *JNSI*, XVI, pp. 95-96 and 280-281.

Bhilsa (Vidisha) :

(a) Lead coins of Vāsiṣṭhīputra Pulumāvī of the Sātavāhana dynasty found. *JNSI*, XI, pp. 1-3.

(b) Coins of Sātavāhana ruler Gautamīputra Yajñaśrī found. *ARASI*, 1914-15, p. 213.

(c) A unique silver portrait coin of Sātavāhana ruler Vāsiṣṭhīputra Pulumāvī acquired and preserved in the Advani collection at Indore. *JNSI*, XIV, pp. 1-3.

Bilaspur District :

Nine types of Sātavāhana coins related to Sātakarṇī, Veda Śrī, Śakti Śrī, Apīlaka and Kumbha Sātakarṇī found in the district makes the history of Sātavāhana rule in South Kosala clear. Possibly the dynasty ruled in two phases interrupted by the Maghas. *PP*, XVI, pp. 101-06.

Dewas (Dewas) :

Six Sātavāhana coins, two of Pulumāvī, two of Sātakarṇī, one of Yajñaśrī Sātakarṇī and one of Kumbha Sātakarṇī noticed. *JNSI*, XV, p. 110.

Indore (Indore) :

(a) Three interesting coins which may possibly may attributed to Sātavāhana family noticed in the Advani collection. *JNSI*, XIII, pp. 209-11; XV, pp. 183-84.

(b) A non-portrait silver coin of Gautamīputra Sātakarṇī in collection of Daulal Johari. *JNSI*, XLVII (1985), pt. I-II, pp. 29-30.

(c) One potin coin of Skanda Sātakarṇī in the Gopaldas Mangaldas collection. *JNSI*, XLVIII (1986), pt. I-II, p. 26.

Jamunia (Hoshangabad) :

A copper coin of the Sātavāhana Śrī Sāta found. *JNSI*, XII, pp. 94-97; *NNM*, No. 5, p. 7.

Maheshwar (West Nimar) :

One new Sātavāhana (?) coin found during excavations at Maheswar and Navadatoli (1952-53). *EMN*, p. 79.

Malhar (Bilaspur) :

Two Sātavāhana coins bearing legend '*Rajño Māgha Sirisa*' discovered. *PP*, IX-X, 1981-82, p. 125.

Raipur (Raipur) :

Five Sātavāhana coins in the collection of the MGM Museum. *JNSI*, XXIII, p. 505.

Tewar (Jabalpur) :

(a) A silver coin of Gautamīputra Śrī Yajña Sātakaraṇī found. *JNSI*, XII, pp. 126-33; XIII, pp. 46-52; *NNM*, No. 5, p. 7.

(b) Two lead coins of Sātakarṇī I discovered. *JNSI*, XIII, pp.35-39; *NNM* No.5, p.7.

Tripuri (Jabalpur) :

(a) A bronze coin of Sātakarṇī of Sātavāhana dynasty found. *JNSI*, XXI, pp. 110-11.

(b) Three lead coins of Siri Sāti of Sātavāhana dynasty found in the excavations of 1951-52 and 1952-53. *JNSI*, XVI, p. 70; *Tripuri-1952*, p. 126 and fn.

(c) Eight Sātavāhana lead coins of uncertain readings found in the excavations during 1951-52 and 1952-53. *JNSI*, XVI, p. 69; *Tripuri-1952*, pp. 126-28.

(d) Six lead coins of '. . . *Yadhana*' found in the excavations of 1951-52. *JNSI*, XVI, pp. 70-71.

(e) Coins of Siri Sāta Kanisa and Siri Sāta found in the excavation of 1968-69. *IAR*, 1969-70.

(f) Sātavāhana coins of six rulers viz. Sātakarṇī I, Śakti Śrī, Sātakarṇī II, Gautamīputra Śrī Yajña Sātakarṇī, Kumbha and Śrī Harṣa found in various excavations and explorations conducted at Tripurī examined. *PP*, IX-X, 1981-82, pp. 149-60.

(g) Five types of Sātavāhana coins found from Tripurī discussed. *ND*, XVI (1992), pp. 29-46.

Ujjain (Ujjain) :

(a) A Sātavāhana coin, tentatively ascribed to Gautamīputra Sātakarṇī found. *JNSI*, XIV, pp. 3-4.

(b) A non-portrait silver coin of Gautamīputra acquired. *JNSI*, VIII, pp. 111 ff; IX, pp. 93-94.

(c) Two re-struck Sātavāhana coins found and preserved in the Wakankar collection. *JNSI*, XVI, pp. 181-82.

(d) Copper coin of Siri Sāta found. Bajpai, K.D., *Coinage of the Sātavāhanas and Coins from Excavations* (Ed. A.M. Shastri), p. 29.

(e) Copper coin of Sātakarṇī. *Ibid.*

(f) Four Sātavāhana coins—two of copper with no legend, third of silver assigned to Vāsiṣṭhīputra Pulumāvī and the fourth of potin assigned to Vāsiṣṭhīputra Sātakarṇī. *JNSI*, XLV (1983), pt. I-II, pp. 31-35.

(g) One silver coin of Skanda Sātakarṇī found. *JNSI*, XLVIII (1986), pt. I-II, pp. 26-29.

(h) One silver coin of Gautamīputra Yajña Sātakarṇī found. *JNSI*, XLVIII (1986), pt. I-II, pp. 26-29.

Vidisha (Vidisha) :

(a) A Sātavāhana copper coin of Śrī Sātakarṇī found. *IAR*, 1967-68, p. 63.

(b) A copper coin of Śrī Sātakarṇī in punch-marked style. Bajpai, K.D., *Coins of the Sātavāhanas and Coins from Excavations* (ed. A.M. Shastri), pp. 27-28.

(F) Coins of the Śakas and the Western Kṣatrapas

Avra (Mandsaur) :

(a) Silver coins of Western Kṣatrapa ruler Rudrasena III found in the excavation of 1960-61. *JMPIP*, No. 4 (1962), pp. 32-33.

(b) Copper coin of Dāmajadaśrī II found in surface exploration during excavation of 1960-61. *JMPIP*, No. 4 (1962), p. 34.

Besnagar (Vidisha) :

(a) Two silver coins, one of Mahākṣatrapa Vīradāman and the other of Rudrasena II found in the excavation. *ARASI*, 1913-14, p. 213.

(b) One copper coin of Īśvardatta of the Western Kṣatrapas of Saurashtra found. *ARASI*, 1914-15, p. 88.

(c) Eight coins of the Western Satraps of Saurastra found. *CASIR*, X, p. 37.

(d) Silver and copper coins of the Western Kṣatrapas found in the excavations of 1913-14 and 1914-15. *ASIR*, 1913-14, pp. 186-226; 1914-15, pp.66-68.

Dangawada (Ujjain) :

Two Kṣatrapa coins found in excavations. *DER*, p. 126.

Gondarmau (Sehore) :

A hoard of 51 silver coins of Western Kṣatrapas—5 coins of M.K. Vijayasena, 6 of M.K. Rudrasena II, 17 of Bhartrdāman, 10 of K. Viśvasena, 3 of K. Rudrasiṁha II and 1 of M.K. Svāmī Rudrasena III, the attribution of the remaining 9 being uncertain, discovered. All the coins are dated, the legible dates ranging from Śaka 157 to 270 (AD 235 to 348). *IAR*, 1954-55, p. 63.

Indore (Indore) :

(a) Indo-Scythian coins in the Advani collection. The coins are the following :

(1) A coin of Maues: Elephant and seated figure.

(2) A coin of Azes with Poseidon.

(3) Another coin of Azes : Elephant and bull type.

(4) A copper coin of Spalyris with Spalagadames.

(5) Indo-Scythian coins with peculiar monograms. *JNSI*, XIV, pp. 47-51.

(b) New coins of Chaṣṭana of the Western Kṣatrapa dynasty in the collection of Shantilal Pardeshi. *JNSI*, XVIII, pp. 169-71.

(c) A copper Kṣatrapa coin noticed in the Advani collection. *JNSI*, XIII, p. 213.

(d) Kṣatrapa potin and copper coins of the following rulers noticed in Shri Daulal Johri collection :

(1) A potin coin of Rudramsiṁha I dated in S.E. 103.

(2) A potin coin of Rudrasena I dated in S.E. 140.

(3) Two potin coins of Dāmasena dated in S.E. 147 and 148.

(4) A copper coin of Yaśodāman II dated in S.E. 252. *JNSI*, XXXVIII (1976), pt. I, pp. 38-45.

(e) A unique coin of M.K. Īśvaradatta dated in S.E. 154 noticed in collection of Prabhachandra Shastri. *JNSI*, XL (1978), pt. I-II, pp. 34-41.

Keolari (Seoni) :

Three silver Western Kṣatrapa coins found. The coins belonged to Mahākṣatrapa Rudrasena II, son of Kṣatrapa Vīradāman, Kṣatrapa Bhartṛdāman, son of Mahākṣatrapa Rudrasena II and Kṣatrapa Rudrasiṁha II, son of Svāmī Jīvadāman. *JNSI*, XVI, pp. 207-09.

Pagara (Dhar) :

Nine silver coins of Kṣatrapa rulers discovered in a hoard. *JNSI*, XLIV (1982), pt. I-II, pp. 52-55.

Pichhore (Gwalior) :

Four silver coins with traces of human head and legend *Śrīdāma* on the obverse and a crude form of Sassanian fire-altar on the reverse found. *ASIR*, 1913-14, pp. 248-60.

Raipur (Raipur) :

Three silver Western Kṣatrapa coins in the collection of MGM Museum. *JNSI*, XXIII, p. 505.

Sanchi (Raisen) :

Forty-one silver coins of the Western Kṣatrapas discovered in 1916-17. These belong to Rudrasena I, Rudrasena II, Viśvasiṁha, Bhartṛdāman, Viśvasena, Rudrasiṁha II, Rudrasena III and some unidentified coins. *Catalogue of the Museum of Archaeology at Sanchi* by John Marshall and others (1922), pp. 60-64.

Seoni (Seoni) :

One silver coin of Rudrasena, son of Svāmī Jīvadāman discovered. *JNSI*, XII, pp. 167-69.

Shivpuri (Shivpuri) :

(a) Twenty-six coins of Western Kṣatrapa ruler Rudrasena found and examined. *JNSI*, XV, pp. 106-07.

(b) Some Western Kṣatrapa coins found in the Muniraj collection. The coins are :

(1) Copper coin of Kṣaharāta Arta (?).

(2) Copper coins of Bhūmaka.

(3) Silver coins of Nahapāna, re-struck by Gautamīputra Sātakaraṇī.

(4) Silver-coated copper coin of Chaṣṭana.

(5) Silver coin of Mahākṣatrapa Rudrasiṁha.

(6) An unattributed copper coin.

(7) An anonymous potin coin of the time of Dāmasena and some more coins of the type. *JNSI*, XVII, pp. 89-98.

Sonepur (Chhindwara) :

A collection of 670 silver coins of the Western Kṣatrapas belonging to kings from Rudrasena I to Swāmī Rudrasena III, with the exception of Sanghadāman found. *NS*, XLVII, Article No. 345.

Ujjain (Ujjain) :

(a) A silver coin of Mahākṣatrapa Chaṣṭana found at and preserved in the Advani collection at Indore. *JNSI*, XIV, pp. 20-21.

(b) A coin of a certain ruler Mahu and two coins bearing the name of Dāsa, both in copper, were discovered and identified. Possibly these two kings belonged to the pre-Bhūmaka house of the Śakas of Malwa. *IAR*, 1965-66, p. 76.

(c) Three copper coins of Early Śaka rulers, Mahu, Dāsa and Sauma respectively. *JNSI*, XXVIII, pp. 49-50.

(d) Two punch-marked coins of the Western Kṣatrapas, belonging respectively to Viśvasena and struck by Rudrasena III found. *JNSI*, XV, pp. 220-22.

Vabachia (Vidisha) :

A hoard of forty-eight silver coins of Western Kṣatrapas discovered. These are grouped into fourteen types. *JNSI*, XLII (1980), pt. I-II, pp. 25-30.

Vidisha (Vidisha) :

(a) A copper coin of Śaka ruler Hamugama, probably of Ujjain branch, with name inscribed in Brāhmī character of early Śunga period found. *IAR*, 1962-63, p. 63.

(b) Two copper coins of Early Śaka rulers Hamugama and Valāka respectively found. *JNSI*, XVIII, p. 46 ff.

(G) Kuṣāṇa Coins

Bilaspur (Bilaspur) :

One copper Kuṣāṇa coin found. *NNM*, No. 5, p. 10.

Harda (Hoshangabad) :

Two gold Kuṣāṇa coins—one quarter stater of Huviṣka and the other, a stater of Kaṇiṣka II or III found. *NMC; JNSI*, XVII, p. 109; *NNM*, No. 5, p. 9.

Jhajhapuri (Bilaspur) :

Fifteen copper coins of Kuṣāṇa rulers Kaṇiṣka and Huviṣka found. *JNSI*, XVII, p. 109; *NNM*, No. 5, p. 10.

Kenda Zamindari (Bilaspur) :

Twenty-five copper Kuṣāṇa coins found. *JNSI*, XVII, p. 109; *TTR*, No. 5 of 1922-23.

Malhar (Bilaspur) :

Kuṣāṇa coins found in excavations. *MER*, p. 34.

Pendharwa (Bilaspur) :

Copper Kuṣāṇa coin found with Yaudheya coins. *JNSI*, XVII, p. 109.

Raipur (Raipur) :

Twenty-four Kuṣāṇa coins in the collection of MGM Museum. *JNSI*, XXIII, p. 505.

Rajgarh (Rajgarh) :

A new Boddo type of gold coin of Kaṇiṣka I found. *JNSI*, XLIV (1981), pt. I-II, pp. 42-45.

Shahdol (Shahdol) :

A big hoard of 757 copper coins of Kuṣāṇa rulers comprising 44 coins of Wema Kadphises, 324 coins of Kaṇiṣka, 362 coins of Huviṣka and rest unidentified found. *JNSI*, XXVII, pp. 118-19; XXVIII, pp. 1-5; *IAR*, 1964-65, p. 70.

Tewar (Jabalpur) :

One copper coin of Kuṣāṇa Vāsudeva found. *MPR*, p. 47.

Vidisha (Vidisha) :

A Kuṣāṇa coin of Wema Kadphises found. *IAR*, 1967-68, p. 63; *JNSI*, XXXII (I), pp. 82-83.

(H) Nāga Coins

Akoda (Bhind) :

Two hundred and seventy copper coins of various types belonging to the Nāga rulers discovered. *IAR*, 1961-62, p. 94.

Besnagar (Vidisha) :

(a) A coin of Vṛṣanāga, a new Nāga king found at and preserved in the Gwalior Museum. *JNSI*, XV, pp. 121-23; XVI, p. 279.

(b) Eight coins of the Nāgas of Narwar found. *CASIR*, X, p. 37.

(c) Copper coins of Gaṇaptināga found in the excavations of 1913-14 and 1914-15. *ASIR*, 1913-14, pp. 186-226; 1914-15, pp. 66-68.

(d) Coins of Nāga rulers found in the excavations of 1963. Obverse of these coins has Nandi and on the reverse the names of rulers with the title of Mahārāja appear. Bajpai, K.D., *Madhya Pradesh Ka Purtattva*, p. 16.

Cheema (Datia) :

A hoard of 1,082 copper coins of the Nāga rulers discovered. *IAR*, 1987-88, p. 132.

Eran (Sagar) :

(a) A new type of Nāga coin of Ravināga found. *JNSI*, XXXI, pt. I, pp. 72-73.

(b) Coins of different Nāga rulers found in excavation and exploration. Bajpai, K.D., *Sagar Through the Ages*, pp. 9, 29.

Gohad (Bhind) :

Nāga coins found. *CASIR*, II, pp. 307 ff.; *JASB*, 1865, pp. 115ff.; *CMA*, pp. 23ff.

Gwalior (Gwalior) :

Two new coins of Śesadatta possibly associated with the Nāgas of Mathura, Padmavati, Kantipuri and Vidisha found. *JNSI*, XXXIV (1972), pt. II, pp. 189-95.

Indore (Indore) :

One Nāga coin in the collection of late Shri Tikekar. *JNSI*, X, pp. 26-42.

Kutwar (Morena) :

A hoard of 18,959 Nāga coins found. *GAR*, 1927-28, p. 16; *CCNP*, p. 60.

Narwar (Shivpuri) :

(a) Fourteen copper coins of Nava Nāga rulers found. *JASB*, XXXIV, p. 115; *CASIR*, II, pp. 307ff; *CMI*, pp. 23ff; *IHQ*, I, p. 255.

(b) One coin of Vyāghranāga found. *CMI*, p. 24; *JASB*, XXXIV, p. 115.

Pawaya (Gwalior) :

(a) Coins of Nāga ruler Bhavanāga and Vibhunāga found. *JNSI*, V, pp. 20-27.

(b) Nāga coins of some new rulers found at and preserved in the Gwalior Museum. The kings represented are — Bhīmanāga, Skandanāga, Bṛhaspatināga, Devanāga, Gaṇapatināga and Prabhākaranāga. *JNSI*, XV, pp. 130-35.

(c) A few coins of the Nāgas of Padmāvatī found and preserved in the Gwalior Museum. The coins belong to the rulers named Makhadata, Mahata, Sabalasena, Amitasena and Yataga (?). *JNSI*, XVII, pp. 53-57.

(d) Two copper coins of Nāga rulers Prabhākara and *'Mahārāja Bh(i)* ? . . .' found. *JNSI*, XVII, pp. 52-53.

(e) Nine Nāga coins representing kings Bhavanāga, Vibhunāga and Vīrasena found and preserved in Gwalior Museum. *JNSI*, XVII, pp. 47-51.

(f) Die-struck copper Nāga coins acquired at and preserved in Indore Museum. The coins belong to Bhavanāga, Vasunāga, Ravināga, Prabhunāga, Skandanāga and Bṛhaspatināga. *JNSI*, XIV, pp. 71-79.

(g) A new type of Gaṇapati Nāga coin found. *ND*, IV, pt. II (Dec. 1980), pp. 24-25.

Raipur (Raipur) :

One hundred forty-four copper coins of the Nāgas of Padmāvatī in the collection of MGM Museum. *JNSI*, XXIII, p. 505.

Tumain (Guna) :

Two coins of Gaṇapati Nāga found in excavation. *EAT*, p. 44.

Ujjain (Ujjain) :

Nāga coins found. *CCNP*, p. XXXIX.

Vidisha (Vidisha) :

Coins of Vṛsa (Nāga), the founder of the Nāgas of Padmāvatī found. *CCNP*, pp. V-VI.

(I) Bodhi Coins

Tripuri (Jabalpur) :

Coins and sealings of the rulers of Bodhi dynasty viz. Śrī Bodhi, Chandra Bodhi, Śiva Bodhi, Vasu Bodhi, Dharma Bodhi, Vīra Bodhi, Vīra Bodhi Datta,

Sirivasaka and Siriśiva found in excavations and explorations. *JNSI*, XXXIV (1972), pt. II, pp. 213-22; XXXVII, pt. I-II (1975), pp. 31-38; XXXVIII, pt. II (1976), pp. 62-72 and 98-99; *Bulletin of Ancient Indian History and Archaeology*, Sagar University, No. 3; *PP*, VI, No. 1, Jan. 1978, pp. 55-67.

(J) Sena Coins

Tripuri (Jabalpur) :

(a) Ten lead coins of Sena dynasty found in personal collection of Dr. M.C. Choubey. Sudarasena (or Sundarasena) is the new ruler known from these coins. Two rulers viz. Sujeṣṭhasena (copper coin) and Mahāsena (clay sealing) were earlier brought to light in Tripuri excavations conducted by Sagar University. *JNSI*, XXXIX (1977), pt. I-II, pp. 157-59.

(b) From coins and seals, seven rulers of the Sena dynasty of Tripuri are known as follows :

Coins

1. Yaśasena
2. Sundarasena
3. Mahāsena-I
4. Sujeṣṭhasena

T.C. Seals

5. Siṁhasena
6. Vitilaya Skanda
7. Mahāsena-II (Mahāsena Govira)

These rulers ruled at Tripuri after Bodhis and before the Guptas. Details discussed. *JNSI*, XLV (1983), pt. I-II, pp. 40-45.

(K) Magha Coins

Bandhogarh (Shahdol) :

Coins of Magha dynasty found. *INC*, III, No. 1 (1962), pp. 11-21.

Kasrawad (West Nimar) :

A Magha coin found along with other indigenous coins in the excavation of 1939-40. *JNSI*, VIII, pp. 99ff.

Jabalpur (Jabalpur) :

A hoard of 2,400 Magha coins acquired by A.M. Shastri. Possibly these were originally found at Umaria in Shahdol district. These contain eight varieties of the coins of Vijayanandin whose relationship with the Magha rulers is unknown. *ND*, VI, pt. I-II (1982), pp. 17-25.

Malhar (Bilaspur) :

Three copper coins of Magha dynasty, of which two were of Śiva Magha and the third Yamagha found. *ND*, IX, pt. I-II (1985), pp. 34-60.

(L) Coins of the Guptas and their Contemporaries

Anuppur (Shahdol) :

Two archer type of gold coins of Chandragupta II found and deposited in MGM Museum, Raipur. *JNSI*, XLI (1979), pt. I-II, p. 123.

Arang (Raipur) :

A silver coated copper coin of Kumāragupta I found. *PP*, V, No. 2, July 1977, p. 198.

Balpur (Bilaspur) :

Two silver (possibly gold) coins of Prasannamātra found. *Pr. AIOC,* V; *IHQ*, IX, XV.

Bamnala (East Nimar) :

Eight coins of Samudragupta, nine of Chandragupta II and four of Kumāragupta found. On the coin of Samudragupta, the epithet used is *Vikrama* instead of his usual one of *Parākrama*. *JNSI*, V, p. 135.

Banabarada (Durg) :

One coin of Kācha, seven of Chandragupta II and one of Kumāragupta I discovered. *Nav Bharat (Daily)*, Jabalpur ed., dt. Jan. 7, 1973.

Besnagar (Vidisha) :

One coin of Chandragupta II found. *CASIR*, X, p. 37.

Bhilsa (Vidisha) :

(a) Six coins of Rāmagupta collected. *JNSI*, XII, pp. 103-11.

(b) Four copper coins of Rāmagupta (?) collected. *JNSI*, XIII, pp. 128-30.

Edenga (Bastar) :

A hoard of thirty-two coins of Nala dynasty of Bastar, datable to 4th-5th century AD found. The names of the kings representated are Varāharāja, Bhavadatta and Arthapati. *JNSI*, I, pp. 29 ff.

Eran (Sagar) :

(a) Copper coins of Rāmagupta, some of them with the border legend Śrī-Rāmaguptaḥ on the obverse and garuḍa on the reverse. *IAR*, 1961-62, p. 94; Bajpai, K.D., *Sagar Through the Ages*, p. 29.

(b) Coin of Hūṇa ruler Toramāṇa. Bajpai, K.D., *Sagar Through the Ages*, p. 30.

Ganeshpur (Jabalpur) :

One gold Gupta coin found. *JNSI*, XVII, p. 110; *TTR*, No. 8 of 1910.

Harda (Hoshangabad) :

One gold coin of Chandragupta II, archer type, found. *JNSI*, XVII, p. 110; *NMC*.

Indore (Indore) :

Nine silver coins of Kumāragupta I in collection of Shri Umrao Singh Babel, acquired from some place in Malwa. Of these, a rare coin depicts lotus symbol on the reverse. It is a new type. *JNSI*, LI (1989), pt. I-II, pp. 16-18.

Khairatal (Raipur) :

Fifty-four gold repoussé coins of Śrī-Mahendrāditya found and distributed in different museums. *JNSI*, X, pp. 137 ff. and XI, pp. 108-10; *TTR*, No. 6 of 1948-49.

Kulia (Raipur) :

Thirty repoussé gold coins discovered in 1977. Of these, twenty-five belong to Mahendrāditya (24 known variety and one new variety), two of Nala ruler Bhavadatta and one of Nala ruler Arthapati. Of the remaining two, one has legend Stambha and the other Śrī Nandanarāja, also Nala rulers of South Kosala and Orissa. *JNSI*, XL (1978), pt. I-II, pp. 108-10; XLV (1983), pt. I-II, pp. 46-50; *PP*, V, No. 1, Jan. 1977, pp. 69-74; V, No. 2, July 1977, pp. 194-96.

Mahasamund (Raipur) :

A repoussé gold coin of Prasannamātra found. *JNSI*, XXXIV (1972), pt. I, pp. 84-85.

Malhar (Bilaspur) :

(a) One copper repoussé coin of Prasannamātra found. *JNSI*, L (1988), pt. I-II, pp. 30-32.

(b) One repoussé gold coin of Mahendrāditya found. *JNSI*, L-II (1990), pt. I-II, pp. 126-30.

Pagara (Dhar) :

Nine gold coins of Gupta kings viz. Kācha, Chandragupta II (archer, lion-slayer and Chhatra types) and Kumāragupta I (archer type) found. *JNSI*, XLIV (1982), pt. I-II, pp. 52-55.

Pattan (Betul) :

One gold coin of Chandragupta II, archer type found. *TTR*, No. 3 of 1938-39.

Pitaiband (Raipur) :

A hoard of 46 coins of Mahendrāditya and three coins of Kramāditya, rulers of S. Kosala found. *JNSI*, XXII, pp. 184-87; XXVI, pp. 31-39; *IAR*, 1959-60, p. 65.

Raipur (Raipur) :

(a) One gold coin of Gupta emperor Narasiṁhagupta in the collection of MGM Museum. *JNSI*, XXIII, p. 505.

(b) Three gold coins of Kramāditya in the collection of MGM Museum. *JNSI*, XXIII, p. 505.

(c) Forty-six gold coins of Mahendrāditya in the collection of MGM Museum. *JNSI*, XXIII, p. 505.

(d) Three copper coins of Jiṣṇu in the collection of MGM Museum. *JNSI*, XXIII, p. 505. For a critical review of Jiṣṇu coins, see *JNSI*, XXXVIII (1976), pt. I, pp. 65-71.

(e) Five copper coins of Rāmagupta in the collection of MGM Museum. *JNSI*, XXIII, p. 505.

(f) One gold coin of Prasannamātra in the collection of MGM Museum. *JNSI*, XXIII, p. 505.

(g) Twenty copper local coins of South Kosala in the collection of MGM Museum. *JNSI*, XIX, pp. 72-73.

(h) Two repoussé gold coins of Mahendrāditya in personal collection of Shri Parasram Soni. *JNSI*, XL (1978), pt. I-II, pp. 108-10.

Riawan (Raipur) :

Thirty-nine repoussé gold coins of Prasannamātra of usual type found in 1975. *JNSI*, XL (1978), pt. I-II, pp. 108-10; *PP*, V, No. 2, July 1977, pp. 194-96.

Runija (Ujjain) :

Coins of Samudragupta and Chandragupta I found. *IAR*, 1979-80, pp. 53-54.

Sagar (Sagar) :

Six gold coins of the Guptas found. *JNSI*, XVII, p. 110; *NMAR*, 1915-16.

Sakaur (Damoh) :

Gold coins of the Gupta rulers, Samudragupta, Kācha, Chandragupta II, and Skandagupta found. *JNSI*, XVII, pp. 103-04, 110; *TTR*, No. 5 of 1914; No. 4 of 1914 and No. 8 of 1909.

Salhepali (Raigarh) :

A silver coin of king Prasannamātra of Śarabhapura, with legend inscribed in box-headed character of 5th-6th century AD found. *IHQ*, IX, p. 595.

Sanchi (Raisen) :

A rare Gupta coin from Sanchi in collection of Shri Pardesi of Indore with legend '*Jitam Bhagavatā Padmanābhena*' may possibly be assigned to Chandragupta II. *JNSI*, XXXIII (1971), pt. I, pp. 120-21; XXXIV (1972), pt. II, pp. 258-59; XXXIX (1977), pt. I-II, pp. 162-64.

Sehora (Guna) :

Gupta coins found. *GAR*, 1924-25, p. 17; *ASIR*, XXIV, p. 168.

Seoni (Seoni) :

One gold coin of Chandragupta II found. *NNM*, No. 5, p. 12.

Sirpur (Raipur) :

One gold coin of Prasannamātra found during excavation. *NNM*, No. 5, p. 13.

Tala (Bilaspur) :

One silver repoussé coin of Prasannamātra found. *JNSI*, L (1988), pt. I-II, pp. 30-32.

Tumain (Guna):

A square coin with legend '*Satyagupta* . . .' in Gupta character found. *IAR*, 1967-68, p. 62.

Ujjain (Ujjain) :

(a) Five new types of the coins of Jiṣṇu, the ruler of Malwa. *JNSI*, XVI, pp. 105-06.

(b) Thirty copper coins of Jiṣṇu, the ruler of Malwa in Advani collection. *JNSI*, XIII, p. 192; XV, pp. 89-93.

(c) Twelve copper coins of Jiṣṇu, the ruler of Malwa. *JNSI*, XIII, pp. 150-51; XV, pp. 89-93.

Vidisha (Vidisha) :

(a) A coin of Rāmagupta bearing his name on one side and figure of a bull on the other found. *IAR*, 1964-65, p. 70.

(b) Lion and garuḍa types of copper coins of Rāmagupta obtained. *JNSI*, XXIII, pp. 340-44.

(c) Sixteen copper coins of Rāmagupta, of which 4 of lion type and the rest of garuḍa type found. *IAR*, 1967-68, p. 63.

(d) Copper coins of Kācha found. *JMPIP*, No. 2, p. 21.

(e) Copper coin bearing the legend '*Jitaṁ Bhagavatā Padmanābhena* (?)'. *JNSI*, XXXIII (Ī), pp. 120-21.

(f) Silver coin of Skandagupta dated in G.E. 141 (460 AD). *JNSI*, XXXVIII (1976), pt. I, pp. 72-73.

(M) Ādivarāha Drammas

Bastar (Bastar) :

Three silver Ādivarāha Drammas found and deposited in Nagpur Museum. *NMC; NNM*, No. 5, p. 14.

Umaria (Jabalpur) :

Five hundred and thirteen silver pieces of Ādivarāha Dramma located, of which only one could be acquired and deposited in Nagpur Museum. *TTR*, No. 3 of 1919-20; *NMAR* for 1919-20.

(N) Indo-Sassanian Coins

Avra (Mandsaur) :

Two Indo-Sassanian coins found in the surface collection during the excavation of 1960-61. *JMPIP*, No. 4 (1962), p. 34.

Bahoriband (Jabalpur) :

A big hoard of 748 silver Indo-Sassanian coins recovered from the Bahoriband area. *JNSI*, XXXIX (1977), pt. I-II, p. 169.

Balaghat (Balaghat) :

Ten silver Indo-Ṣassanian or Gadhiya coins discovered. *Balaghat District Gazetteer* (1907), p. 69.

Bardia (Mandsaur) :

A hoard of Indo-Sassanian (Gadhiya) coins found. *JNSI*, XV, p. 104.

Bhat Pachlana (Ujjain) :

A new variety of Indo-Sassanian coins found. *GAR*, 1927-28, p. 97.

Chanderi (Guna) :

A hoard of Indo-Sassanian coins found. *JNSI*, X, p. 104.

Chhindwara (Chhindwara) :

Thirty-one silver Indo-Sassanian coins found. *NMC; NNM*, No. 5, p. 15.

Devatpur (Shajapur) :

A hoard of Indo-Sassanian coins found. *JNSI*, XV, p. 104.

Eran (Sagar):

Indo-Sassanian coins found. Bajpai, K.D., *Sagar Through The Ages*, p. 30.

Ghataoda (Dhar) :

A hoard of Indo-Sassanian coins found. *JNSI*, XV, p. 104.

Guida (Nimar) :

Eleven silver Indo-Sassanian coins found. None of them could be acquired. *TTR*, No. 9 of 1916; *NNM*, No. 5, p. 15.

Harsud (East Nimar) :

A hoard of 1,226 silver Gadhiya coins discovered. *JNSI*, XXVIII, pp. 213-14.

Hoshangabad (Hoshangabad) :

Thirty-eight silver Indo-Sassanian coins found and deposited in the Nagpur Museum. *NMC*; *NNM*, No. 5, p. 16.

Indore (Indore) :

(a) Rare Gadhiya coins—eight of silver, two of copper and one of lead, noticed in the Advani collection. Some silver and copper coins bear the legend '*Oṁkāra*' on the reverse. *JNSI*, XIII, pp. 205-06.

(b) One thousand one hundred and fifty silver Gadhia coins of the state treasury of Indore examined. About seventy of them bear on the obverse the usual crude Sassanian head and on the reverse there is the figure of a horse-rider fighting with sword raised out his hand against one or more foot soldiers. *JNSI*, VIII, pp. 66-71.

Kherua (Damoh) :

Three hundred and twelve silver Indo-Sassanian coins found, of which only 65 acquired and deposited in the Nagpur Museum. *TTR*, No. 8 of 1930-31; *NNM*, No. 5, p. 14.

Maharajpur (Sagar) :

Eighteen copper Indo-Sassanian coins found and deposited in the Nagpur Museum. *TTR*, No. 9 of 1954-55; *NNM*, No. 5, p. 15.

Mandhata (East Nimar) :

Indo-Sassanian coins with legend '*Śrī-Oṁkāra*' found. *JNSI*, XI, p. 58.

Mohania Khurd (East Nimar) :

(a) A large hoard of silver Gadhiya coins was collected. *IAR*, 1961-62, p. 94.

(b) A hoard of 200 copper mixed silver Gadhiya coins found. *JNSI*, XXV, pp. 36-38.

Multai (Betul) :

One thousand six hundred and forty silver Indo-Sassanian coins of which only twelve could be acquired, found and deposited in the Nagpur and other museums. *TTR*, No. 12 of 1935-36; *NNM*, No. 5, p. 15.

Murwara (Jabalpur) :

Silver Indo-Sassanian coins found. *Jabalpur District Gazetteer* (1909), p. 73; *NNM*, No. 5, p. 14.

Patan (Jabalpur):

Six hundred and ninety-two copper Indo-Sassanian coins found at and deposited in Nagpur Museum. *Frag. TTR*, No. 8 of 1919-20; *NMAR* for 1919-20; *NNM*, No. 5, p. 14.

Raipur (Raipur) :

Eleven silver and four copper coins of Indo-Sassanians in the collection of the local museum. *JNSI*, XXIII, p. 505.

Seoni (Seoni) :

Eight silver Indo-Sassanian coins found. *NMC; NNM*, No. 5, p. 15.

Sirsa (Durg) :

One hundred and thirty-nine copper Indo-Sassanian coins found at and deposited in Nagpur and other museums. *TTR*, No. 8 of 1954-55; *IAR*, 1954-55, p. 63.

Tumain (Guna) :

A hoard of 582 coins of Gadhiya type found in excavation. Of these seven were inscribed with legend *'Ajoyadeva'*. *EAT*, p. 38.

Ujjain (Ujjain) :

Two inscribed copper Gadhiya coins found at and preserved in Wakankar collection. *JNSI*, XVI, pp. 281-82.

(O) Coins of the Chandellas

Ajaigarh (Panna) :

This rare coin of Chandella Trailokyavarman acquired at Ajaigarh has on obverse legend of Śrīmat Trailokyavarmadeva and on reverse seated Lakṣmī. *JNSI*, XXXIV (1972), pt. II, pp. 262-63.

Khajuraho (Chhatarpur) :

(a) A unique gold dramma of Chandella ruler Vīravarman. *CCIMC*, pt. I, p. 254.

(b) A rare half-dramma copper coin of Chandella Jayavarmadeva found. *JNSI*, XXXVII (pt. I-II), 1975, pp. 100-05.

Rewa (Rewa) :

A hoard of forty-eight silver coins of the Chandella ruler Madanavarman found. *NS*, XXII (131), 1914.

Tripuri (Jabalpur) :

(a) A gold coin of Chandella Vīravarman found. *JNSI*, XVI, pp. 236-38.

(b) Three coins of king Paramardideva — two of base gold and one of copper found. *JNSI*, XLIII (1981), pt. II, pp. 74-75.

Tulapar (Raisen) :

Nine gold coins of Chandella ruler Sallakṣaṇavarman found during excavations. *ND*, XI (Dec. 1987), p. 126.

(P) Coins of the Paramāras of Malwa

Indore (Indore) :

(a) One coin each of gold and copper of Paramāra king Naravarman in the collection of Sri Padamsingh and Sri Santilal Pardeshi. *JNSI*, XXX, p. 208. For another coin of Udayāditya, see *NS*, pt. XXXIII, Art. No. 203.

(b) Gold and silver coins respectively of Udayāditya and Ajayavarman in collection of Padamsingh Shyamsukh. *MPSG*, p. 451.

(c) Gold coin of Naravarman in personal collection of Dr. Nagu. *MPSG*, p. 451.

Tulapar (Raisen) :

Twenty-seven gold coins of Paramāra ruler found during excavations. Of these ten were of Jayavarman, two of Udayāditya and fifteen of Naravarman. *ND*, XI (Dec. 1987), p. 126.

Tulsipur (Raisen) :

Thirty-six circular gold coins bearing the legends of the Paramāra and Chandella rulers found as a treasure trove. *IAR*, 1982-83, p. 130.

(Q) Coins of the Kalachuris

Bachchhauda (Bilaspur) :

Nine gold Kalachuri coins found. *NNM*, No. 5, p. 17.

Balpur (Bilaspur) :

(a) Three silver Kalachuri coins found at and deposited in the Mahakoshal Historical Society, Raigarh. *JNSI*, III, pp. 41-42.

(b) Twelve copper coins of king Pratāpamalla found. *IHQ*, III, p. 173.

(c) One coin with name Vikram Sāi, evidently a late chief of Kalachuri dynasty of Ratanpur found. *IAR*, 1958-59, p. 66.

(d) Three coins of the Kalachuris found. *IAR*, 1958-59, p. 66.

Barela (Jabalpur):

A hoard of about 125 gold coins of Gāṅgeyadeva found. *JNSI*, XVI, p. 281; XVIII, pp. 110-11; *IAR*, 1955-56, p. 66.

Baretha (Jabalpur) :

A hoard of 54 silver coins of Kalachuri ruler Gāṅgeyadeva found. *JNSI*, XVIII, pp. 205-06.

Besnagar (Vidisha) :

(a) Kṛṣṇarāja Rūpaka of the Kalachuri dynasty found. *ARASI*, 1913-14, pp. 208, 214.

(b) Seven silver coins of Kalachuri Kṛṣṇarāja found in the excavation of 1913-14. *ASIR*, 1913-14, pp. 186-226.

Bhagaund (Bilaspur) :

Twelve gold and three copper coins of Pṛthvīdeva of Kalachuri dynasty found.

NNM, No. 5, p. 17.

Dalal-Seoni (Raipur) :

One hundred and thirty-six gold coins (of which only 124 acquired) of the Kalachuri kings Pṛthvīdeva, Jājalladeva and Ratnadeva found. *ITR*, No. 5 of 1940-41; *NNM*, No. 5, p. 17.

Dewas (Dewas) :

Two gold coins of Pṛthvīdeva and one of Jājalladeva found in the state treasury. *JNSI*, XV, p. 110.

Dhanpur (Bilaspur) :

A hoard of 3,900 copper coins of the Kalachuri dynasty of Ratanpur discovered. *JNSI*, XVIII, pp. 111-12.

Dungaria (Seoni) :

Forty-two gold coins of Gāṅgeyadeva discovered and preserved in Rani Durgavati Museum, Jabalpur. This hoard is important as three types of Gāṅgeyadeva coins 9—big sized, 18 middle sized and 15 smaller sized—discovered. *PP*, V, No. 2 (July 1977), pp. 92-93.

Geji (Sarguja) :

Three coins of Gāṅgeyadeva found. *HC*, p. 42.

Isurpur (Sagar) :

Eight gold coins of Gāṅgevadeva found and deposited in the Nagpur Museum. *NS*, XVII, Article No. 101.

Jabalpur District :

Fifty-eight coins of Kalachuri Gāṅgeyadeva and two of Chandella Madanavarman found. *IAR*, 1987-88, p. 132.

Jargawan (Panna) :

A new hoard of twenty-two gold coins of Gāṅgeyadeva found. A new variety is added in this hoard. *JNSI*, XXXIX (1977), pt. I-II, p. 172.

Kaira (Bilaspur) :

A hoard of one hundred and three gold coins of the Kalachuris of Ratanpur discovered. The hoard consisted of big and small coins of Jājalladeva (one coin), Ratnadeva II (nine coins) and Pṛthvīdeva II (ninety-three coins). *PP*, V, No. 2 (July 1977), p. 93.

Khairagarh (Rajnandgaon) :

Eleven copper coins of Kalachuri king Jājalladeva found. *ND*, XIV (1990), p. 112.

Mandu (Dhar) :

A gold coin of Gāṅgeyadeva of Kalachuri dynasty obtained. *JNSI*, XV, p. 105.

Old Khairagarh State (Rajnandgaon) :

Two hundred copper coins of the Kalachuri dynasty found (further details lacking). *JNSI*, III, p. 28, fn. 43; *NNM*, No. 5, p. 18.

Old Raigarh State (Raigarh) :

Forty-three copper coins of the Kalachuri dynasty found at (further details not known). *NNM*, No. 5, p. 18.

Old Sarangarh State :

Fifty-six gold coins of the Ratanpur Kalachuris found. *PRASB*, 1893, p. 92.

Pattan (Betul) :

Two silver coins of Kṛṣṇarāja found. *TTR*, No. 3 of 1938-39; *NNM*, No. 5, p. 14.

Raipur (Raipur) :

Three gold, two silver and one hundred and ten copper coins of the Kalachuris in the collection of MGM Museum. *JNSI*, XXIII, p. 505.

Sagar (Sagar) :

Eight gold coins of Kalachuri king Gāṅgeyadeva found. *NS*, XVII (101), 1912.

Sonsari (Bilaspur) :

A hoard of six hundred gold coins comprising those of Kalachuri rulers Gāṅgeyadeva, Jājalladeva, Ratnadeva and Pṛthvīdeva and of Nāga ruler Someśvara found. Two coins of Govindachandra were also found. *JAHRS*, XII, pt. III, pp. 177-78; *JNSI*, III, p. 27 ff; XVII, pt. II, pp. 54 ff.

Tewar (Jabalpur) :

(a) A silver coin of Kṛṣṇarāja of the Kalachuri dynasty found. *JNSI*, XVI, pp. 107-08.

(b) One gold coin of Gāṅgeyadeva of Kalachuri dynasty found. *NNM*, No. 5, p. 16.

(c) Two rare silver coins of Gāṅgeyadeva and Ratnadeva collected. *JNSI*, XLIII (1981), pt. II, pp. 70-71.

Tingamali (Rajanandgaon) :

A hoard cointaining four gold coins of Gāṅgeyadeva discovered. *JNSI*, XLIII (1981), pt. II, pp. 72-74; *PP*, VIII, No. 1-2, Jan.-July, 1980, pp. 33-35.

Tripuri (Jabalpur) :

One small silver coin of Kalachuri ruler Gāṅgeyadeva found during excavations of 1952-53. *JNSI*, XIX, p. 74.

(R) Coins of the Chhindaka Nāgas of Bastar

Sonsari (Bilaspur) :

Four coins of Someśvara, the ruler of Chhindaka Nāga dynasty of Bastar in the hoard of 600 gold coins found in 1921. *JNSI*, XVII, pp. 54-57.

(S) Padmaṭaṅkas of the Yādava Kings of Devagiri

Dewas (Dewas) :

The Padmaṭaṅka of Yādava king Rāmadeva found in the state treasury. *JNSI*, XV, p. 110.

Kotha (East Nimar) :

Twenty-four gold Padmaṭaṅkas of Yādava king Siṅghaṇa discovered. *JNSI*, XXVIII, pp. 214-15.

Parsadih (Raigarh) :

Four gold Padmaṭaṅkas of the Yādava rulers (three of Singhaṇa and one unidentified) found. *JNSI*, VIII, pp. 148 ff.

(T) Coins of the Kachchhapaghātas

Gwalior (Gwalior) :

A coin of Vīrasimhadeva of the Kachchhapaghāta dynasty of Narwar found. *NS*, XLVI, p. 333.

(U) Coins of the Yajvapālas

Gwalior (Gwalior) :

(a) Seven hundred and ninety-one coins of Jajapella dynasty found in the Gwalior State discussed. The names of the kings represented are Chāhaḍadeva, Āsalladeva and Gopāladeva who ruled in the 13th century AD. *NS*, XXXIII (201), 1918; *JNSI*, XXVII, pp. 192-93; XXXIII (1971), pt. I, pp. 128-29.

(b) Coins of the Yajvapālas found in the state treasury at Gwalior. *CMI*, pp. 92-93; *NS*, XXXIII, art. 201; XL, art. 268.

(V) Miscellaneous Coins

Balpur (Bilaspur) :

(a) One gold coin of Kesari found. *JAHRS*, III, p. 181.

(b) Three silver and one copper Chinese coins found. *JNSI*, X, p. 161.

Bhopal (Bhopal) :

New coins of Simhendrapāla, an unknown ruler of Central India, datable to c. 13th-14th cent. AD found. *JNSI*, XL (1978), pt. I-II, pp. 128-29.

Bilaspur (Bilaspur) :

(a) One gold coin of Roman emperor Serverus found. *NMC; NNM*, No. 5, p. 23.

(b) Three gold coins of Roman emperors found. *NNM*, No. 5, p. 23.

Chakarbedha (Bilaspur):

Two gold coins of Roman emperors Commodus and Divus Marcus Aurelius found. *JNSI*, VII, pp. 6 ff.

Gwalior (Gwalior) :

Five copper coins found. Four of them have been assigned to king Paśupati and the fifth of Śrī Guhilapati (?). In one of the Gwalior inscriptions, king Paśupati is stated to be a mighty sovereign, the son of Toramāṇa. *JASB*, XXXIV, p. 115.

Indore (Indore) :

(a) A copper coin of Dāmasena (?) noticed in the Advani collection. *JNSI*, XIII, p. 213.

(b) Two Rāmaṭanki coins found. *JNSI*, XV, pp. 236-38.

Mamdakhedi (Sehore) :

A Roman gold coin of Augustus Imperator VII found. *JNSI*, XXXVII (pt. I-II), 1975, p. 158; XXXVIII (1976), pt. II, pp. 100-101.

Raipur (Raipur) :

One Pāñchāla coin in the collection of the MGM Museum. *JNSI*, XXIII, p. 505.

Riapur (Raipur) :

Thirty-two gold Fanams of Anantavarman-Choḍagaṅga found. *TTR*, No. 17 of 1908; *NNM*, No. 5, p. 20.

Shivpuri (Shivpuri) :

A silver coin of Raṇahastin found at and preserved in the Muniraj collection. *JNSI*, XVI, pp. 282-83.

Sirpur (Raipur) :

One copper Chinese coin found during excavation. *JNSI*, XVIII, pp. 64-66; *NNM*, No. 5, p. 21.

Tripuri (Jabalpur):

A small lead coin of Chandra (?) found in the excavations of 1951-52. *JNSI*, XVI, pp. 69-70.

Ujjain (Ujjain):

(a) A copper coin of Śrī-Jayāsra(ya) of about 2nd century AD found. *JNSI*, XX, p. 219; XXI, pp. 135-36.

(b) A Karttikeya coin preserved in Bharatiya Kala Bhavan. *INC*, pt. III, pp. 182-88.

Vidisha (Vidisha) :

(a) Repoussé coins found at and preserved in the MGM Museum, Raipur. *JNSI*, XXIII, p. 305.

(b) One coin of Śivagupta of c. 2nd-1st cent. BC. *JMPIP*, II, p. 21; *JNSI*, XXII, p. 132.

(c) A coin of Sakhadeva of c. 3rd century AD. *JNSI*, XXII, p. 132.

(W) Seals, Sealings and Impressions

Avra (Mandsaur) :

(a) Impression of a Roman coin on a terracotta bull found in the excavation of 1960-61. *JMPIP*, No. 4 (1962), p. 25.

(b) A terracotta sealing with legend '*(a) parāya*' [of (the city of) Aparā] in Brāhmī of about 2nd cent. BC found in the excavation of 1960-61. *JMPIP*, No. 4 (1962), p. 36.

(c) A prism - shaped terracotta sealing with legends '*Samarasatasa*' on one side and '*Yasomitasa*' on the other in Brāhmī of about 4th cent. AD. *JMPIP*, No. 4 (1962), p. 36.

(d) An oval shaped terracotta sealing with legend '*Gosamasa*' in Brāhmī characters of about second century AD. *JMPIP*, No. 4 (1962), p. 36.

(e) A small round sealing with legend *'Jidhavasa'* in Mauryan Brāhmī characters. *JMPIP*, No. 4 (1962), p. 23.

Balpur (Bilaspur) :

One seal of Rāṇaka Śrī Bālakesarī found. *NNM*, No. 5, p. 24; *JOHRS*, IV, pp. 58-59; *JNSI*, XXXVI (1974), pp. 122-26.

Besnagar (Vidisha) :

(a) Twenty-six terracotta sealings found in the excavations of 1914-15. Of these, two were of officers and the rest of individuals. One sealing was of Mahārāja Viśvāmitra. *ASIR*, 1914-15, pp. 66-68.

(b) A stone seal with legend *'Nikubha Nāgasya'* in Brāhmī characters of 1st century BC found in excavations of 1963. *IAR*, 1963-64, p. 17.

Dangawada (Ujjain) :

The following seals discovered in the excavations conducted in 1966:

(1) A seal of Bhaṭṭāraka

(2) A seal of Vedisa

(3) A seal of Dāmodara

(4) A sealing of Mahārāja Śiva

(5) A seal of Jīva Mataṅgasa

(6) A *dhvaja-daṇḍa* Ujjayinī sealing. *JNSI*, XLVII (1985), pt. I-II, pp. 97-98; *DER*, pp. 126-27.

Dhamnar (Mandsaur) :

Clay seal found with inscription *'Chandanagiri-Mahāvihāra'* in the script of c. 5th-6th century AD. *IAR*, 1960-61, p. 60.

Eran (Sagar) :

(a) Coin-die of Indragupta found in excavation. The king's name is inscribed in Mauryan Brāhmī characters with the title. *'raño'*. *IAR*, 1960-61, p. 55; *JUPHS*, VIII (2), 1960.

(b) A clay sealing bearing Brāhmī legend *'Rajño Īśvaramitra Putrasya Rajño Siṁhaśrīsenasya'* in the character of 3rd century AD with a river symbol and three-arched hill discovered. It seems to belong to a Śaka ruler of Malwa. *IAR*, 1964-65, p. 57.

(c) A black clay sealing bearing Brāhmī legend *'Rajño siṁha-Śrīsenasya'* (i.e. of king Siṁhaśrīsena), found in the excavation. *JNSI*, XXVIII, pp. 48ff.

(d) A terracotta seal bearing the figure of standing Gaja-Lakṣmī and an inscription below in two lines of embossed writing in characters of about 5th century AD mentioning *'Airikiṇa'* and *'Gomika'* found. *IAR*, 1962-63, p. 51.

(e) A clay sealing with legend *'Mahādaṇḍanāyaka Siṁhanandi'* in Gupta Brāhmī characters. *INHAC*, p. 82.

(f) Fifteen coin-moulds of four Śaka-Kṣatrapas viz. Vijayasena, Rudrasena II, Viśvasiṁha and Rudrasiṁha discovered in course of excavations. Two coin moulds of Vijayasena are dated in Śaka era 170 (248 AD) and those of Rudrasena II have three dates 180, 185 and 189 corresponding to AD 258, 263 and 267 respectively. *IAR*, 1964-65, p. 70.

Indore (Indore) :

A copper seal of Gupta period with legend *'Jitam Dovyi'* found. *JNSI*, XXXI, pt. I, pp. 74-75.

Kesur (Dhar) :

A terracotta sealing of Ballāla found and preserved in the Dhar museum. *JNSI*, XV, pp. 124-25.

Maheshwar (West Nimar) :

A seal impression on a glass tablet, datable to c. 4th century BC found in the excavation (1953) of Trench II of Mandalkho mound. *JNSI*, XV, pp. 201-02.

Malhar (Bilaspur) :

The following seals located in collection of Shri Gulab Singh :

(a) A jasper stone seal bearing the legend *'Chandrakara'* in negative in box-headed character of Brāhmī script.

(b) A lime stone seal bearing the legend *'Keśavadevasya'* in negative, in box-headed character of Brāhmī script.

(c) A clay sealing of Prasannamātra of Śarabhapurīya dynasty with legend *'Śrīprasan(na)'* in box-headed character of Brāhmī script. *JNSI*, LII (1990), pt. I-II, pp. 126-30.

(d) A small nearly oval shaped terracotta sealing with Kharoshti-Brahmi legend *'Raṇe Mahalaje Esara (d) / Sa / . . .'* meaning 'The king, the Great King Esarad(asa)' i.e., Īśvaradāsa. Īśvaradāsa was possibly a local ruler of South Kosala in 1st century AD to whom this sealing has been assigned. *ND*, XVI (1992), pp. 128-31.

(e) An inscribed clay sealing bearing legend *'Vedasirisa'* (of the King Vedaśrī), a Satavahana ruler recovered in surface collection of Garhi mound. *PAI*, p. 226.

(f) A clay sealing with legend *'Gāmasakosalīya'* (of village Kosala) in Brāhmī script of 2nd cent. AD found. *Ibid.*

(g) A clay sealing with inscription *'Mahārāja Mahendrasya'* in Gupta Brāhmī script of 4th cent. AD found. *Ibid.*

(h) A cylindrical clay seal inscribed at three places bearing the legend *'Śrī Kalyānarchi'* in 7th-8th century characters found. *Ibid.*

(i) Several Buddhist clay sealings found. *Ibid.*

Mandsaur (Mandsaur) :

Two glass sealings bearing the legend *'Śrī Prakāśa Dharma'* discovered in the excavations of 1974-76. Prakaśa Dharma was predecessor of Yaśodharman, the Aulikara ruler of Malwa. *JNSI*, XLVII (1985), pt. I-II, p. 98.

Manpur (Shahdol) :

Ten terracotta sealings bearing Buddhist mantra found in exploration of the stupa found at this site. *Nav Bharat*, Jabalpur, July 20, 1993.

Nandur (Sehore) :

(a) Eight seals discovered during excavations conducted at the site. These seals bear the following legends:

1. Dharasya
2. Devadasa
3. Mahādata Nayaka
4. Mahārāja Ya Ha Sa
5. Mivijapa
6. Grata Rala Suti
7. Nigamasa
8. . . . t tanāga. *JNSI*, XLVII (1985), pt. I-II, pp. 98-99.

(b) Baked clay seals and sealings of Kṣatrapa and Gupta rulers mentioning the names of *Mahākṣatrapa Rajño Īśvaravarmā, Mahākṣatrapa Swāmi*

Vijayasena, Rudra Sena, Bhartṛdāman and *Parikshita* found. The baked clay sealings of the Gupta rulers with legends, *Śrī Vikramāditya, Devadāsa, Mahādanḍanāyaka Parṇaka, Viṣayādhikaraṇasya, Kiṣkindhā* and *Mātṛviṣṇu* etc. found in excavations.

A few more clay sealings belonging to Kṣatrapa, Nāga and Gupta rulers were also recovered. One sealing reads '. . . . ta *Nāga*' (Bhavadatta Nāga), the second reads '*Daśagāma Devadāsa*', the third sealing has the legend '*Mahārāja Raut*'. The fourth of Śuṅga period reads '*Nigamasa*'. *PAI*, p. 227.

Raipur (Raipur) :

A clay sealing of Dhanadeva of Kauśāmbī (or Ayodhyā) in the collection of MGM Museum. *JNSI*, XXI, pp. 187-88.

Tripuri (Jabalpur) :

(a) A tiny ivory seal stamp of Virāka, datable to about 300 BC found in the excavation of 1953. *JNSI*, XVI, pp. 73-74.

(b) Clay sealings of Vasu Bodhi, Śiva Bodhi, Chandra Bodhi, Śrī Bodhi and Dharma Bodhi of Bodhi dynasty of Tripuri found during excavation. *IAR*, 1967-68, pp. 23-24; 1968-69; *JNSI*, XXXVII, pp. 35ff.

(c) An ivory seal of '. . . Mara' datable to about 1st-2nd century AD found during excavation of 1953. *JNSI*, XVI, p. 74.

(d) A terracotta seal of Śaka Vithuḍa, datable to about the latter half of 2nd century AD found during excavation of 1951. *JNSI*, XVI, pp. 24-26.

(e) Clay sealing of Mahāsena found in the excavation of 1968-69. Mahāsena was possibly ruler in c. 350 AD. *IAR*, 1968-69.

(f) A Mauryan seal bearing swastika, conch, taurine symbols found in the excavation of 1968-69. *IAR*, 1968-69.

(g) A terracotta sealing of the *Ārya Bhikṣu Saṁgha* of Nālandā Mahāvihāra found in exploration. *JNSI*, XXXIV (I).

(h) Terracotta seals of Sena rulers Siṁhasena, Vitilaya Skanda and Mahāsena II found in excavations. *JNSI*, XLV (1983), pt. I-II, pp. 40-45.

(i) A Mauryan seal found in excavation of 1969 bears symbols of *Swastika, Yava, Hala* and *Nandipada*. *JNSI*, L-II (1990), pt. I-II, pp. 124-125.

(j) A Sātavāhana clay sealing of Śrī Harṣa (the son of Kumbha Sātavāhana) found in the excavation. *PAI*, p.225.

(k) Sealings and coins of a few rulers like Mahāsena, Vilavatasa, Sivarakhita, Revatimitra and Ānanda found in excavations. *PAI*, p. 225.

Tumain (Guna) :

Two terracotta sealings found, of which one bears the legend '*Siṁhasya*' in Gupta Brāhmī characters. *EAT*, p. 38.

Ujjain (Ujjain):

(a) A glass seal found in the Pipal Khodra, nala near Gad Kalika, datable probably to pre-Mauryan period. *INC*, III, pp. 155-57.

(b) A copper sealing with legend *apramada* datable to about 4th century AD found in the hoard of coins discovered. *JNSI*, XIII, pp. 74-75.

(c) A terracotta sealing with legend '*Yavanikānām*' in Brāhmī of about 2nd century AD. *IAR*, 1968-69, p. 46.

(d) A terracotta sealing with legend '*asadevasa*' in Brāhmī of about 1st century AD found in excavations of 1957-58. *IAR*, 1957-58, pp. 32-36.

(e) A terracotta lid with legend '*nāgabudhisa pravajitasa*' in Brāhmī of about 1st century AD found in excavations of 1957-58. *IAR*, 1957-58, pp. 32-36.

(f) A terracotta coin die with figure of Roman ruler Augustus found in excavations of 1957-58. *IAR*, 1957-58, pp. 32-36.

(g) An ivory seal with legend '*gothajasatisakasa*' in Brāhmī of about 3rd century BC found in excavations of 1957-58. *IAR*, 1957-58, pp. 32-36.

(h) Two ivory seals bearing respectively the legends of '*gosahitakasa*' and '*pattilasa*' in Brāhmī of about 3rd-2nd cent BC. *IAR*, 1956-57, pp. 20-28.

(i) A terracotta seal from Gadkalika area with legend '*Katasa Ujeniya*'. *JNSI*, XLVII (1985), pt. I-II, p. 93.

(j) A sealing from the rain gullies of Gada area with a lion figure. *Ibid.*, pp. 93-94.

(k) Roman sealing on an amphora found from Gada mound. *Ibid.*, p. 94.

(l) A bronze sealing of Amātya Nanda now in collection of Shri Mangalji Gopal of Indore. *Ibid.*

(m) A terracotta sealing from Gada mound with legend '*Śravani Grāma*' in late Gupta Brāhmī characters *Ibid.*

(n) A terracotta sealing with legend '*Dharasa*' in Śuṅga-Brāhmī characters. *Ibid.*

(o) A terracotta seal from Gadakalika mound with legend '*Varadamanoha Bala*' in Śuṅga–Kṣatrapa Brāhmī. *Ibid.*, p. 95.

(p) A bronze seal with box-headed Brāhmī legend reading '*Bappilasya*'. *Ibid.*

(q) A seal bearing lion symbol. *Ibid.*, pp. 95-96.

(r) A seal bearing garuḍa symbol. *Ibid.*, p. 96.

(s) Three glass seals of Śunga-Sātavāhana period. *Ibid.*

(t) A seal bearing bull impression from Gadakalika found. *Ibid.*

Vidisha (Vidisha) :

A unique seal inscribed on the reverse side of a human face reading '*Yogeśvara*' written in box-headed Brāhmī in 4th-5th centuries AD in reverse order. *HI*, pt. I, pp. 165-67.

VI
Art and Architecture

Madhya Pradesh is famous for its rich heritage of monuments and sculptures of sectarian and non-sectarian character built during various phases of its history. A study of the vast literature existing on the subject coupled with field-work conducted at various sites helps us to conclude as follows:

Architectural pieces related to Buddhism are mostly stūpas. Major stūpas dating back to pre-Christian era have been located at Sanchi and Bharhut. The stūpa of Sanchi exists at the site while only remains of the Bharhut stūpa now exist in different museums of repute. Remains of numerous stūpas have been located in either explorations or excavations. The concerned sites are: Andher, Ujjain, Udayagiri, Kasrawad, Khejaria Bhop, Gyaraspur, Bigan, Besnagar, Bhojpur, Pataura, Navdatoli, Rajapur, Vidisha, Satdhara and Sonari. Remains of Buddhist monasteries have been found at Sirpur, Sanchi, Bigan and Khejaria Bhop. Rock-cut monastic establishments related to Buddhism exist at Khejaria Bhop, Dhamnar, Poladongar and Bagh.

Sculptures of Buddhist pantheon are in abundance in M.P. and varieties of them have been noticed both in stone and metal. Stone sculptures have been located at Akaha, Arang, Indragarh, Ujjain, Khirki, Gyaraspur, Gwarighat, Gopalpur, Tilwarghat, Turturia, Tewar, Durg, Nandur Khurd, Bagrol, Bagh, Besnagar, Bharhut, Bheraghat, Malhar, Manda, Rewa, Sheorinarayan, Sanchi, Sirpur, Sohagpur and Hirapur. Rare bronze images of Buddhist deities have been located at Phopnar Kalan and Sirpur.

Temples and images of Jaina Tīrthaṅkaras as well as Śāśanadevīs were also built during all the phases of the ancient history of Madhya Pradesh. More than 150 sites have been located in M.P. where architectural and sculptural remains of Jaina faith exist.

The Jaina temples of different periods built in different forms of Nāgara style and conforming to regional variations exist at Arang, Indhar, Indor, Unhel, Urwaha, Un, Karera, Kalan, Kukreshwar, Kurra, Kethuli, Kota-Udhamre, Kothri, Kotwal, Koni, Koladit, Khola, Khajuraho, Khandwa, Gandhawal, Gwalior, Gyaraspur,

Gujarra, Guril-ka-Pahad, Gudar, Gangli, Ghusai, Chitara, Chait, Jabalpur, Tewar, Thoban, Dungarpura, Dubkund, Dhonakona, Dhanpur, Nagpura, Naderi, Narwar fort, Nimthur, Nohta, Pataura, Panagar, Pachrai, Padhavali, Pali, Pipalrawan, Pujaripali, Paitha, Bagher, Badoh, Banadya, Barai, Balarpur, Baro or Barnagar, Budhi Chanderi, Budhi Rai, Berad, Baijnath, Banda, Bhimpur, Bhuraoda, Bhojpur, Magroni, Machalpur, Madanpur, Malhargarh, Makshi, Mandhata, Mamon, Mehsana, Mohanpur, Radeb, Lakhnadaun, Vidisha, Siddhawarkut, Sandor, Sandhara, Sahajai, Sirpur, Siroha, Suhania, Sesai, Sohagpur and Singhna. Miscellaneous architectural pieces exist at Katni, Khajuraho, Ghusai, Tewar, Barahta and Suhania.

Images of different Tirthankaras, both inscribed and uninscribed have been found at Ajaigarh, Adbhar, Amrol, Ahar, Arang, Ashapuri, Uchehra, Un, Karitalai, Kulan, Khajuraho, Khutiani-Behad, Gwalior, Gyaraspur, Guril-ka-Pahad, Gudar, Ghansaur, Chait, Chainpur, Choli, Jakhoda, Jabalpur, Jaso, Jura, Tiktoli-Dumdar, Timarni, Tikamgarh, Tola, Dongargarh, Tigawa, Tumain, Terahi, Tewar, Deori, Dhonakona, Dhanpur, Dhanacha, Dhanach, Narwar, Panagar, Panihar, Papaura, Pendra, Bajrangarh, Bargaon, Barehta, Bahoriband, Balaghat, Bawangaja, Bijawar, Bithala, Bilahari, Burhikhar, Bortalao, Bhilsa, Bhojpur, Majholi, Malhar, Maihar, Rakhetra, Ratanpur, Ramban, Lakhnadaun, Vidisha, Shahdol, Sakti, Sarangpur, Sidhawarkut, Sleemnabad, Sunahra, Suhania, Sohagpur and Singhpur.

Sculptures of Jaina deities have been discovered at Khajuraho, Tewar and Barehta.

Rock-cut caves related to Jaina faith may be found at Udayagiri.

A bronze image of Adinatha datable to c. 9th century AD has been unearthed at Sirpur.

Madhya Pradesh also abounds in architectural and sculptural remains of Vaiṣṇava faith. These exist in the form of temples, rock-cut caves, monasteries and images, built and carved in different styles and as per regional variations.

Remains of Vaiṣṇava temples have been found at Achera, Afzalpur, Amjhera, Amarkantak, Agar, Ashapuri, Indor, Ujjain, Umaria, Eran, Kachrod, Kanjarda, Kagpur, Kambli, Karitalia, Kalamadh, Kukreshwar, Kethuli, Koni, Kohla, Khajuraho, Kharavada, Gyaraspur, Gwalior Fort, Gudar, Ghusai, Janjgir, Tongra, Tigawa, Thoban, Devkani, Dharahar, Dhunderi, Narsingha, Narayanpal, Nimthur, Pathari, Padhavali, Panihar, Paraini, Palnagar, Pawaya, Panvihar, Pipalrawan, Peprol, Badoh, Badakalan, Badher, Bamora, Barmanghat, Balarpur, Bandogarh, Baro, Bilahari, Bilauni, Madankheri, Mahidpur, Makundpur, Mandhata, Mitauli, Mohanpur, Mohendra, Rajim, Ramgarh, Sheorinarayan, Satanwara, Sandhara,

Sirpur, Sonari and Sohagpur.

Specimens of rock-cut architecture and sculpture of Vaiṣṇava faith may be noticed at Udayagiri, Pargarh, Piploda and Sindursi.

Sculptures related to Viṣṇu and his incarnations as well as other deities pertaining to Vaiṣṇava faith have been discovered from Amarkantak, Arang, Ashapuri, Ishwarpur, Indor, Eran, Katni, Karanpura, Kawardha, Karitalai, Kethuli, Koni, Khajuraho, Khamaria-Bakal, Khoh, Gwalior Fort, Gudar, Gurah, Gopalpur, Janjgir, Jiran, Timarni, Tongra, Dongar, Tatapani, Tigawa, Turturia, Tewar, Dudhia, Deo Baloda, Deori, Deola, Dharampuri, Nachna, Naderi, Pathari, Padhavali, Panagar, Palnagar, Panihar, Piparia, Babai, Bamora, Barehta, Bandogarh, Bilahri, Burhikhar, Besnagar, Bhilsa, Bhita, Bheraghat, Majholi, Madanpur, Marai, Malhar, Rithi, Rewa, Rehli, Vidisha, Shamshabad, Sheorinarayan, Sheopur, Sakri, Singhpur, Sindursi, Sirpur, Silchat, Suvasra, Sohagpur and Hoshangabad.

A stone pillar of historical importance, containing inscription of Heliodorus exists at Besnagar.

Abundance of Śaivite temple remains, caves and monasteries as well as sculptures have been located at more than 225 sites in different parts of Madhya Pradesh. Temple remains exist at Anghora, Achana, Adbhar, Afzalpur, Amjhera, Amarkantak, Amrol, Amledha, Arang, Asukhedi, Indor, Ujjain, Udayapur, Un, Ekalbara, Kanjarda, Karnawad, Kadwaha, Kanoda Bari, Karai-Ahmadpur, Karena, Kakarshisha, Kagpur, Karohan, Kalamdh, Kukreshwar, Kundalpur, Kurra, Kulwar, Kuna, Keldhar, Khajuraho, Khajuha, Kharod, Khalari, Khera, Kherat, Gandai, Gurgi, Gudar, Gurur, Ghusai, Chandrehe, Chanchol, Champajhar, Churli, Chikalda, Chirmoli, Chorpura, Choli, Chaura, Chada, Chhitara, Chhoti Deori, Jakhoda, Jamli, Jharoda, Timarni, Thakurai, Dangarwa, Terahi, Digthan, Deokani, Deodungri, Deotalao, Deo Baloda, Depalpur, Dehri, Dundapura, Dulhagaon, Dhandholi, Dhanwantri, Dharampuri, Dhunderi, Nachna-Kuthra, Naresar, Navli, Nand Chand, Narayanpur, Nimthur, Nemawar, Nohta, Pathari, Padhavli, Parkhera, Paharo-khurd, Pali, Pithoria, Piprai, Piparghar, Pipalrawan, Pujaripali, Pohri, Fatehpur, Bagrod, Bajrangarh, Barwani, Badnawar, Bargaon, Barahta, Balarpur, Bagh, Bara, Barod, Bichrod, Bijwar, Bilahri, Bilav, Bina, Budhi-Rai Baijnath, Bhaktar, Bharaoli, Bharoli, Bhitarwar, Bhumra, Bheraghat, Bhairongarh, Bhainsoda, Bhojpur, Bhopali, Madha-Guruharu, Mandsaur, Marai, Malhar, Mahasamund, Mahidpur, Mahua, Mahuvan, Mahu, Makanganj, Mandhata, Mamon, Mitaoli, Miyan, Murpa, Modi, Rapeth, Rai, Rajim, Rithora, Rithi, Rewa, Lakhari, Lavan, Lanji, Shankhudhar, Shanichara, Sheorinarayan, Sakarra,

Satanwara, Sandhor, Samli, Sirpur, Sultanpur, Suhania, Semarkheri, Semuldha, Seondha, Desai, Sonkach, Sohagpur and Harankheri.

Rock-cut caves related to Śaivism have been found at Udayagiri, Khatama, Bilaoa, Manda, Mandu and Mara. Śaiva monasteries have been located at Khundalpur, Bisesra, Ranod, Survaya and Chandrehe. Rock-cut images may be seen at Piploda and Shankargarh. Sculptures related to different aspects of Śaivism exist at Adbhar, Antara, Amarkantak, Amarpatan, Eran, Karitalai, Kundeshwar, Kulwar, Kulan, Khajuraho, Khajuha, Khandwa, Khamaria Bakal, Kharod, Khilchipura, Khoh, Gwalior Fort, Gurgi, Gudar, Gurah, Gurur, Chanchoda, Jaso, Jiran, Joba, Terahi, Tewar, Deogawan, Deodah, Devargaon, Dudhia, Dhanpur, Dhamnar, Nayi-Soyan, Pali-Bachhra, Pandra, Bagor, Bina, Bhanpura, Bheraghat, Bhairamgarh, Mau, Majholi, Marai, Malhar, Mehsaun, Makla, Mandhata, Rakhetara, Ratanpur, Rajim, Ramgarh, Rewa, Rupnath, Lapha, Shamshabad, Sakarwara, Sakarra, Satna, Sanpuhi, Singhpur, Sinawad, Sirpur, Sundarsi, Suwasra, Suhania, Sewai, Sohagpur and Hoshangabad.

Śākta monuments and sculptural remains thereof have similarly been located at more than 85 sites in Madhya Pradesh. Temple remains exist at Adbhar, Amjhera, Amrol, Antari, Arang, Karedi, Kagpur, Karitalai, Kolaras, Kundalpur, Khajuraho, Kharod, Khalari, Gwalior Fort, Girwani, Gandhawal, Chanderi, Tigawa, Tumain, Terahi, Dudakheri, Nachna Khuthra, Naresar, Navli, Pachavali, Bagrod, Barwani, Bari-Delchi, Badoh, Balakwada, Bichrod, Boria, Bhilsa, Bheraghat, Malhar, Makanganj, Maihar, Ratanpur, Laphagarh, Sagaur, Siroha and Suhania.

Sculptures of various Śaktis and their manifestations have been found from Ajaigarh, Adbhar, Antara, Afzalpur, Indragarh, Eran, Karimganj, Kolaras, Khajuraho, Khajuha, Gadia, Girwani, Gurgi, Gandhawal, Chhuri, Tigawa, Tewar, Deobaloda, Dhar, Nagaria, Pathari, Pali, Pali-Bachhara, Panchgawan, Panchmatha, Bargaon, Bahoriband, Bagh, Bilaspur, Budhikhar, Baijnath, Bhanpura, Malhar, Mandhata, Morwan, Ratanpur, Ramgarh, Rewa, Larai-Lohari, Lavan, Vidisha, Sakarra, Sakri, Satna, Singhpur, Silchat, Sewai and Tripuri.

Architectural and sculptural remains related to the worship of Sūrya have been located at more than twenty sites. Remains of Sūrya temples exist at Khajuraho, Tongra, Narayanpur, Bharauli, Mankhera and Sesai. Saura sculptures have been found at Ajaigarh Fort, Umri, Karitalai, Kotgarh, Koni, Tatapani, Narayanpur, Panagar, Barhata, Bheraghat, Manora, Masaun, Sakarra, Samatpur, Sewai and Sohagpur.

Other art and architectural pieces of miscellaneous nature comprising temple remains, pillars, toraṇas, sati-stones, stepped-wells, male, female, animal and mythical figures, fort-remains and rock-cut caves have been discovered at more than 500 sites. In addition to these archaeological museums maintained by the Central Govt., the State Govt., Universities, Research Centres, private and personal acquisitions have rich collection of art and architectural pieces of different phases of the ancient history and culture of Madhya Pradesh.

List of Monuments and Sculptures

(A) Buddhist Monuments and Sculptures

Akaha (Satna) :

Buddhist sculptures found at the village which is at a short distance from Bharhut. *CASIR*, XIII, p. 1.

Andher (Vidisha) :

Remains of Buddhist stūpas found. *BT*, pp. 221-26.

Arang (Raipur) :

An image of Buddha in *Bhūmisparśa-mudrā* datable to c. 9th cent. AD. *IAR*, 1968-69.

Bagh (Dhar) :

(a) Nine rock-cut Buddhist caves of about 4th-6th cent. AD with fresco paintings and sculptures. *Bagh Caves* by Marshall and others, Reprinted, Delhi, 1972; *GAR*, 1985, No. 1; *IHQ*, XXI, p. 79; *Vikram Smriti Granth*, p. 649; *Marg*, XXV, No. 1, June 1972 (Bagh Special No.).

(b) Aśoka Pillar at. *ASIR*, II, 16.

Bagrol (Hoshangabad) :

Buddhist sculptures found. *IAR*, 1962-63, p. 68.

Besnagar (Vidisha) :

(a) Ruins of a stūpa datable to 3rd century BC found. *CASIR*, X, pp. 38-39.

(b) Ruins of a stūpa found in the excavations of the mound locally known as 'Khera'. *CASIR*, X, p. 45.

(c) A pillar capital with Kalpavṛkṣa, now preserved in Indian Museum, Calcutta. *MP*, p. 13.

Bharhut (Satna) :

(a) Remains of Buddhist stūpa found. Cunningham, A. *The Stupa of Bharhut* (1879); Barua, B.M., *Barhut*, pts. I-III, Calcutta, 1934; Hultzsch, Jatakas at Bharhut, *JRAS*, 1912, pp. 399 ff; Kala, S.C., Bharhut sculptures . . .

etc., *JUPHS*, XVIII, p. 91; *Guide to Calcutta Museum; Guide to Allahabad Museum; CASIR*, IX, pp. 2-3.

(b) Buddhist sculptures found. *ASIR*, VI, 147-48.

Bhatanwara (Satna) :

Preserved remains of Bharhut stūpa containing Jātaka scenes and Brāhmī inscriptions. *JMIP*, No. 5 (1967), p. 3.

Bheraghat (Jabalpur) :

An image of Tārā with inscription kept in the *garbhagṛha* of the temple of Chaunsaṭha Yoginī. *Hiralal List*, No. 50.

Bhojpur (Raisen):

Remains of a Buddhist stūpa. *BT*, pp. 211-20.

Bigan (Vidisha) :

(a) Two Buddhist stūpas. *GAR*, 1914-23.

(b) Buddhist monastery. *GAR*, 1914-23.

Dhamnar (Mandsaur) :

Buddhist rock-cut caves, fourteen in number excluding subsidiary cells, datable to about 7th-9th century AD. *CASIR*, II, pp. 270-76; *ASIR*, 1905-06, p. 110; Fergusson, *Rock-cut Caves of India.*

Durg (Durg) :

Fragments of Buddhist sculptures. *CASIR*, XVII, p. 3; *CLAR*, p. 50.

Gopalpur (Jabalpur) :

Five Buddhist sculptures datable to c. 11th-12th cent. AD. Of these, three are inscribed. *EI*, XVIII, pp. 73-74; Hiralal, *Jabalpur Jyoti*, p. 141; *Bhandarkar List*, No. 1903; *Hiralal List,* No. 52.

Gwalior (Gwalior) :

Images of Buddha, seated and standing, railings and cross-bars of stūpa preserved in the local museum. *Catalogue of Sculptures in the Gwalior Museum*, Gwalior.

Gwarighat (Jabalpur) :

Gandhara sculputres consisting of stray images of Buddha and Bodhisattva made of blue schist found. *IAR*, 1962-63, p. 69.

Gyaraspur (Vidisha) :

(a) A Buddhist stūpa of about 9th century AD built of stone on a raised platform with niches enshrining figures of Buddha on four sides. *AG*, p. 92.

(b) Inscribed image of Buddha found. *GAR*, 1992, No. 35.

Hirapur (Hoshangabad) :

Buddhist sculptures found. *IAR*, 1962-63, p. 68.

Indragarh (Mandsaur) :

Sculptures of Padapani Avalokiteśvara with figure of Dhyāni Buddha, Amitābha on the elaborate *jaṭā*, lower part of Buddha's image seated in *padmāsana*, Buddha subduing Nāgarāja Apalata etc. discovered. *IAR*, 1965-66, p. 22.

Jafer Kheda (Vidisha) :

Remains of a group of stūpas located. *IAR*, 1987-88, p. 139.

Kasrawad (Nimar) :

Stūpas of about Ist-2nd century BC, two miles to the south-west of the town, discovered in excavations. *IHQ*, XXV, p. 1.

Khajuraho (Chhatarpur) :

Ruins of a Buddhist monastery on a mound locally known as Satdhara. *CASIR*, II, No. 15, p. 428.

Khejaria Bhop (Mandsaur) :

(a) A Buddhist monastery of about 9th-10th century AD consisting of 28 rock-cut cells. *AG*, pp. 97-98.

(b) A Buddhist rock-cut stūpa of about 9th-10th century AD. *AG*, pp. 97-98.

Khirki (Hoshangabad) :

Buddhist sculptures found. *IAR*, 1962-63, p. 68.

Malhar (Bilaspur) :

Buddhist images found in explorations. *MER*.

Manda (Sidhi) :

An image of Buddha preserved in the local Rest House. *Madhya Pradesh Sandesh*, Sept. 5, 1970, pp. 12-15.

Nachna (Panna) :

An image of Buddha of c. 6th cent. AD. *IAR*, 1987-88, p. 139.

Nandur Khurd (Raigarh) :

An image of Bodhisattava with inscription in 8th-9th century character found. *IAR*, 1958-59, p. 72, pl. LXXIB-B.

Navdatoli (West Nimar) :

Remains of a Buddhist stūpa datable to c. 3rd century BC. *EMN*, pp. 29-30.

Pangoraria (Sehore) :

Group of stūpas located. *IAR*, 1975-76, pp. 28-30; 1976-77, pp. 31-32.

Pataura (Satna) :

Remains of Bharhut stūpa. *JMPIP*, No. 5, p. 6.

Phopnar Kalan (East Nimar) :

Four well-preserved standing Buddha bronzes having inscriptions on their pedestal in South Indian character of about 6th century AD. *IAR*, 1965-66, p. 62; *Lalit Kala*, No. 12, p. 16.

Poladongar (Mandsaur) :

Buddhist rock-cut caves of about 8th-9th century AD. One of the caves is a chaitya and the others were meant for their use as residence of monks. *ISG*, p. 56.

Raipur (Raipur) :

Buddhist sculputres of Pāṇḍuvaṁśī period (8th-9th century AD) from the Sirpur excavations, of the Kalachuris of Tripuri from Karitalai and of the Kalachuris of Ratanpur from Ratanpur, preserved in the local museum. *Catalogue of Sculptures in the M.G.M. Museum*, Raipur, 1960 (in Hindi).

Rajapur (Shivpuri) :

Brick-built Buddhist stūpa of about 9th-10th century AD. *AG*, p. 117.

Ramban (Satna) :

Bharhut sculptures found in the area around; on two of them hitherto unknown Champeyya and Ghatasena-Jatakas. *IAR*, 1961-62, p. 100.

Rewa (Rewa) :

Buddhist sculptures on one of which is an inscription datable to c. 10th cent. AD found. *CASIR*, XXI, p. 144.

Sanchi (Raisen) :

(a) Buddhist stūpas and other Brahmanical ruins including stūpas Nos. 1, 2, 3; monasteries Nos. 36, 37, 38, 45, 46, 47, 51; buildings Nos. 8, 32, 43, 44, 49, 50; temples Nos. 40, 45, pillars and fencing of stūpa etc. Marshall, J. and Foucher, A., *Monuments of Sanchi*, Vols. I-III, Rep. Ed. Delhi (1982); Cunningham, A., *The Bhilsa Topes*; Burgess, *The Great Stūpa at Sanchi-*

Kanakhera; *JRAS*, 1902, pp. 29-45; Maisey, F.C., *Sanchi and Its Remains* (1892); Marshall J., *A Guide to Sanchi,* (1918); Hamid, *Excavation of Maurya Monastery at Sanchi, Bhopal State* — Annual Bibliography of Indian Archaeology for the year 1937, pp. XII, pp. 25, 28 and 1936-37, pp. 84, 87.

(b) Buddhist images and other archaeological remains preserved in the museum. Marshall and others, *Catalogue of the Museum of Archaeology at Sanchi* (1922), pp. 1-7.

(c) Votive stūpas datable to late medieval period preserved in the museum. *Catalogue of the Museum of Archaeology at Sanchi*, by Marshall and others (1922), pp. 17-18.

Satdhara (Raisen) :

Buddhist topes found. *BT*, pp. 207-10.

Shankargarh :

Stone pillars similar to that of Bharhut found. *CASIR*, IX, pp. 4-5.

Sheorinarayan (Bilaspur):

Buddhist sculptures in the Kalachuri temple. *CASIR*, VII, pp. 197-98.

Sirpur (Raipur) :

(a) A Buddhist sculpture datable to about 5th-6th century AD found. *CASIR*, VII, p. 31.

(b) A number of bronze images of Buddha, Tara etc. datable to about 8th-9th century AD discovered. *KV*, pp. 286, 296.

(c) Buddhist image in Gandheśvar temple with an inscription of c. 8th-9th cent. AD. *Hiralal List*, No. 184.

(d) Remains of two Buddhist monasteries found in the excavation of 1955. *SAG*, p. 189.

(e) A large image of Buddha found in the excavation of 1955. *SAG*, p. 189.

Sohagpur (Shahdol) :

A 20-armed female statue containing the image of Buddha with two Bodhisattvas. *CASIR*, VII, p. 245.

Sonari (Raisen) :

Buddhist topes found. *BT*, pp. 199-206.

Tewar (Jabalpur) :

(a) Buddhist images datable to c. 11th-12th cent. AD. *KV*, pp. 300-308.

(b) Image of Bodhisattva of Kalachuri period found. *HTM*, pp. 93-94; *CASIR*, IX, p. 58.

(c) Image of Vajrapāṇī which is inscribed. *CASIR*, X, p. 58.

Turturia (Raipur) :

(a) Early Buddhist sculptures found. *CASIR*, XIII, p. 146; *KV*, pp. 298-99.

(b) Numerous Buddhist sculptures found. *CASIR*, XIII, pp. 147-48.

Tilwaraghat (Jabalpur) :

An inscribed image of Tārā located. *Hiralal List*, No. 51.

Udayagiri (Vidisha) :

(a) Remains of a Buddhist stūpa found. *CASIR*, X, p. 55.

(b) A pillar with Mauryan polish and lion capital. *Ibid.*

Unchahra (Satna) :

Remains of stūpa at Bharhut which are now preserved in the Bharat Kala Bhawan, Varanasi. *JMPIP*, No. 5, pp. 6-7.

Ujjain (Ujjain) :

(a) Remains of a stūpa discovered in the excavations of Vaishya Tekri, a mound three miles to the north-east of the present city. The excavations which were conducted in 1938-39 revealed it to be the biggest stūpa so far known, with 350′ diameter and 100′ height. Punch-marked coins were also discovered. The stūpa was probably built by Mauryan emperor Aśoka. *GAR*, 1938-39, p. 13.

(b) Remains of a small stūpa discovered in the excavation of a mound about 100 yards to the west of Vaishya Tekri. The excavations were carried out in 1938-39. *GAR*, 1938-39, p. 14.

(c) Remains of a stūpa discovered in the excavation of Pallevali Tekri or Kankar Tekri, about 100 yards to the south-west of Vaishya Tekri. *GAR*, 1938-39, p. 14.

Vidisha (Vidisha) :

Remains of a Buddhist stūpa of Śuṅga period. *CASIR*, IX, pp. 4-5.

(B) Jaina Monuments and Sculptures

Adbhar (Bilaspur) :

Image of Pārśvanatha found. *PP*, V, No. 2, p. 166.

Ahar (Tikamgarh) :

(a) Number of Jaina images containing inscriptions dated V.S. 1123 and 1169. *Anekanta*, Vols. IX and X.

(b) Jaina image on which inscription of the Paramardideva dated V.S. 1237 is carved. *Premi Abhinandan Granth*, pp. 624-26; *Nagri Pracharini Patrika*, Vol. XVII, pp. 15-19.

Ajaigarh (Panna) :

(a) Rock-cut Jaina figures in the fort. *CASIR*, XXI, p. 47.

(b) Jaina image of Sumatinātha with an inscription of Chandella Vīravarmadeva dated in V.E. 1331. *CJT*, Appdx. A, No. 54.

(c) Colossal Jaina image of Śāntinātha with an inscription of Chandella Vīravarman dated in V.E. 1335. *Ibid.*, No. 55.

Amrol (Gwalior) :

Jaina images near the temple of 'Behmata'. *GAR*, 1940-41, p. 21.

Arang (Raipur) :

(a) A Jaina temple locally known as Bhand Dewal, said to have been built by the Haihaya rulers, datable to about 11th century AD. *CASIR*, VII, pp. 161-62; *KV*, pp. 150, 162; *CLAR*, pp. 48-49; *RDG*, pp. 35-36.

(b) A number of Jaina sculptures found. *CASIR*, VII, p. 164; XVII, pp. 20-21.

Ashapuri (Raisen) :

An ancient image of Śāntinātha. *MPS*, p. 51.

Badnapur (Damoh) :

A few Jaina sculptures of medieval period found in course of clearance of site. *IAR*, 1985-86, p. 110.

Badoh (Vidisha) :

Jaina temples of about 10th-11th century AD consisting of a group of 25 cells enclosing an oblong courtyard, with a raised platform in its centre. The two pilgrim records dated in V.S. 1134 and 1113 are carved on the door frames. *GAR*, 1923-24, pp. 8-10; *AG*, pp. 58-59.

Bagher (Shivpuri) :

A Jaina temple with an inscription dated in V.S. 1532 (1475 AD), referring to its construction by Mahārājādhirāja Kīrtisiṁha and his minister Harichand of Bagher. *GAR*, 1935-36, p. 12.

Bahoriband (Jabalpur) :

A colossal stone image of Śāntinātha on which an inscription of Rāṣṭrakūṭa Golhaṇa is inscribed. It is of the period of the rule of Kalachuri king Gayākarṇa. *CASIR*, IX, pp. 39-40; *PRASIWC*, 1903-04, p. 54; *HTM*, p. 107; *KV*, p. 137; *CLAR*, p. 27.

Baijnath (Rewa) :

Early medieval Jaina temples found. *IAR*, 1960-61, p. 62.

Bajrangarh (Guna) :

Two Jaina temples, one bearing an image with inscription dated in V.S. 1236 (1179 AD). *GAR*, 1929-30.

Balaghat (Balaghat) :

A number of Jaina sculptures found. *KV*, p. 141.

Balarpur (Shivpuri) :

An old Jaina temple. *GAR*, 1914-15.

Banadya (Indore) :

Jaina temple having inscriptions dated V.E. 1548 and 1659. *HMIM*.

Banda (Sagar) :

An ancient Jaina temple. *SDG*, p. 522.

Barai (Gwalior) :

(a) Two groups of Jaina temples to the north of the village, datable to c. 15th century AD. A Jaina colossal image exists in one of them. *GAR*, 1940-41, pp. 22-23.

(b) A group of four Jaina temples to the south of the village datable to about 15th cent. AD. These contain Jaina Tīrthaṅkara images. *Ibid.*

Barhata (Hoshangabad) :

(a) Remains of a Jaina memorial pillar and other Jaina remains. *SAG*, pp. 206-07.

(b) A colossal image of Ṛṣabhadeva. *Ibid.*, p. 208.

(c) An image of Pārśvanātha. *Ibid.*, p. 208.

(d) A rare image of Jaina Saraswati. *Ibid.*, p. 210.

Barheta (Narsimhapur) :

Six huge images of Jaina Tīrthaṅkaras. *NDG*, p. 456.

Baro or Barnagar (Vidisha) :

(a) Jaina restoration of a Brahmanical shrine, datable to about 8th-10th century AD, locally known as Gadarmal temple. *CASIR*, X, pp. 73ff.

(b) Ruins of a group of Jaina temples to the north-west of the Gadarmal temple. *CASIR*, VII, p. 78.

Bawangaja (West Nimar) :

A colossal Jaina image of Ṛṣabhanātha locally known as Bāwan-gajā (i.e. 52 yds. or 72 feet in height) of about 13-14th century AD. It is about 8 km south of Barwani on a hilltop. *MAR*, 1949-50; *WNDG*, p. 435.

Berad (Shivpuri) :

Remains of a Jaina temple of about 10th-12th century AD with part of a wall and a few sculptures. *GAR*, 1928-29, p. 13.

Bhilsa (Vidisha) :

Jaina image with inscription dtd. V.E. 1132. *GAR*, *Saṁ*. 1980, No. 4.

Bhimpur (Shivpuri) :

A Jaina temple with inscription referring to its construction by Jaittrasiṁha, an officer of Jajjapella king Āsalladeva of Narwar, and installation of an image by Nāgadeva in V.S. 1319 (1226 AD). *GAR*, 1914-15.

Bhind District :

Jaina sculptures of late medieval period found at Aithar, Barhi, Kosh and Ramakot. *IAR*, 1978-79, p. 11.

Bhojpur (Raisen) :

(a) An image of Pārśvanātha having an inscription of the reign of Paramāra Narvarman. *IAR*, 1959-60, p. 57.

(b) A Tīrthaṅkara image in an old Jaina temple having an inscription of the reign of Paramāra Bhoja. *IAR*, 1959-60, p. 57.

(c) A Jaina temple possibly constructed during the reign of Paramāra Bhoja. *MPS*, p. 1.

Bhurwada (Shivpuri) :

Remains of a Jaina temple of about 11th-12th century AD at a deserted village called Puranakheda, one mile from Bhurwada. *GAR*, 1935-36, p. 12.

Bijwad (Dewas) :

(a) Ruins of a Jaina temple datable to about 11th-12th century AD. *PRASIWC*, XX, p. 106; *ISD*, II, p. 9; *RAHS*, 1932, p. 95.

(b) A Jaina temple of about 11th-12th century AD on a hillock near the village. *Ibid.*

Bilahari (Jabalpur) :

(a) Jaina image of about 12th cent. AD. *KV*, pp. 169-71.

(b) A Tīrthaṅkara image. *KV*, pp. 182-83.

Bithala (Guna) :

Jaina temple of about 12th century AD with a shrine and a porch. A large image of Tīrthaṅkara with head damaged, and four other Jaina images are preserved in the shrine. A group of four shrines, probably subsidiary to the main temple, exists nearby. *GAR*, 1924-25, pp. 14-15; *ASIR*, XXIV, p. 166.

Bortalao (Durg) :

A headless image of Ṛṣabhadeva with an inscription dated in V.E. 1548. *KV*, p. 148.

Budhi-Chanderi (Guna):

A group of five Jaina temples of about 11th-12th century AD now in ruins. *ASIR*, XXIV, p. 166; *CASIR*, II, p. 403; *GC*, p. 4.

Budhi-Rai (Shivpuri) :

An ancient Jaina temple. *GAR*, 1914-23.

Chainpur (Mandsaur) :

A colossal Jaina image with inscription. *PRASIWC*, XIX, p. 87; *ISG*, II, p. 11.

Chait (Gwalior) :

(a) A Jaina temple datable to 11th-12th cent. AD on the slope of the hill to the south-west of the village. It has a *garbhagṛaha* and a *sabhāmaṇḍapa* and its *śikhara* resembles the Sāsbahu temple of Gwalior fort. *GAR*, 1933-34, pp. 11-12.

(b) Remains of Jaina temples on the hill to the south-west of the village.

Number of Jaina sculptures are available. *Ibid.*

(c) Memorial pillars with inscriptions dtd. V.S. 1182 and 1183. *Ibid.*

(d) Two colossal Jaina images datable to c. 11th cent. AD. *Ibid.*

Chanderi (Guna) :

Rock-cut Jaina images carved on hill situated between the fort and Katighati, with inscriptions datable to 13th century AD. *GC*, p. 30.

Chhitara (Shivpuri) :

Ruins of an old Jaina temple. *GAR*, 1916-17.

Choli (West Niwar) :

Remains of ancient Jaina temples. *WNDG*, p. 440.

Dadur (Dhar) :

Jaina temples in ruins with colossal images of Tīrthaṅkara. *GAR*, 1940-41, p. 23.

Dehri (Dhar) :

An old Jaina temple. *HMIM*.

Deori (Sagar) :

Medieval Jaina sculptures datable to 11th-12th cent. AD noticed. *IAR*, 1964-65, p. 74.

Dhanaich (Shivpuri) :

Fifteen Jaina image inscriptions dated V.S. 1390. *GAR*, Sam. 1973, No. 63, 70, 71, 72, 74, 75, 76, 77, 78, 79, 84, 85, 87, 88; *Ibid.*, Sam. 1986, No. 68.

Dhanacha (Morena) :

A colossus Jaina unfinished image on the bank of nala in jungle. *GAR*, 1916-17.

Dhanpur (Shahdol) :

(a) A group of four Jaina temples in ruins, datable to about 9th century AD. *CASIR*, VII, p. 237; *CLAR*, p. 60.

(b) A number of Jaina sculptures on the bank of tank locally known as Sobhnath. *Ibid.*

Dhonakona (Shivpuri) :

(a) Ruins of a Jaina temple in a jungle, lined with shrines sheltering images of Tīrthaṅkaras. A large image of Supārśvanātha of about 10' in height is available in the main shrine. Inscriptions dated between 11th-14th centuries AD are inscribed on the images. *GAR*, 1935-36, p. 13.

(b) An unfinished colossus Jaina image of a Tīrthaṅkara, datable to about 13th-14th century AD lying in the bed of a stream. *GAR*, 1935-36, p. 13.

Dongargarh (Durg) :

(a) Image of Ṛṣabhadeva located. *KV*, pp. 142-44.

(b) Image of Pārśvanātha locate., *KV*, p. 145.

Dubkund (Shivpuri) :

(a) Remains of a huge Jaina temple from which a large stone slab containing inscription of Kachchhapaghāta Vikramsingh dated V.S.1145 were found. *GAR*, 1915-16; *CASIR*, XX, p. 99.

(b) Footprints in a Jaina temple below which is carved inscription dated V.S. 1152. *CASIR*, XX, p. 102; *GAR*, Sam. 1973, No. 48; *Bhandarkar List*, No. 161.

Dundapura (Gwalior) :

Ancient Jaina temple which has an inscription dated V.S. 1598 (?). *GAR*, 1929-30, p. 15.

Gandhaval (Ujjain) :

Ruins of a group of two Jaina temples of about 11th-12th century AD with large images of Tīrthaṅkaras. *GAR*, 1942-46, pp. 22-23.

Gangli (Dhar) :

Remains of three Jaina temples datable to c. 11th-12th century AD. *GAR*, 1916-17.

Ghansor (Seoni) :

A fine Jaina statue preserved. *CLAR*, p. 38.

Ghusai (Mandsaur) :

(a) Two memorial pillars of the Jainas, one having an inscription dated in V.S. 1323 (1266 AD). *GAR*, 1916-17.

(b) Ruins of a Jaina temple with an inscription dated in V.S. 1313 (1256 AD). *GAR*, 1916-17.

Gudar (Shivpuri) :

(a) A group of three colossal Jaina images, the central one measuring 9' in height and the side one are each 6'-6" in height. The inscription on one dated in V.S. 1206 (1149 AD) mentions the images as of Śāntinātha, Kunthanātha and Aranātha. *GAR*, 1929-30, pp. 23, 61.

(b) Ruins of a Jaina temple, 2 furlongs to the north-west of the above-mentioned images. An image of Tīrthaṅkara of 7' in height and a *chaumukha* are lying in the shrines. *GAR*, 1929-30, p. 24.

(c) A Jaina temple built out of material of a temple of about 11th-12th century AD. Images of Tīrthaṅkaras available. Three of these images contain inscriptions dated in V.S. 1390 (1333 AD). *GAR*, 1929-30, p. 23.

Gujarra (Rewa) :

Early medieval Jain temple found. *IAR*, 1960-61, p. 62.

Guril-ka-Pahad (Guna) :

(a) Jaina temple on a hilltop, of about 14th century AD belonging to Digambara sect, enshrining an image of Śāntinātha of 11'-9" in height. *GAR*, 1924-25, p. 13; *ASIR*, XXIV, p. 167.

(b) A Jaina temple of about 11th-12th century AD belonging to Digambara Jaina sect on a hilltop. Twenty-six images of Tīrthaṅkaras are preserved of which the central one is that of Ādinātha. On the wall is inscribed a pilgrim's record dated in V.S. 1307 (1250 AD). *GAR*, 1924-25, p. 13.

Gwalior Fort (Gwalior) :

(a) Three rock-cut Jaina colossal images near Urwahi gate with inscriptions on pedestals referring to Tomara kings Dungar Singh and Kirtti Singh. *DFGS*, p. 54; *CASIR*, II, p. 356.

(b) Many rock-cut Jaina colossal images at a short distance from Urwahi gate by the side of the ascent to the fort, one measuring 57' in height with inscriptions on the pedestals referring to Tomara kings Dungar Singh and Kirtti Singh. *Ibid.*

(c) Many rock-cut colossal Jaina images in the north of the fort hill, with inscriptions on the pedestals referring to the Tomara kings Dungar Singh and Kirtti Singh. *DFGS*, p. 57.

(d) Rock-cut colossal Jaina images in the south-west of the fort hill. *Ibid.*

(e) Rock-cut colossal Jaina images in the south-east of the fort hill near

Marimata with inscription on pedestals referring to Tomara king Kirtti Singh. *Ibid.*

(f) Remains of Jaina temple. *DFGS*, p. 50.

(g) Jaina temple with inscription dated V.S. 1165. *CASIR*, II, pp. 362-63.

Gyaraspur (Vidisha) :

Temple to the south-west of the village on the slope of a hill, locally called as Maladevi Mandir, once originally dedicated to a goddess but now enshrining Jaina images datable to 9th-10th cent. AD. *AG*, pp. 91-92; *CASIR*, VII, pp. 90-93; *ibid.*, X, pp. 31-34.

Indhar (Shivpuri) :

Remains of a group of Jaina temples to the north and east of the village, datable to about 8th-10th century AD. *GAR*, 1925-26, p. 8.

Indor (Guna) :

Ruins of an old Jaina temple with sculptures lying about. *GAR*, 1914-15.

Indore (Indore) :

Jaina sculptures in stone and metal preserved in the Central Museum. *Guide Book of the Central Museum*, Indore, p. 6.

Jabalpur (Jabalpur) :

(a) Jaina images preserved in the Digambar Jaina temple at Hanumantal. *KV*, pp. 32-35.

(b) Jaina images noticed in the garden of M/s. Cursetjee & Co. *CLAR*, p. 27.

(c) A rare Jaina image datable to Kalachuri period. *HTM*, p. 106.

Jakhoda (Guna) :

Remains of an ancient Jaina temple found. *GAR*, 1914-23.

Jaso (Satna) :

A large number of Jaina images comprising Ādinātha, Pārśvanātha, Neminātha, Śāntinātha, Mallinātha, Ṛṣabhadeva, Ambikā etc. found. *KV*, pp. 258-64.

Jura (Rewa) :

A beautifully carved fragmented Jaina image found. *HTM*, pp. 106-07, pl. XLVI, b.

Kalan (Rewa) :

Early medieval Jaina temple found. *IAR*, 1960-61, p. 62.

Karera (Shivpuri) :

Ancient Jaina temple. *GAR*, 1927-28, p. 13.

Karitalai (Jabalpur) : Five Jaina sculptures on which the names of the donors are inscribed. *Hiralal List*, No. 71.

Katni (Jabalpur) :

Toraṇa of Jaina temple. *KV*, pp. 173-75.

Kethuli (Mandsaur) :

An old Jaina temple. *ISG*, p. 28.

Khajuraho (Chhatarpur) :

(a) Jaina temple of Pāraśvanātha built during the reign of Chandella ruler Dhaṅga whose inscription has been found in the temple. There are a number of pilgrim records also in the temple. Originally the temple contained image of Ādinatha but later on the present image of Pārśvanātha was installed. *KD*, pp. 13-35; *KKD*, pp. 51-60; *KDP*, pp. 12-22; *KSS*, pp. 10-18; *KZ*, pp. 87-160; *AI*, No. 15; *KKC*; *KDI*; *KVJ*; *KVP*.

(b) Temple of Ādinātha to the north of Pārśvanātha temple. This is a *Nirādhāra Prāsāda* whose *garbhagṛaha* with *śikahara* and *antarāla* only are remaining. In plan, style and art, it is very close to Vāmana and it is likely that it was built a decade or two after it. *Ibid.*

(c) Jaina temple of Ghantai, so named possibly on account of chain and bell carvings profusely found on the pillars of the temple. It is datable to later part of 10th cent. AD, *Ibid.*

(d) Modern temple of Śāntinātha to the south of Pārśvanātha temple. A huge image of Ādinatha is installed in its garbhagṛha. *KSS*, p. 15, No. 17.

(e) The following Jaina sculptures may be noticed at the site.

Tīrthaṅkara images :

(i) Adināthā in the small temple near Pisanari-ki-Madhia.

(ii) Ajitanātha in the Pārśvanātha temple and Khajuraho Museum.

(iii) Śambhavanātha in the small temple near Pisanari-ki-Madhia.

(iv) Abhinandanātha in the small temple near Pisanari-ki-Madhia.

(v) Padmanābha in Khajuraho Museum.

(vi) Śāntinātha in the Śānti temple.

(vii) Mahavīra in the Śāntinātha temple.

Yakṣa and Yakṣiṇī Images :

(i) Yakṣa in Pārśvanātha temple and Khajuraho Museum.

(ii) Yakṣiṇī in Pārśvanātha temple.

Images of Bāhubalī in Pārśvanātha temple. Ambikā images in Śāntinātha and Ādinātha temples.

Images of Jaina goddesses:

(i) Kandarpā and Mānasī images in Khajuraho Museum.

(ii) Eight-armed goddess in Ādinātha temple.

(iii) Eight-armed goddess on lion in Ādinātha temple. Images of Agni in Pārśvanātha temple. Some unidentified images in Viśvanātha, Jagadambī and Śāntinātha temples. Gomedha couple in Śāntinātha temple. *KSS*, pp. 107-10.

Khandwa (East Nimar) :

Numerous remains of Jaina temples and sculptures. *CLAR*, p. 40; *CASIR*, IX, p. 114.

Khargone (Raisen) :

Ruins of a Jaina temple datable to c. 10th-11th cent. AD discovered. *IAR*, 1986-87, p. 119.

Khutiani Behad (Morena) :

Mound with Hindu and Jaina sculptures. *GAR*, 1916-17.

Kohala (Mandsaur) :

Jaina temples of about 13th-14th century AD. *ISG*, p. 70.

Koladit (East Nimar) :

Remains of ancient Jaina temples. *East Nimar District Gazetteer* (1969), p. 468.

Koni (Kalan) (Jabalpur) :

A cluster of Jaina temples of Digambara sect. The Jains regard it as one of their *Atiśaya Kṣetras*. *Jabalpur District Gazetteer* (1968), pp. 685-86.

Kota Udhamade (Shivpuri) :

A group of Jaina temples of about 8th-10th century AD. *GAR*, 1922-23.

Kothadi (Mandsaur) :

A Jaina temple of about 13th-14th century AD. *ISG*, 36; *PRASIWC*, XIX, p. 81.

Kotwal (Morena) :

An ancient Jaina temple. *GAR*, 1914-23.

Kukarramath (Mandla) :

Medieval Jaina (?) temple. *Mandla District Gazetteer* (1919), p. 240.

Kukdesvar (Mandsaur):

A Jaina temple of Pārśvanātha, originally of 13th-14th century AD with inscriptions of later date. *ISG*, p. 37; *ASIR*, XIX, pt. I, p. 44; *PRASIWC*, XIX, p. 95.

Kura (Raipur) :

Remains of two ancient Jaina temples, now dismantled. *Raipur District Gazetteer* (1973), p. 551.

Lakhari (Guna) :

Ruins of a Jaina temple datable to about 11th-12th century AD to the east of the village. *GAR*, 1924-25, p. 14.

Lakhnadon (Seoni) :

(a) A number of Jaina sculptures found. *KV*, p. 139; *CLAR*.

(b) Ruins of Jaina temples. *Ibid.*

Machalpur (Mandsaur) :

Two Jaina temples. *HMIM*.

Madanpur (Sagar) :

Remains of Jaina temples. *CLAR*, p. 35.

Magroni (Shivpuri) :

An ancient Jaina temple with an image of Pārśvanātha. *GAR*, 1914-15.

Mahalpurapatha (Raisen) :

A colossal broken image of Śāntinātha noticed at Khonia Kakar. *IAR*, 1986-87, p. 119.

Maihar (Satna) :

A number of Jaina images. *KV*, pp. 265-66.

Majholi (Jabalpur) :

Jaina sculpture found. *JDG*, p. 688.

Maksi (Ujjain) :

Ancient Jaina temple. *GAR*, 1934, pp. 23-29.

Malhar (Bilaspur) :

A standing Jaina image of Mahāvīra datable to about 8th century AD noticed. *IAR*, 1960-61, p. 59; *PP*, V, No. 2, p. 165.

Malhargarh (Guna) :

Ancient Jaina temple. *GAR*, 1914-15.

Mamon (Guna) :

Ruins of a group of about 6-7 Jaina temples of about 10th century AD to the south-west of the old site of the village. A colossal image of the Tīrthaṅkara of about 8'-10" in height stands in the ruins of one of the temples. *GAR*, 1925-26, p. 10.

Mandhata (East Nimar) :

Remains of ancient Jaina temple. *ENG*, p. 471.

Mehsana (Rewa) :

Early medieval Jain temples found. *IAR*, 1960-61, p. 62.

Mohanpur (Guna) :

Remains of an old Jaina temple of about 10th century AD used in the construction of the modern Jain temple called Chaityalaya. *GAR*, 1924-25, p. 13.

Naderi (Guna) :

Remains of an ancient Jaina temple. *GAR*, 1924-25, p. 25.

Nagpura (Durg) :

An ancient Jaina temple. *DDG*, p. 447.

Narwar (Shivpuri) :

One hundred and sixty Jaina images found in an underground chamber. *GAR*, 1914-15; *Anekanta*, XIX, No. 1-2 (April-June, 1960), pp. 81-83.

Narwar Fort (Shivpuri) :

Five Tīrthaṅkara images bearing dates of V.S. 1213, 1316, 1340 and 1348 found in a Jaina temple built in 17th-18th cent. AD. *GAR*, 1925-26, p. 7.

Nimthur (Mandsaur) :

Ruins of a Jaina temple with old sculptures lying about. *GAR*, 1917-18.

Nohta (Damoh) :

Ruins of a number of Jaina temples. *CLAR*, p. 32.

Pachrai (Shivpuri) :

A group of Jaina temples with sculptures dated in V.S. 1122 (?), 1210, 1213, 1222, 1231 respectively and other inscriptions on pillars dated V.S. 1132, 1210 respectively. *GAR*, 1914-15.

Padhavali (Morena) :

(a) A group of two Jaina temples of about 10th century AD. *GAR*, 1915-16.

(b) A group of Jaina temples of about 10th century AD locally called Gupha. *GAR*, 1922-23.

(c) A temple of Śāntinātha of about 10th century AD. *GAR*, 1915-16.

(d) Ruins of a group of two Jaina temples of about 10th century AD in the Batesvara valley. *GAR*, 1915-16.

Paitha (Morena) :

Remains of Jaina temple. *GAR*, 1940-41, p. 23.

Pali (Shivpuri) :

Ruins of a Jaina temple to the south of the village with images of Tīrthaṅkaras. *GAR*, 1939-40, p. 17.

Panagar (Jabalpur) :

A number of ancient Jaina sculptures found in Jaina temple. *KV*, p. 138.

Panagar (Hoshangabad) :

Remains of a Kalachuri Jaina temple. *SAG*, pp. 207-08.

Panihar (Gwalior) :

Jaina image bearing inscription dated V.S. 1529 referring to Kīrtisiṁha. *GAR*, Sam. 1997, No. 1.

Papaura (Tikamgarh) :

Jaina image of Chandella period with inscription of Madanavarman dated V.S. 1202. *Papaura,* p. 20.

Pataura (Satna) :

A Jaina temple of Gupta period. *Anekanta*, Vol. XIX, No. 6, Feb. 1967, pp. 340-46.

Paytha (Morena) :

Ruins of a Jaina temple with images of Tīrthaṅkaras lying at the site. *GAR*, 1940-41, p. 23.

Pendra (Bilaspur) :

Image of Pārśvanātha noticed. *PP*, V, No. 2, p. 166.

Pipalarawan (Ujjain) :

A Jaina temple of early date. *GAR*, 1917-18.

Pujaripali (Raigarh) :

Remains of a Jaina temple. *CASIR*, XIII, p. 144.

Radeb (Shivpuri) :

Originally a Jaina temple of about 11th century AD to the east of the village probably dedicated to Śāntinātha. A mutilated image of Śāntinātha lying at the site bears an inscription dated in V.S. 1078 (1021 AD). The temple was later repaired and converted to a Śaiva shrine. *GAR*, 1935-36, p. 13.

Rai (Budhi) (Shivpuri) :

An old Jaina temple, locally called the temple of Naga-Madha. *GAR*, 1916-17.

Raipur (Raipur) :

Jaina images of the Pāṇḍuvaṁśī period from Sirpur excavations, of the period of the Kalachuris of Tripurī from Karitalai and of the period of the Kalachuris of Ratanpur from Ratanpur and Arang preserved in the M.G.M. Museum. *Catalogue of Sculptures in the M.G.M. Museum, Raipur* (1960) (in Hindi).

Rakhetra (Guna) :

Rock-cut colossal Jaina images of about 14th century AD. *GAR*, 1924-25, pp. 35-36, 15-38.

Ramban (Satna) :

A number of Jaina images preserved. *KV*, pp. 256-58.

Ratanpur (Bilaspur) :

Images of Ṛṣabhanātha and Chandraprabha found. *PP*, V, No. 2, pp. 165-66.

Rewa (Rewa) :

A number of Jaina images noticed. *KV*, pp. 242-56.

Sahajai (Shivpuri) :

Remains of ancient Jaina temples. *GAR*, 1922-23.

Sakti (Raigarh) : A colossal Jaina image. *KV*, p. 151.

Sandhara (Mandsaur) :

Three Jaina temples datable to about 11th-12th century AD. *ISG*, p. 60.

Sandor (Guna) :

Ruins of an old Jaina temple. *GAR*, 1918-19.

Sarangpur (Rajgarh) :

Jaina goddess and other images datable to c. 10th-11th cent. AD. *IAR*, 1964-65, p. 74.

Shajapur (Shajapur) :

Marble Jaina sculptures of Śvetāmbara sect datable to c. 13th-17th cent. AD unearthed in the compound of the local Girls' H.S. School examined. *IAR*, 1985-86, p. 111.

Sesai (Shivpuri) :

Ruins of a Jaina temple of about 11th-12th century AD to the south-east of the village. *GAR*, 1914-15.

Siddhawarkut (East Nimar) :

(a) Eight modern Jaina temples in which remains of ancient Jaina temples are installed. *ENG*, p. 474.

(b) Image of Chandraprabha on the pedestal of which an inscription of 13th cent. AD is carved. *Ibid.*

Singhna (Dhar) :

Ancient Jaina temple. *HMIM*.

Siroha (Shivpuri) :

Remains of a Jaina temple datable to about 10th-12th cent. AD. *GAR*, 1925-26, p. 8.

Sirpur (Raipur) :

(a) A unique bronze image of Ādinātha datable to about 9th century AD found. *KV*, pp. 152-54.

(b) Remains of an old Jaina temple near the Gandhesvara temple. *CASIR*, VII, p. 170.

Sleemnabad (Jabalpur) :

(a) A number of Jaina sculptures found. *KV*, p. 139.

(b) A Jaina image with Navagrahas datable to about 13th century AD found. *KV*, p. 139; *SAG*, p. 211.

Sohagpur (Shahdol) :

(a) Ruins of a group of two Jaina temples. *CASIR*, VII, p. 244.

(b) Jaina image of Tīrthaṅkara and Śāśanadevī datable to Kalachuri period preserved in Thakur's palace. *HTM*, p. 100; *CASIR*, VII, p. 240.

Suhania (Morena) :

(a) A Jaina temple of Neminātha datable to about 11th century AD. *GAR*, 1936-37, p. 23.

(b) Ruins of a group of Jaina temples on the slope of a hill to the north of the village, datable to about 10th cent. AD. Images of Ādinātha, Pārśvanātha and of other Tīrthaṅkaras may be found on the site. *GAR*, 1929-30, p. 16.

(c) A group of two Jaina temples on the bank of nala, opposite the above-mentioned temples. Images of Tīrthaṅkaras are available on the site. *GAR*, 1929-30, p. 17.

(d) A temple to the north of the second group of Jaina temples, in total ruins, with images of Tīrthaṅkaras on the site, datable to about 10th century AD. *GAR*, 1929-30, p. 17.

(e) A group of three Jaina figures, the central one of about 15' in height and the other two flanking of 6' height. The central one is dated in Saṁ. 1467 (1410 AD). *CASIR*, II, p. 401.

(f) A Jaina pillar of about 10th cent. AD. *GAR*, 1929-30, p. 16.

Sunahra (Jabalpur) :

Jaina image with inscription dated V.S. 1363 referring to Mahārāja Mudriṅgadeva. *Hiralal List*, No. 59.

Sundarsi (Shajapur) :

Jaina sculptures in the vicinity of Mahakaleshwar temple noticed. *IAR*, 1985-86, p. 111.

Terahi (Shivpuri) :

An ancient Jaina *Chaumukhi*. *MPS*, p. 34.

Tewar (Jabalpur) :

(a) Jaina sculptures found. *KV*, pp. 135-36, 167-68; *CASIR*, IX, pp. 54-60.

(b) Torana of a Jaina temple found. *Ibid.*, pp. 171-73.

(c) A Jaina image of Ṛṣabhadeva dated in (K) E. 951. *Ibid.*, pp. 175-76.

(d) An image of Ambikā found. *Ibid.*, pp. 177-78.

(e) An image of Neminātha found. *Ibid.*, p. 179.

(f) A Jaina image with inscription referring to Jayadeva Jasadhavala. *MPR*, p. 70.

Tigowa (Jabalpur) :

An image of Pārśvanātha found. Hiralal, *Jabalpur Jyoti*, p. 140; *KV*, p. 137.

Tikamgarh (Tikamgarh) :

Jaina image with inscription dated V.S. 1216. *CJT*, Appendix B, No. 10.

Tiktoli-Dumdar (Morena) :

Rock-cut Jaina image on which an inscription dated V.S. 1542 is carved. *GAR*, 1916-17.

Timarni (Hoshangabad) :

A Jaina image on which an inscription dated V.S. 1265 is carved. *Hiralal List*, No. 130.

Thoban (Guna) :

Five groups of Jaina temples, comprising thirty-nine temples in all. *GAR*, 1914-15; *PP*, V-2, p. 181.

Tola (Jabalpur) :

Jaina images. *JDG*, p. 677.

Tumain (Guna) :

A colossal seated Jaina image of about 11th-12th century AD locally called Baitha Deva. *GAR*, 1918-19.

Uchahara (Satna) :

A number of Jaina images. *KV*, pp. 264-65; *CASIR*, IX, pp. 5-6.

Udayagiri (Vidisha) :

(a) Jaina rock-cut cave (Cave No. 1) datable to about 4th century AD. *MUH; CASIR*, X, p. 47.

(b) Jaina rock-cut cave of about 5th century AD with an inscription recording its excavation during the reign of the Gupta ruler Kumāragupta. *CASIR*, X, pp. 53-55.

Un (West Nimar) :

(a) Ruins of a Jaina temple locally called *Natal Avara Ka Dera*, datable to about 11th century AD built during the reign of the Paramāras of Malwa. *ISG*, p. 86; *ARASIWC*, 1918-19, p. 17; Ganguli, D.C., *The Paramaras of Malwa*, p. 265.

(b) A Jaina temple, locally called Goalesvara Mahadeva, built during the reign of the Paramāras of Malwa. *Ibid.*

(c) A temple of about 11th century AD locally called *Chaubara Dera*, built during the reign of the Paramaras of Malwa presently enshrining Jaina sculptures. *ISG*, p. 68; *ARASIWC*, 1918-19, p. 17; Ganguli, D.C., *The Paramaras of Malwa*, p. 263.

Unhel (Ujjain) :

Ancient Jaina temple. *GAR*, 1917-18.

Urwaha (Shivpuri) :

Ancient Jaina temple. *GAR*, 1922-23.

Vidisha (Vidisha) :

(a) Head of a Jaina Tīrthaṅkara and miscellaneous sculptures of the Paramāra period discovered. *IAR*, 1964-65, p. 74.

(b) Image of Chandraprabha with inscription of *Mahārājādhirāja Rāmagupta* on the pedestal. *MP*, p. 14; *JOI*, XVIII, No. 3, pp. 247-54.

(c) Second image of Chandraprabha with inscription of *Mahārājādhirāja Rāmagupta* on the pedestal. *Ibid.*

(d) Image of Puṣpadanta with inscription of *Mahārājādhirājā Rāmagupta* on the pedestal. *Ibid.*

(C) Vaiṣṇava Monuments and Sculptures

Amarkantak (Shahdol) :

(a) Ruins of a Vaiṣṇava temple. *CASIR*, VII, p. 231; *HIM*, p. 59.

(b) The large Vaiṣṇava temple of the Kalachuri period locally known as the Kesava-Narayan temple. *CASIR*, VII, p. 230; *HTM*, pp. 57-58, pl. XV; *CLAR*, p. 58.

Achera (Mandsaur) :

Ancient Vaiṣṇava temple. *GAR*, 1929-30, p. 18.

Afzalpur (Mandsaur) :

Two ancient Vaiṣṇava temples. *GAR*, 1914-22.

Agar (Ujjain) :

Temple of Varāha in which an image of Varāha datable to c. 10th-11th cent. AD is installed. *GAR*, 1929-30, p. 28.

Amjhera (Dhar) :

(a) Ancient Vaiṣṇava temple of Chaturbhujānātha. *GAR*, 1916-17.

(b) Ancient Vaiṣṇava temple of Lakṣmīnārāyaṇa. *Ibid.*

Arang (Raipur) :

Viṣṇu image near Narayantal. *RDG*, p. 536.

Ashapuri (Raisen) :

Ancient Vaiṣṇava temple with image of Varāha. *MPS*, p. 51.

Babai (Narsimhapur) :

A four-armed Viṣṇu image in an ancient fort. *NDG*, 1906, p. 205.

Badher (Vidisha) :

Ruins of two Vaiṣṇava temples of about 9th-12th cent. *AD*. *GAR*, 1940-41, p. 23.

Badoh (Vidisha) :

A group of Vaiṣṇava temples of about 9th-10th century AD, locally known as Daśāvatara temple. *AG*, pp. 57-59.

Bahoriband (Jabalpur) :

Rock-cut Vaiṣṇava sculptures of Gupta period, comprising Śeṣaśāyī-Nārāyaṇa, Narasiṁha, and four-armed Viṣṇu, akin to Udaigiri caves (Vidisha) found at Sindursi, adjoining Bahuriband. *IAR*, 1962-63, p. 68.

Balarpur (Shivpuri) :

Remains of ancient Vaiṣṇava temple. *GAR*, 1918-19.

Bamora (Sagar) :

Remains of an ancient temple in which a Varāha image exists. *SDG*, p. 522.

Bandhogarh (Shahdol) :

(a) A colossal rock figure of Ādivarāha to the west of which is incised an inscription of the reign of Kalachuri king Yuvarājadeva I. *CII*, IV, pt. I, p. 183.

(b) A fish temple in the fort at, containing an inscription of the reign of Kalachuri king Yuvarājadeva I. *CII*, IV, pt. I, p. 182.

Barahata (Hoshangabad) :

A rare image of Viṣṇu. *SAG*, p. 212.

Bara Kalan (Bhind) :

Ruins of old brick-built Vaiṣṇava temple probably of 7th-8th century AD. *GAR*, 1929-30, p. 8.

Baro or Baranagar (Vidisha) :

A group of eight small sized Vaiṣṇava temples. *CASIR*, X, pp. 74-75.

Barmanghat (Narsinghpur) :

Ancient temple of Laxmī–Nārāyaṇa and Rāma-Lakṣmaṇa. *NDG*, p. 458.

Besnagar (Vidisha) :

(a) Heliodorus pillar, locally called Kham Baba with Brāhmī inscription of about 2nd-Ist century BC. *ASIR*, VII, p. 127; XIII, p. 186; XXIII, p. 99; XXIV, p. 128; *IHQ*, VIII, p. 610; *GAR*, Saṁ. 1974, No. 66; *JOR*, XV (1945-46), pp. 135-37.

(b) Broken Viṣṇu image found near Kham Baba. *ASIR*, 1915-16, pp. 195-96; *MBI*, p. 623.

(c) Two fragmentary pieces of a pillar capital. *MBI*, pp. 624-25.

(d) Pedestal of an image of Garuḍa. *Ibid.*

Bheraghat (Jabalpur) :

Image of Viṣṇu and Lakṣmī in the temple of Chaunaṭha Yoginī. *HTM*, p. 91.

Bhilsa (Vidisha) :

An image of Viṣṇu with an inscription dated V.S. 1242, recording installation of the image. *GRA*, p. 17.

Bhita (Jabalpur) :

(a) Sculptures of the 10th-12th century AD in the Kalachuri style found. *IAR*, 1959-60, p. 69.

(b) A colossal image of Varāha. *Ibid.*

Bilaoni (Shivpuri) :

Ruins of an old Vaiṣṇava temple. *GAR*, 1915-16.

Bilahari (Jabalpur) :

(a) The Kalachuri temple of Viṣṇu-Varāha datable to about 12th century AD. *KV*, p. 321; *CASIR*, IX, pp. 35-38.

(b) Fine image of the boar incarnation of Viṣṇu in the compound of the temple of Viṣṇu-Varāha. *HTM*, p. 94, pl. XXXVII-b.

(c) A number of Vaiṣṇava images found. *KV*, pp. 338-40.

Burhikhar (Bilaspur) :

A Viṣṇu image of c. 2nd cent. AD with an inscription recording donation by a lady named Prajāvatī. *MPR*, p. 46.

Chhapri (Durg) :

Viṣṇu temple of about 12th-13th cent. AD locally known as Boramdeo temple. *CASIR*, XVII, p. 34; Mirashi, *CII*, IV, pt. II, p. 380; *Hiralal List,* No. 174.

Deokani (Guna) :

Ruins of a Vaiṣṇava temple of about 12th-13th century AD. *GAR*, 1925-26, p. 9.

Deori (Sagar) :

Vaiṣṇava sculptures of medieval period found. *IAR*, 1959-60, p. 70.

Devala (Dhar) :

An ancient temple of Narasiṁha. *GAR*, 1916-17.

Dharampuri (Dhar) :

Colossi images of Viṣṇu, Narasiṁha and Balarāma (?). *MAR*, 1949-50.

Dhunderi (Ujjain) :

Ruins of a Vaiṣṇava temple. *TSG*, p. 22.

Dongar (Bastar) : Viṣṇu and other images. *IAR*, 1968-69.

Dudhia (Rewa) :

(a) An image of Viṣṇu datable to Kalachuri period found. *HIM*, p. 108, pl. L,a.

(b) An image of Viṣṇu in the temple of Keśavanārāyaṇa. *HIM*, p. 108, pl. XLIX, b.

Eran (Sagar) :

(a) Temple of Varāha Avatāra of Viṣṇu erected by Dhanyaviṣṇu. *CASIR*, X, pp. 82-83.

(b) Temple of Viṣṇu with colossal image of the god belonging to the Gupta age. *CASIR*, X, pp. 85-87.

(c) A small temple of Viṣṇu to the north of the above-mentioned temple. *Ibid.*, p. 87.

(d) Vaiṣṇava temple of Gupta period dedicated in the Narasiṁha Avatāra form of Viṣṇu, near the above-mentioned temple. *Ibid.*, pp. 88-89.

(e) Inscribed statue of Viṣṇu datable to Gupta period. *Ibid.*, p. 87.

(f) A number of Vaiṣṇava sculptures datable to Gupta period found. *IAR*, 1959-60, p. 70.

(g) Colossal Boar with inscription of Toramāṇa. *CASIR*, VII, p. 89; X, pp. 83-84.

(h) Toraṇa in front of Varāha temple. *CASIR*, X, pp. 83-84; *CLAR*, pp. 34-35.

(i) Inscribed pillar set up in the reign of Gupta ruler Budhagupta by Mātṛviṣṇu and Dhanyaviṣṇu. *CASIR*, X, p. 81; *ibid.*, VII, p. 88; *CLAR*, pp. 34-35.

(j) Rare stone slabs with Kṛṣṇa-līlā scenes. *MB*, III, No. 3 (1960), pp. 1-5.

(k) Gāja-Lakṣmī image of Gupta period. *Ibid.*, p. 5.

Ghusai (Mandsaur) :

An ancient Vaiṣṇava temple. *GAR*, 1916-17.

Gopalpur (Rewa) :

A Śeṣaśāyī image of Viṣṇu at the back of which is incised an inscription of the reign of Kalachuri king Yuvarājadeva I. *CII*, IV, pt. I, p. 185.

Gudar (Shivpuri) :

(a) Ruins of an old Vaiṣṇava temple, with a large size image of Viṣṇu measuring 7.75' in height. *GAR*, 1929-30, p. 24.

(b) A Vaiṣṇava temple at Hanumān Kho, 2 miles to the south-west of the village, with a life-size image of Hanumān. *GAR*, 1929-30, p. 24.

(c) A colossal Vaiṣṇava image of about 7.5'. in height. *GAR*, 1929-30, p. 23.

Gwalior (Gwalior) :

Images of Viṣṇu, Lakṣmī-Nārāyaṇa and all the incarnations of Viṣṇu preserved in the State Govt. Museum. *Catalogue of Sculptures in the Archaeological Museum*, Gwalior.

Gwalior Fort (Gwalior) :

(a) Vaisnava (?) temple of about 8th-10th century AD locally named as Teli-Ka-Mandir with oblong shrine and barrel-shaped *śikhara* in South Indian style. Richly carved door frames with figures of Ganga and Yamuna. *CASIR*, II, pp. 357 ff; *AG*.

(b) Rock-cut Vaiṣṇava temple, called Chaturbhuj Mandir built on the ascent to fort from Gwalior gate. There are two inscriptions dated V.S. 932 and V.S. 933, the former referring to the excavation of the temple by Alla during the reign of Gurjara Pratihāra king Ādivarāha (Bhojadeva) and the other recording the construction of the other temple nearby. *CASIR*, II, p. 356; *EI*, I, p. 156.

(c) Two Vaiṣṇava temples near the eastern rampart of the fort, the one known as the larger Sāsbahu temple and the second known as the smaller Sāsbahu temple. A large inscription in the former dated in V.S. 1150 (1093 AD) during the reign of Mahipāla, refers to the dynastic line of the Kachchhapaghāta rulers of Gwalior. *AG*, p. 80; *CASIR*, II, p. 347.

Gyaraspur (Vidisha) :

(a) Vaiṣṇava temple to the south-west of the village, locally called as Bājrā Maṭha datable to about 9th century AD. It consists of three shrines, originally dedicated to Śiva, Sūrya and Viṣṇu, but Jaina images are presently enshrined in them. *AG*, pp. 91-92; *CASIR*, VII, pp. 90-93; *ibid.*, X, pp. 31-34.

(b) Vaiṣṇava temple in the eastern part of the village datable to about 9th-10th century AD. Only its platforms, pillars with brackets, sculptures etc. and a very richly carved toraṇa, locally called as Hinḍolā Toraṇa now exist. Two fragmentary inscriptions discovered from here refer to Chāmuṇḍarāja and Mahendrapāladeva. *AG*, pp. 94-95; *GAR*, 1932-33, p. 20; *CASIR*, VII, pp. 90-93; *ibid.*, X. pp. 31-34.

Hoshangabad (Hoshangabad) :

Medieval Vaiṣṇava sculptures found. *IAR*, 1964-65, p. 74.

Indor (Guna) :

Ruins of a Vaiṣṇava temple of about 9th-10th century AD with sculptures of Viṣṇu, Lakṣmī etc. lying seattered about. *GAR*, 1936-38, p. 9.

Indore (Indore) :

Images of the Boar incarnation of Viṣṇu, of Lakṣmī Nārāyaṇa and Yoga

Nārāyaṇa preserved in the Central Museum. *Guide Book to the Central Museum*, Indore, pp. 3-4.

Ishwarpur (Sagar) :

Statues of Lakṣmī-Nāryāṇa and Varāha discovered. *IAR*, 1961-62, p. 100.

Janjgir (Bilaspur) :

(a) The great unfinished Vaiṣṇava temple datable to about 10th century AD. *CASIR*, VII, pp. 209-11; *CLAR*, p. 60.

(b) Two Vaiṣṇava temples datable to about 10th century AD. *Ibid.*, pp. 204-09; *PRASIWC*, 1904, p. 29.

(c) Vaiṣṇava sculptures found. *Ibid.*, pp. 204-05.

Jiran (Mandsaur) :

Four-armed Viṣṇu, Lakṣmī–Nārāyaṇa and Narasiṁha images found. *IAR*, 1965-66, p. 81.

Kachrod (Ujjain) :

An old Vaiṣṇava temple and a Nṛsiṁha temple. *GAR*, 1917-18.

Kadvada (Mandsaur) :

Ruins of an old Vaiṣṇava temple of Chaturbhuja with later repairs. *HMIM*.

Kagpur (Vidisha) :

Ruins of a Vaiṣṇava temple of about 8th century AD (probably of later Gupta period). *GAR*, 1931-32, p. 6.

Kalamadh (Shivpuri) :

Ruins of a Vaiṣṇava temple of about 10th-11th century AD with old sculptures lying about. The style of architecture resembles the temple of Tongra (see below). *GAR*, 1928-29, p. 13.

Kambli (Mandsaur) :

A Vaiṣṇava temple. *HMIM*.

Kanjarda (Mandsaur) :

Sculptures of about 11th-12th century AD fixed in the modern Vaiṣṇava temple of Chaturbhuja. *HMIM*.

Karanpura (Jabalpur) :

A colossal image of the Boar incarnation of Viṣṇu. *CLAR*, p. 28.

Karitalai (Jabalpur) :

(a) Ruins of temples, Varāha and other Vaiṣṇava sculptures. *MPR*, p. 83; *CASIR*, IX, pp. 7-8.

(b) Vaiṣṇava images found. *KV*, p. 329.

(c) A temple probably dedicated to the Boar incarnation of Viṣṇu, from which was discovered the stone inscription of Kalachuri king Lakṣmaṇarāja II. *CII*, IV, pt. 1, pp. 178-86.

Katni (Jabalpur) :

A Daśāvatarī Viṣṇu image found. *KV*, pp. 369-74.

Kawardha (Durg) :

Remains of old temple fixed in the modern temple of Rāma. *CASIR*, XVII, p. 34.

Kethuli (Mandsaur) :

Vaiṣṇava temple of about 13th-14th century AD with an image of Śeṣaśāyī Viṣṇu. *ISG*, p. 28.

Khadavada (Mandsaur) :

Ancient Vaiṣṇava temple, known as Chaturbhuj temple. *HMIM*.

Khajuraho (Chhatarpur) :

(a) Brahmā temple datable to c. 10th cent. AD built on the bank of Khajuraho Sagar. *KD*, pp. 13-35; *KKD*, pp. 51-60; *KDP*, pp. 12-22; *KSS*, pp. 10-18; *KZ*, pp. 87-160; *AI*, No. 15.

(b) Temple of Varāha avatāra of Viṣṇu close to Lakṣmaṇa temple datable between 900-925 AD. *Ibid.*

(c) Lakṣmaṇa temple which is of pañchāyatana style, built by Chandella ruler Yaśovarman during 930-950 AD. *Ibid.*

(d) Vāmana temple in which an image of Vāmana avatāra of Viṣṇu is installed. It was built during 1050-1075 AD. *Ibid.*

(e) Javārī temple in which four-armed image of Viṣṇu is installed, datable between 1075-1100 AD. *Ibid.*

(f) Chaturbhuja temple in which a colossal image of Viṣṇu is installed, datable to c. 1100 AD. *Ibid.*

(g) A ruined temple of Viṣṇu to the east of Vāmana temple, locally known as Khakhrā Maṭha. *Ibid.*

(h) Sthānaka Viṣṇu images located in Lakṣmaṇa temple, Jagadambī temple, Khajuraho Museum, Mātangeśvara temple, Chaturbhuja temple, Javārī temple, Viśvanātha temple, Dhubela Museum, Chitragupta temple, Pratāpeśvara temple, Vāmana temple, Pārśvanātha temple and Kandariyā temple. *KDP*, pp. 150-51, No. 1-186, pp. 57-149; *Ibid.*

(i) Āsana Viṣṇu images located in Lakṣmaṇa temple, Khajuraho Museum, Brahmā temple, Vāmana temple, Viśvanātha temple, Kandariyā temple, Pratāpeśvara temple, Dulādeva temple, Chaturbhuj temple, Javārī temple, Mahādeva temple, Jagadambī temple and Pārvati temple. *KDP*, p. 152, No. 87-124; *Ibid.*, pp. 57-149.

(j) Find spots of Viṣṇu Śayana images are Khajuraho temple, Dhubela Museum, Lakṣmaṇa temple, Brahmā temple, Vāmana temple, Viśvanātha temple, Pratāpeśvara temple, Kandariyā temple, Dulādev temple, Chaturbhuja temple, Javārī temple and Mahādeva temple. *Ibid.*

(k) Find spots of the Daśāvatāra images of Viṣṇu are Lakṣmaṇa temple, Varāha temple, Jagadambī temple, Chitragupta temple, Khajuraho Museum, Vāmana temple, Javārī temple, Viśvanātha temple, Kandariyā temple, Pārśvanātha temple and Hanumāna temple. *KDP*, pp. 154-56, No. 129-203; *Ibid.*, pp. 57-149.

(l) Images of other avatāras and forms of Viṣṇu may be located in Khajuraho Museum, Lakṣmaṇa temple, Kandariyā temple, Viśvanātha temple, Pārśvanātha temple, Chitragupta temple, Jagadambī temple, Vāmana temple, Kandariyā temple, Javārī temple and Dūlādeva temple. *KDP*, pp. 156-57, No. 204-47; *Ibid.*, pp. 57-149.

(m) Find spot of the Garuḍa and Āyudha Puruṣas are Khajuraho Museum, Lakṣmaṇa temple, Pārśvanātha temple and Viśvanātha temple. *KDP*, pp. 157-58, No. 248-49; *Ibid.*, pp. 57-149.

Khoh (Panna) :

A fine image of Boar incarnation of Viṣṇu found. *PRASIWC*, 1920, pl. XXIX; *CASIR*, IX, pp. 6-7.

Kohala (Mandsaur) :

Three Vaiṣṇava temples of about 13th-14th century AD. *ISG*, pp. 30 ff.

Koni (Bilaspur) :

Images of Viṣṇu and Gaṇeśa found in the ruins of the Kalachuri temple. *EI*, XXVII, pp. 276 ff.

Kukdesvar (Mandsaur) :

Temple of Viṣṇu of about 13th-14th century AD repaired later. *ISG*. p. 37.

Madankhedi (Guna) :

Temple of Viṣṇu of about 11th-12th century AD. *GAR*, 1918-19.

Madanpur (Sagar) :

A colossal boar and two inscribed sati stones. *CLAR*, p. 35.

Mahidpur (Ujjain) :

Temple of Chaturbhuja Viṣṇu, with inscription dated in V.S. 1344 (1287 AD). *HMIM*.

Maihar (Satna) :

Image of Narasiṁha on a plateau of Kaimur range. *HIM*, pp. 77-78.

Majholi (Jabalpur) :

(a) Varāha statue found. *CASIR*, IX, p. 48.

(b) Ruins of other temple sculptures. *CLAR*, p. 29.

Makundpur (Rewa) :

Ruins of a Kalachuri temple, probably dedicated to Viṣṇu, yielding an inscription of the reign of Gāṅgeyadeva dated in (K) E. 722. *CASIR*, XIII, pp. 4-5.

Malhar (Bilaspur) :

A beautifully carved image of Viṣṇu with inscription datable to about 2nd century BC. *IAR*, 1960-61, p. 59.

Mandhata (East Nimar) :

A Vaiṣṇava temple of avatāras of Viṣṇu. *ENG*, p. 471.

Marai (Rewa) :

A beautiful image of Śeṣaśāyin datable to Kalachuri period. *HIM*, p. 94, pl. XIV, b.

Mitaoli (Morena) :

Ruins of a Vaiṣṇava temple to the east of the Mahādeva temple, on a hill, datable to about 11th-12th century AD. *GAR*, 1918-19; 1942-46, p. 67.

Mohanpur (Guna) :

Remains of an old Vaiṣṇava temple of about 10th century AD used in the construction of a temple of later date. *GAR*, 1924-25, p. 13.

Mohendra (Panna) :

A medieval Brahmanical temple with sculptures found. Among them the figure of a *nāgī* holding a child is interesting. *IAR*, 1960-61, p. 61 and pl. LXXIIIA.

Nachna (Panna) :

(a) Vaiṣṇava sculptures datable to the Gupta and Kalachuri-Chandella periods found. *IAR*, 1962-63, p. 69.

(b) About half a dozen Gupta panels depicting Rāmāyaṇa scenes found. *IAR*, 1960-61, p. 61.

Naderi (Guna) :

Old sculptures representing the avatāras of Viṣṇu fixed in Jain temple. *GAR*, 1924-25, p. 25.

Narasimha (Balaghat) :

An old temple of Narasiṁha. *CLAR*, p. 26.

Nimthur (Mandsaur) :

A Vaiṣṇava temple with illegible inscription. Also sculptures of Varāha, Trimurtī etc. fixed in *bāolī*. *GAR*, 1917-18.

Padhavali (Morena) :

(a) Ruins of a Vaiṣṇava temple of about 10th century AD in the Batesvara valley. *GAR*, 1915-16.

(b) Ruins of a group of two Vaiṣṇava temples of about 10th century AD in the Batesvara valley. *GAR*, 1915-16.

(c) Ruins of a Vaiṣṇava temple, with Trimurtī, of about 10th century AD in the Batesvara valley. *GAR*, 1915-16.

Palanagar (Dewas) :

Vaiṣṇava temple with collection of old sculptures datable to about 13th-14th century AD. *MAR*, 1949-50.

Panagar (Jabalpur) :

(a) A number of Vaiṣṇava images found. *KV*, pp. 327-69.

(b) Three images of Viṣṇu datable to 11th-12th century AD found. *Ibid.*, p. 369.

(c) A colossal Varāha image. *MPR*, p. 83.

Panihar (Gwalior) :

An ancient Vaiṣṇava temple. *GAR*, 1933-34, p. 13.

Panvihar (Ujjain) :

(a) Old sculptures of Śeṣaśāyī Viṣṇu, Gaṇeśa etc. built into the construction of a gate. *GAR*, 1917-18.

(b) An old Vaiṣṇava temple. *GAR*, 1917-18.

Paraini (Rewa) :

Remains of a Kalachuri temple and a Varāha image. *CASIR*, XXI, p. 158.

Pepraul (Sarguja) :

A Vaiṣṇava temple. *CASIR*, VIII, pp. 64-65.

Piploda (Dhar) :

Rock-cut Vaiṣṇava sculptures found in the midst of Narmada. *IAR*, 1958-59, p. 72.

Paragadh (Guna) :

Rock-cut sculptures of Śeṣaśāyī Viṣṇu with inscription dated in V.S. 1300 (1243 AD). *GAR*, 1915-16.

Pathari (Bhilsa) :

(a) A colossal Varāha (13' x 11') to the east of the village, left incomplete. *GAR*, 1923-24, p. 10.

(b) Stone pillar with an inscription dated V.S. 917 recording installation of a *Garuḍadhavaja* in front of a temple of Śauri (Viṣṇu or Kṛṣṇa) by Rāṣṭrakūṭa Parabala. *CASIR*, X, p. 70; *JASB*, XVII, pt. I, p. 305; *ASIR*, X, p. 70; *EI*, IX, p. 252; *IA*, XL, p. 239; *GAR*, Saṁ. 1970, No. 7; *Bhandarkar List*, No. 29.

Pawaya (Gwalior) :

Remains of a Vaiṣṇava temple datable to c. 3rd-5th cent. AD found in the excavation. *GAR*, 1940-41, pp. 17-20.

Pipalarawan (Ujjain) :

Two Vaiṣṇava temples of early date. *GAR*, 1917-18.

Piparia (Satna) :

Vaiṣṇava sculptures found in the excavation of Gupta temple by the University of Sagar. *IAR*, 1968-69.

Raipur (Raipur) :

Vaiṣṇava images of the period of the Kalachuris of Tripurī, from Karitalai and those of the period of the Kalachuris of Ratanpur and from Sirpur preserved in the MGM Museum. *Catalogue of Sculptures in the M.G.M. Museum*, Raipur (1960) (in Hindi).

Rajim (Raipur) :

(a) Rajiv Lochan temple, dedicated to the worship of Viṣṇu, datable to about 5th century AD. *CASIR*, XVII, pp. 9-12; *Ibid.*, VII, pp. 151-53; *KV*, p. 357; *CLAR*, p. 53.

(b) Temple of Jagannātha to the east of the Rajiva-Lochana temple, dedicated to Viṣṇu as Jagannātha. *Ibid.*, pp. 13-14; *CLAR*, p. 54.

(c) Temple of Rāmachandra bearing a small pilgrim's record of about 8th-9th century AD. *CASIR*, XVIII, p. 14; *CLAR*, p. 54.

Ramgarh Hill (Sarguja) :

Remains of Vaiṣṇava temple. *CASIR*, XIII, pp. 36-37.

Rehli (Sagar) :

Vaiṣṇava sculptures of medieval period found. *IAR*, 1959-60, p. 70.

Rewa (Rewa) :

A standing figure of Viṣṇu. *CASIR*, XXI, p. 144.

Rithi (Jabalpur) :

Ancient image of Varāha. *JDG*, p. 690.

Sakri (Guna) :

Vaiṣṇava images built in a temple of about 11th cent. AD. *GAR*, 1927-28, p. 10.

Sandhara (Mandsaur) :

Temple of Chaturbhuja Viṣṇu datable to about 11th-12th century AD. *ISG*, p. 60.

Sarguja District :

A unique image of Vaikuṇṭha discovered from the temple complex at Deepadih, an ancient mound located at the top of Ramgarh hills. *IAR*, 1987-88, p. 139.

Satanwada (Shivpuri) :

Ruins of a Vaiṣṇava temple datable to about 10th-11th century AD to the east of the village. Ruins of another temple nearby. *GAR*, 1923-24, p. 14.

Shamshabad (Vidisha) :

Vaiṣṇava sculptures of medieval period discovered. *IAR*, 1959-60, p. 71.

Sheopur (Mandsaur) :

A Viṣṇu image of 10th-11th century AD found. *IAR*, 1954-55, p. 62.

Sheorinarayan (Bilaspur) :

The brick-temple of Nārāyaṇa datable to about 9th-10th century AD with sanctum on a circular plan, facing the stone temple. *CASIR*, VII, pp. 199-201; *PRASIWC*, 1904, pp. 30-31; *CLAR*, p. 62.

Sindursi (Jabalpur) :

Rock-cut images of Anantaśāyī-Viṣṇu, Mahiṣāsura-Mardinī, Viṣṇu, and Narasiṁha in the Gupta style discovered near the Bahoriband rest house. *IAR*, 1960-61, p. 60.

Sirpur (Raipur) :

(a) Ruins of a Vaiṣṇava temple datable to about 5th-6th century AD. *CASIR*, VII, p. 174.

(b) Ruins of another contemporary Vaiṣṇava (?) temple about 50' to the south of the above. *Ibid.*

(c) Ruins of a large Vaiṣṇava temple. *Ibid.*, p. 175.

(d) Ruins of another Vaiṣṇava temple. *Ibid.*, p. 179.

(e) Remains of a Vaiṣṇava temple. *Ibid.*, p. 180.

(f) Ruins of a huge temple forming a mound, locally known "Surang". *CASIR*, VII, pp. 182-85; XVII, pp. 29-30.

(g) A Vaiṣṇavite brick temple locally known as Lakṣmaṇa temple datable to about 6th century AD. *CASIR*, VII, pp. 186-92; *XVII*, p. 27; *PRASIWC*, 1904, pp. 20-23; *ARASI*, 1909-10, pp. 11-18, pl. I-III, fig. I; *CLAR*, p. 55; *KV*, pp. 253-555.

(h) Remains of two other brick temples nearby. *Ibid.*

(i) Ruins of a temple. *CASIR*, VII, p. 174.

(j) Ruins of another temple 30' to the south-east of the above. *Ibid.*

(k) Ruins of a small temple. *Ibid.*, p. 177.

(l) Rāma temple. *CASIR*, VII, pp. 185-86; *KV*, p. 255.

Sohagpur (Shahdol) :

(a) Ruins of a group of a two Vaiṣṇava temples. *CASIR*, VII, p. 244.

(b) Ruins of two groups of Vaiṣṇava temples on the bank of a rivulet. *Ibid.*

(c) Images of Viṣṇu Nārāyaṇa lying on Śeṣa, and Garuda, datable to Kalachuri period found in the palace of Thakur. *HIM*, pp. 99-100, pls. XL, b; XLII-a; XL-a.

Suhania (Morena) :

A Vaiṣṇava temple of about 11th century AD. *GAR*, 1914-23; *CASIR*, II, p. 401.

Sunari (Vidisha) :

Ruins of a Vaiṣṇava temple with an image of the Buddha avatāra of Viṣṇu. *GAR*, 1923-24, p. 8.

Suvasra (Mandsaur) :

Early medieval Vaiṣṇava sculptures found. *IAR*, 1965-66, p. 81.

Tatapani (Sarguja) :

Vaiṣṇavite sculptures found. *CASIR*, XIII, p. 63.

Tewar (Jabalpur) :

(a) An image of four-armed Viṣṇu discovered. *IAR*, 1965-66, p. 80.

(b) A large number of Vaiṣṇava sculptures near bāoli. *MPR*.

(c) Vaiṣṇava images found. *KV*, p. 320.

Thoban (Guna) :

Ruins of a Vaiṣṇava temple. *GAR*, 1914-15.

Tigwan (Jabalpur) :

Nṛsiṁha avatāra image and other Vaiṣṇava sculptures kept in a Gupta temple and ruins near about. *JDG*, p. 698.

Timarni (Hoshangabad) :

An image of Lakṣmīnārāyaṇa on which an inscription dated 1203 is inscribed. *Hiralal List*, No. 130.

Tongra (Shivpuri) :

(a) Four Vaiṣṇava temples of about 10th-11th century AD with architecture similar to the Sun temple existing here. *GAR*, 1928-29, pp. 11-12.

(b) Nṛsiṁha image on which an inscription of V.S. 1082 is inscribed. *GAR*, Saṁ, 1985, No. 60.

Udayagiri (Vidisha) :

(a) A Vaiṣṇava rock-cut cave (cave No. 5) locally called Varāha Guphā (the name is derived from the scene of Varāha incarnation of Viṣṇu carved in the cave) datable to about 4th century AD. *MUH; CASIR*, X, pp. 48-49.

(b) Eleven rock-cut caves (caves Nos. 8-18) datable to about 4th-5th century AD with images of Viṣṇu enshrined in some of them. Śeṣāśāyī Viṣṇu is carved in cave No. 13. *MUH*; CASIR, X, p. 52.

Ujjain (Ujjain) :

A group of Vaiṣṇava temples at Gomatī Kuṇḍa datable to about 10th-11th century AD. *GAR*, 1917-18.

Umaria (Jabalpur) :

Sculputres of Lakṣmī and Garuḍa. *JDG*, p. 699.

Vidisha (Vidisha) :

(a) A highly artistic Viṣṇu head of the Gupta period and a complete statue of Surasundarī noticed. *IAR*, 1962-63, p. 69.

(b) A statue of Hari-hara discovered on a mound near the Heliodorus pillar. *IAR*, 1965-66, p. 81.

(c) Śeṣaśāyī image with an inscription of Śrī Lābhadeva. *GAR*, Saṁ. 1986, No. 3.

(D) Śaiva Monuments and Sculptures

Achana (Dhar) :

Ancient Śaiva temple. *GAR*, 1916-17.

Afzalpur (Mandsaur) :

An ancient Śaiva temple. *GAR*, 1914-22.

Ainti (Morena) :

(a) Śaiva temple of about 11th-12th century AD. *GAR*, 1914-15, p. 27.

Amarkantak (Shahdol) :

(a) Ruins of a large Śaiva temple with its maṇḍapa supported on sixteen pillars. *CASIR*, VII, p. 231; *HTM*, p. 57; *CLAR*, p. 58.

(b) Ruins of a similar large Śaiva temple. *CASIR*, VII, p. 232.

(c) A Śaiva temple built by Kalachuri king Karṇa, locally known as Karan Mandir. *CASIR*, VII, pp. 227-29; *HTM*, pp. 54-57, pl. XIII; *CLAR*, p. 57.

(d) Three small Śaiva temples near the Karan Mandir. *CASIR*, VII, p. 230; *HTM*, p. 57; *CLAR*, p. 57.

(e) The temple of Machchhendranātha datable to the Kalachuri period. *HTM*, p. 58, pl. XVI b.

(f) The Kalachuri temple of Pātāleśvara. *HTM*, pp. 59-60, pl. XVI, a.

(g) An image of Kārttikeya datable to Gupta period. *IAR*, 1968-69.

Amjhera (Dhar) :

An ancient Śaiva temple. *GAR*, 1916-17.

Amledha (Morena) :

Ruins of Śaiva temples of about 11th-12th century AD (?). One of the temples is half-buried in ground and the other is somewhat well preserved. *GAR*, 1929-30, pp. 30-31.

Amrol (Gwalior) :

(a) Temple of Rāmeśvara Mahādeo of about 7th-8th century AD. *GAR*, 1916-17, p. 13.

(b) Mound called Ganesh Pahadi datable to 9th-10th century AD. *GAR*, 1929-30, p. 13.

(c) Śaiva temple of about 11th-12th century AD locally known as Dhane-Baba-Ki-Madhi. *GAR*, 1916-17, p. 13.

(d) Śaiva temple of about 11th-12th century AD locally called Mata-Ki-Madhi. *GAR*, 1929-30, p. 13.

Anghora (Guna) :

(a) Śaiva temple originally dedicated to goddess Mahiṣamardinī, with sanctum and a porch probably added later. A pilgrim's record dated in V.S. 1157 (1100 AD) is inscribed on floor slab. *GAR*, 1927-28, p. 9.

(b) Śaiva temple, two miles to the north-west of the village. *GAR*, 1927-28, p. 26.

Antri (Gwalior) :

Śaiva temple locally called Turka Gol (?). The modern name of the village is believed to be derived from the old village Antikāpurī existing in about 6th century AD. *GDG*, p. 357.

Arang (Raipur) :

The Śaiva temple possibly originally a Jaina temple, locally known as Bagh Deval, datable to about 11th century AD. *CASIR*, VII, pp. 162-64.

Adbhar (Raigarh) :

A Kalachuri Śaiva temple found. *CASIR*, XIII, p. 145; *PRASIWC*, 1904, pp. 32-33; *CLAR*, p. 63.

Asukhedi (Dhar) :

Ruins of an ancient Śaiva temple. *GAR*, 1920-21.

Badi-delchi (Ujjain) :

Śaiva temple locally called as the temple of Hinglajmata. *HMIM*.

Badnawar (Dhar) :

Śaiva temple of about 11th-12th century AD. *MAR*, 1948-49.

Bagar (Rewa) :

Old Śaivite sculptures found. *CASIR*, XIII, p. 5.

Bagh (Dhar) :

(a) Temple of Mahākala of about 10th-11th century AD. *AG*, 61; *ASIAR*, II, 16.

(b) Ruins of Śaiva temple on a hill to the south-west of the village. *GAR*, 1930-31, p. 8.

Bagrod (Vidisha) :

A Śaiva temple. *GAR*, 1932-33, pp. 7-8.

Baijnath (Rewa) :

The temple of Vaidyanātha Mahādeva, probably the same as that given by the Kalachuri ruler Lakṣmaṇarāja to the Śaiva ascetic Hṛdayaśiva as mentioned in the Bilahari stone inscription. *CASIR*, XXI, pp. 154-55; *HTM*, pp. 61-62; *CII*, IV, pt. I; *EI*, I, pp. 259, 268.

Bajrangarh (Guna) :

Śaiva temple of about 10th-12th century AD presently in ruins. *GAR*, 1929-30.

Balarpur (Shivpuri) :

An ancient Śaiva temple. *GAR*, 1914-15.

Balod (Durg) :

A group of seven Śaiva temples. *CASIR*, VII, pp. 133-34, pl. XV; *CLAR*, p. 49.

Bara (Bhind) :

A group of ruined old temples, probably dedicated to Śiva. *GAR*, 1929-30, pp. 7-8.

Barahata (Hoshangabad) :

Ruins of Śaiva temples. *SAG*, pp. 206-07.

Bargaon (Jabalpur) :

(a) Lintel of a Śaiva temple datable to Kalachuri period found close to the temple of Somanātha. *HIM*, p. 107, pl. XXXIX, b.

(b) Śaiva temple of Somanātha datable to Kalachuri period, containing inscription of Śabara. *CASIR, XXI*, pp. 101, 163; *CLAR*, p. 27; *HTM*, p. 66, pl. 18-a.

Baro or Barnagar (Vidisha) :

A Śaiva temple locally known as Gadarmal temple with a group of seven subsidiary shrines, later used by the Buddhists or Jainas datable to about 8th-10th century AD. *CASIR*, VII, pp. 69-79; X, pp. 71-74.

Barod (Gadhi) (Shivpuri) :

An ancient Śaiva temple. *GAR*, 1922-23.

Barwani (West Nimar) :

(a) The ancient temple of Siddhanātha which was originally a Jaina temple. *WNDG*, p. 434.

(b) The temple of Gaṇapati locally known as 'Vani-Vinayaka'. *Ibid.*

Bhairamgarh (Bastar) :

Images of Kārttikeya, Bhairava, Pārvatī found. *IAR*, 1968-69.

Bhaktar (Shivpuri) :

Śaiva temple with a pilgrim's record dated in V.S. 970 (?). *GAR*, 1914-23.

Bhanpura (Mandsaur) :

Sculputres of Śiva holding a double-faced heavy mace in his right hand and standing in dvibhaṅga pose, Naṭarāja and Skanda discovered. *IAR*, 1965-66, p. 22.

Bharaoli (Morena) :

Ancient Śaiva temple at. *GAR*, 1929-30, p. 31.

Bharoli (Bhind) :

A Śaiva temple datable to 11th-12th century AD. *GAR*, 1914-15.

Bhejratala (Rajnandgaon) :

Ruins of a Śiva temple and sculptures of Bhairava, Nāga, Hanumān, and Gaṇeśa datable to c. 12th-13th century AD discovered. *IAR*, 1988-89, p. 105.

Bhensoda (Morena) :

(a) Ruins of a Śaiva temple of about 10th century AD to the north-west of the village. *GAR*, 1929-30, p. 329.

(b) Ruins of a Śaiva temple to the south of the village, datable to about 10th century AD. *GAR*, 1929-30, p. 329.

Bheraghat (Jabalpur) :

Images of Vareśvara Mahādeva, Śiva, Gaṇapati etc. in the temple of Chausaṭha Yoginī. *HTM*, pp. 86, 87, 91; *TCYB*.

Bherongarh (Ujjain) :

Śaiva temples of Kāla Bhairava, Ukreśvara Mahādeo, Tārakeśvara Mahādeo and of Siddhadeo. *GAR*, 1926-27, p. 18.

Bhitarwar (Gwalior) :

An old Śaiva temple, locally called Golesvar Mahadeo. *GAR*, 1914-23.

Bhojpur (Raisen) :

Large Śiva temple of Paramāra period in which a colossal liṅga is installed. *MPS*, p. 51.

Bhopal (Bhopal) :

A Śiva jalaharī, terracotta human bust, beads, toy objects and medieval pottery, discovered. *IAR*, 1988-89, p. 105.

Bhopali (Betul) :

An old cave-temple of Mahādeva on a hill. *CLAR*, p. 44.

Bhumra (Panna) :

Gupta Śaiva temple. *MASI*, No. 16; *Modern Review* (Calcutta), XLV, pp. 57-58.

Bichrod (Ujjain) :

A group of two Śaiva temples. *GAR*, 1917-18.

Bijawad (Dewas) :

A Śaiva temple of about 11th-12th century AD. *ISG*, p. 9.

Bilao (Shivpuri) :

A group of old Śaiva temple, now in ruins. *GAR*, 1914-15.

Bilaua (Gwalior) :

Rock-cut cells about a mile from the village, some having images of Śiva etc. carved and datable to 10th-12th century AD. *GAR*, 1947-48.

Bilahari (Jabalpur) :

The temple of Kāmakandalā datable to the early period of the rule of the Kalachuri kings. *HTM*, pp. 46-47, pl. VII b; *CASIR*, IX, pp. 34-35, pl. VII; *PRASIWC*, 1904, p. 33.

Bina (Sagar) :

Remains of a Kalachuri temple with Śaiva sculptures found. *IAR*, 1959-60, p. 70.

Bisesara (Bilaspur) :

Remains of a Śaiva monastery. *BDG*, p. 263.

Budhi-Rai (Shivpuri) :

(a) A Śaiva temple, locally called as Rameshwar Mahadeo. *GAR*, 1914-23.

(b) A Śaiva temple, locally called as Bhairavji. *GAR*, 1914-23.

Champajhar (Raipur) :

Ancient temple of Champakeśvara Mahādeva. *RDG*, p. 540.

Chanchoda (Guna) :

Temple of Bāgeshwar Mahādeo containing ancient Śaiva sculptures. *GAR*, 1929-30, p. 10.

Chanchol (Morena) :

Ancient Śaiva temple locally known as Mahadeo-Ki-Madhi. *GAR*, 1915-16.

Chandrehe (Rewa) :

Ramains of a temple of Śiva datable to Kalachuri period. *CASIR*, XIII, pp. 6-9; *HTM*, pp. 32-35, pl. I, a and b.

Chhade (Morena) :

A Śaiva temple of about 10th-12th century AD. *GAR*, 1916-17.

Chhitara (Shivpuri) :

An old Śaiva temple. *GAR*, 1916-17.

Chhoti Deori (Jabalpur) :

Pillar of a Śaiva temple containing the inscription of Kalachuri king Śaṅkaragaṇa I. *CASIR*, XXI, p. 100; *HTM*, p. 77; *CLAR*, p. 28.

Chikalda (Dhar) :

A Śaiva temple of early date. *HMIM*.

Chirmolia (Mandsaur) :

Śaiva temple, locally known as the temple of Jagannātha Mahādeva. *GAR*, 1914-23.

Choli (Indore) :

Three Śaiva temples. *HMIM; WNDG*, p. 440.

Chorpura (Shivpuri) :

A Śaiva temple of about 11th-12th century AD. *GAR*, 1914-23.

Churli (Gwalior) :

Ruins of a Śaiva temple of about 8th-10th century AD to the east of the village. *GAR*, 1929-30, p. 14.

Dangarwa (Ujjain) :

An ancient Śaiva temple. *GAR*, 1916-17.

Dasai (Dhar) :

Two Śaiva temples, one called the temple of Mukteśvara Mahādeva. *GAR*, 1916-17.

Deepa Dih (Sarguja) :

Plans of medieval temples and sculptures of Pāśupata sect discovered in the temple complex. *IAR*, 1988-89, p. 106.

Dehri (Dhar) :

An old Śaiva temple. *HMIM*.

Deo-Baloda (Raipur) :

Śaiva temple of Kalachuri period datable about 11th century AD. *CASIR*,

XVII, pp. 4-6; *PRASIWC*, 1904, p. 27; *CLAR*, p. 49; *DDG*, pp. 444-45.

Deodungari (Ujjain) :

Site of an ancient Śaiva temple where the modern temple of Devadharma-raja has been constructed. *GAR*, 1925-26, p. 11.

Deogavan (Chhatarpur) :

A Śiva liṅga with inscription of Bhaṭṭāraka Mahārāja Bangeśvara Jāngat, year 1980. *GSMD*, p. 2.

Deokani (Guna) :

A group of Śaiva temples of about 12th-13th century AD. *GAR*, 1925-26, p. 9.

Deotalao (Rewa) :

Two Śaiva temples, locally known as the temple of Somanātha and the temple of Bhairava, datable to later Kalachuri period. *HTM*, pp. 70-71, pls. XXIV, a, b; *PRASIWC*, 1921, pp. 75-76.

Depalpur (Indore) :

A Śaiva temple of about 13th century AD locally called Mangaleśvara Mahādeva. *ISG*, p. 13.

Devargaon (Durg) :

A colossal liṅga with inscription of 'Magardhaja — Jogi'. *Hiralal List*, No. 303.

Dhamdhauli (Shivpuri) :

A Śaiva temple of about 11th-12th century AD to the west of the village near Kalipahadi. *GAR*, 1937-38, pp. 11-12.

Dhamnar (Mandsaur) :

Rock-cut Śaiva temple of Dharmanātha, with seven subsidiary shrines, datable to about 7th-9th century AD. *CASIR*, II, pp. 276-79; *ASIAR*, 1905-06, p. 110; Fergusson, *Rock-cut Temples of India*.

Dhanvantari (Ujjain) :

An ancient Śaiva temple. *HMIM*.

Dharampuri (Dhar) :

A group of four Śaiva shrines, datable to about 12th-13th century AD. *MAR*, 1949-50.

Dhunderi (Ujjain) :

Ruins of a Śaiva temple. *ISG*, 22.

Digthan (Dhar) :

A Śaiva temple, locally known as Mukteśvara Mahādeva. *GAR*, 1916-17.

Dudhia (Rewa) :

Śaiva sculptures of the Kalachuri period found. *HTM*, p. 108, pl. L-b; *PRASIWC*, 1921, p. 76.

Dulhagaon (Bhind) :

A Śaiva temple, locally known as Bhoreśvara Mahādeva. *GAR*, 1916-17.

Dundapura (Gwalior) :

Ruins of a Śaiva temple. *GAR*, 1928-30, p. 15.

Ekalbara (Dhar) :

An old Śaiva temple, locally known as Baijnath Mahādeva. *GAR*, 1915-16.

Eran (Sagar) :

A liṅga bearing inscription of Mādhava and Bhānugupta dated in Gupta Era 191. *CASIR*, X, pp. 89-90.

Fatehpur (Shivpuri) :

An old Śaiva temple, locally known as Rāmeśvara Mahādeva. *GAR*, 1915-16.

Ghatiyari (Rajnandgaon) :

Four rare Śaiva images of Tripurāntakamūrti (two images) Andhakāsuravadhamūrti discovered and preserved in MGM Museum, Raipur. *PP*, VI, No. 1 (Jan. 1978), pp. 31-37.

Ghusai (Mandsaur) :

Three old Śaiva temples. *GAR*, 1916-17.

Gowror (Durg) :

(a) A temple possibly a Śaivic, roofed in the style of intersecting square and mounted by tower roof. *CASIR*, VII, p. 139; *CLAR*, p. 50; *DDG*, pp. 448-49.

(b) Ruins of a much larger temple possibly Śaivic, to the north of the above-mentioned temple. *Ibid.*

(c) Ruins of a temple possibly Śaivic, to the east of the village. *Ibid.*, pp. 140-41.

(d) A large image of Gaṇeśa. *Ibid.*

Gudar (Shivpuri) :

(a) A group of three Śaiva temples to the east of the village, with sculptures of Gaṇeśa, Brahmā, Lakṣmī, Viṣṇu, etc. *GAR*, 1929-30, p. 23.

(b) A Śaiva temple of about 11th century AD with an image of Lakulīśa Śiva having illegible inscription. *GAR*, 1929-30, p. 25.

(c) Ruins of an old Śaiva temple on a rocky mound, with sculptures of Ganesa, Kali etc. *GAR*, 1929-30, p. 24.

Gumad Ral (Bastar) :

A Śiva temple of the Kākatīya period datable to 15th century AD discovered. *IAR*, 1988-89, p. 105.

Gurgi (Rewa) :

(a) The Gurgaj mound containing the remains of a Śaiva Kalachuri temple and yielding an inscription of the reign of Kokalladeva II. *CASIR*, XIX, pp. 151-52; *HTM*, pp. 43-44, pl. V; *PRASIWC*, 1920-21, pp. 51ff.

(b) Image of Śiva-Durgā found from the Gurgaj mound. *HTM*, pp. 76-77, pl. XXVII b.

Gwalior (Gwalior) :

Images of Śiva-Pārvatī, Gaṇeśa, Bhairava, Ardha-nārīśvara, Trimurtī and Liṅga preserved in the local museum. *Catalogue of Sculptures in the Archaeological Museum*, Gwalior.

Gwalior Fort (Gwalior) :

Śaivite sculptures at some distance from Lakṣmaṇa gate. *CASIR*, II, p. 336.

Harankhedi (Ujjain) :

An old Śaiva temple. *GAR*, 1917-18.

Hoshangabad (Hoshangabad) :

(a) Medieval Śaiva sculptures found. *IAR*, 1964-65, p. 74.

(b) An image of four-armed Śiva seated on in *lalitāsana* discovered. *IAR*, 1988-89, p. 105.

Indor (Guna) :

Śaiva temple with star-shaped plan of its garbhagṛaha, datable to about 8th-9th century AD locally known as Garagaj Mahadeo. *GAR*, 1936-38, p. 9.

Indore (Indore) :

Śaiva images preserved in the local museum. *Guide Book to the Central Museum*, Indore, pp. 5-6.

Jakhoda (Gwalior) :

Total ruins of an ancient Śaiva temple. *GAR*, 1929-30, p. 16.

Jamli (Dhar) :

Śaiva temple of about 10th-11th century AD. *GAR*, 1940-41, pp. 13-14.

Jaso (Satna) :

Śaivite and other sculptures discovered. *IAR*, 1960-61, p. 62, pl. LXXI, B.

Jharda (Ujjain) :

Śaiva temple of about 10th-11th century AD. *ISG*, p. 25.

Jiran (Mandsaur) :

Four-faced image of Śiva datable to 10th-11th century AD found. *IAR*, 1965-66, p. 81.

Joba (Sarguja) :

Śaivite sculptures noticed. *CASIR*, XIII, p. 63.

Kadwaha (Guna) :

(a) Śaiva temple of about 10th century AD with a Sanskrit inscription referring to king Jayantavarman and to another king named Gopāla. *AG*, p. 96; *GAR*, 1939-40, p. 20.

(b) Śaiva temple of about 10th-11th century AD locally called Chandal Madhi, a mile to the north of the village. *GAR*, 1914-23.

(c) A group of Śaiva temples of about 10th-11th century AD locally known as Murayatas, on the river bank. *AG*, p. 96.

(d) A group of Śaiva temples of about 10th-11th century AD to the east of the village. *GAR*, 1914-23.

(e) A group of Śaiva temples of about 10th-11th century AD to the north of the village. *GAR*, 1914-23.

(f) A group of Śaiva temples of about 10th-11th century AD to the west of the village. *GAR*, 1914-23, p. 13.

(g) A Śaiva monastery of about 10th century AD built for the Śaiva ascetics of the Mattamayūra clan. Three inscriptions recovered from the debris give information about the Śaiva ascetics of the sect. *AG*, p. 96; *GAR*, 1939-40, p. 18; *GAR*, 1942-43, p. 23.

Kagpur (Vidisha) :

(a) Ruins of a Śaiva temple of about 9th-10th century AD which originally consisted of a principal shrine surrounded by four or six shrines. *GAR*, 1931-32, p. 6.

(b) Sculptures of about 8th-10th century AD built into a modern Śaiva temple locally known as Mata-ki-Madhi. *GAR*, 1931-32, p. 6.

Kaildhar (Shivpuri) :

Ruins of two Śaiva temples of about 10th century AD. *GAR*, 1927-28, p. 12.

Kakarshisha (Rewa) :

Ruins of about twelve Śaiva temples. *CASIR*, XIII, pp. 19-20.

Kalamadh (Shivpuri) :

Ruins of a Śaiva temple, mostly buried in ground, datable to about 10th-11th century AD. The site is about three furlongs to the north of Kalamadh. *GAR*, 1928-29, p. 13.

Kanjarda (Mandsaur) :

An old Śaiva temple locally called Godya Mahadeva. *HMIM*.

Kanoda (Bari) (Damoh) :

Medieval Śiva temple enshring image with inscription. *Hiralal List*, No. 120.

Karari-Ahmadpur (Shivpuri) :

Ruins of a Śaiva temple of about 12th century AD. *GAR*, 1928-29, p. 11.

Karera (Shivpuri) :

An old Śaiva temple locally known as the temple of Trimbakeśvara Mahādeva. *DFGS*, pp. 66ff; *GAR*, 1927-28.

Karitalai (Jabalpur) :

Imager of Śiva-Pārvatī. *JDG*, p. 683.

Karnavad (Ujjain) :

Śaiva temple called Karṇeśvara Mahādeva with inscription dated in V.S. 1275 (1218 AD) referring to a grant in the reign of Paramāra Devapāladeva. *GAR*, 1917-18.

Karohan (Ujjain) :

An old temple of Śiva, one of the eighty-four Śaiva temples which the pilgrims visit in course of their circumambulation of the holy city of Ujjayini. An 11th century image of Varāha may be seen fixed in the well near the temple. *GAR*, 1934-35, p. 11.

Khajuraho (Chhatarpur) :

(a) Lalguhān Mahādeva temple situated about 1 km to the west of Chausaṭha Yoginī Temple. *KD*, pp. 13-35; *KKD*, pp. 51-60; *KDP*, pp. 12-22; *KSS*, pp. 10-18; *KZ*, pp. 87-160; *AI*, No. 15.

(b) Mātaṅgeśvara temple which is a plain structure enshrining a colossal Śiva liṅga, datable to c. 900-925 AD. *Ibid.*

(c) Viśvanātha temple which on stylistic basis may be placed between Lakṣmaṇa and Kandariyā temples. Two inscriptions fixed in the temple are dated V.S. 1058 and 1059. *Ibid.*

(d) Nandī temple built in front of the Viśvanātha temple contains a colossal Nandī. It is contemporary of Viśvanātha temple. *Ibid.*

(e) Kandariyā Mahādeva temple which is the largest temple of Khajuraho. It was built in the later part of the reign of Vidyādhara Chandella, around 1025-50 AD. *Ibid.*

(f) Dulādeva temple datable between 1100-50 AD. *Ibid.*

(g) The small temple of Mahādeva situated between Kandariyā and Jagadambī temples. *Ibid.*

(h) Modern temple of Pratāpeśvara containing ancient Śaiva sculptures. *Ibid.*

(i) Four-armed śānti images of Śiva located in temples of Viśvanātha, Jagadambī, Kandariyā, Chitragupta, Lakṣmaṇa, Pārśvanātha, Nandī, Javārī, Vāmana, Śāntinātha, Pratāpeśvara and Khajuraho Museum. *KSS*, pp. 45-51.

(j) Jaṭarāja images of Śiva located in Dulādeva temple and Khajuraho Museum. *Ibid.*, pp. 51-53.

(k) Śiva Pārvatī images exhibiting their marriage located in Khajuraho Museum, Vāman and Chitragupta temples. *Ibid.*, p. 53.

(l) Śiva in Āliṅgana-mudrā located in Chitragupta temple. *Ibid.*, p. 52.

(m) Saṁhāra mūrtis of Śiva located:

(i) Nīlakaṇṭha images in the temples of Kandariyā, Chitragupta, Jagadambī, Pārśvanātha and Khajuraho Museum. *Ibid.*, p. 53.

(ii) Aghora images located in the temples of Jagadaṁbī, Pārśvanātha, Kandariyā, Viśvanātha and Dulādeo. *Ibid.*, p. 54.

(iii) Gaja-Saṁhāra images located in the temples of Kandariyā, Visvanātha, Duladeo and Khajuraho Museum. *Ibid.*, pp. 54-55.

(iv) Image of Bhairava with Bhairavī in Pārśvanātha temple. *Ibid.*, p. 55.

(v) Tripurānataka Śiva in Pārśvanātha temple. *Ibid.*, p. 55.

(vi) Bhairava images in the temples of Kandariyā, Vāmana, Chaturbhuja, Jagadambī, Chitragupta, Lakṣmaṇa, Viśvanātha, Ādinatha, Duladeo and Khajuraho Museum. *Ibid.*, pp. 56-57.

(vii) Gaṇeśa images located in the temples of Lakṣmaṇa, Jagadambī, Mātangeśvara, Pārvatī, Duladeo, Javārī, Kandariyā, Viśvanātha, Laxmaṇa, Chitragupta and in Khajuraho Museum. *KDP*, pp. 52-53, No. 1-39 and pp. 31-55.

(viii) Gaṇeśa with the Saptamātṛkās located in Lakṣmaṇa and Dulādeo temples and in Khajuraho Museum. *KDP*, p. 53, No. 40-43 and pp. 31-51.

(ix) Gaṇeśa with Pārvatī images in Lakṣmaṇa temple and Khajuraho Museum. *KDP*, p. 53, No. 40-49 and pp. 31-51.

(x) Gaṇeśa with Umā-Maheśvara in Lakṣmaṇa, Jagadambī and Chitragupta temples and Khajuraho Museum. *KDP*, p. 53, No. 50-55 and pp. 31-51.

(xi) Skanda or Kārttikeya images in Kandariyā Mahādeva temple and Khajuraho Museum. *KSS*, pp. 86-87.

Khalari (Raipur) :

(a) Remains of an old Śaiva temple of Kalachuri period having an inscription of Haribrahmadeva dated in (V) E. 1470. *CASIR*, VII, pp. 156-58; *CLAR*, pp. 50-51.

(b) Ruins of two other temples, one being a Śaivic. *Ibid.*

Khalwa (East Nimar) :

Remains of a Śaiva temple of Paramāra period in Bhūmija style. *PP*, XI (1983), pp. 181-84, pl. 52-57.

Khandwa (Nimar) :

Śaiva sculptures found. *CLAR*, p. 40.

Kharod (Bilaspur) :

A Śaiva brick temple locally known as the temple of Lakhaneśvara, datable to Kalachuri period. In the wall of the temple is built an inscription of Ratnadeva III dated in Chedi year 933. *CASIR*, VII, p. 202; *PRASIWC*, 1904, pp. 31-32; *ASIAR*, 1909-10, pp. 11-18, pl. IV; *CLAR*, pp. 60-61.

Khatama (Hoshangabad) :

Ancient Śaiva cave. *CLAR*, p. 42.

Khera (Morena) :

Ruins of a Śaiva temple of about 10th century AD with sculptures of Śiva, Gaṇeśa, Sūrya, Mahiṣamardinī etc. *GAR*, 1925-26, p. 9.

Kherat (Bhind) :

Śaiva brick-temple of about 10th century AD to the south-east of the village in the ravines of the river Chambal. *GAR*, 1930-31, p. 3.

Khilchipura (Mandsaur) :

Rudra-Śiva sculptures with heavy *jaṭā* datable to Gupta period discovered. *IAR*, 1965-66, p. 22.

Khoh (Panna) :

Ekamukha liṅga of Gupta period. *PRASIWC*, 1920, pp. 106-07, pl. XXIX; *MASI*, No. 16, p. 5.

Khoti (Satna) :

Plan of a Śiva temple discovered during debris clearance work. *IAR*, 1988-89, p. 106.

Kukdesvar (Mandsaur) :

Śaiva temple of Sahasra Mukheśvara, originally of 13th-14th century AD, repaired later. *ISG*, p. 37.

Kulwar (Guna) :

Remains of Śaiva temple with sculptures, datable to about 11th century AD. *GAR*, 1930-31, p. 9.

Kuna (Mandsaur) :

Remains of a large Śaiva temple datable to c. 9th-10th cent. AD. *GSP*, p. 7.

Kundalpur (Shivpuri) :

(a) Śaiva monastery, double-storeyed with a large pillared hall in centre surrounded by rooms; locally believed to be the hall where Rukminī was married to Kṛṣṇa. The structure resembles the Surwaya monastery (see below). *GAR*, 1922-23.

(b) Two Śaiva temples (No. 1 and No. 2) in ruins, datable to about 10th century AD. *GAR*, 1922-23.

Kundeshwar (Tikamgarh) :

Image of Nandī with inscription dated V.S. 1201. *CJT*, Appendix-B, No. 4.

Kura (Raipur) :

Remains of ancient Śaiva temple. *RDG*, p. 551.

Lakhari (Guna) :

A group of two Śaiva temples on a common plinth, datable to about 9th-10th century AD with an inscription dated in V.S. 1000 (943 AD). *GAR*, 1924-25, pp. 13-14.

Lanji (Balaghat) :

An old Śaiva temple. *CLAR*, p. 25.

Lapha (Bilaspur) :

An ancient liṅga in a cave. *BDG*, pp. 274-75.

Lavan (Bhind) :

A Śaiva temple with fine carving noticed. *IAR*, 1960-61, p. 59.

Mahasamund (Raipur) :

Two Śaiva temples of about 14th century AD. *CASIR*, VII, p. 159; *CLAR*, p. 51; *RDG*, pp. 552-53.

Mahidpur (Ujjain) :

(a) Temple of Nārakeśvara Mahādeva. *HMIM*.

(b) Temple of Dhurjaṭeśvara Mahādeva. *Ibid.*

Mahu (Ujjain) :

Śaiva temple of an early date. *GAR*, 1917-18.

Mahua (Shivpuri) :

(a) Śaiva temple No. 1 with an inscription datable to about 7th century AD referring to one Vatsarāja and his ancestors. *AG*, p. 100; *GAR*, 1914-15.

(b) Śaiva temple No. 2 of about 7th-8th century AD. *AG*, p. 100; *GAR*, 1914-15.

Mahuvan (Guna) :

(a) Śaiva temple to the south-west of the village with a Nandī shrine, datable to about 10th-12th century AD. *GAR*, 1925-26, pp. 9, 20, 21.

(b) Śaiva temple of about 10th-12th century AD with a liṅga and a sculpture of Mahiṣamardinī. *GAR*, 1925-26, pp. 9, 20-21.

(c) Ruins of three Śaiva temples on mound on the river bank. *GAR*, 1925-26.

Maihar (Satna) :

The Śaiva temple of Kalachuri period, datable to c. 11th-13th cent. AD, locally known as Golāmaṭha. *PP*, IX-X (1981-82), pp. 47-53.

Majholi (Jabalpur) :

Image of Śiva Pārvatī. *JDG*, p. 688.

Makanganj (Mandsaur) :

Śaiva temple of about 5th-7th century AD to the east of the village. The Chaturmukhi liṅga of this temple is said to have been removed to Bardun in Rajasthan. *GAR*, 1929-30.

Makla (Ujjain) :

(a) Colossus of Trimurtī locally worshipped as Kālī or Mātā. *ISG*, p. 42.

(b) Śaiva temple of Mahākāleśvara of about 11th-12th century AD. *Ibid.*

Maljhir (Raisen) :

A Śiva temple of Pratihāra period located. *IAR*, 1986-87, p. 119.

Mamon (Guna) :

Ruins of a Śaiva temple of about 10th century AD to the south-east of the village with an image of Śiva-Pārvatī. *GAR*, 1925-26, p. 21.

Manda (Sidhi) :

Image of Śiva installed in a rock-cut cave of c. 7th cent. AD. *MPS*, Sept. 5, 1970, pp. 12-15.

Mandhata (East Nimar) :

(a) The temple of Onkāreśvara containing ancient sculptured pillars and

Jyotirliṅga. *ENG*, p. 469.

(b) Incomplete ancient temple of Siddheśvara. *Ibid*, pp. 469-70.

(c) Ancient temple of Gaurī-somanātha enshrining colossal liṅga. *Ibid.*, p. 470.

(d) Remains of many ancient temples. *Ibid.*, p. 470.

(e) Amareśvara temple on the south coast of the Narmada, having four inscriptions of 11th cent. AD. *Ibid.*

(f) Another ancient temple near Amareśvara temple. *Ibid.*

Mandsaur (Mandsaur) :

(a) Ancient temple of Ghumaṭeśvara Mahādeva. *GAR*, 1922-23.

(b) Ancient temple of Gaṇeśa. *GAR*, 1916-17.

(c) Aṣṭamukhi liṅga on the bank of Sivna river. *MBI*, p. 360; *MPS*, p. 13.

Mandu Fort (Dhar) :

(a) Śaiva rock-cut cells, seven in a group, called Sat-Kothari, with a liṅga inside. Yazdani, *Dhar and Mandu*, p. 122.

(b) Śaiva rock-cut cells called Lohānī caves. *HMM*.

Mara (Sidhi) :

Four groups of rock-cut caves locally known as Jagdaliya Mara, Hanuman Mara, Vivaha Mara and Rawan Mara with Śaiva sculptures. *CASIR*, XIII, pp. 20-31; *PP*, XIII, pp. 48-56.

Marai (Rewa) :

(a) A fine image of Śiva and Durgā of Kalachuri period found. *HTM*, p. 94, pl. XLVII-a.

(b) A Kalachuri Śaiva temple. *HTM*, pp. 62-64, pl. XX-a.

Mau (Balaghat) :

Śaiva sculptures found. *CLAR*, p. 25.

Mitaoli (Morena) :

Śaiva temple called 'Ekottaraso-Mahadeo' with an inscription dated in V.S. 1380 (1323 AD) referring to its construction by Mahārāja Devapāla. *GAR*, 1918-19; 1942-46, p. 67.

Miyana (Guna) :

Ancient Śaiva temple. *GAR*, 1918-19.

Modi (Mandsaur) :

Temple of Lakulīśa Śiva with inscription dated in V.S. 1317 (1251 AD). *ISG*, p. 43.

Murpar (Raipur) :

Ruins of old temples yielding Śaivite and Vaiṣṇavite sculptures. *CASIR*, VII, p. 147; *CLAR*, pp. 51-52.

Nachna-Kuthara (Panna) :

Temple of Chaturmukha Mahādeva datable to 7th-8th century AD. *CASIR*, XXI, pp. 98-99.

Nand-Chand (Jabalpur) :

Ruined Śaiva temple of Mṛtaṅgeśvara-Mahādeva, possibly belonging to the Kalachuri period. *CASIR*, XXI, p. 161.

Narayanpur (Bilaspur) :

A Śaiva temple of the Kalachuri period. *CASIR*, VII, pp. 193-95, pl. XIX; *ASIAR*, 1930-34, pl. LXXVII a-d; *RDG*, p. 554.

Naresar (Gwalior) :

(a) Eight Śaiva temples on the bank of a tank, datable to about 12th-13th century AD. *GAR*, 1947-48.

(b) Four Śaiva temples of about 12th-13th century AD with a common platform in front. *GAR*, 1947-48.

(c) Four Śaiva temples of about 8th-10th century AD with barrel vaulted roof. *GAR*, 1947-48.

(d) Ruins of a Śaiva temple with a small shrine and a *śikhara* datable to about 8th-10th century AD. *GAR*, 1947-48.

Navli (Mandsaur) :

A Śaiva temple locally called Nandikeśvara Mahādeo, datable to about 12th-13th century AD. *ISG*, p. 46.

Nayi Soyan (Shivpuri) :

An image of Gaṇesa with inscription of V.S. 1229. *GAR*, Saṁ. 1973, No. 33.

Nemawar (Dewas) :

Śaiva temple of Sidheśvara Mahādeva on the bank of Narmada, datable to about 10th-11th century AD. *ARASIWC*, 1921, p. 98.

Nimthur (Mandsaur) :

Śaiva temple of "Pañchamukhī Mahādeva" with an inscription dated in V.S. 102(8) (971-AD ?) referring to its construction by one Padmajā during the reign of Mahārājadhirāja Chāmuṇḍarāja. *GAR*, 1917-18; *CASIR*, XXIII, p. 125.

Nohta (Damoh) :

Śaiva temple of Kalachuri period. *DMDG*, p. 386.

Padhavali (Morena) :

(a) Śaiva temple to the north of the village, datable to about 10th-12th century AD. *GAR*, 1914-15.

(b) Ruins of a Śaiva temple of about 10th century AD locally called Baṭeśvara Mahādeva, with later additions. *GAR*, 1915-16.

(c) Ruins of a Śaiva temple of about 10th century AD in Batesvara valley. *GAR*, 1915-16.

(d) Śaiva temple of about 10th century AD in Garhi. *GAR*, 1925-26.

Pahado-Khurd (Gwalior) :

Śaiva temple with inscription dated in V.S. 1350 (1293 AD), referring to one Gaṇapatideva. *GAR*, 1918-19.

Pajdhar :

An old Śaiva brick-temple. *CASIR*, XIII, p. 143.

Pali (Bilaspur) :

(a) A Śaiva temple of the Kalachuri period, bearing three inscriptions of the reign of Jājalladeva I recording his unspecified Kīrti (meritorious work). *CASIR*, VII, p. 217-19; *CLAR*, pp. 61-62; *CII*, IV, pt. II, pp. 417-19; *KV*, p. 150.

(b) Ruins of a number of small temples near about. *CASIR*, VII, p. 217.

Pali (Sagar) :

Śaiva temple of Chandella period. *SDG*, p. 541.

Pathari (Vidisha) :

(a) A Śaiva temple of about 9th-10th century AD in front of the Bhīmagajā pillar. *MAR*, 1949-50.

(b) A Śaiva temple of about 9th-10th century AD near Bhīmgaja pillar, lying half-buried in the ground. *MAR*, 1949-50.

(c) A Śaiva temple of about 10th-11th century AD to the east of the village, locally called Kukdeśvara Mahādeva. *MAR*, 1949-50.

(d) Rock-cut Śaiva caves of about 5th century AD with images of Saptamātṛkas and an inscription referring to Mahārāja Jayantasena. *GAR*, 1925-26, pp. 12-25.

Perkheda (Dhar) :

Two Śaiva temples, locally called Bhogīśvara Mahādeva and Nīlakaṇtheśvara Mahādeva. *GAR*, 1916-17.

Pipadi (Bhind) :

Ruins of a Śaiva temple of about 10th century AD. *GAR*, 1928-29, p. 27.

Pipalarawan (Ujjain) :

A Śaiva temple of early date. *GAR*, 1917-18.

Pipargarh (Shivpuri) :

A Śaiva temple of about 11th-12th century AD with three attendant shrines. *GAR*, 1914-15.

Piploda (Dhar) :

Rock-cut Śaiva sculptures found in the midst of the Narmada. *IAR,* 1958-59, p. 72.

Pithoria (Sagar) :

Remains of a Kalachuri Śaiva temple found. *IAR*, 1959-60, p. 70.

Pohri (Shivpuri) :

An old Śaiva temple, locally called the temple of Kedārnātha. *GAR*, 1914-15.

Pujaripali (Raigarh) :

(a) Remains of two Kalachuri Śaiva temples. *CASIR*, XVII, p. 68; *PRASIWC*, 1904, p. 32; *CLAR*, p. 65.

(b) Remains of two other Śaiva temples in the village Pajdhar, one km to the west. *CASIR*, XIII, p. 144; *CLAR*, p. 65.

Rai (Budhi) (Shivpuri) :

Ruins of two Śaiva temples, called Rāmeśvara and Bhairava, with old sculptures lying about. *GAR*, 1916-17.

Raipur (Raipur) :

Śaiva images of the Pāṇḍuvaṁśī period from Ratanpur, Bilaspur and Sirpur, of the period of the Kalachuris of Tripurī from Karitalai and Bilahari and of the Kalachuri of Ratanpur from Ratanpur and Sirpur excavations preserved in the local M.G.M. Museum. *Catalogue of the Sculptures in the M.G.M. Museum,* Raipur (1960) (in Hindi).

Rajim (Raipur) :

(a) Temple of Rājeśvara on the west of the Rajiv Lochan temple, dedicated to the worship of Śiva. *CASIR*, XVII, pp. 12-13; *CLAR*, p. 53.

(b) Temple of Dāneśvara to the south of Rājeśvara, dedicated to the worship of Śiva. *Ibid.*, p. 13; *CLAR*, p. 53.

(c) Temple of Kuleśvara bearing an inscription of Jagat Rau who was living in 1145 AD. *Ibid.*, pp. 15-16; *Ibid.*, Vol. VII, p. 149; *KV*, p. 358; *CLAR*, p. 54.

(d) Temple of Rajiv Telin under worship. *CLAR*, p 53.

Rakhetra (Guna) :

A number of rock-cut images of Śiva, Pārvatī, Gaṇeśa etc. and a number of rock-cut niches. *GAR*, 1924-25, pp. 15, 16, 38.

Ramgarh Hill (Sarguja) :

(a) Śaiva sculptures collected. *CASIR*, XIII, pp. 34, 35.

(b) Image of an eight-armed Śiva. *Ibid.*, p. 35.

(c) Remains of a Śaiva temple. *CASIR*, XIII, pp. 35-36.

Ranod (Guna) :

A Śaiva monastery locally called Khokhai Maṭha. It is built of large stone slabs and is two-storeyed. An inscription found here records its construction by the Śaiva ascetics Vyomakeśa of Mattamayūra clan. The inscription refers to the line of ascetics of the sect and mentions king Avantivarman. Though the inscription is undated, on palaeographic grounds, it has been assigned to 10th-11th century AD. *GAR*, 1914-15; *AG*, p. 121; *CASIR*, II, pp. 303-06; *EI*. I, p. 354; *JMPIP*, IV, pp. 3-12.

Rapeth (Morena) :

Ruins of an old Śaiva temple. *GAR*, 1914-23.

Rehi (Rewa) :

A Pratihāra Śiva temple datable to c. 8th-9th cent. AD discovered. *IAR*, 1988-

89, p. 44.

Rewa (Rewa) :

(a) A bas-relief with the images of Śiva and Pārvatī sculptured at the top. *CASIR*, XXI, p. 144.

(b) The huge toraṇa (gateway) of a Śaiva temple brought from Gurgi and set up in front of the palace. *CASIR*, XXI, pp. 143-44; *Ibid,* XIX, p. 80; *HTM*, pp. 72-76, pl. XXV-XXVI.

Rithi (Jabalpur) :

Ruins of some ten or twelve temples, with Śaivite and Vaiṣṇavite sculptures and jambs and lintels of richly carved doorways scattered about. *CASIR*, XXI, p. 160; *HTM*, p. 31; *CLAR*, p. 29; *JDG*, p. 690.

Rithora (Morena) :

Ruins of a Śaiva temple with peculiar carvings on one of its pillars. *GAR*, 1925-26, p. 9.

Rupnath (Jabalpur) :

Lingam of Śiva. *CASIR*, IX, p. 38.

Sakarra (Guna) :

A Śaiva temple on the western bank of a tank, datable to about 11th century AD. Images of Gaṇeśa, Brahmā, Sūrya, Mahisamardinī etc. also available. *GAR*, 1927-28, p. 9.

Sakarwara (Jabalpur) :

Dancing Gaṇapati image found. *IAR*, 1960-61, p. 60.

Samarkund (Mandsaur) :

A Śiva temple of Pratihāra period (c. 9th cent. AD) discovered. *IAR*, 1986-87, p. 119.

Samli (Mandsaur) :

Ruins of an old Śaiva temple. *GAR*, 1917-18.

Sandor (Guna) :

Ruins of an old Śaiva temple. *GAR*, 1918-19.

Satanwada (Shivpuri) :

A Śaiva temple, originally of about 11th century AD rebuilt in 15th-16th century AD. *GAR*, 1923-24, p. 14.

Satna (Satna) :

Sculputres of Śiva as Ardhanārīśvara found. *IAR*, 1967-68, p. 67.

Semakhedi (Shivpuri) :

Ruins of a group of two Śaiva temples of about 12th century AD. Image of a forty-armed goddess from one of these temples is built up in a platform nearby. *GAR*, 1928-29.

Semuldha (Shivpuri) :

Ruins of a Śaiva temple. *GAR*, 1916-17.

Serwasa (Vidisha) :

A Śaiva temple assignable to 9th cent. AD discovered. *IAR*, 1986-87, p. 120.

Sesai (Shivpuri) :

Ruins of a Śaiva temple of about 10th-12th century AD. *GAR*, 1929-30, p. 26.

Sewai (Gwalior) :

Images of Śiva, Gaṇeśa, Kārttikeya etc. datable to c. 10th-12th cent. AD found. *GAR*, 1933-34, p. 14.

Sewandha (Datia) :

An ancient temple of Śiva on the bank of Sindh river. *MPS*, p. 28.

Shamshabad (Vidisha) :

Śaiva sculptures of medieval period discovered. *IAR*, 1959-60, p. 71.

Shanichara (Morena) :

Old Śaiva temple, locally called 'Parvati-ki-Jagah'. *GAR*, 1914-15.

Shankargarh Hills (Satna) :

Rock-cut Śaivite Gupta sculptures found. *IAR*, 1967-68, p. 67.

Shankhoddhar (Mandsaur) :

An old Śaiva temple. *HMIM*.

Sheorinarayan (Bilaspur) :

The stone temple of Chandra-Chuḍeśvara datable to about 9th-10th century AD. Close to is fixed into a wall the stone inscription of Jājalladeva II dated in Chedi year 919. *CASIR*, VII, pp. 197-98; *CII*, IV, pt. II, pp. 519 ff; *PRASIWC*, 1903-04, pp. 30-31.

Sinaval (Datia) :

An image of Pārvatī with an inscription in Siddhamātṛakā character of c. 8th cent. AD. *IAR*, 1962-63, p. 50.

Sirpur (Raipur) :

(a) Scattered Śaivite sculptures within an enclosure. *CASIR*, VII, p. 173.

(b) Śaiva temple locally known as the Gandheśvara temple. *CASIR*, VII, pp. 169-70; XVII, p. 25; *CLAR*, p. 55; *KV*, pp. 152, 356.

(c) Ruins of a Śaiva temple. *Ibid.*, p. 179.

(d) Ruins of a brick temple and a beautifully carved fragment of a door jamb and a *chaturmukha-liṅga* found. *IAR*, 1960-61, p. 61.

(e) Remains of a Śaiva temple found in the excavation of 1954. *SAG*, p. 188.

(f) A huge Śiva liṅga found in the above-mentioned excavation. *Ibid.*

Sohagpur (Shahdol) :

(a) The temple of Virāṭeśvara Śiva belonging to the reign of the Kalachuri kings, datable to about 11th century AD. *CASIR*, VII, pp. 240-43; *HTM*, pp. 48-53.

(b) Ruins of a group of two Śaiva temples. *CASIR*, VII, p. 244.

Sonkach (Ujjain) :

An old Śaiva temple. *GAR*, 1917-18.

Suhania (Morena) :

(a) A Śaiva temple, locally called Kakanmadha, built by Kacchyāhā king Kīrttirāja of Gwalior in about 11th century AD. The temple is named after Kakanāvatī, the queen of Kīrttirāja. The Gwalior Fort (Sās-Bahu temple) inscription refers to the construction of this temple. *AG*, p. 124; *CASIR*, II, pp. 399-400.

(b) Ruins of a Śaiva temple of about 10th century AD on the slope of a hill to the north of the village. *GAR*, 1929-30, p. 16.

Sultanpur (Dhar) :

Ruins of two old Śaiva temples. *GAR*, 1916-17.

Sundarsi (Ujjain) :

A Śaiva temple of Mahākāleśvara with an inscription on one of its pillars, dated in V.S. 1224 (1167 AD). *GAR*, 1917-18.

Surwaya (Shivpuri) :

(a) A double-storeyed Śaiva monastery built of large stone slabs, datable to about 10th-11th century AD. *GS*, pp. 8-9.

(b) A group of three Śaiva temples of about 10th-11th cent. AD. *Ibid.*

Suvasra (Mandsaur) :

Early medieval Śaiva sculptures datable to 10th-11th century AD found. *IAR*, 1965-66, p. 81.

Terahi (Shivpuri) :

(a) Ruins of a Śaiva temple, a mile to the east of the village. *GAR*, 1914-15; *CASIR*, XXI, p. 177.

(b) A huge Śiva liṅga with eigth faces carved on it, in a forest to the south of the village. *MPS*, p. 34.

(c) A huge image of Gaṇapati near the above-mentiond Śiva liṅga. *Ibid.*

Tewar (Jabalpur) :

(a) Śaiva sculptures on the bank of Balasagar tank. Lower part of a Śiva image, Liṅga, Gaṇapati, Śiva-Pārvatī, Chāmuṇḍā, Kārttikeya.

(b) Four-armed Śiva, Chāmuṇḍā and Gaṇapati under a tree near Balasagar tank.

(c) Four-armed Śiva-Pārvatī, Gaṇapati and Liṅga in temple near well.

(d) Fragmentary Śiva, Nṛtya Gaṇapati, Śiva Pārvatī, Gaṇapati, Kārttikeya and Andhakāsura Vadha images near ancient well.

(e) Śiva head, Nṛtya Gaṇapati, Śiva-Pārvatī and Umā-Maheśvara images in the ruins of Tripureśvara temple.

(f) Śiva, Gaṇapati, Śiva-Pārvatī images under a pipal tree. *PE*.

(g) Gaṇeśa images. *KV*, pp. 377-78.

(h) Images of Śiva-Pārvatī. *IAR*, 1965-66.

(i) Number of Śaiva images. *KV*, pp. 370-74.

(j) Gaṇeśa image found in the excavation of Tripuri. *IAR*, 1968-69.

Thakurai (Mandsaur) :

Ruins of a Śaiva temple, datable to about 10th century AD to the west of the village. *GAR*, 1929-30, pp. 21-22.

Timarni (Hoshangabad) :

Śiva image with an undated inscription. *Hiralal List*, No. 130.

Udayagiri (Vidisha) :

(a) Three Śaiva rock-cut caves (cave Nos. 2, 3, 4) datable to about 4th century AD with sculptures of Dvārapālas, Viṣṇu, Gaṇeśa, Sapta Mātṛakās, Skanda etc. *MUH; CASIR*, X, p. 52.

(b) One Śaiva rock-cut cave (cave No. 6) datable to about 4th century AD with carved doorway and sculptures of Dvārapālas, Viṣṇu, Gaṇeśa, Sapta-Mātrakās etc.

An inscription carved in the cave refers to its construction during the reign of the Gupta ruler Chandragupta II. *MUH*; *CASIR*, X, pp. 49-50.

(c) One Śaiva rock-cut cave (cave No. 7), locally called 'Tawa cave' with an inscription recording its construction during the reign of the Gupta ruler Chandragupta II. The inscription refers to the tribe of the Sanakānikas. *MUH; CASIR*, X, p. 51.

(d) A Śaiva rock-cut cave (cave No. 19) locally called 'Amrita cave' (the name is derived from the scene of Amṛta Manthana carved on the lintel of its door frame) with pilgrims' records datable to about 4th-5th century AD. *MUH; CASIR*, X, pp. 52-53.

Udayapur (Vidisha) :

Saiva temple of Nīlakaṇṭheśvara Mahādeva, with inscription, one of which records its construction by Paramāra king Udayāditya in V.S. 1116 (1050 AD). *AG*, p. 133; *GAR*, 1917-18; 1923-24, p. 5; *CASIR*, VII, pp. 83-88; *Ibid*, X, pp. 68-69.

Ujjain (Ujjain) :

(a) Śaiva temple of Mahākāleśvara destroyed by Altamash in 1235 AD. The present temple was rebuilt by Rāmachandra, the Diwan of Peshwa in 1745 AD. *UDG*, pp. 373-74.

(b) Two Śaiva temples of an early date, locally called Puṣpadanteśvara Mahādeva and Rupeśvara Mahādeva. *GAR*, 1926-27, p. 17.

(c) A Śaiva temple locally known as Kilkileśvara Mahādeva. *GAR*, 1922-23, p. 17.

(d) An ancient temple similar in plan to the Mahākāleśvara temple discovered. *IAR*, 1967-68.

Un (Nimar) :

(a) A Śaiva temple, locally called Mahākāleśvara Mandir, datable to about 11th cent. AD, built during the reign of the Paramāras of Malwa. *ISG*, p. 68; *ARASIWC*, 1918-19, p. 17; D.C. Ganguli, *The Paramaras of Malwa*, p. 264.

(b) A Śaiva temple, locally called Gupteśvara Mahādeva built during the reign of the Paramāras of Malwa. *Ibid.*

(c) A Śaiva temple locally called Vallabheśvara Mahādeva, built during the reign of the Paramāras of Malwa. *Ibid.*

(d) A Śaiva temple locally known as the Nīlakaṇṭheśvara Mahādeva. *Ibid.*

(e) A Śaiva temple called Mahākāleśvara Mahādeva. *Ibid.*

(E) Śākta Monuments and Sculptures

Adbhar (Bilaspur) :

(a) Remains of an ancient Devī temple. *BDG*, p. 255.

(b) Image of Mahiṣāsuramardinī. *Ibid.*

Afzalpur (Mandsaur) :

Ancient sculptures in the temple of Āśādevī. *GAR*, 1914-22.

Ajaigarh (Panna) :

Rock-cut images of eight goddesses (aṣṭa-śaktis) with their names inscribed at the bottom at the Tarhoni gate of the fort. *CASIR*, XXI, p. 47.

Amjhera (Dhar) :

Temple of Chāmuṇḍā and Ambikā. *GAR*, 1916-17.

Amrol (Gwalior) :

A modern temple of goddess called Behmata of about 11th-12th century AD. *GAR*, 1940-41, p. 21.

Antra (Shahdol) :

(a) Brahmanical sculptures collected in the debris clearance at the site. *IAR*, 1987-88, p. 139.

(b) Sculptures of Śakti cult discovered. *IAR*, 1988-89, p. 106.

Antri (Ujjain) :

Modern temple of Devī which is built of the remains of an ancient temple datable to c. 10th-12th cent. AD. *ISG*, p. 6.

Antri (Gwalior) :

Ancient temple of Turki-Golaki-Mata. *GDG*, p. 357.

Arang (Raipur) :

A modern temple of goddess Pārvatī built with extensive alterations of an old temple. *CASIR*, VII, p. 160.

Badoh (Vidisha) :

A temple of goddess of about 9th-10th century AD or earlier, locally known as Gadarmal temple. The famous large image of mother and child, now preserved in the Gwalior Museum was originally found in the debris of this temple. *GAR*, 1923-24, p. 8; *AG*, p. 24; *CASIR*, VII, pp. 69-79; X, pp. 71-74.

Bagh (Dhar) :

Temple of Bāgheśvarī Devī. *GAR*, 1914-22.

Bagrod (Vidisha) :

Ruins of a temple of goddess, locally called Bijāsanī Devī. *GAR*, 1932-33, pp. 7-8.

Bahoriband (Jabalpur) :

Rock-cut image of Mahiṣamardinī of Gupta period noticed. *IAR*, 1962-63, p. 68.

Balakwada (Nimar) :

An old temple of goddess Bhawānī. *HMIM*.

Bari-Delchi (Ujjain) :

Ancient temple of Hinglājmātā. *HMIM*.

Barwani (West Nimar) :

Ancient temple of Kālikā-mātā. *WNDG*, p. 434.

Bhanpura (Mandsaur) :

Images of Vārāhī, Indrāṇī, Skandamātā, Vīṇādhara discovered. *IAR*, 1965-66, p. 81.

Bheraghat (Jabalpur) :

Circular temple of Chaunsaṭha Yoginī, with 81 images placed in the enclosure and the temple of Gaurī Śaṅkara in the centre of the enclosure. *CASIR*, IX, pp. 60 ff; *HIM*, pp. 66-70 and 78-92; *KV*, pp. 323-26; *Annual Report of Indian Epigraphy*, 1964-65, Nos. C. 2083-2147; Bloch, *Conservation Notes on Bheraghat; CLAR*, p. 27; *ASIAR*, 1907-08, p. 234; Sharma, R.K., *The Temples of Chausatha Yogini at*

Bheraghat, Delhi, 1978.

Bhilsa (Vidisha) :

Ruins of an old temple of goddess Charchikā and pillar with inscription datable to 11th century AD referring to Paramāra king Naravarman, in the mosque called Bijamandal. *AG*, p. 65; *ARASIWC*, 1913-14; Sharma, R.K., *Art of the Paramaras of Malwa*, Delhi, 1979, pp. 54 ff.

Bichrod (Ujjain) :

An old temple of goddess; locally called Śītalā-Mātā. *GAR*, 1917-18.

Bilaspur (Bilaspur) :

Several medieval sculptures including that of Vīrāsanadevī discovered. *IAR*, 1962-63, p. 69.

Boria (Durg) :

Ruins of a temple of the goddess Kaṅkālī, 3 miles to the north-west of Boria. *CASIR*, XVII, pp. 44-46.

Chanderi (Guna) :

An ancient temple of goddess, locally called Jogeśvarī. *GAR*, 1914-23.

Chhuri (Bilaspur) :

Temple of Devī in the Kosgain fort. *BDG*, p. 264.

Dhar (Dhar) :

Image of Saraswatī with inscription of Paramāra Bhoja dated V.S. 1081 on the pedestal, now in collection of British Museum, London. *EI*, XVIII, p. 320, No. 3; *Rupam*, 1924, p. 2; *Bhandarkar List*, No. 120.

Dudakhedi (Mandsaur) :

An ancient temple of goddess. *ARASIWC*, 1920-21, p. 8.

Eran (Sagar) :

A sculpture of Gaja-Lakṣmī datable to Gupta period found. *IAR*, 1960-61, p. 62, pl. LXXI A.

Gadia (Sehore) :

An image of Mahiṣāsurmardinī originally belonging to the temple at. *IAR*, 1960-61, p. 62.

Gandhaval (Ujjain) :

Old sculptures of about 11th-12th century AD in the temple of Śītalā Mātā. *GAR*, 1942-46, pp. 22-23.

Girwani (Shivpuri) :

A temple of goddess Kālī, with sculptures of Indrāṇī, Pārvatī, Kaumārī etc. The style of the construction of the temple resembles that of the temples at Tongra (see below). *GAR*, 1928-29, p. 14.

Gurgi (Rewa) :

Image of Durgā as Umā found in the Gurgaj mound. *HTM*, p. 77, pl. XXVII, a.

Gwalior (Gwalior) :

Śakti images representing its various forms preserved in a large number in the local museum. *Catalogue of Sculptures in the Archaeological Museum*, Gwalior.

Gwalior Fort (Gwalior) :

Temple of Mātā Devī (Mother Goddess) datable to about 12th century AD. *CASIR*, II, pp. 363-64.

Indragarh (Mandsaur) :

Sculpture of a seated Gaja-Lakṣmī, discovered. IAR, 1965-66, p. 22.

Jabalpur (Jabalpur) :

An image of Śrī-Kalyāṇadevī, with the name inscribed on the pedestal found. *IAR*, 1964-65, p. 56.

Jagdalpur (Bastar) :

Medieval sculptures viz. aṣṭadhātu image of eight-armed Mahiṣmardinī, two stone images of Bhairava and dancing Śiva noticed in the local Mavali Devī temple. In the Collectorate office, image of Bhairava, Śiva-Pārvatī, Sūrya, Gaṇeśa, Navagraha and seated Bhairavī noticed. *IAR*, 1987-88, p. 137.

Kagpur (Vidisha) :

Temple of goddess Durgā (?) of about 9th-10th century AD to the west of the village near roadside. *GAR*, 1931-32, p. 7.

Karedi (Ujjain) :

An old temple of goddess, locally called the temple of Mahākālī. *HMIM*.

Karitalai (Jabalpur) :

The temple of Devī Maḍhia having an inscription of Kalachuri king

Lakṣmaṇarāja I dated in (K) E. 953. *CII*, IV, pt. 1, p. 178.

Khajuraho (Chhatarpur) :

(a) The rectangular temple of Chaunsaṭha Yoginī to the south-west of Sibsagar datable to c. 9th cent. AD, containing originally 67 cells of which 45 only remain at present. Only three images of Mahiṣāsuramardinī, Māheśvarī and Brahmāṇī now exist. Of these two are inscribed. *KD*, pp. 13-35; *KKD*, pp. 51-60; *KDP*, pp. 12-22; *KSS*, pp. 10-18; *KZ*, pp. 87-160; *AI*, NO. 15.

(b) Devī Jagadambī temple originally dedicated to Viṣṇu, datable to 1000-1025 AD. An image of Pārvatī is now installed in the temple. *Ibid.*

(c) Temple of Pārvatī situated to the south of Viśvanātha temple. Originally it was a Vaiṣṇava temple. *Ibid.*

(d) Śākta images which may be located as follows :

(i) Lakṣmī images found in the temples of Vāman, Lakṣman, Kandariya, Visvanatha and Khajuraho Museum. *KSS*, pp. 57-59.

(ii) Saraswatī images found in the temples of Parsvanatha, Kandariya, Visvanatha, Chaturbhuja, Vamana, Jagadambi, Lakṣman and Khajuraho Museum. *Ibid.*, pp. 59-60.

(iii) Durgā in the forms of —

1. Durgā in Visvanatha, Lakṣmana and the neighbouring temple.
2. Vana-Durgā in Visvanatha temple.
3. Nandā in Khajuraho Museum.
4. Devī in Jagadambi and Parsvanatha temple.
5. Bhuvaneśvarī in Lakṣman temple.
6. Sarva Maṅgalā in Kandariya temple.
7. Ghaṇṭakarṇī in Visvanatha temple.
8. Mahiṣāsurmaradinī in Khajuraho Museum, Lakṣman and Chausaṭha Yogini temples.

(iv) Other forms of Devī —

1. Ambikā in Lakṣman temple.
2. Tripurā in Khajuraho Museum.
3. Pārvatī in Parvati temple, Lakṣman temple and Khajuraho

Museum.

4. Ambā in temples of Lakṣman, Jagadambi, Kandariya and Vishwanatha.

5. Śivā in Jagadambi.

6. Yogeśvarī in Lakṣman and Duladeo temples and Khajuraho Museum.

(v) Saptamātṛkā images —

1. Vaiṣṇavī in the temples of Adinatha, Jagadambi, Chaturbhuja and Vaman, and the Museums at Khajuraho and Chhatarpur.

2. Brahmāṇī in the temples of Devi, Chausaṭha Yogini, Lakṣmi, Kandariya and Khajuraho Museum.

3. Māheśvarī in Kandariya temple.

4. Chāmuṇḍā in Duladeo temple and Khajuraho Museum.

5. Vārāhī in Khajuraho Museum.

6. Kaumārī in the temples of Kandariya, Adinatha, Jagadambi and Parsvanatha. *KSS*, pp. 57-70.

(vi) Other goddesses —

1. Vāruṇī in Jagadambi temple.

2. Narasiṁhī in Chaturbhuja temple.

3. Kālī in Pratapesvara temple.

4. Sadyojāta in Khajuraho Museum.

5. Manasā in Gandhi Museum, Chhatarpur and Lakṣman temple.

6. Gaṅgā-Yamunā in temples of Brahmā, Visvanatha, Kandariya and Khajuraho Museum.

7. Mahākālī in temples of Lakṣman and Visvanatha.

8. Manonmanī in Pratapesvara temple.

(vii) Unidentified images of goddesses —

1. Saraswatī or Bālā in Visvanatha temple.

2. Aparājitā or Kālī in Pratapesvara temple.

3. Chāmuṇḍā or Kālī in Lakṣman temple and Khajuraho

Museum. *KSS*, pp. 80-84.

Khallari (Raipur) :

Temple of Khallari Devī with few sati pillars. *RDG*, pp. 548-49.

Khargone District :

Images of Brāhmī, Māheśvarī, Kaumārī, Vaiṣṇavī, Vārāhī, Vīrabhadra and Aindrī noticed in the Bagheśvarī Mātā temple at Borut. Two Chāmuṇḍā sculptures noticed in Hirai Mātā temple, Hirapur. *IAR*, 1987-88, p. 138.

Kharod (Bilaspur) :

Two brick-temples, one dedicated to devī (Kālī ?) and the other in ruinous condition. Collection of a number of sculptures in the temple of devī. *CASIR*, VII, p. 203; *PRASIWC*, 1904, pp. 31-32; *ASIAR*, 1909-10, pp. 11-18, pl. IV.

Kolaras (Shivpuri) :

Temple of goddess, locally called Śītalā Mātā, with a collection of old carvings datable to 11th-12th century AD. *GAR*, 1918-19.

Kundalpur (Shivpuri) :

(a) A temple of Devī datable to c. 10th cent. AD containing images of Mahiṣamardinī etc. *GAR*, 1922-23.

(b) A flat-roofed Gupta temple located. *IAR*, 1971-72, p. 27.

Laphagarh (Bilaspur) :

The great fort with a temple of Durgā. *CASIR*, VII, pp. 219-23; *CLAR*, p. 61; *BDG*, p. 274.

Lotkhedi (Mandsaur) :

Sculptures of Mahiṣamardinī, Narasiṁha, Agni, Hanumāna and Gaṇeśa datable to 8th-9th cent. AD kept on the platform of Śītalā Mātā temple. Remains of a Pratihāra temple noticed to the east of the temple. *IAR*, 1988-89, p. 105.

Lavan (Bhind) :

A Devī temple with fine carvings noticed. *IAR*, 1960-61, p. 59.

Maihar (Satna) :

The temple of Śārdā Devī with a 10th century inscription referring to construction of the temple of Saraswatī by a Brāhmaṇa Devadhara. *CASIR*, IX, pp. 33-34; *IAR*, 1959-60, p. 57.

Makanganj (Mandsaur) :

Temple of Mahiṣamardinī with an inscription in 5th-7th century characters. The carvings are similar to the one on the toraṇa pillar from Mandsaur. *GAR*, 1929-30.

Malhar (Bilaspur) :

(a) An image of Durgā of medieval period found. *IAR*, 1962-63, p. 68.

(b) An image of Ambikā noticed. *IAR*, 1960-61, p. 59.

Mandhata (East Nimar) :

Ten-armed huge image of Mahākālī near Ravan nala. *ENG*, p. 471.

Morwan (Mandsaur) :

Temple of Durgā with collection of old sculptures datable to about 11th-12th century AD. *GAR*, 1929-30, pp. 20-21.

Nachna Kuthara (Panna) :

Pārvatī temple of the Gupta age. *CASIR*, XXI, pp. 96-98.

Naresar (Gwalior) :

Temple of goddess on a hill, datable to about 8th-10th century AD. *GAR*, 1947-48.

Navli (Mandsaur) :

A temple of goddess datable to about 12th-13th century AD. *HMIM*.

Pachaoli (Shivpuri) :

Ancient temple of Mahiṣamardinī. *GAR*, 1922-23.

Pathari (Vidisha) :

Rock-cut caves of about 5th cent. AD containing Saptamātṛkā images. *GAR*, 1925-26, pp. 12, 25.

Ramgarh-Hill (Sarguja) :

Image of twelve-armed Durgā. *CASIR*, XIII, p. 35.

Rewa (Rewa) :

A seated figure of a four-armed goddess with an inscription on the pedestal, datable to about 10th century AD. *CASIR*, XXI, p. 144.

Sagaur (West Nimar) :

Ancient temple of Bāgheshwari Devī. *WNDG*, p. 457.

Sakarra (Guna) :

Images of Vārāhī, Vaiṣṇavī, Pārvatī etc. installed on the walls of an 11th century temple. *GAR*, 1927-28, p. 10.

Sakri (Jabalpur) :

An image of Chāmuṇḍā noticed. *IAR*, 1960-61, p. 60.

Sewai (Gwalior) :

Devi images of 10th-12th cent. AD. *GAR*, 1933-34, p. 14.

Silchat (Rewa) :

A peculiar images of Kālī, datable to Kalachuri period found. *HTM*, pp. 98-99, pl. XXXIX, a.

Siroha (Shivpuri) :

Temple of goddess, probably of Pārvatī, datable to about 10th-12th century AD. *GAR*, 1925-26, p. 8.

Suhania (Morena) :

A temple of goddess, locally called Ambikā Devī, datable to about 11th century AD. *AG*, p. 125; *CASIR*, II, p. 401.

Terahi (Shivpuri) :

Temple of a goddess, locally called Mohaj Mātā, datable to about 10th-11th century AD. *GAR*, 1934-35, p. 7; *CASIR*, XXI, p. 177.

Tewar (Jabalpur) :

Four-armed Devī images near old Baodi and in the remains of Tripureśvara temple. *PE*.

Tigwan (Jabalpur) :

Ancient Devi images preserved in the Kankālī Devī temple. *JDG*, pp. 697-98.

Tripuri (Jabalpur) :

Image of Mahiṣamardinī found in excavation. *IAR*, 1968-69.

Tumain (Guna) :

Temple of goddess, locally called the temple of Vindhyavāsinī, datable to about 10th-11th century AD. *GAR*, 1918-19.

Vidisha (Vidisha) :

Fragment of a Saptamātṛkā panel, datable to the Paramāra period discovered. *IAR*, 1964-65, p. 74.

(F) Saura Monuments and Sculptures

Ajaigarh (Panna) :

Sūrya image in the Ajaigarh Fort. *MPS*, p. 75.

Barehta (Narsimhapur) :

A rare image of Sūrya. *NDG*, pp. 456-57.

Bharauli (Bhind) :

A medieval Sūrya temple discovered. *IAR*, 1961-62, p. 98.

Bheraghat (Jabalpur) :

Image of Sūrya in the temple of Chausaṭha Yoginī. *HTM*, pp. 91-92, pl. XXXIV.

Gwalior (Gwalior) :

Sūrya images preserved in the State Govt. Museum. *Catalogue of Sculptures in the Archaeological Museum*, Gwalior.

Indore (Indore) :

Image of Rathārūḍa Sūrya preserved in the Central Museum. *Guide Book to the Central Museum*, Indore, pp. 4-5.

Karitalai (Jabalpur) :

Sūrya images found. *KV*, p. 329.

Khajuraho (Chhatarpur) :

(a) Chitragupta temple enshrining an image of Sūrya 5' 8" in height, dated between 1000-1025 AD. *KD*, pp. 13-15; *KKD*, pp. 51-60; *KDP*, pp. 12-22; *KSS*, pp. 10-18; *KZ*, pp. 87-160; *AI*, No. 15.

(b) Sūrya images located in the temples of Lakṣmana, Chitragupta, Chaturbhuj, Pratapesvara, Duladeo, Jawari, Visvanatha and Khajuraho Museum. *KDP*, pp. 185-85, No. 1-32; *Ibid.*, pp. 161-83.

Koni (Bilaspur) :

A Sūrya image in the ruins of the Kalachuri temple. *EI*, XXVII, pp. 276 ff.

Markhera (Tikamgarh) :

Sun temple belonging to Pratihāra period found. *PP*, VII (No. 1-2), (1979), pp. 83-87; *MPS*, p. 17.

Manora (Rewa) :

An image of Revanta, datable to Kalachuri period. *HIM*, p. 106, pl. XLVI, a.

Masaun (Rewa) :

A block of stone carved to represent a Sūryanārāyāṇa discovered on the bank of a tank. *HTM*, p. 93, pl. XXXVII, a.

Narayanpur (Bilaspur) :

Ruins of three small temples, one dedicated to Āditya (Sun). *CASIR*, VII, p. 195; *CLAR*, p. 52.

Panagar (Jabalpur) :

A Sūrya image datable to about 10th-12th century A.D. found. *KV*, p. 327.

Sakarra (Guna) :

Sūrya image installed in the temple of about 11th century AD. *GAR*, 1927-28, p. 10.

Sesai (Shivpuri) :

A temple of Sūrya datable to about 10th-12th century AD. *GAR*, 1914-15.

Sewai (Gwalior) :

Sūrya images datable to c. 10th-12th cent. AD. *GAR*, 1933-34, p. 14.

Sohagpur (Shahdol) :

A Sūrya image. *CASIR*, VII, p. 245.

Tatapani (Sarguja) :

Sūrya sculptures found. *CASIR*, XIII, p. 63.

Tongra (Shivpuri) :

A temple of Sūrya, datable to about 10th-11th century AD with peculiar architecture comprising an oblong and narrow flat-roofed shrine, a sabhāmaṇḍapa and a porch with raised seats. *GAR*, 1928-29, pp. 11-12.

Umri (Tikamgarh) :

Sūrya temple of Pratihāra period. *MPS*, June 20, 1970, p. 7.

(G) Other Monuments and Sculptures

Achal (Chhatarpur) :

Early medieval sculptures discovered. *IAR*, 1961-62, p. 98.

Afzalpur (Mandsaur) :

Ancient images and other remains installed in a well. *PRASIWC*, 1905, p. 64.

Agar (Ujjain) :

Ancient remains built on the embankment of a tank. *GAR*, 1914-15, p. 27.

Ahalwara (Hoshangabad) :

Medieval sculptures discovered. *IAR*, 1961-62, p. 99.

Ainti (Morena) :

Two temples locally called 'Baradari' datable to c. 11th-12th cent. AD. *GAR*, 1914-15, p. 27.

Ajaigarh (Panna) :

(a) Ruins of three temples of the Chandella period. *CASIR*, XXI, p. 47.

(b) Ancient tanks of Chandella period. *CASIR*, XXI, pp. 46-47.

(c) Chandella fort. *CASIR*, VII, pp. 46 ff. *Ibid.*, XXI, pp. 46 ff.

(d) Sati memorial with inscription of the reign of Chandella Hammīravamadeva dated in V.S. 1368. *EI*, XX, p. 134; *Madhuri*, Vol. V, pt. II, No. 2.

(e) Sati memorial of Chandella period with inscription dated in V.S. 1348. *CASIR*, XXI, p. 53.

Akaltara (Bilaspur) :

Modern temple built of the ruins of an ancient temple. *BDG*, p. 256.

Aketa (Guna) :

Sati stone in Mātā temple with inscription dated in V.S. 1369 (1312 AD) recording its erection by Patwari Chahada (?). GAR, 1929-30, p. 53.

Alapur (Morena) :

Ruins of a temple of about 11th-12th century AD. *GAR*, 1917-18.

Alhaghat (Rewa) :

Remains of Kalachuri sculptures. *CASIR*, XXI, pp. 114-15.

Amadpur (Vidisha) :

Ruins of an old temple on a hill to the north-west of the village. *GAR*, 1914-15.

Amarkantak (Shahdol) :

(a) Ruins of a small temple containing four-armed female statue of Narmadā Māi. *CASIR*, VII, p. 231; *HTM*, p. 58; *CLAR*, p. 57.

(b) The great temple of Narmadā Māi. *CASIR*, VII, p. 234; *CLAR*, p. 59.

(c) Remains of an old reservoir, supposed to be the source of Narmada. *CASIR*, VII, p. 232; *HTM*, pp. 58-59; *CLAR*, p. 58.

(d) Ruins of small temples near Savitri nala. *CASIR*, VII, pp. 234-35.

(e) Images of two riders datable to Kalachuri period. *HTM*, p. 108, pl. LI, a-b.

(f) Statue of a male seated in the posture of adoration, having an inscription on its pedestal dated in (K) E. 922 (1170-71 AD). *Asiatic Researches*, Vol. XV, p. 506; *CASIR*, VII, pp. 233 ff; *PRASIWC*, 1920-21, p. 55; *HTM*, p. 107, pl. XLIX, a.

(g) A similar inscribed statue as above, but without any date. *Ibid.*

(h) Ruins of a temple about 200' to the north of Karan Mandir. *CASIR*, VII, p. 230.

Amar-khoha (Shivpuri) :

Ruins of temples and sculptures of Jaina and Brahmanical faith and datable to medieval period discovered. *IAR*, 1985-86, p. 112.

Amarpatan (Rewa) :

A fine image of dancing Gaṇeśa of Kalachuri period found on the steps of a tank. *HIM*, pp. 94-95, pl. XLVII-b.

Amera (Vidisha) :

(a) An old tank with an inscription dated in V.S. 1151 (1094 AD) fixed in its embankment. The inscription records the construction of the embankment by a Brahmin named Vikrama during the reign of Paramāra ruler Naravarman. *GAR*, 1923-24, p. 7.

(b) Ruins of an old temple of about 11th-12th cent. AD locally called as Vedi. *GAR*, 1923-24, p. 7.

(c) A pillared hall of about 11th-12th century AD square in plan with 12 pillars. *GAR*, 1923-24, p. 7.

Amjhera (Dhar) :

Temples of Śiva, Chāmuṇḍa, Ambikā, Ratneśvara, Chaturbhujanātha and Laxmī-Nārāyaṇa. Also old tanks, wells and sati stones. *GAR*, 1916-17.

Amledha (Morena) :

A group of two sati stones with crudely carved panels and a worn out inscription.

GAR, 1929-30, p. 31.

Amrol (Gwalior) :

Sati pillar on which an inscription of Vallaṇadeva is carved. *GAR*, Saṁ. 1999, No. 5.

Andalkhera (Rajgarh) :

Sati pillar with inscription dated in V.S. 644. *ISG*, p. 162.

Ankaleshwar (Mandsaur) :

A pillar with eight sides on which an inscription of c. 2nd-3rd cent. BC is carved. *Nav Bharat (Daily)*, Jabalpur, dated, October 19, 1970.

Antaralia (Mandsaur) :

Ruined temples. *GAR*, 1916-17.

Arang (Raipur) :

(a) Ruins of a small temple behind the Bhand Deval temple. *CASIR*, VII, p. 162.

(b) Ancient mound yielding bricks, pottery etc. *CASIR*, VII, p. 160; XVII, p. 21.

Ardoni (Morena) :

(a) Ruins of an ancient temple. *GAR*, 1929-30, p. 31.

(b) Ruins of an old well. *GAR*, 1929-30, p. 31.

(c) A group of two sati stones, one dated in V.S. 1442 (1385 AD). *GAR*, 1929-30, p. 31.

Avra (Mandsaur) :

Ruins of an ancient temple. *HMIM*.

Badegaon (Betul) :

Some old temples. *CLAR*, p. 44.

Badhotar (Shivpuri) :

Memorial pillar with inscription of Gopāladeva dated in V.S. 134(?). *GAR*, Sam. 1975, No. 93.

Badkeshvara (Hoshangabad) :

Remains of a group of temples of Paramāra period noticed. *IAR*, 1987-88, p. 138.

Badkeshwar (East Nimar) :

A group of small temple shrines noticed on the bank of the Narmada. *IAR*, 1988-89, p. 105.

Badoh (Vidisha) :

(a) Pillared hall of about 9th century AD locally known as Solah Khambi, from its sixteen pillars supporting its flat roof. AG, p. 57.

(b) A group of temples locally called *satmadh* (i.e. the seven shrines) of about 10th-12th century AD. Only six shrines are now existing, but the ruins at the site indicate the existence of more than seven shrines. *GAR*, 1923-24, pp. 8-10; *AG*, pp. 58-59.

(c) Remains of an old tank of about 10th-12th century AD. *AG*, p. 55.

(d) Memorial pillar of about 10th-12th century AD near the Solah Khambi. *GAR*, 1914-22.

Badoh-Pathari (Vidisha) :

Stone images of Sūrya, Kārttikeya, Kubera and Buddha, datable to 9th-10th cent. AD discovered. *IAR*, 1986-87, p. 120.

Badokhar (Morena) :

(a) A group of two sati memorials having date of V.S. 1548. *GAR*, 1935-36, p. 14.

(b) Ancient memorial pillar. *Ibid.*, p. 15.

(c) Pillar with inscription dated in V.S. 1598. *GAR*, Sam. 1992, No. 46.

(d) Ancient well. *GAR*, 1935-36, p. 14.

Badoni (Datia) :

(a) A site of early historical period with find of typical Gupta pottery and a few pieces of Roman pottery located at. *IAR*, 1971-72, p. 27.

(b) About 2 km to the south of Badoni, remains of three Buddhist stūpas along with a large number of clay-sealings of two sizes with inscriptions located. *IAR*, 1971-72, p. 27.

Badon-rajpur (Shivpuri) :

Memorial pillar with worn out inscriptions and sculptures. *GAR*, 1934-35, p. 22.

Bagh (Dhar) :

(a) An image of Brahmā with inscription of Bhāminī, sister of Paramāra Yaśodhavala, dated in V.S. 1210. *GAR*, Sam. 1983, No. 35.

(b) Two ancient tanks locally known as 'Ganga-Kui' and 'Brahma-Kui'. *GAR*, 1914-22.

Baghoria (Shivpuri) :

A group of sati stones with worn out inscriptions to the south-west of the village. *GAR*, 1925-26, p. 8.

Bahoriband (Jabalpur) :

(a) Images and architectural fragments of Kalachuri style found in the vicinity of the inscribed colossal image of Śāntinātha. *IAR*, 1965-66, p. 80.

(b) A large number of medieval sculptures found. *IAR*, 1960-61, p. 60.

Baijnath (Rewa) :

(a) Early medieval Brahmanical temples found. *IAR*, 1960-61, p. 62.

(b) An old brick temple between Bela and Baijnath found. *CASIR*, XIII, p. 2.

Balarpur (Shivpuri) :

(a) Memorial pillars. *GAR*, 1914-15.

(b) Three sati stones with inscriptions dated in 13th century AD. The first inscription dated in V.S. 1342 (1285 AD) records the committing of sati by the three widows of Ratna Arjuna who died in battle in the time of Gopāladeva of Narwar. The second inscription dated in V.S. 1356 (1299 AD) refers to Gaṇapatideva of Nalapura. The third inscription dated in VS. 1357 (1300 AD) refers to Gaṇapatideva and to committing of sati at village Palasai. *GAR*, 1914-15.

(c) A group of two memorial pillars, one with inscription dated in V.S. 957 (900 AD). *GAR*, 1918-19.

(d) A group of two sati stones. *GAR*, 1918-19.

(e) Two ancient temples in ruined condition. *GAR*, 1914-15.

(f) Four ancient temples in ruined condition. *GAR*, 1918-19.

(g) Remains of two ancient tanks. *GAR*, 1914-15, 1918-19.

Balod (Durg) :

(a) The earliest known sati pillar, datable to 2nd century AD. *CASIR*, VII, pp. 136-37; *CLAR*, p. 49; *KV*, p. 360.

(b) A number of old tanks. *CASIR*, VII, pp. 133-34; *CLAR*, p. 49.

(c) A number of ancient pillars. *CASIR*, VII, pp. 136-37; *CLAR*, p. 49.

Bamaur (Shivpuri) :

Memorial pillar with inscription dated in V.S. 957. *GAR*, 1915, No. 97.

Bamhni (Damoh) :

Sati pillar with inscription of Chandella ruler Hammīravarmadeva and his feudatory Vāghadeva dated in V.S. 1365. *EI*, XVI, p. 10; XX, p. 135; *PAIOC*, Allahabad, pt. I; Hiralal, *Damoha Dipaka*, pp. 95-96; *Bhandarkar List*, No. 660.

Bandakpur (Sagar) :

(a) Ruins of Kalachuri temples. *MPR*, p. 84.

(b) A number of sculptures of c. 10th-12th cent. AD (Chandella-Kalachuri period) located at. *IAR*, 1971-72, p. 27.

Bangla (Shivpuri) :

A group of memorial pillars and sati stones lying scattered between the village and the river Barua. Some of them are inscribed with sculptural panels depicting various scenes of life after death. Two inscriptions dated in V.S. 1338 (1281 AD) refer to Brahmadeva, the Chief Minister of Gopāladeva of Nalapura. The memorial pillars commemorate the battle that took place between king Gopāladeva of Nalapura (Narwar) and Vīravarman of Jejākabhukti (Bundelkhand) in V.S. 1338, in which the former was victorious. *GAR*, 1934-35, pp. 88 ff.

Bara (Chhatarpur) :

Late medieval temple discovered. IAR, 1961-62, p. 98.

Bara (Shivpuri) :

(a) Sati stone with inscription dated in V.S. 1539 (1482 AD.). *GAR*, 1928-29, p 25.

(b) Sati pillar with inscription dated in V.S. 1487. *GAR*, 1929-30, p 8.

Bara (Bhind) :

(a) A group of four memorial pillars, locally called as Joginis. *GAR*, 1929-30, pp. 7-8.

(b) A group of two sati stones, one of them dated in V.S. 1487 (1430 AD). *GAR*, 1929-30, p. 8.

Barai (Gwalior) :

Ancient 'Ras-Leela-Ghar'. *GAR*, 1946-47.

Baraka (Gwalior) :

Ancient brick temple. *HMIM*.

Baredi (Morena) :

(a) Temple of about 13th century AD. *GAR*, 1940-41, p. 23.

(b) Old well of about 13th century AD. *GAR*, 1940-41, p. 23.

Barehat (Bhind) :

Interesting terracotta figurines in typical Gupta style found. *IAR*, 1959-60, p. 69, pl. LVIII-C.

Bargaon (Jabalpur) :

(a) The temple of Somanātha datable to the Kalachuri period, with an inscription of Śabara. *CASIR*, XXI, pp. 101, 163 ff; *HTM*, p. 66, pl. XVIII-a; *CLAR*, p. 27.

(b) Ruins of temple datable to the early Kalachuri period. *HTM*, pp. 47-48, pl. XI-a, g.

(c) A temple of Kalachuri period. *HTM*, p. 107.

Barha (Gwalior) :

Early medieval rock-cut caves found. *IAR*, 1958-59, p. 72.

Baro or Barnagar (Vidisha) :

(a) A number of Śaiva, Vaiṣṇava, Buddhist and Jaina sculptures found. *CASIR*, VII, pp. 69 ff.

(b) A group of sati pillars of an early date. *CASIR*, X, p. 75.

(c) An open pillared building, locally known as 'Solah-Khambhi' (Sixteen pillared), datable to about 7th-8th century AD. *CASIR*, X, p. 75.

Barod-Budhi (Shivpuri) :

(a) A group of sati stones on the bank of tank south of the village. *GAR*, 1922-23.

(b) An old well with an inscription dated in V.S. 1336 (1279 AD), recording its construction by Chhalia, Minister of Jajjapella Āsalladeva of Narwar at Vitapatra. *GAR*, 1922-23.

(c) Remains of an old fort. *Ibid.*

Barod (Gadhi) (Shivpuri) :

Memorial pillars with sculptured panels and inscriptions datable to 10th century AD. *GAR*, 1922-23.

Bagrol (Hoshangabad) :

Brahmanical sculptures found. *IAR*, 1962-63, p. 68.

Bartara (Jabalpur) :

Sati stone with inscription of Pratihāra Vāghadeva dated in V.S. 1357. *Hiralal List*, No. 78.

Barukheda (Mandsaur) :

A group of four ancient temples. *GAR*, 1914-22.

Barwani (West-Nimar) :

(a) Four ancient sati pillars. *WNDG*, p. 434.

(b) Remains of ancient monasteries. *Ibid.*

Bastar District :

(a) In course of exploration of Indrawati river valley medieval Nāga, Somavaṁśī and Kākatīya groups of temples and sculptures, mostly in ruins were located at Chitrakot, Chhindgaon, Kuruspal, Jagdalpur, Narayanpal, Mundgaon, Dharaur, Bhairamgarh, Singhanpur, Bersu, Nagpani and Dantewara. *IAR*, 1985-86, p. 47.

(b) Ruins of a medieval Śiva temple and memorial pillars discovered at six sites in the submergence area of the Indra-Sagar Hydel Project. *IAR*, 1987-88, p. 41.

Behati (Guna) :

A monastery of about 10th century AD having a pillared hall, an open courtyard and an enclosed wall. *GAR*, 1936-37, p. 9.

Behir (Balaghat) :

Some old temples. *CLAR*, p. 25.

Belaras (Durg) :

Remains of an old temple. *CLAR*, p. 49.

Benai Ko (Guna) :

Ruins of temples. *GAR*, 1930-31.

Besani (Panna) :

Ruins of temple yielding a stone inscription dated in (K) E. 958. *CASIR*, XXI, p. 102.

Besnagar (Vidisha) :

(a) Female statue datable to Mauryan age found. *CASIR*, X, p. 44.

(b) 'Makara' capital and 'Kalpa-druma' capital found. *CASIR*, X, pp. 42-43.

(c) Sculptures of Gupta period found. *CASIR* X, p. 41.

(d) Ruins of an old temple found in the excavation of a mound. *CASIR*, X, pp. 45-46.

(e) Ruins of old city on the western end of the city. *CASIR*, X, pp. 36 ff; *BT*, p. 95.

(f) Ancient mounds near the Helidorus pillar site, partly excavated by Dr. Bhandarkar in 1913-14. *ARASI*, 1913-14. pp. 186 ff.; *GAR*, 1935-36, pp. 7-8.

(g) Colossal Yakṣa and Yaksī images of Śuṅga period, now preserved in Indian Museum, Calcutta and State Museum, Gwalior. *JMPIP*, II, p. 20; *SIS*, p. 52, pl. 43.

(h) Images of Ganga now in collection of Museum of Fine Arts, Boston. *SIR*, p. 197, pl. 97.

Betul District :

Sculptures of Pratihāra, Rāṣṭrakūta and Paramāra periods collected in course of explorations. *IAR*, 1985-86, pp. 48-49.

Bhadera (Shivpuri) :

A number of sati memorials with inscriptions dated in V.S. 1495, 1535, 1565 and 1668. *GAR*, 1928-29, p. 14.

Bhailipura (Hoshangabad) :

Medieval sculptures discovered. *IAR*, 1961-62, p. 99.

Bhairamgarh (Bastar) :

Remains of medieval temples. *IAR*, 1968-69.

Bhaktar (Shivpuri) :

A group of four sati stones with inscriptions dated in VS. 1304 (1247 AD). V.S. 1384 (1327 AD), V.S. 1519 (1462 AD) and V.S. 1767 (1710 AD). *GAR*, 1914-23.

Bhander (Gwalior) :

Ancient tank locally known as 'Son Talaiya' of Mahābhārata fame. *GAR*, 1914-23.

Bhanpur (Raipur) :

A ruined temple of Somavaṁśī period and a damaged mud fort 7th-8th cent. AD discovered. *IAR*, 1988-89, p. 105.

Bhanpura (Mandsaur) :

(a) Stone sculptures of Brahmanical and Jaina faith datable to c. 11th cent. AD identified. *IAR*, 1985-86, p. 110.

(b) An ancient site, 2 miles to the north-east, close to the foot of the extensive table land called 'Pathar' found to be rich in remains like sculptures, ruined habitations and fortification walls. *IAR*, 1954-55, p. 62.

Bharaoli (Morena) :

A group of sati memorials with inscriptions dated in V.S. 1439, 1539, 1594 and 1675. *GAR*, 1929-30, p. 32.

Bharhut (Satna) :

A temple of Khajuraho style located on a hill near the fortress of Naro Pahad. *IAR*, 1955-56, p. 73.

Bhatanwara (Satna) :

A complete Bharhut lintel depicting the procession of elephant riders discovered. *IAR*, 1962-63, p. 69.

Bhatnawar (Shivpuri) :

(a) Ruins of an old temple of about 10th century AD to the west of the village. *GAR*, 1928-29, p. 13.

(b) Sati stones with crude carvings, but without any inscriptions. *GAR*, 1928-29, p. 13.

Bheraghat (Jabalpur) :

Two sculptures of Kuṣāṇa age with inscriptions referring to their installation by the daughter of Bhūmaka or Bhūvaka. Hiralal, *Jabalpur Jyoti*, p. 162; Director General, ASI, Report, 1918-19, p. 33; *Hiralal List,No.* 45.

Bhesarwas (Guna) :

A group of five sati stones datable to about 13-14th century AD. Two of them bear inscriptions dated in VS. 1352 (1295 AD), one referring to Gaṇapatideva of Nalapura. *GAR*, 1926-27, p. 18.

Bhesdehi (Betul) :

An old temple with five sculptures. *CLAR*, p. 44.

Bhichor (Mandsaur) :

Ruins of a temple of about 14th century AD. *GAR*, 1929-30, pp. 18-19.

Bhidari-Kalan (Jabalpur) :

Sculptures of the 10th-12th centuries in Kalachuri style found. *IAR*, 1959-60, p. 69.

Bhilsa (Vidisha) :

(a) Sculptures of about 8th-10th century AD in the Bhairon Singh Haveli area of the fort. *GAR*, 1946-47.

(b) Capital of a pillar with the figure of a lion, datable to about 3rd century BC on the Lohangi hill. *AG*, p. 65.

(c) Image with inscription of Kumarsi dated in V.S. 1154 (?). *GAR*, Sam. 2000, No. 4.

Bhind District :

(a) Medieval Brahmanical sculptures found at Baderi Bhadakhur, Bijora Jabai, Jari, Kachongra, Kanawar, Koshand, Pachokhra, Paraya, Parsona, Phupkalan, Pur, Sakraya, Sapar Sonhra. *IAR*, 1978-79, p. 11.

(b) In the explorations conducted, remains of a Pratihāra temple found at Boreswar; sculptures of Pratihāra and Kachchhapaghāta times found at Baderi, Jor-Brahmana, Kanawar and Kanchogar; and sati-pillars bearing inscriptions of 14th-15th century AD located at Levan, Sakraya and Sagar. *IAR*, 1979-80, p. 41.

Bhojpur (Raisen) :

Remains of embankments of an ancient tank named 'Bhojatāla' built by Paramāra Bhoja. *MPS*, p. 51.

Bhonrasa (Vidisha) :

(a) An old tank, marking the source of the river Markundi, locally believed to be the site of the hermitage of the legendary sage Mārkaṇḍeya. *GAR*, 1935-36, p. 10.

(b) Sati pillar with inscription dated in V.S. 1564. *GAR*, 1935-36, pp. 8-9.

Bhopal (Bhopal) :

A stone pillar bearing shell charactered inscription in old Umrao Dulla's Garden. *IAR*, 1957-58, p. 68, pl. LXXXII-B.

Bhopali (Betul) :

Ancient cave situated 23 km to the east of Betul. *MPR*, p. 92.

Bhurwada (Shivpuri) :

Temple of about 11th-12th century AD locally called as Maḍhi. *GAR*, 1935-36, p. 12.

Bihar Kotra (Rajgarh) :

(a) Site of a Hindu temple of about 11th-12th century AD where a modern mosque has been built out of the material of the temple. *MAR*, 1949-50.

(b) A pillared-hall of about 10th-12th century AD locally called as Solah Khambi. *Ibid.*

Bijagad (West Nimar) :

(a) Two large rock-cut caves, each consisting of a pillared hall, respectively of 40' x 30' and 30' x 20'. *IAR*, 1959-60, p. 69.

(b) Sculptural remains of the Paramāra period noticed in the fort. *Ibid.*

Bijairaghogarh (Jabalpur) :

Pillar with inscription of Magadhadeva dated in V.S. 1154. *Hiralal List*, No. 72.

Bijri (Guna) :

Ruins of a group of three temples of about 11th-12th century AD. *GAR*, 1918-19.

Bilaigarh (Bilaspur) :

Remains of ancient temples and a fort. *CLAR*, p. 59; *RDG*, p. 539.

Bilao (Shivpuri) :

(a) An old sati stone with illegible inscription. *GAR*, 1914-15.

(b) A small temple with old sculptures lying about. *GAR*, 1914-15.

Bilaspur (Bilaspur) :

Sculptural remains of Kalachuri period found. *PRASIWC*, 1904, p. 27.

Bilaspur District :

Sculptures datable between c. 2nd cent. BC and 12th cent. AD belonging to

Buddhist, Jaina and Brahmanical pantheon noticed at Malhar. At Burhikhar, close to the above site, a number of temples and sculptural remains of Buddhist and Jaina faith were noticed. *IAR*, 1973-74, pp. 18-19.

Bilahari (Jabalpur) :

(a) The Laksmanasagar tank said to have been built by Kalachuri king Lakṣmaṇarāja. *KV*, p. 330; *HTM*, p. 46, pl. VII-a; *CLAR*, p. 28; *CASIR*, IX, pp. 35-38.

(b) Remains of an old monastery. *KV*, pp. 331-32.

Bina (Sagar) :

A number of well-preserved sculptures found. *IAR*, 1961-62, p. 100.

Birpur (Morena) :

Ruins of an old temple, datable to about 11th-12th century AD. *GAR*, 1935-36, p. 12.

Boram Deo (Rajnandgaon) :

(a) Sati monument dated in Saṁ. 1432 (1365 AD). *CASIR*, XVII, p. 37.

(b) Sati pillar with date in Vikram Samvat. *CASIR, XVII*, p. 41

(c) Brick-temple of peculiar plan. *CASIR*, XVII, p. 38.

(d) Other temples. *Ibid.*, p. 39.

(e) Temple of Boram Deo with five inscriptions. *CASIR*, XVII, pp. 34 ff; *CLAR*, p. 59.

Boreshwar (Bhind) :

Remains of a Pratihāra temple at. *IAR*, 1978-79, p. 11.

Boria (Durg) :

Two statues of bearded males having inscriptions of Jasarājadeva, dated in (K). E. 910 (1158-59 AD) on their pedestals. *CASIR*, XVII, p. 44.

Borpend (Betul) :

An old temple situated in the jungle. *CLAR*, p. 44.

Budhera (Shivpuri) :

A pillar on a hillock near Jhaloni tank, with an inscription dated in V.S. 1351 (1294 AD) referring to Chanderi and its Bundela rulers. *GAR*, 1929-30, p. 22.

Budhi-Mandu (Dhar) :

(a) Plans of Pratihāra and Paramāra temples and Brahmanical sculptures discovered. *IAR*, 1987-88, p. 138.

(b) A total of 350 sculptures of Pratihāra - Paramāra period discovered during clearance work of a temple by the Deptt. of Archaeology & Museums, M.P. Govt. *IAR*, 1988-89, p. 105.

Budhi-Rai (Shivpuri) :

Sati pillars with inscription dated in V.S. 1545. *GAR*, 1914-23.

Chainpur (Mandsaur) :

Numerous antiquities found. *IAR*, 1954-55, p. 62.

Chamo (Bhind) :

Remains of temples and sculptures of medieval period found. *IAR*, 1962-63, p. 68.

Chanchoda (Guna) :

(a) Remains of a temple of about 11th-12th cent. AD. *GAR*, 1929-30, p. 10.

(b) A monolithic pillar on the bank of local tank. *Ibid.*

Chandankhera (Jabalpur) :

Inscribed sati pillar. *Hiralal List*, No. 78.

Chanderi (Guna) :

A tank, locally called Kirti Sagar, built by Pratihāra king Kīrttirāja in 11th century AD. *GC*, pp. 28-29; *CASIR*, II, p. 405.

Chandrehe (Rewa) :

Remains of a monastery datable to the Kalachuri period. An inscription in its wall records its construction in Kalachuri Era 724 (973 AD). *CASIR*, XIII, pp. 9-11; *HTM*, pp. 36-41, pls. II-IV.

Chapka (Bastar) :

Six inscribed sati memorials. *EI*, *IX*, p. 166; *Hiralal List*, No. 297.

Chhanka (Bhind) :

Ruins of an old temple. *GAR*, 1915-16.

Chhapara (Vidisha) :

Gupta and post-Gupta shrines found. *IAR*, 1958-59, p. 71.

Chhapera (Rajgarh) :

Remains of a Jaina temple. *CISG*, p. 166.

Chhapri (Durg) :

(a) Statue of a bearded male seated in the posture of adoration, on the pedestal of which is incised an inscription of Gopāladeva dated in (K) E. 840 (1048-49 AD). *CASIR*, XVII, p. 34; *CII*, IV, pt. II, pp. 580-82; *Hiralal List*, No. 304.

(b) A number of sati pillars of which two have inscriptions dated V.S. 1430 and 1445. *CASIR*, XVII, p. 41; *Hiralal List,* No. 179.

Chhatarpur (Chhatarpur) :

Jaina image of Chandella period with inscription of Madanavarman dated in V.S. 1203. *ASIAR*, 1935-36, p. 94.

Chhatarpur District :

A large number of ancient mounds, structural remains, water reservoirs and wells located at Bamanaura, Beniganj, Jatakara, Khajuraho and Shivpuri during explorations at these places. *IAR*, 1969-70, p. 16.

Chhayan (Dhar) :

Ruins of an old temple locally called Deva Dharmaraja. *GAR*, 1914-23.

Chhind Kharak (Bastar) :

Ruins of a fort built in Saṁ. 1180. *CLAR*, p. 49.

Chhitara (Shivpuri) :

(a) A group of three memorial pillars with sculptured panels. *GAR*, 1916-17.

(b) A pillar with inscription dated in V.S. 1238 (1181 AD). *GAR*, 1916-17.

(c) A pillar with inscription dated in V.S. 1118. *GAR*, Saṁ. 1973, No. 55.

Chhote Dongar (Bastar) :

(a) Remains of a temple and sculptures of Kākatīya period unearthed. *IAR*, 1987-88, p. 137.

(b) Plan of a temple datable to medieval period exposed by the Deptt. of Archaeology & Museums, M.P. *IAR*, 1988-89, p. 104.

Chhoti Deori (Jabalpur) :

Ruins of an extensive group of small temples, 30 to 40 in number, datable to about early Kalachuri period (7th century AD). *CASIR*, XXI, pp. 100, 158, pl. XXXII- a; *HTM*, p. 77, pl. XXVIII-a.

Chikalda (Dhar) :

Two temples of snake-god, locally known as the temples of Taksakesvara and Bhilatdeva. *HMIM*.

Chiplipara (Raipur) :

An ancient temple of about 12th-13th century found. *IAR*, 1964-65, p. 13.

Chinochi (Bhind) :

Remains of temples and sculptures of medieval period found. *IAR*, 1962-63, p. 68.

Chirodia (Vidisha) :

Ruins of an old temple of about 10th-12th century AD to the east of the village. *GAR*, 1923-24, p. 68.

Chitrakhera (Damoh) :

A number of sculptures of c. 10th-12th century AD (Chandella-Kalachuri period) located. *IAR*, 1971-72, p. 27.

Chopda Pati (Chandi Chopda) (Damoh) :

An image kept in an ancient temple, with inscription of the reign of Narasiṁhadeva on its pedestal. *Hiralal List*, No. 102.

Chopera (Vidisha) :

Image of Yakṣī datable to c. 2nd cent. BC. *JMPIP*, No. 2, pp. 19-20.

Chorkho (Guna) :

A group of about a dozen temples in ruins datable to about 10th century AD. *GAR*, 1930-31, pp. 8-9.

Chorpura (Shivpuri) :

(a) Ruins of a group of two temples of about 11th-12th century AD. *GAR*, 1914-23.

(b) Ruins of a group of another two temples near the Railway watering station. *Ibid.*

(c) Ruins of a temple near the hill. *Ibid.*

(d) Ruins of another temple with its pillared hall still existing. *Ibid.*

Churli (Gwalior) :

An ancient mound to the east of the village, covered with potsherds, brick-bats etc. datable to about 7th-8th century AD. *GAR*, 1929-30, p. 14.

Culna (Dhar) :

A step-well of Paramāra period noticed. *IAR*, 1987-88, p. 138.

Dedur (Dhar) :

Damaged temple containing colossal Tīrthaṅakara and Kubera images. *GAR*, 1940-41, p. 23.

Daimapur (Jabalpur) :

(a) Loose sculptures of Brahmanical gods and goddesses found. *IAR*, 1962-63, p. 68.

(b) Sati pillar with inscription dated. V.S. 1288. *Hiralal List,* No. 78.

Damoh (Damoh) :

Sati pillars with inscriptions dated in V.S. 1336 and 1341. *CASIR*, XXI, p. 168.

Damoh District :

Sculptures belonging to the Chandella and Kalachuri periods found in exploration at Abhana, Badgawan, Bahmori, Balakot, Bandakpur, Chhaparat, Chhita-Kheda, Damoh, Dumar, Khajuri, Khamaria, Khera, Kodal, Marhia, Sarkhodi, Sihora, Tendukhera and Tharraka. *IAR*, 1979-80, p. 41.

Damru (Raipur) :

An old temple. *CLAR*, p. 49.

Dande-Ki-Khidak (Gwalior) :

(a) A group of temples of about 11th-12th century AD to the north of the village near hillside, with fragments of sculptures etc. *GAR*, 1929-30, pp. 15-16.

(b) Ruins of a group of temples in the local jungle, datable to about 11th-12th century AD. *GAR*, 1929-30, pp. 15-16.

(c) Sati stone with inscription dated in V.S. 1454 (1397 AD). *GAR,* 1929-30, pp. 15-16.

Dang (Bhind) :

(a) Brick-temple of about 9th-10th century AD. *GAR*, 1916-17.

(b) A group of sati stones. *GAR*, 1946-47.

Dantewada (Bastar) :

(a) Stone pillar with an inscription of Chhindaka Nāga ruler. *Hiralal List*, No. 166.

(b) Stone pillar with inscription of Nāga ruler of Bastar, dated in SE 1147. *EI*, X, p. 40; *Hiralal List*, No. 168.

Datia District :

In the village-to-village survey of Datia district, sculptures of early historical and medieval pottery found form 91 villages. *IAR*, 1987-88, pp. 41-44.

Dehri (Dhar) :

An ancient Jaina temple. *HMIM*.

Dehta (Jabalpur) :

Memorial pillar with inscription of V.S. 1299. *Hiralal List*, No. 77.

Dewas District :

(a) Sculptures of Paramāra period found in thirty villages during the course of exploration conducted by the University of Sagar. *IAR*, 1978-79, p. 42.

(b) Medieval sculptures and sati pillars located in explorations at : Balakheri, Bhasundi, Dhabla, Jangli, Khajuria, Mundabera, Nalesara, Sinduria, Sumrakhera, Sunwanigopal, Sutli and Tumraoda. *IAR*, 1978-79, p. 27.

(c) In the exploration of the river Chhoti Kali Sindh and its tributaries, medieval mounds with red ware, sculptures and pillars located at : Barkheri, Bhaturi, Kaneria, Karvia, and Parlia — all in Sonkachh taluk. *IAR*, 1980-81, p. 33.

(d) Temples and sculptures explored. *IAR*, 1979-80, pp. 41-42; 1985-86, p. 110.

Deogaon (Mandla) :

Ruins of an ancient temple. *CLAR*, p. 37.

Deokani (Guna) :

(a) A temple, about 2 furlongs to the east of the local Gadhi, datable to about 12th-13th century AD. *GAR*, 1925-26, p. 9.

(b) A step-well of about 12th-13th century AD near the local Gadhi. *GAR*, 1925-26, p. 9.

(c) Memorial pillars and remains of an old temple datable to c. 11th-12th cent. AD. *Ibid.*

Deokhut (Raipur) :

Four small but old temples on the bank of river with a number of sculptures scattered about. *CASIR*, VII, pp. 146-47; *CLAR*, p. 49; *RDG*, p. 542.

Deoras (Sidhi) :

A brick temple and sculptures discovered. *IAR*, 1988-89, p. 106.

Deori (Jabalpur) :

A temple with an exquisitely carved doorway bearing Ganga and Yamuna, mithuna and navagraha panels discovered. *IAR*, 1962-63, p. 69.

Deori (Sagar) :

Medieval Brahmanical sculptures of 11th-12th cent. AD. *IAR*, 1964-65, p. 74.

Depalpur (Indore) :

A lake called Depalasagara, constructed by Paramāra ruler Devapāladeva in 13th century AD. *ISG*, p. 13.

Dhamnar (Mandsaur) :

Two stone pillars on hill, one with inscription dated in V.S. 1363. *CASIR*, II, p. 279.

Dhamora (Chhatarpur) :

Remains of an early temple discovered. *IAR*, 1961-62, p. 98.

Dhamtari (Raipur) :

(a) A group of four temples, one belonging to an earlier date and three of later date built out of older material. *CASIR*, VII, pp. 142-45; *CLAR*, pp. 49-50.

(b) Temples of Ramachandra and Bilai Mata. *RDG*, pp. 543-44.

(c) An image with illegible inscription. *Hiralal List,* No. 194.

Dhanacha (Morena) :

A ruined temple in jungle. *GAR*, 1916-17.

Dhanaich (Shivpuri) :

Stone pillar with inscription dated in V.S. 1351. *GAR*, Sam. 1988, No. 17.

Dhankhedi (Mandsaur) :

(a) Two rock-cut cells in a hill south-east of the village. *GAR*, 1916-17.

(b) Two rock-cut cells in Gaṇeśa Pahāḍī with carved image of Gaṇeśa. *Ibid.*

(c) A small rock-cut temple to the west of the village. *Ibid.*

Dhanora (Betul) :

Ancient cave situated on the south bank of river Tapi, 12 km from Atner. *MPR*, p. 97.

Dhanpur (Bilaspur) :

(a) A group of six Brahmanical brick temples in ruins datable to about 9th century AD on the bank of tank locally known as Katha Talao. *CASIR*, VII, p. 237; *CLAR*, p. 60.

(b) A group of four Brahmanical temples in ruins, datable to about 9th century AD. *Ibid.*

(c) A number of smaller isolated shrines near the above-mentioned temples. *Ibid.*

Dhar (Dhar) :

(a) The Kamal Maula mosque built out of the material of the temple of Saraswati built by Paramāra Bhoja of Dhar in 11th century AD. *Dhar and Mandu*, by Luard.

(b) The Lat mosque built out of the material of an old Hindu temple of about 11th century AD. Pieces of an iron pillar that was once erected in front of the temple are now lying at the site on a ruined platform. The name of the mosque is derived from this pillar, known as *Lat*. *Dhar and Mandu*, by Luard.

Dhar District :

(a) Brahmanical sculptures noticed in course of explorations at Bhirotakot, Budhi-Mandu, Kesur, Mahatpura, Murorka, Nagora, Panch-Ghat, Suli-Bardi and Undakho. *IAR*, 1984-95, pp. 40-41.

(b) Ruins of medieval temples, sculptures and forts explored. *IAR*, 1986-87, pp. 47-48; 1985-86, pp. 48-50.

Dharampuri (Dhar) :

(a) Colossus image of a Hindu god, of about 12th-13th century AD. *MAR*, 1949-50.

(b) Ruins of an old temple to the south-west of the village, near the Sangam, datable to about 11th-12th century AD. *Ibid.*

(c) Rock-cut cells near Sangam. *Ibid.*

(d) Colossus image of Hanumāna, datable to about 12th-13th century AD. *Ibid.*

(e) A colossal image of a bearded sage with a dagger tied at his belt discovered. *IAR*, 1987-88, p. 138.

Diagarh (Jabalpur) :

Loose sculptures of Brahmanical gods and goddesses found. *IAR*, 1962-63, p. 68.

Dighori (Seoni) :

Ancient cave on the bank of Thal river. *MPR*, p. 92.

Dongargarh (Rajnandgaon) :

Ruins of temples found. *CLAR*, p. 50.

Dundapura (Gwalior) :

A group of three memorial pillars on the bank of river, datable to about 10th-11th century AD. *GAR*, 1929-30, p. 15.

Dungarpura (Shajapur) :

Brahmanical and Jaina sculptures of c. 10th-11th cent. AD located. *IAR*, 1985-86, p. 111.

Durg (Durg) :

Remains of a mud fort. *DDG*, p. 447.

Durg District :

Explorations in the Durg district conducted by the University of Sagar led to notice of sculptures of the Kalachuri period at Balod, Bhoramdeo, Chaurel, Dhamdha, Gurur, Lohara, Rajauli and Sahaspur. The temples at Bhoramdeo and Gurur were closely examined. Sati pillars discovered at Bhoramdeo, Ghaurel and Deokar. *IAR*, 1972-73, pp. 14-15.

Durgapur (Rewa) :

A small temple built of old material datable to 10th-11th century AD. *CASIR*, XIII, p. 6.

East Nimar District :

(a) Temples and sculptures of medieval period explored in course of Indira

Sarovar survey by the State Deptt. of Archaeology. *IAR*, 1985-86, p. 110.

(b) Temple remains, structural remains and loose sculptures located at a large number of sites in course of explorations of the submergence area of the Narmada Sagar Project. *IAR*, 1987-88, pp. 44-49.

(c) Exploration of the submersible area under Indira Sagar Project of the Narmada valley led to discovery of medieval remains including habitation mounds, dilapidated temples, disturbed tombs, loose sculptures and a few memorial pillars at various localities in the Harsud tehsil of the district. *IAR*, 1987-88, pp. 55-57.

(d) Exploration in the Khandwa taluk led to discovery of loose sculptures of Śiva Pārvatī, Śiva liṅga, Nandī, Chāmuṇḍā, Viṣṇu, Lakṣmī, Narasiṁha, Gaṇeśa and broken pieces from the villages Bangarda, Bhongani, Bir, Chiktikhal, Dharikotla Madhi, Jamoti, Piplani, Richhi and Sarlia. *IAR*, 1987-88, p. 59.

(e) In course of exploration of 29 villages under submersion in the Narmada Sagar Dam, Śiva temple, sati stones and sculptures of Nandī, Pārvatī, Viṣṇu, Paraśurāma, Narasiṁha, Bhairava and Kārttikeya noticed. *IAR*, 1988-89, p. 43.

Eran (Sagar) :

(a) A squared stone with a long inscription of Samudragupta engraved on it. *CASIR*, X, p. 89.

(b) Various sati monuments. *Ibid.*, pp. 89-90.

(c) Torso of a Nāga image of c. 3rd cent. AD. *MB*, III, No. 3 (1960), pp. 1-5.

Fingeshwar (Raipur) :

Medieval temple with inscription in two lines. *IAR*, 1969-70.

Fular (Jabalpur) :

Sculptures of 10th-12th century in the Kalachuri style found. *IAR*, 1959-60, p. 69.

Gadajar (Morena) :

Ruins of an ancient temple. *GAR*, 1914-15.

Godhala (Shivpuri) :

A memorial pillar dated in V.S. 1353 (1296 AD), mentioning one Bhaṭṭāraka Kumārapāla and a certain Jaina. *GAR*, 1916-17.

Gandhaval (Ujjain) :

(a) Temple of Gandharvasena of about 11th-12th century AD. *GAR*, 1942-46, pp. 22-23.

(b) Sculptures of about 11th-12th century AD fixed in the Muslim tomb called Dargah. *GAR*, 1942-46.

(c) Memorial pillar with illegible inscription. *GAR*, 1917-18.

Ganeshpura (Vidisha) :

Two Yakṣa torsos datable to 2nd-1st century BC discovered from ancient habitation site on southern bank of the Bes, between Ganeshpura and the Bes river bridge discovered. *IAR*, 1964-65, p. 74.

Gataura (Bilaspur) :

Ruins of several ancient temples and statues. *CLAR*, p. 60.

Gatwaya (Shivpuri) :

Ruins of a temple of about 11th century AD. *GAR*, 1922-23.

Gaznipur (Mandsaur) :

Ruins of a group of ancient temples. *HMIM*.

Ghansor (Seoni) :

Ruins of about twenty-five Kalachuri temples. *CASIR*, VII, pp. 107-08; *MPR*, p. 84; *CLAR*, p. 38.

Ghirongi (Bhind) :

A beautifully carved stone jamb with the remains of a temple noticed. *IAR*, 1960-61, p. 59.

Ghusai (Mandsaur) :

(a) A group of old temples on the bank of a tank. *GAR*, 1916-17.

(b) Two sati stones, one with inscription dated in V.S. 1334 (1277 AD) mentioning the ancient place name as Ghoṣavatī. *Ibid.*

Gohadi (Bhind) :

Ruins of old temple. *GAR*, 1929-30, p. 9.

Gopaltalai (Betul) :

Ancient cave 9 km to the south of Betul. *MPR*, p. 92.

Gorakhpur (Raisen) :

Ruins of a large Paramāra temple. *IAR*, 1986-87, p. 119.

Gudar (Shivpuri) :

(a) Collection of old sculptures of about 11th-12th century AD in the temple of Mātā. *GAR*, 1929-30, p. 23.

(b) Sati stone with illegible inscription on the same. *GAR*, 1929-30, p. 24.

(c) Ruins of an old temple with sculptures nearby. *GAR*, 1929-30, p. 25.

(d) Ruins of two temples of about 11th century AD on the western bank of irrigation tank. *GAR*, 1929-30, p. 25.

(e) Ruins of an old temple, with sculptures. *GAR*, 1929-30, p. 25.

(f) Pillar in a hamlet called Nayagaon, with inscription dated in V.S. 144(5). *GAR*, 1929-30, p. 62.

Gujra (Rewa) :

Early medieval Brahmanical temples found. *IAR*, 1960-61, p. 62.

Guna District :

Exploration under the Rajghat Survey yielded sculptures of Pratihāra and Kachhapaghāta art at Pancham Nagar, Sirsod, Bari Sona Umariya, Laheri, Kannaota, Bhattiya, Ghurisia, Dimroli; ancient baoli and inscription at Bari, royal palace of Bundelas at Pancham Nagar; and Jain sculptures with temple remains at Laderi, Tanda and Ghorapahad. *IAR*, 1985-86, p. 50.

Gurgi (Rewa) :

(a) A large enclosure, locally known as Rehuta Fort, containing ruins of a number of temples of Kalachuri period. *CASIR*, XIX, p. 98; *HTM*, p. 44, pl. V-a.

(b) Foundations of two temples. *HTM*, p. 44.

Gurji Dasarni (Jabalpur) :

Remains of Sculptures. *MPR*, p. 84.

Gurur (Durg) :

(a) Numerous sati pillars of early dates. *CASIR*, VII, p. 141; *DDG*, p. 49.

(b) Remains of a number of temples. *Ibid.*

(c) Pillar on which an inscription of Vāgharāja, ruler of Somavaṁśī dynasty of Kanker is found. *IA*, 1926, p. 44; *Hiralal List*, p. 137; *Bhandarkar List*,

No. 1091.

Gwalior (Gwalior) :

Images of Yakṣa and Yakṣiṇī, Rāhu-Ketu, Dvārapāla, Aṣṭadikpāla, Gandharva, Yama, Mother and Child, Vāyu, Goblin couple, Drummer, preserved in the local museum. *Catalogue of Sculptures in the Archaeological Museum*, Gwalior.

Gwalior Fort (Gwalior) :

An old tank, locally known as Surajkund, datable to about 3rd-4th century AD. *CASIR*, II, pp. 342, 353.

Gyaraspur (Vidisha) :

(a) Temple of about 9th century AD near the roadside now known as Aṭhakhambhā - Mandir. All the pillars are richly carved, one containing a trifoil design. One of the pillars bears a pilgrim record dated in V.S. 1039. *AG*, pp. 91-92; *CASIR*, VII, pp. 90-93; X, pp. 31-34.

(b) Ruins of a group of old temples datable to about 9th-10th century AD on the eastern slope of a hill, north of Mānsarovar tank. *AG*, p. 92; *CASIR*, VII, pp. 90-93; X, pp. 31-34.

(c) Memorial pillar near the enclosure of Katarmal, half a mile to the east of the village, with sculptured panels and worn out inscriptions datable to about 10th century AD. *GAR*, 1931-32, p. 4.

(d) A group of sati memorial to the south-east of Mansarovar tank. *AG*, p. 94.

Handia (Harda) :

Brahmanical temples and Indo-Islamic monuments noticed in exploration. *IAR*, 1985-86, pp. 53-54.

Harchauka (Sarguja) :

Rock-cut cave temple on the bank of Mabai river, the pillars of which contain inscriptions of Kalachuri period. *Hiralal List*, No. 188.

Hasalpur (Shivpuri) :

Pillar with inscription of Nāgavarman in Gupta characters. *GAR*, Sam. 1973, No. 21.

Hatta (Damoh) :

Sculptures of medieval period found at several sites. *IAR*, 1967-68, p. 66.

Hindoria (Damoh) :

(a) An inscribed sati pillar dated Sam. 1113. *CLAR*, p. 31.

(b) Remains of old temples. *CLAR*, p. 31.

(c) A number of sculptures of c. 10th-12th century AD (Chandella-Kalachuri period) located. *IAR*, 1971-72, p. 27.

Hinglajgarh (Mandsaur) :

(a) Sculptures and architectural pieces of about 11th-12th century AD found. *IAR*, 1965-66, p. 81.

(b) Numerous antiquities found. *IAR*, 1954-55, p. 62.

(c) Medieval sculptures of Brahmanical faith noticed and identified. *IAR*, 1985-86, p. 110.

Hirapur (Hoshangabad) :

Brahmanical sculptures found. *IAR*, 1962-63, p. 68.

Hoshangabad District :

In course of exploration of Narmada valley submergence coming under Indira Sarovar Dam, mound, brick temple, Śiva temple and Brahmanical sculptures located at eleven sites. *IAR*, 1986-87, p. 49.

Imli Tikra (Sarguja) :

Sculptures and sati pillar noticed. *CASIR*, XIII, p. 61.

Indhar (Shivpuri) :

(a) Two ancient sites yielding large-size bricks, pottery etc., datable to 8th-12th century AD on the western and northern outskirts of the village. *GAR*, 1925-26, p. 8.

(b) Remains of a group of temples to the north and east of the village, datable to about 8th-12th century AD. *GAR*, 1925-26, p. 8.

(c) A memorial pillar with illegible inscription dated in V.S. 1345 (1288 AD), lying half-buried in western approach to the village. *GAR*, 1925-26, pp. 20-24.

Indor (Guna) :

(a) Three memorial pillars with inscriptions dated in V.S. 902 (845 AD), V.S. 920 (863 AD) and V.S. 1177 (1120 AD). *GAR*, 1936-37, p. 25.

(b) Memorial pillars on the bank of Airapat river to the north of the village, with carved panels, some bearing inscriptions datable from 10th to 12th cent. AD. *GAR*, 1936-37, p. 9.

(c) Memorial pillar with inscription dated in V.S. 1345. *GAR*, Sam. 1980, No. 9.

Jakhoda (Gwalior) :

Remains of a temple and sati pillar. *GAR*, 1929-30, p. 57.

Janjgir (Bilaspur) :

A cave in hill containing sculptures, pillars etc., about 16 miles due north of Janjgir. *CASIR*, VII, pp. 210-11.

Jeeran (Mandsaur) :

Pillar with inscription of V.S. 1053. *GAR*, Sam. 1970, No. 25.

Jhapal (Betul) :

An ancient cave, about 60 km from Betul. *MPR*, p. 92.

Jharda (Ujjain) :

(a) Ancient well datable to c. 11th-12th cent. AD. *ISG*, p. 25.

(b) Medieval Brahmanical sculptures identified. *IAR*, 1985-86, p. 112.

Jharna (Shivpuri) :

Ruins of an old temple of about 10-11th century AD, a furlong south-west of road at 4th mile from Satanwada to Narwar road. *GAR*, 1923-24, p. 14.

Jonapura (Gwalior) :

(a) Ruins of an old temple with sculptures scattered about. *GAR*, 1918-19.

(b) Memorial pillars with illegible inscriptions on some of them. *Ibid.*

Kabulpur (Vidisha) :

A flat-roof temple with a portico having decorated pillars discovered. *IAR*, 1985-86, p. 112.

Kadwaha (Guna) :

(a) A sati stone with inscription dated in V.S. 1451 (1394 AD). *GAR*, 1918-19.

(b) A sati stone near tank with illegible inscription dated in V.S. 1120 (?) (1063 AD). *Ibid.*

Kagpur (Vidisha) :

Ruins of a group of temples of about 11th century AD to the west of the village near roadside. *GAR*, 1931-32, p. 7.

Kaildhar (Shivpuri) :

'Kapil Gupha', which according to local tradition, was used by sage Kapila. *ISG*, p. 75.

Kajli Kanojia (Betul) :

Ruins of old temples. *CLAR*, p. 45.

Kakarari (Rewa) :

An open pillared hall, locally called 'Darwaza', possibly belonging to the age of the Kalachuris of Tripuri. *CASIR*, X, p. 15.

Kalakot (Mandsaur) :

Sculptures datable to about 11th-12th century AD found. *IAR*, 1965-66, p. 81.

Kalan (Rewa) :

Early medieval Brahmanical temples found. *IAR*, 1960-61, p. 62.

Kali-baodi (Dhar) :

A tank, baoli and sculptures located. *IAR*, 1988-89, p. 41.

Kalipith (Rajgarh) :

A Nāgī image datable to about 10th-11th century AD discovered. *IAR*, 1964-65, p. 74.

Kamed (Ujjain) :

Ruins of an old temple of about 10th century AD with sculptures scattered about. *GAR*, 1934-35, p. 10.

Kandadongar (Raipur) :

Remains of an old fort. *RDG*, p. 547.

Kanker (Bastar) :

Remains of an old fort and temples. *CLAR*, p. 50.

Kanoda (Damoh) :

(a) Remains of an old sculptured temple. *CLAR*, p. 31.

(b) Three memorial pillars with inscriptions dated in V.S. 1342, 1350 and 1360. *Hiralal List*, No. 115.

Kanorabari (Damoh) :

Remains of Kalachuri sculptures. *PRASIWC*, 1894, p. 7.

Kanvan (Dhar) :

A stone pillar with dateless inscription. *CIGS*, p. 514.

Kapu (Sarguja) :

Ruins of some single-celled temples and sati pillars. *CASIR*, XIII, p. 59.

Karnavad (Ujjain) :

An ancient mound, locally called Vaisya Tekri, strewn over with brickbats and ancient pottery. *GAR*, 1917-18.

Kasdol (Raipur) :

Remains of an old fort. *RDG*, p. 548.

Kayatha (Ujjain) :

Ruins of old temples. *HMIM.*

Kenri (Chhatarpur) :

Remains of an early temple discovered. *IAR*, 1961-62, p. 98.

Kerban Piparia (Jabalpur) :

Memorial pillar with inscription of V.S. 1308. *Hiralal List*, No. 77.

Kesur (Dhar) :

Ancient mound yielding large size bricks and pottery. *MAR*, 1949-50.

Kethuli (Mandsaur) :

(a) Sculptures datable to about 11th-12th century AD found. *IAR*, 1965-66, p. 81.

(b) Numerous antiquities found. *IAR*, 1954-55, p. 62.

Kevati-Kund (Rewa) :

(a) An old cave bearing Pali inscription of about 200 BC. *CASIR*, XXI, p. 116.

(b) Three pillars with inscriptions dated in V.S. 1397. *Bhandarkar List*, No. 702.

Khachrod (Ujjain) :

A building of about 11th-12th century AD locally called as Mahal. *GAR*, 1917-18.

Khadlai (Dhar) :

Ancient rock-cut sculptures. *GAR*, 1916-17.

Khairi (Betul) :

Five ancient caves, about 18 km to the west of Betul. *MPR*, p. 92.

Khajuraho (Chhatarpur) :

(a) Ancient tank locally known as 'Chopra-tal', with steps all around and a *maṇḍapa* in the centre. *KD*, pp. 13-35; *KKD*, pp. 51-60; *KDP*, pp. 12-22; *KSS*, pp. 10-18; *KZ*, 87-160; *AI*, No. 15.

(b) Navagrahapaṭṭas located in the temples of Lakṣman, Jagadambi, Duladeo, Chaturbhuj, Javari, Ghantai, Parsvanatha, Shantinatha, Kandariya and in museums at Khajuraho and Dhubela. *KDP*, pp. 197-98, No. 1-36; *Ibid.*, pp. 189-96.

(c) Aṣṭadikpālas located in the temples of Lakṣman, Jagadambi, Chitragupta, Duladeo, Chaturbhuj, Vaman, Javari, Parsvanatha, Adinatha, Kandariya, Visvanatha and Khajuraho Museum. *KDP*, pp. 239-40, No. 1-29; *Ibid.*, pp. 203-10.

(d) Agni images located in the temples of Lakṣman, Jagadambi, Chitragupta, Duladeo, Chaturbhuj, Vaman, Javari, Parsvanatha, Adinatha, Kandariya, Visvanatha and Khajuraho Museum. *KDP*, pp. 240-41, No. 1-36; *Ibid.*, pp. 210-16.

(e) Yama images found in the temples of Lakshman, Jagadambi, Chitragupta, Duladeo, Chaturbhuj, Vaman, Javari, Parsvanatha, Adinatha, Kandariya and Visvanatha. *KDP*, p. 241, No. 1-23; *Ibid.*, pp. 216-18.

(f) Nirti images located in the temples of Lakshman, Jagadambi, Chitragupta, Duladeo, Chaturbhuj, Vaman, Javari, Parsvanatha, Adinatha, Kandariya and Khajuraho Museum. *KDP*, p. 242, No. 1-25; *Ibid.*, pp. 219-23.

(g) Images of Varuṇa located in the temples of Lakṣman, Jagadambi, Chitragupta, Duladeo, Chaturbhuj, Vaman, Javari, Parsvanatha, Adinatha, Kandariya, Visvanatha and Khajuraho Museum. *KDP*, pp. 242-43, No. 1-25; *Ibid.*, pp. 224-27.

(h) Vāyu images. *KDP*, pp. 242-43, No. 1-22; *Ibid.*, pp. 227-30.

(i) Kubera images located in the temples of Lakṣman, Jagadambi, Duladeo, Chaturbhuj, Vaman, Parsvanatha, Kandariya, Visvanatha and Khajuraho Museum. *KDP*, pp. 244-45, No. 1-37; *Ibid.*, pp. 230-36.

(j) Īśāna images located in the temples of Lakṣmana, Jagadambi, Chitragupta, Duladeo, Chaturbhuj, Vaman, Javari, Parsvanatha, Adinatha, Kandariya and Visvanatha. *KDP*, p. 245, No. 1-23; *ibid.*, pp. 236-38.

(k) Images of Brahmā located in the temples of Vaman, Nandi, Kandariya, Lakṣman, Parsvanatha, Adinatha, Visvanatha, Chaturbhuja, Javari, Duladeo, Jagadambi and Khajuraho Museum. *KSS*, pp. 87-89.

(l) Vāyu-Varuṇa images in Kandariya temple. *KSS*, p. 103.

(m) Bṛhaspati - Śukra image in the Lakṣman temple. *Ibid.*, pp. 103-04.

(n) Rāhu-Ketu image in Khajuraho Museum. *Ibid.*, p. 104.

(o) Yama-Vāyu image in the Adinatha temple. *Ibid.*, p. 104.

(p) Varuṇa-Vāyu image in the Jagadambi temple. *Ibid.*, pp. 104-05.

(q) Viṣṇu (?) image in Kandariya temple. *Ibid.*, p. 105.

(r) Sūrya-Śiva image in Kandariya, Jagadambi and Duladeo temples. *Ibid.*, pp. 105-06.

(s) Sūrya-Viṣṇu-Śiva image in Lakṣman and Chaturbhuj temples. *Ibid.*, p. 106.

(t) Sūrya-Viṣṇu-Śiva - Brahmā image in Pratapesvara temple. *Ibid.*, p. 106.

(u) Bhauma or Śani image in the Parsvanatha temple and Khajuraho Museum. *Ibid.*, pp. 106-07.

(v) Lady writing letter preserved in Indian Museum, Calcutta. *SIS*, p. 109, pl. 175.

Khajuri (Jabalpur) :

Memorial pillar with an inscription dated V.S. 1354. *Hiralal List,* No. 58.

Khalari (Jabalpur) :

(a) Images of Brahmanical gods and goddesses found. *IAR*, 1962-63, p. 68.

(b) An image with inscription reading *'Mahārājā Bhumiraṇa'*. Hiralal, *Jabalpur Jyoti*, p. 144; *Hiralal List*, No. 68.

Khallari (Raipur) :

(a) Temple of Kalachuri period built by a *'mochi'*. *RDG*, pp. 548-49.

(b) Sati pillars. *Ibid.*

Khama (Jabalpur) :

A garuḍa pillar of about 11-12th century AD discovered. *IAR*, 1958-59, p. 72.

Khamaria (Jabalpur) :

A large number of medieval sculptures found. *IAR*, 1960-61, p. 60.

Khamtara (Jabalpur) :

Images of Brahmanical gods and goddesses found. *IAR*, 1962-63, p. 68.

Khandwa (East Nimar) :

(a) Ancient *'Padma-Kuṇḍa'*, *'Bhairava-tal'* and *'Kilala-Kunda'*. *CASIR*, IX, p. 113.

(b) Ancient 'Bhim-Kunda', 'Suraj-Kunda' and 'Rameshwara-Kunda'. *ENDG*, p. 467.

Khandwa District :

Nine sites explored in Harsud tehsil in course of village-to-village survey by the ASI led to discovery of ruins of temples, sculptural remains, garhi, baoli and fort-walls. *IAR*, 1986-87, p. 54.

Khanpur (Guna) :

Number of sati pillars on the eastern outskirts of the village. *GAR*, 1924-25, p. 12.

Khargone (West Nimar) :

Ancient temple of Navagrahas. *GAR*, 1924-25, p. 12; *WNDG*, p. 445.

Kharod (Bilaspur) :

(a) A group of five small temples in ruin, datable to about 7th century AD. *CASIR*, VII, p. 203; *CLAR*, pp. 60-61.

(b) Temple of Lakṣmeśvara from where an inscription of K.E. 933 was found. *BSG*, p. 272.

Kherat (Bhind) :

Ruins of an old brick temple of about 10th century AD on a mound in the midst of Chambal ravines. *GAR*, 1934-35, p. 11.

Khirki (Hoshangabad) :

Brahmanical sculptures found. *IAR*, 1962-63, p. 68.

Khopra :

Fragmentary sculptures and pillars found. *CLAR*, p. 51.

Khor (Mandsaur) :

(a) More than ten temples of about 10th-11th century AD, some intact and others in ruins. *GAR*, 1918-19.

(b) A group of 28 memorial pillars. *GAR*, 1918-19.

Khudaoli (Gwalior) :

Three groups of temples of about 12th century AD, locally called as Rathas in ruins. *GAR*, 1929-30, p. 16.

Khudgaon (Mandsaur) :

Ruins of old temples. *GAR*, 1918-19.

Kirari (Bilaspur) :

A broken wooden pillar with inscription datable to c. 2nd cent. AD. *EI*, XVIII, p. 152; *Hiralal List*, No. 214.

Kirnapur (Balaghat) :

Some old temples. *CLAR*, p. 25.

Kod (Dhar) :

A temple with an inscription. *CIGS*, p. 514.

Kọlaras (Shivpuri) :

Sati stone with inscription dated in V.S. 1348 (1291 AD). *GAR*, 1918-19.

Koni (Bilaspur) :

Remains of a Kalachuri temple yielding a stone inscription of Pṛthvīdeva II dated in (K)E. 900. *EI*, XXVII, pp. 276 ff.

Korba (Bilaspur) :

An ancient cave situated about 40 km from Ratanpur. *MPR*, p. 92.

Kosgain (Bilaspur) :

(a) An old fort of the Kalachuri period, having sculptures and inscriptions. Two inscriptions found from the fort refer to the Kalachuri king Vāhara. Of these, one is dated in V.E. 1570. *CASIR*, XIII, pp. 153-57; *CLAR*, p. 61.

(b) Remains of an old fort and sculptural remains of Kalachuri period. *CASIR*, XIII, pp. 153-57.

Kota Udhamade (Shivpuri) :

A group of temples of about 8th-10th century AD. *GAR*, 1922-23.

Kotgarh (Bilaspur) :

An old fort containing ruins of an older temple and bearing an inscription in one of its gates datable to 10th century AD. *CASIR*, VII, pp. 212-13; *CLAR*, p. 61; *BDG*, p. 273.

Kotwal (Morena) :

(a) Ancient mound of about 2nd-3rd century AD, yielding Nāga coins. Some scholars believe it to be the site of ancient Kāntipurī, one of the capitals of the Nāga rulers. *GAR*, 1914-23.

(b) Stone pillar on which exists an inscription dated in V.S. 1339. *GAR*, Sam. 1972, No. 24.

Kulon (Jabalpur) :

A large number of medieval sculptures found. *IAR*, 1960-61, p. 60.

Kulwar (Guna) :

Sati stone with inscription dated in V.S. 1329 (1272 AD), commemorating the committing of sati by two wives Kuvalayādevī and Kuntādevī of Kacchavāha prince named Sihadeva. The pillar is said to have been erected by Devapāladeva, brother of the deceased. *GAR*, 1927-28, p. 8.

Kumbhi (Jabalpur) :

Remains of several old temples, probably belonging to the Kalachuri period. *CLAR*, p. 28; *JDG*, p. 686.

Kunda (Jabalpur) :

(a) Flat-roofed temple of Gupta period. *Hiralal List* (1932), p. 45.

(b) Sculptures of 10th-12th century AD in the Kalachuri style found. *IAR*, 1959-60, p. 69.

(c) Memorial stone with undated inscription. *Hiralal List*, No. 77.

Kundalpur (Damoh) :

(a) A flat-roofed Gupta temple. *CASIR*, VII, p. 58; XXI, p. 167.

(b) Remains of a number of old temples. *CLAR*, p. 32.

Kundalpur (Shivpuri) :

(a) Ruins of an ancient gadhi, locally believed to be situated in Kuntalapura of Harivaṁśa, the birthplace of Rukminī, wife of Kṛṣṇa. *GAR*, 1922-23.

(b) Ruins of temple of about 10th century AD on the banks of a tank. *Ibid.*

(c) Temple of a Nāga god, of about 10th century AD with a large image of Nāga lying nearby. *Ibid.*

Kunwara (Raipur) :

Remains of old temples. *CLAR*, p. 51.

Kura (Raipur) :

Remains of buildings of Kalachuri period. *RDG*, pp. 550-51.

Kurwai (Bilaspur) :

An ancient brick-temple datable to about 6th-7th century AD. *CASIR*, VII, p. 196.

Lakhari (Guna) :

(a) Rectangular well near the temples, with an inscription dated in V.S. 1124 (1067 AD) referring to Mahārājādhirāja Abhyadeva and princes Chandrāditya and Jalhanadeva. *GAR*, 1924-25, p. 14.

(b) A temple, locally called as Maḍh to the east of the village datable to about 11th-12th century AD. *Ibid.*

Lal-Pahad (Rewa) :

A pillar or altar scratched on rock having Kalachuri inscription of Narasiṁhadeva dated in K.E. 909 (1155 AD). *HTM*, p. 109, pl. LIII b; *CASIR*, IX, pp. 1-2.

Lalvadi (Betul) :

Ancient cave, 6 km to the north of Bhopali. *MPR*, p. 109, pl. 53-b.

Lanji (Balaghat) :

Pillar with inscription of Yādava Rāmanāyaka, the ruler of Devagiri. *Hiralal List*, No. 28.

Lown (Raipur) :

Modern temple built out of the remains of old temple. *CLAR*, p. 51.

Madankhedi (Guna) :

Ruins of a temple of about 11th-12th century AD. *GAR*, 1918-19.

Madanpur (Sagar) :

(a) Ruins of Kalachuri temples. *PRASIWC*, 1894, p. 7.

(b) Ruins of six old temples. *CLAR*, p. 35.

Made Devara (Jabalpur) :

Ten temples (one in dilapidated condition) datable to later Gupta period discovered in a jungle close to the village. *IAR*, 1988-89, pp. 39-40.

Madhia (Jabalpur) :

Flat-roofed temple of Gupta period. *IAR*, 1968-69.

Madhogarh :

Old sculptures over the doorway of the fort. *CASIR*, XIII, p. 1.

Maheshwar (West Nimar) :

(a) Ancient mound called Navda-Ki-Todi, where archaeological excavations were conducted. *MAR*, 1949-50; *EMN*; *CN*; *WNDG*, pp. 453-54.

(b) Ancient-mound in the area called 'Mandal-Kho' with bricks, pottery etc. datable to about 3rd century BC. *MAR*, 1949-50.

(c) A cave locally known as *'Bhartihari-Gupha'* enshrining sculptures of Paramāra age. *EMN*, p. 17.

(d) A few Brahmanical images discovered during clearance work at a village in Maheshwar tehsil. *IAR*, 1984-86, p. 112.

Mahori (Rewa) :

Sati pillars, one having the date Sam. 1421. *CASIR*, XIII, p. 3.

Mahuvan (Guna) :

A group of two sati stones, one with inscription dated in V.S. 1443 (1386 AD). *GAR*, 1925-26, pp. 9, 20-21.

Maihar (Satna) :

(a) Remains of Kalachuri sculptures found. *ARASI*, 1922-23, pl. XLC.

(b) Remains of a temple on the top of nearby hill range. *HTM*, p. 77.

Majhgawan (Jabalpur) :

(a) Two sati pillars with inscriptions dated V.S. 1246 and 1290. *Hiralal List*, No. 78.

(b) Image with inscription referring to a Pāśupatāchārya. *Hiralal List*, No. 69.

(c) Ruins of ancient temples. *JDG*, p. 687.

Majholi (Rewa) :

Ruins of temples of about 10th century AD. *CASIR*, XIII, p. 15.

Makanganj (Mandsaur) :

Ancient well repaired later. *GAR*, 1929-30, p. 20.

Makhwa (Shivpuri) :

A group of four sati stones, one with inscription dated in V.S. 1356 (1299 AD) referring to one Kalpana, son of Palhana. *GAR*, 1922-23.

Makla (Ujjain) :

Brahmanical sculptures noticed near Śiva temple. *IAR*, 1985-86, p. 112.

Makni (Dhar) :

Ancient mound yielding bricks, pottery etc. *MAR*, 1949-50.

Makundpur (Rewa) :

Remains of Hindu temple. *CASIR*, XIII, pp. 3-4.

Malhar (Bilaspur) :

(a) A Gupta sculpture showing a mother-and-child. *IAR*, 1962-63, p. 68.

(b) Remains of two temples of Kalachuri period. *CASIR*, VII, p. 204.

(c) Pillar with inscription in *Siddhamatṛkā* script of about 8th cent. AD. *IAR*, 1964-65, p. 56.

Mamon (Guna) :

(a) Ruins of a group of temples of about 10th-12th century AD to the north of the old site of the village. *GAR*, 1925-26, p. 10.

(b) Ruins of a group of temples of about 10th-12th century AD to the south of the old site of the village. *GAR*, 1925-26, p. 10.

(c) Two broken memorial pillars with damaged inscriptions, one dated in V.S. 1351 (1294 AD) and the other with date illegible but referring to Kīrasiṁha and Vīradeva. *GAR*, 1925-26, pp. 21, 25.

Mandhata (East Nimar) :

(a) Medieval statues of Brahmanical gods and goddesses discovered. *IAR*, 1961-62, p. 99.

(b) Ancient temples. *CLAR*, pp. 40-41.

Mandsaur (Mandsaur) :

(a) Ancient mound of about 5th century AD with ring-wells and yielding pottery and large-size bricks. *GAR*, 1946-47.

(b) Ruins of ancient temples in the fort area. *GAR*, 1922-23 and 1916-17.

(c) A pillar with inscription of V.S. 1283. *GAR*, Sam. 1975, No. 43.

(d) Stone sculptures of Brahmanical and Jaina faith of c. 11th cent. AD kept in the open-air museum identified. *IAR*, 1985-86, p. 111.

Mandsaur District :

Rich sculptures of 10th-11th century AD found at the sites of Bhanpura, Nevli, Kethuli, Taksakeswar, Hinglajgarh, Chainpur etc. *IAR*, 1954-55, p. 62.

Mandu Fort (Dhar) :

(a) Remains of a temple of about 10th century AD on a mound near Lohani gate. Yazdani, *Dhar and Mandu*, pp. 122-23.

(b) Old tank of about 10th century AD locally called Munja tank, built and named after the Paramāra king Muñja. Yazdani, *Dhar and Mandu*, pp. 6, 68.

(c) Monolithic pillar of about 10th century AD, 16' in height on a mound near Lohani gate, the crowning member is lost. Yazdani, *Dhar and Mandu*, p. 122.

(d) Gate of about 13th-14th century AD locally called Bhangi Darwaza. Yazdani, *Dhar and Mandu*, p. 41.

(e) Hindu carvings of about 12th century AD near Lohani Darwaza, originally built by the Paramāras of Malwa. Yazdani, *Dhar and Mandu*, p. 121.

(f) The Rampal Darwaza, originally built by the Paramāras of Malwa in 12th century AD. Yazdani, *Dhar and Mandu*, p. 121.

(g) Remains of a temple and a well near 'Sant Kothri'. *Ibid.*, p. 123.

Manipur (Bilaspur) :

Remains of old temples. *CLAR*, p. 61.

Maniya Garh (Chhatarpur) :

An ancient Chandella fort. *CASIR*, XXI, p. 69.

Marai (Rewa) :

Peculiar pillars of Kalachuri period found. *HTM*, pp. 95-98, pl. XXXVII, a-b.

Marhpiparia (Sagar) :

A number of well-preserved sculptures found. *IAR*, 1961-62, p. 100.

Masaun (Rewa) :

(a) Ruins of a circular-type Kalachuri temple. *HTM*, pp. 45-46, pl. VI, a-b.

(b) Foundains of two temples. *HTM*, p. 44.

Maser (Vidisha) :

Ruins of an ancient temple of about 11th century AD. *GAR*, 1930-31, p. 8.

Mayapur (Shivpuri) :

Remains of an old temple with an inscription dated in Sam. 1297 (1240 AD) found. *CASIR*, II, p. 302.

Mehsana (Rewa) :

Early medieval Brahmanical temples found. *IAR*, 1960-61, p. 62.

Mitaoli (Morena) :

Ruins of an old temple datable to about 11th-12th century AD. *GAR*, 1918-19.

Modi (Mandsaur) :

Ruins of a group of three temples of about 13th century AD. *ISG*, p. 43.

Mohanpur (Vidisha) :

Ruins of an old temple of about 10th-12th century AD. *GAR*, 1920-21.

Mohna (Gwalior) :

A group of three sati memorials of which one contains an inscription dated in V.S. 1462. *GAR*, 1923-24, p. 12.

Morena District :

(a) Medieval Brahmanical sculptures, sati-pillars, Jaina sculptures and historical pottery found in course of exploration conducted by Shri K.S. Bhadoria of the ASI in the following villages :

Aisaha, Arron, Bawadipura, Bhakroli, Bhirosa, Bhonpura, Budhara, Chapak, Dharmgarh, Dondri, Garhi Durgadas, Ikhera, Jotai, Kamtari, Kandauli, Katelhakapura, Kicoola, Kirranch, Kontharkalan, Kudona, Kukthari, Karetha, Mahua, Mai, Mehdora, Nunhera, Orethe, Purawaskalan, Rached, Ritwari, Ruariya, Rupehati, Sangoli, Senthra-Ahir, Senthra-Badhai, Sihoniya, Sikrodi, Thara, Tutwas. *IAR*, 1979-80, p. 44.

(b) In course of debris clearance at Dubkund, Jaina sculptures of Tirthankaras, Ambika etc. and Śaiva sculptures datable to c. 9th-10th cent. AD discovered. *IAR*, 1987-88, pp. 138-39.

Norwan (Mandsaur) :

Ruins of an old temple of about 11th-12th century AD. *GAR*, 1929-30, pp. 20-21.

Motalsir (Raisen) :

Ruins of two temples of Pratihāra period noticed. *IAR*, 1986-87, p. 119.

Mukhwasa (Shivpuri) :

A group of four sati pillars, of which one contains an inscription in V.S., 1356, referring to Kalhana, son of Palhana. *GAR*, 1922-23.

Nachna (Panna) :

(a) Two temples and a mosque constructed out of the material from the existing Gupta shrines of the area noticed at the south of the village. *IAR*, 1962-63, p. 69.

(b) Further south, at a distance of about 3 km, Gupta and post-Gupta pillars, a Chaturmukhaliṅga and a door-frame with mātṛkas and other deities found within the old Lakhura fort. *IAR*, 1962-63, p. 69.

Nagda (Dewas) :

(a) Old sculptures fixed in the temple of Sitala Mata. *MAR*, 1949-50.

(b) Ancient mound of about 2nd-3rd century BC to the south-west of the village, yielding pottery and brickbats. Punch-marked coins also discovered from the mound. The local belief is that the snake sacrifice of king Janamejaya of Mahābhārata was performed at this place. *MAR*, 1949-50.

(c) Excavations of the above-mentioned mound carried out. *IAR*, 1955-56; *NER*.

Nagjhiri (Betul) :

Ancient cave, about 8 km to the south of Betul. *MPR*, p. 92.

Nala (Damoh) :

A number of sculptures of c. 10th-12th century AD (Chandella-Kalachuri period) located at. *IAR*, 1971-72, p. 27.

Nand Chand (Jabalpur) :

(a) Ruins of more than fifteen temples, possibly belonging to the Kalachuri period. *CASIR*, XXI, p. 161.

(b) Ruins of two toraṇas (gateways). *CASIR*, XXI, p. 161; *CLAR*, p. 29.

Nanhwara (Jabalpur) :

Kalachuri sculptures. *ARASI*, 1930-34, pl. LXXVI, b-c.

Naresar (Gwalior) :

(a) A group of two temples datable to about 8th-10th century AD. *GAR*, 1947-48.

(b) A group of four temples datable to about 8th-10th century AD. *GAR*, 1947-48.

(c) Gateway with stone post having inscription dated in V.S. 1316 (1259 AD), referring to one Vastupāladeva and to the village Naleshwar. *GAR*, 1924-13.

Narsimhapur (Narsimhapur) :

Archictectural and sculptural pieces preserved in the public garden. *CLAR*, p. 43.

Narwar (Shivpuri) :

A step-well in a field, a mile to the north-east of the town with an inscription dated in V.S. 1341 (1284 AD), recording its construction by a bania named Rāma of Bansala *gotra* of the village Sevayika during the reign of Mahārāja Gopāladeva. *GAR*, 1937-38, pp. 12-39.

Narwar Fort (Shivpuri) :

(a) An old tank of about 11th-12th century AD, square and enclosed by massive retaining walls lined with steps, locally believed to have been constructed by legendary Makaradhvaja. *DFGS*, p. 84.

(b) An ancient well with an inscription dated V.S. 1338 (1281 AD) referring to its construction by one kāyastha Āśāditya of Chāhaḍa of Nalapura. The inscription is presently preserved in Gwalior Museum. *GAR*, 1927-28, pp. 40-41.

(c) An ancient well with an inscription dated in V.S. 1339 (1282 AD), recording its construction by one Gaṅgadeva in the reign of Jajjapella Gopāladeva of Nalagiri. The inscription is now in Gwalior Museum. *GAR*, 1914-15.

Navli (Mandsaur) :

Numerous antiquities found. *IAR*, 1954-55, p. 62.

Navagaon (Raipur) :

Two stone temples and two brick temples built of material from Arang. *CASIR*, XVII, p. 22; *CLAR*, p. 52.

Navagarh (Durg) :

Ancient temple said to have been constructed in Samvat 704 (647 AD) as per an inscription available in it. *DDG*, p. 453.

Nemawar (Dewas) :

An incomplete temple on a hillock. Locally it is believed that the Siddheśvara temple was to be originally built here, but was left incomplete. *ARASIWC*, 1921, p. 98.

Nilagarh (Raisen) :

Ruins of a large temple of the Paramāras discovered amidst forest. *IAR*, 1986-87, p. 120.

Nilakanthi (Chindwara) :

A pillar, which seems to be a component of a temple, with an inscription which refers to Rāṣṭrakūṭa Kṛṣṇa-III. *Hiralal List*, No. 169.

Nimar District :

An image with an inscription dated. V.S. 1149. *IAR*, 1961-62, p. 81.

Nimthur (Mandsaur) :

A step-well with sculptures of Bhairava, Varāha, Trimurtī etc. built in its walls. *GAR*, 1917-18.

Niwas (Mandla) :

A sarvatobhadrikā image found and preserved in State Museum, Mandla. *PP*, XI (1983), pp. 185-90, pl. 58-61.

Pachaoli (Shivpuri) :

Ruins of two old temples. *GAR*, 1922-23.

Pachrai (Shivpuri) :

(a) A number of sati stones with inscriptions dated in V.S. 1319 (1262 AD); V.S. 1339 (1282 AD); V.S. 1345 (1288 AD); V.S. 1362 (1305 AD); V.S. 1374 (1317 AD); V.S. 1388 (1321 AD) and V.S. 137 (?) etc. *GAR*, 1929-30, p. 61; 1914-15.

(b) A group of old temples and a well. *GAR*, 1914-15.

Padampur (Bilaspur) :

Sati stone on which an inscription dated V.S. 1403 is inscribed. *Hiralal List*, No. 231.

Padhavali (Morena) :

(a) Temple of about 10th century AD with an image of Kubera in the shrine. *GAR*, 1914-15.

(b) A group of four temples of about 10th century AD with flat roofs. *GAR*, 1922-23.

(c) A group of three temples of about 10th century AD to the south of the village. *GAR*, 1922-23.

(d) Ruins of a temple of about 10th century AD in the Batesvara valley. *GAR*, 1915-16.

(e) Ruins of seven temples of about 10th century AD locally called Satmadhi, in the Batesvara valley. *Ibid.*

(f) Ruins of a group of four temples of about 10th century AD in the Batesvara valley. *Ibid.*

(g) An ancient well, locally called *Chhau Kua*, datable to about 9th century AD and a temple close by. *AG*, p. 113.

(h) Two ancient wells in the Batesvara valley. *GAR*, 1929-30, p. 31.

(i) Sculptures in the wall of the old tank in the Batesvara valley. *AG*, p. 113.

(j) Two memorial pillars of about 5th-6th century AD with sculptured panels and illegible inscriptions in Gupta characters. *GAR*, 1929-30, p. 33.

Pahargaon (Chhatarpur) :

Late medieval shrine discovered. *IAR*, 1961-62, p. 98.

Pahado Bujrug (Gwalior) :

A flat-roofed temple. *GAR*, pp, 1918-19.

Pala (Balaghat) :

An old small temple. *CLAR*, p. 26.

Palari (Raipur) :

Ancient brick temple on the bank of a tank called Bal Samudra. *RDG*, p. 555.

Pali (Sagar) :

An inscription dated V.S. 1162 in Mahadeo temple. *Hiralal List*, No. 94.

Pali (Shivpuri) :

(a) Ruins of a temple with richly carved door-frames and sculptures. *GAR*, 1918-19.

(b) Ruins of three temples in a group. *Ibid.*

Panna (Panna) :

Some interesting *gaṇa* figures. *Lalit Kala,* No. 10, Oct. 1961, pp. 22-24.

Papet (Sagar) :

A number of well-preserved sculptures found. Amongst them the life size figure of mother *Nagi* in *varada mudrā* is particularly interesting. *IAR,* 1961-62, p. 100.

Para (Bhind) :

Remains of temples and sculptures of medieval period found. *IAR,* 1962-63, p. 68.

Paroli (Morena) :

(a) A group of four temples with loose sculptures lying about. *GAR,* 1915-16; CASIR, XX, p. 105.

(b) Sugarcane press with inscription. *GAR,* 1915-16.

Parsora (Vidisha) :

Gupta and post-Gupta shrines found. *IAR,* 1958-59, p. 71.

Patan (Rajgarh) :

Some sati pillars with inscriptions. *CIGS,* p. 169.

Patan (Jabalpur) :

(a) Sculptures of 10th-12th centuries in the Kalachuri style found. *IAR,* 1959-60, p. 69.

(b) Sati stone with an inscription dated V.S. 1361 mentioning Rājaputra Vāghadeva. *EI,* XXVI, p. 11; *Hiralal List,* No. 78; *Bhandarkar List,* No. 653.

Pathapur (Chhatarpur) :

Remains of an early temple discovered. *IAR,* 1961-62, p. 98.

Pathari (Vidisha) :

A monolithic pillar of about 40' in height locally called Bhīmagajā, with an inscription recording its erection during the reign of Rāṣṭrakūṭa king Parabala, in front of a temple of Śauri (i.e., Kṛṣṇa) and dated in V.S. 917 (860 AD). *GAR,* 1923-24, p. 10; *JASB,* XVII (I), p. 305; *CASIR,* X, 70; VII, p. 67; *EI,* IX, p. 252; *IA,* XL, p. 239; *ASIAR,* XVIII, p. 116; *PRASIWC,* XVIII, p. 22; *Bhandarkar List,* No. 29.

Pawai (Bhind) :

Remains of temples and sculptures of medieval period found. *IAR*, 1962-63, p. 68.

Pawaya (Gwalior) :

(a) Remains of a brick-built structure of about 3rd-5th cent. AD with three terraces placed receding one above the other, with terracotta sculptures and an image of Viṣṇu discovered in excavations. *GAR*, 1940-41, pp. 17-20.

Pawaya is identified with ancient Padmāvatī, one of the capitals of the Nāgas; see Garde, M.B., *Padmavati* (Gwalior, 1952). Also *Madhya Bharata ka Itihasa* (in Hindi) by H.N. Dwivedi, pp. 600 ff. and *M.P. District Gazetteer, Gwalior* (Bhopal, 1965), pp. 373-74; *ARASI*, 1915-16, pp. 101-09, pls. 55-58.

(b) Life size statue of Yakṣa Maṇibhadra with a Brāhmī inscription of about 1st century AD. Garde, *Padmavati*; *GDG*, p. 373.

(c) Miscellaneous finds including the statue of a Nāga king, a palm capital, a large carved fragment of a huge gateway lintel. Garde, *Padmavati*; *GDG*, p. 373.

(d) Ancient mounds datable to about 2nd-3rd century AD to the south and west of the village, yielding pottery and Nāga coins. *MAR*, 1947-48.

(e) Ancient mound to the south of the village, locally called Badila Tila, datable to about 2nd-3rd century AD with traces of brick-built structures found in a trial pit. *GAR*, 1942-46, p. 15.

Pipadi (Bhind) :

Ruins of a group of temples of about 10th century AD on the bank of tank. *GAR*, 1928-29, p. 27.

Piparghar (Shivpuri) :

A group of temples and six sati memorials, *GAR*, 1914-15.

Piparia (Raisen) :

A flat-roofed Gupta temple found. *IAR*, 1967-68, p. 67.

Piparia (Jabalpur) :

(a) Images of Brahmanical gods and goddesses found. *IAR*, 1962-63, p. 68.

(b) A large temple of Kalachuri period found. *IAR*, 1958-59, p. 72.

(c) Sculptures of 10th-12th century AD in the Kalachuri style found. *IAR*, 1959-60, p. 69.

Piparia (Damoh) :

Stone pillar with an inscription recording war between Rāṣṭrakūṭa Mahāmāṇḍalika Rāṇaka Jayatasiṁha and Hemasiṁha. *Hiralal List*, No. 98.

Piparseva (Morena) :

Ruins of a temple of early date. *GAR*, 1915-16.

Pipla (Ujjain) :

Sati stone with inscription dated in V.S. 1395 (1338 AD) mentioning the name of the village as Piplu. *GAR*, 1915-16.

Pipria (Shivpuri) :

Ruins of an old temple with sculptures of Trimurtī etc. lying at the site. *GAR*, 1923-24, p. 15.

Pura Gilana (Mandsaur) :

An image with dateless inscription. *PRASIWC*, XIX, pp. 25, 81.

Radev (Shivpuri) :

Sati pillar with inscription dated V.S. 1497. *GAR*, Sam. 1992, No. 38.

Rai (Budhi) (Shivpuri) :

Sati stone in the temple of Bhairava with an inscription dated in V.S. 1327 (1270 AD) referring to Yagva(jva)pāla Āsalladeva. *GAR*, 1916-17.

Raibor (Hoshangabad) :

Medieval sculptures discovered. *IAR*, 1961-62, p. 99.

Raipur (Raipur) :

Numerous old sculptures preserved. *CLAR*, p. 48.

Raipur District :

Sati pillars and mithuna figures of 14th-15th century AD found at Barpader and a terracotta bull of early medieval period found at Suabahra in course of exploration. *IAR*, 1979-80, p. 44.

Raisen District :

(a) During the course of exploration Narayan Vyas of the ASI brought to light the following sites with stupas; Śuṅga, Gupta, Paramāra and medieval temple ruins and Brahmanical sculptures:

Bari, Barikhurd, Chaukigarh, Ambari, Anori, Balarkho, Balori, Barkheritunda Colony, Besar, Bhanwarkheri, Bhartipur, Binjorikhera, Bhagwanpura, Biskhera, Chirholi, Dargawan, & Dhakna, Eran, Firozpur, Fatehpur-Marmata, Gulgaon, Kachnarya, Khabai, Khamkhera, Kharetia, Khemkheri, Kulharia, Manchi, Mandha, Mandwai, Mehgaon, Mendori, Mundiakhera, Murelkhurd, Murlikheri, Mushkabad, Nagori, Naroda, Nimkhera, Pagnesar, Ratanpur, Ratalalai, Sakasen, Salamatpur, Sanchi, Sarchampa, Satdhara, Semra, Shahpur, Suakheri, Tajalpur, Tigra, Uncher. *IAR*, 1978-79, pp. 13-15.

(b) The following historical sites found in course of exploration: stupa and remains of vihāras belonging to 2nd-1st century BC at Bidpur and Patandeo, sculptures of Śuṅga period, notable being a bell capital, yakṣa and railing bearing inscription in Brāhmī characters at Bera, sculpture of Balarāma belonging to c. 4th century AD at Mehagaon and medieval sculptures at Bhagwanpura colony. *IAR*, 1979-80, p. 46.

(c) Historical mounds, Brahmanical sculptures, sati pillars and ruins of medieval structures noticed at Berkhedi, Dhanora, Gahukhedi, Katsara, Sothis, Tilakhedi and Veerajpur. *IAR*, 1985-86, pp. 55-56.

Rajgarh (Chhatarpur) :

Early medieval sculptures discovered. *IAR*, 1961-62, p. 98.

Rajgarh (Rajgarh) :

Medieval sculptures of ten-armed Gaṇeśa, eight-armed dancing Bhairava, two aśvinikumāras and a fragmentary *aṣṭadhātu* panel noticed. *IAR*, 1987-88, p. 139.

Rakhetra (Guna) :

Remains of an ancient temple. *GAR*, 1924-25, pp.16, 38.

Rajor (Dewas) :

Ruins of an old temple. *HMIM*.

Ramgarh Hill (Sarguja) :

(a) Jogimārā cave with an inscription in Aśokan Brāhmī character. *CASIR*, XIII, pp. 40-41; *ASIAR*, III, pp. 123-31, p. 43.

(b) An old cave locally known as Sītā Bengrā, containng inscription in Aśokan Brāhmī character. *CASIR*, XIII, pp. 39-40.

Rampur (Satna) :

Sati pillar containing inscription of the queens of Mahārājā Vīrarājadeva (?) dated in V.S. 1404. *CASIR*, IX, p. 34; *Bhandarkar List,* No. 705.

Rampura (Mandsaur) :

Medieval sculptures of Paramāra period noticed. *IAR*, 1985-86, p. 111.

Raneh (Damoh) :

Remains of an old temple, probably datable to Chandella period. *CLAR*, p. 33.

Ranod (Shivpuri) :

An ancient image of Nāga. *MPS*, p. 33.

Ratangarh (Mandsaur) :

Sati-stone with inscription dated in V.S. 1142 (1085 AD) referring to a woman Gaṅgā. *IAR*, 1922-23.

Ratanpur (Bilaspur) :

(a) Pillars and sculptures of Kalachuri temples datable to about 11th-12th century AD utilised in the adornment of the gates and parts of the palace in the fort of medieval period existing at this place. *CASIR*, VII, pp. 214-26; *PRASIWC*, 1904, pp. 31-32; *CLAR*, p. 62; *BDG*, p. 269.

(b) A number of sati memorials. *EDG*, p. 289.

(c) A stone image of twenty-armed Rāvaṇa datable to c. 13th cent. AD noticed. *IAR*, 1986-87, p. 118.

Repura (Bhind) :

Remains of temples and sculptures of medieval period found. *IAR*, 1962-63, p. 68.

Rewa District :

Brahmanical sculptures with ruins of temples and forts along with historical mounds yielding Gupta pottery noticed at seven villages in Teonthar tehsil in course of village-to-village survey of the ASI. *IAR*, 1985-86, p. 55.

Rithora (Morena) :

(a) Four memorial pillars datable to about 8th-9th century AD. *GAR*, 1925-26, p. 9.

(b) A memorial pillar to the west of the above-mentioned pillars. *Ibid.*

Rond (Jabalpur) :

Flat-roofed Gupta temple. *Damoha Dipaka* by Hiralal (2nd Edn.), p. 104.

Rupnath (Jabalpur) :

Lakṣman-kund near which the Edict of Aśoka is inscribed on a large stone. A vent in the rock close by enshrines a small liṅgam. *CASIR*, VII, p. 59; IX, p. 38; *CLAR*, p. 29.

Sagor (Dhar) :

(a) Ancient mound with sculptures scattered about. *GAR*, 1916-17.

(b) Pillars and sati stones with illegible inscriptions. *Ibid.*

Sahaspur (Durg):

An image, locally known as Sahasrabāhu or that of Sahasrājuna bearing the inscription of Yaśorāja dated in Kalachuri Era 934 (1182 AD). *CASIR*, XVII, pp. 42-45, pl. XXIII; *CII*, IV, pt. II, pp. 595-96; *CLAR*, p. 54.

Sakarra (Guna) :

(a) Ancient tank of about 11th century AD to the west of the village. *GAR*, 1927-28, p. 9.

(b) Three temples datable to about 11th century AD on the western and northern banks of an old tank, with a number of sculptures. *GAR*, 1927-28, p. 10.

(c) A sati stone behind the temples, datable to about 10th-11th century AD. *GAR*, 1927-28, p. 10.

(d) A group of four sati stones near Mata's temple to the east of village, each bearing an inscription dated in V.S. 1304 (1247 AD). *GAR*, 1927-28, pp. 11-39.

(e) A group of eight sati stones near Mata's temple with illegible inscriptions dated in V.S. 1237, 1281, 128 (?), 1341, 1342, 1375, and 1377. *Ibid.*

(f) A group of three sati stones near a temple with inscriptions dated in V.S. 1342, 1375 and 1397. *Ibid.*

(g) A sati stone near a temple with an inscription dated in V.S. 1400. *Ibid.*

(h) A sati stone near a temple wih an inscription dated in V.S. 1501. *Ibid.*

(i) A memorial pillar on the north bank of tank with three sculptured panels, datable to about 10th-11th century AD. *GAR*, 1927-28, p. 10.

Sakaur (Damoh) :

Flat-roofed Gupta temple at, having a pilgrim record of Sam. 1361 (AD 1304). *Damoh Dipak* by Hiralal (2nd Edn.), pp. 107-08; *Hiralal List*, No. 119; *CLAR*, p. 33.

Salaiya (Damoh) :

Sati stone bearing inscription of V.S. 1362 referring to Pratihāra Mahārājaputra Vāghadeva. *EI*, XVI, p. 11; *Bhandarkar List*, No. 656. *Hiralal List*, No. 101.

Salkhan (Bilaspur) :

A hoard comprising five bronze images, two metal pots, 4 bells and 3 metal lamps found and preserved in different museums. *DP*, p. 13; *Pragati* (Nagpur), March-April, 1956, pp. 99-100, pl. 1, 3.

Salmania (Shivpuri) :

(a) A temple of about 12th-13th century AD built on a platform. Rich carvings on walls and pillars. *GAR*, 1935-36, pp. 13, 14.

(b) Sati stones near the temple. *GAR*, 1935-36, p. 27.

Samantukhedi (Morena) :

(a) Ruins of two temples of about 9th-10th century AD scattered about in the Chambal ravines. *GAR*, 1940-41, p. 22.

(b) Ancient mound of about 5th century AD yielding large sized bricks datable to Gupta period. *GAR*, 1940-41, p. 22.

Sanchi (Raisen) :

(a) Fragmentary sculptures from the gateways of the Stūpa, I, II and III preserved in the museum. *Catalogue of the Museum of Archaeology at Sanchi*, by John Marshall and others (1922), pp. 20-29, 37-38.

(b) Sculptures of (1) the Early school, (2) Kuṣāṇa and Gupta schools and (3) of later medieval period preserved in the museum. *Ibid.*, pp. 28-36, 38-42.

(c) Sculptures and minor antiquities discovered from: (1) gateways of Stūpa I, (2) gateways of Stūpa III, (3) railing of Stūpa II, (4) around and about Stūpa I, (5) near Temple 18, (6) west of Monastery 47,(7) inside Monastery 47, (8) near about temple 45, (9) near about Stūpa 2. *Ibid.*, pp. 65-73.

(d) Miscellaneous antiquities preserved in the museum, comprising (1) iron objects, (2) monastic and household utensils, (3) agricultural implements, (4) artisans tools, (5) household fittings, (6) bronze objects, (7) copper objects, (8) early glazed pottery, (9) miscellaneous pottery of the Gupta and the medieval periods, (10) terracottas, (11) terracotta plaque and (12) other miscellaneous objects. *Ibid.*, pp. 43-59.

(e) Fragmentary pillars, door jambs and other architectural pieces datable between Gupta and late medieval periods preserved. *Ibid.*, pp. 14-17; *ASIAR*, 1913-14, p. 20.

(f) Mauryan sculptures preserved in the museum. *Ibid.*, pp. 19-20; *ASIAR*, XIII, pp. 18, 20.

Sandhara (Mandsaur) :

Sculptures datable to about 11-12th century AD found. *IAR*, 1965-66, p. 81.

Sandor (Guna) :

A memorial pillar with inscription dated in V.S. 1072 (1015 AD). *GAR*, 1918-19.

Sarangpur (Rajgarh) :

A four-handed image of Brahmā datable to about 10th-11th century AD discovered. *IAR*, 1964-65, p. 74.

Satanwada (Gwalior) :

(a) Memorial pillar, half buried in earth to the west of the village. *GAR*, 1923-24, p. 14.

(b) A memorial pillar with sculptured panel to the north-west of the village. *Ibid.*

(c) Ancient well datable to c. 11th century AD. *GAR*, 1923-24, p. 14.

(d) Four sati stones to the south-west of the village. *Ibid.*, pp. 25-28.

(e) Remains of an ancient temple near Viṣṇu temple. *Ibid.*, p. 14.

(f) Sati stone with inscription dated V.S. 1016. *CASIR*, VII, p. 94.

Satna (Satna) :

Remains of Kalachuri period. *ASIAR*, 1925-26, pl. LIX a-b.

Saugor (Sagar) :

A number of Kalachuri sculptures built up into a small imitation kiosks in the four corners of the garden of Artillery mess-house. *SDG*, p. 546; *CII*, IV, pt. I, p. 174; *CLAR*, p. 34.

Sehore (Sehore) :

A few Brahmanical sculptures noticed on the outskirts of the city. *IAR*, 1985-

86, p. 111.

Sendhwa (Nimar) :

A temple of about 11th-12th century AD. *GAR*, 1914-15.

Sesai (Shivpuri) :

(a) A memorial pillar datable to about 6th-7th century AD with inscription recording the self-immolation of a mother sorrowing for her two sons who were killed in battle. *GAR*, 1929-30, pp. 26, 63.

(b) Two sati-stones with illegible inscriptions. *GAR*, 1929-30, pp. 26, 63.

Sewai (Gwalior) :

(a) Remains of a temple comprising sculptures datable to about 10th-12th century AD scattered on a hillock and some placed on a platform to the east of the village. *GAR*, 1933-34, p. 14.

(b) Sati-stones with illegible inscriptions. *Ibid.*

Sheorinarayan (Bilaspur) :

Statue of a male person in a small shrine in the courtyard of the temple of Narayana bearing an inscription dated in (K.) E. 898. *CASIR*, VII, p. 197; *CII*, IV, pt. II, p. 582; *Asiatic Researches*, Vol. *XV*, pp. 505-06; *PRASIWC*, 1903-04, p. 53; *Hiralal List*, p. 132.

Shukalpura (Bhind) :

Remains of temples and sculptures of medieval period found. *IAR*, 1962-63, p. 68.

Sihawa (Raipur) :

(a) Remains of six old temples. *CLAR*, p. 54.

(b) Remains of a Kalachuri temple. *CASIR*, VII, pp. 145-46.

Silbara Khurd (Guna) :

Remains of an old temple comprising sculptures, carved fragments etc. *GAR*, 1936-37, pp. 10, 25.

Simga (Raipur) :

Old sati pillars discovered. *CASIR*, XVII, p. 33; *CLAR*, p. 55.

Simra (Jabalpur) :

(a) Ruins of four Kalachuri temples to the east of the village. *CASIR*, XXI, p. 159; *JDG*, p. 692; *CLAR*, p. 29.

(b) Remains of a fifth temple on the embankment of the Great Tank, with Śaivite and Vaiṣṇavite sculptures. *Ibid.*

(c) Sati memorial bearing record dated in V.S. 1355 (1298 AD). *CASIR*, XXI, p. 101.

Singorgarh (Damoh) :

(a) A fort with memorial pillar dtd. Sam. 1364 (1307 AD). *CASIR*, IX, pp. 49-54.

(b) Sati stone bearing dates in V.S. 1357, 1363 and 1366. *Ibid.*

Siroha (Shivpuri) :

Ancient well datable to c. 10th-12th cent. AD. *GAR*, 1925-26, p. 8.

Sirpat (Bilaspur) :

Sati pillar bearing inscription of V.S. 1401. *Hiralal List*, No. 231.

Sirpur (Raipur) :

(a) Ruins of an unusual temple datable to about 5th-6th century AD dedicated to Indra. *CASIR*, VIII, p. 176.

(b) Remains of a group of old temples. *CASIR*, VII, p. 172.

Sodhangha (Ujjain) :

Broken elephant capital of Aśokan pillar found. *Puratattva*, Vol. II, p. 65.

Sohagpur (Shahdol) :

Interesting reliefs datable to Kalachuri period preserved in the palace of Thakur. *HTM*, pp. 100-06, pl. XLVA; XLII, B.; XLIII; XLIV.

Sohagpur (Hoshangabad) :

(a) A colossal statue found. *ČLAR*, p. 42.

(b) Sati stone with illegible inscription. *Hiralal List*, No. 135.

Sondhni (Mandsaur) :

(a) Two victory pillars, monolithic, 40' in length and 3½' in section in broken condition, recording their erection by king Yaśodharman of Malwa in commemoration of his victory over the Hūṇa ruler Mihirakula. *AG*, 104; *GAR*, 1925-26, p. 5; Fleet, *CII*, III, pp. 142-46; *Dasapura Janapada Sanskriti* (Mandsaur, 1962), pp. 1-264.

(b) An ancient tank, locally called Bhairava Kuṇḍa. *GAR*, 1914-23.

Sonkach (Ujjain) :

A pillar in the market-place with an illegible inscription. *GAR*, 1917-18.

Sorar (Durg) :

(a) Remains of a Kalachuri temple. *CASIR*, VII, p. 137; *CLAR*, p. 56.

(b) A pillar with illegible inscription. *Hiralal List*, No. 236; *DDG*.

Suhania (Morena) :

(a) A stone pillar datable to about 11th century AD. *AG*, p. 125.

(b) A pillar near a modern *madhi* on the slope of the hill. *GAR*, 1929-30, p. 17.

(c) A memorial pillar datable to about 11th century AD. *GAR*, 1929-30, p. 17.

(d) Wells datable to about 10th-11th century AD. *GAR*, 1929-30, p. 18.

(e) A pillar (Jaina) sculptured over on its four sides, datable to about 10th century AD. *GAR*, 1929-30, p. 16.

(f) A stone slab inscribed with numeral figures from 1 to 14, datable to about 5th-6th century AD. *CASIR*, II, p. 401.

Sukulgaon (Rewa) :

Ruins of an old temple noticed. *CASIR*, XIII, p. 3.

Sunaj (Shivpuri) :

(a) An old tank with a stone built dam, datable to about 13th-14th century AD. *GAR*, 1922-23.

(b) A sati stone with an inscription dated in V.S. 1313 (1256 AD). *Ibid.*

Supia (Rewa) :

Memorial pillar bearing inscription of Skandagupta dated in Gupta Era 141. *IAR*, 1959-60, p. 57.

Surwaya (Shivpuri) :

Ancient well with inscription of V.S. 1341. *GS*, p. 25; *Bhandarkar List*, No. 607.

Takshakeswar (Mandsaur) :

Numerous antiquities found. *IAR*, 1954-55, p. 62.

Talagaon (Bilaspur) :

(a) Plan of an early medieval temple on a raised *Jagati* having sanctum, pillared maṇḍapa was unearthed by the Directorate of Archaeology, M.P. Govt. at the temple complex of Jethani and Deorani. A life-size stone sculpture identified as that of Rudra Paśupati was also found along with some other Śākta sculptures which are datable to post-Gupta period. *IAR*, 1987-88, p. 137.

(b) A rare stone image of Naigamesha noticed around the Deorani temple. *IAR*, 1986-87, p. 118.

Tarnod (Mandsaur) :

Remains of a temple datable to about 11th-12th century AD scattered about the village. *GAR*, 1916-17.

Temra (Bastar) :

Sati stone bearing inscription of Chhindaka Nāga ruler Harischandradeva dated in S.E. 1246. *EI*, IX, pp. 39-40; *Hiralal List*, No. 165; *Bhandarkar List*, No. 1118.

Teonda (Vidisha) :

(a) A Gupta sculpture datable to 6th cent. AD discovered. *IAR*, 1986-87, p. 120.

(b) A memorial pillar of about 11th-12th cent. AD. *GAR*, 1932-33, p. 8.

Terahi (Shivpuri) :

(a) A *toraṇa* in front of the Mohaj Mata temple, with rich carvings, datable to about 10th-12th century AD. *GAR*, 1934-35, p. 7; *CASIR*, XXI, p. 177.

(b) A memorial pillar with an inscription dated in V.S. 960 (903 AD) probably recording the battle between Guṇarāja and Undabhaṭṭa, in which *koṭṭapāla* Chandiyana was killed. *GAR*, 1914-15.

(c) A memorial pillar to the south-west of the village, with four carved panels. *GAR*, 1927-28, p. 13.

(d) A group of four memorial pillars. *GAR*, 1914-15.

(e) A group of sati pillars. *Ibid.*

Tewar (Jabalpur) :

(a) Ruins of ancient Tripurī, the capital of the Kalachuris, presently known as the mounds of Karanbel, Hathiagarh, Karisuri, Chaugan etc., extending within an area of 4 square miles. *CASIR*, IX, pp. 54-77; XVII, p. 72; *CLAR*, p. 30; *PRASIWC*, 1894, p. 5; *HTM*, pp. 64-66; M.G. Dixit: *Tripuri*

(Excaation Report) : 1952; Sankalia, *Tripuri Excavations : 1966—A Brief Report.*

(b) A number of Gaṇeśa images found. *KV*, pp. 377-78.

(c) An image of sura-sundarī with elaborate headgear and heavy ornaments discovered. *IAR*, 1965-66, p. IV, 81.

(d) A beautiful image of Kārttikeya on the platform now known as the shrine of Kher Mai. *HTM*, p. 92, pl. XXXV, b.

(e) Ruins of a Kalachuri temple on the Karnbel mound near Tewar. *HTM*, p. 64.

(f) Remains of two Kalachuri temples on the Karanbel mound near Tewar. *HTM*, pp. 65-66, pl. XIX, a-b.

(g) Remains of two Kalachuri temples on Kari Suri mound noticed by Beglar in 1873-74, but presently missing. *CASIR*, IX, p. 59; *HTM*, pp. 64-65.

(h) Ruins of a stepped well datable to Kalachuri period. *HTM*, p. 66, pl. XXI, 6.

(i) A beautiful bas-relief of Kalachuri period kept on a platform now known as the Kher Mai. *HTM*, p. 92, pl. XXXIV, b.

(j) A sculpture representing Andhaka-vadha etc. of Kalachuri period found. *HTM*, p. 93, pl. XXXIV, a.

(k) A panel representing a scene of Gāthā Śaptasati now preserved in Rani Durgavati Museum, Jabalpur. *PE*.

Thana (Raisen) :

Medieval Brahmanical sculptures found. *IAR*, 1967-68, p. 67.

Thoban (Guna) :

Ruins of nine temples. *GAR*, 1914-15.

Tidni (Chhatarpur) :

Late medieval shrine discovered. *IAR*, 1961-62, p. 98.

Tigwan (Jabalpur) :

(a) Ruined temples of Gupta age. *CASIR*, IX, pp. 41-47; *JDG*, pp. 697-98; *CLAR*, p. 30.

(b) Standing Gupta temple. *Ibid.*

Tilori (Morena) :

(a) Ruins of a temple of about 11th century AD. *GAR*, 1917-18.

(b) A flat-roofed temple to the south-west of an old tank, datable to about 11th century AD. *GAR*, 1917-18.

(c) A similar temple to the west of the tank. *Ibid.*

(d) A similar tank on a hillock. *Ibid.*

(e) Ruins of a group of temples of about 10th-12th century AD. *GAR*, 1917-18.

(f) An old tank of about 11th century AD. *GAR*, 1917-18.

(g) An old well of about 10th-11th century AD. *Ibid.*

(h) Pillars with inscriptions datable to about 11th century AD recording the genealogies of the Kacchavāhā and Chāhamāna dynasties of Gwalior. *GAR*, 1917-18.

(i) A pillar of about 11th century AD. *Ibid.*

(j) Two sati stones with inscriptions dated in V.S. 1402. (1345 AD?) and 1419 (?) (1362 AD?). *GAR*, 1917-18.

Timurni (Hoshangabad) :

Medieval sculptures discovered. *IAR*, 1961-62, p. 99.

Tola (Jabalpur) :

(a) Images of Brahmanical gods and goddesses found. *IAR*, 1962-63, p. 68.

(b) Image with inscription in K.E. 907. *Hiralal List*, No. 44.

Tongra (Shivpuri) :

Pillared hall of about 10th-11th century AD with raised seats and back-rests on three sides. *GAR*, 1928-29, pp. 11-12.

Tuman (Bilaspur) :

Toraṇa of an ancient temple. *BDG*, p. 299.

Tumain (Guna) :

(a) Mounds to the west of the village on the other side of the river, locally known as *Nāgar Tor* and *Polā Tor*. Buddhist literature refers to this place as Tumbavana. *GAR*, 1934-35, p. 11.

(b) Fragments of a *toraṇa* of an early date. *GAR*, 1934-35, p. 11

(c) Rock-cut cells of an early date. *GAR*, 1918-19.

Tulaheda (Ujjain) :

Ruins of a temple of an early date. *GAR*, 1917-18.

Udayagiri (Vidisha) :

(a) Remains of a temple datable to the Gupta period. *MUH*.

(b) Remains of a Lion Pillar found. *CASIR*, X, p. 56.

Udayapur (Vidisha) :

(a) A mosque called Bījā Maṇḍala originally a temple datable to about 11th-12th century AD, with four inscriptions. *AG*, p. 138; *CASIR*, VII, pp. 84-85.

(b) Ruins of a temple of about 11th-12th century AD with only its *maṇḍapa* now existing. Locally it is called Bārākhambī from its twelve-pillared hall. *AG*, p. 139.

(c) Sculptures of Brahmanical and Jaina pantheon viz. Viṣṇu and Gaṇeśa in Hajariya temple. Ganesa fixed on Bada Darwaza, and seated Jaina Tīrthaṅkara image in Nāth Mohalla discovered. *IAR*, 1987-88, p. 139.

Ujjain (Ujjain) :

(a) An ancient gate, locally called Chaubis Khambha Darwaza, datable to about 11th-12th century AD. *AG*, p. 144.

(b) A mound locally called *Gadh*, to the north of the modern city, datable to about 2nd-3rd century BC. Excavations conducted here in 1938-39 yielded ring-wells, jars, clay seals, terracotta toys, punch-marked coins etc. *GAR*, 1938-39, p. 13.

(c) A mound, locally known as *Kumhar Tekri* or Potter's hill (so called after the abundance of pottery on its surface) about a mile to the east of Vaishya Tekri. Excavations conducted here in 1938-39 indicated it to be a burial-cum-cremation ground. *GAR*, 1938-39, p. 14.

(d) Brahmanical sculptures of medieval period identified. *IAR*, 1985-86, p. 112.

Ujjain District :

(a) Explorations conducted by the Central Circle of the ASI led to discovery of remains and temples of the Paramāra period at Banyakheri, Bhat Pachlana, Chirola, Dangawara, Kanthar-kheri, Kharotia, Kharsodkalan, Ordi and Pachlana Bil in tahsil Barnagar; Baijnath, Indokh and Jharda in tahsil Mahidpur; Amodia, Barwai, Jamalpur, Karochan, Tajkheri and Tumraoda in tahsil Ujjain. *IAR*, 1971-72, p. 31.

(b) Explorations conducted by the Central Circle of the ASI led to discovery of the historical sites at:

Baranagar, Bhondwas, Dhureri, Dunalja, Harnaoda, Itawa, Kajailana, Khandoda, Palsoda, Pachilana Bil, Paiwa, Similauda, Jahangirpura, Sarsana in tahsil Barnagar; Banfana, Berwan, Jadodia, Makla, Metwas, Nividia Khurd, Rupeta and Unhel in tahsil Khachrod. *IAR*, 1971-72, p. 31.

(c) In the explorations conducted by the Northern Circle of the ASI, Paramāra period temples and sculptures were noticed at the following sites:

Bhesoda, Chintamani, Dablagori, Dhulatia, Ghattia, Gunaia, Kaliadeh, Kamer, Khemlasa, Khilchipur, Nanakheri, Panbihar, Pingleshwar, Piploda-Dwarikadish, Sodang and Undasa in Ujjain taluk; Akyadhaga, Balkhera Ghat, Delchi Buzurg *alias* Badi Delchi, Dhulet, Ghosla, Jorimalakha, Makla and Mahidpur in Mahidpur taluk; Bamnapati, Barnagar, Datarwa, Gaznikheri, Guraoda, Igoria, Jahangirpura, Jamalpura, Kantharia, Kharotia, Kharsodkhurd, Kheranarain, Molana, Nimboda, Palsora, Paslod, Ranaoda, Singaoda and Suwasa in Barnagar taluk; Jalodia, Khachruad, Min and Rajgarh in Khachraud taluk; Aurangpur, Baghera, Kareri, Kathbaroda, Mergarh, Nainawad, Naleshri, Shamnera and Tukral in Tarana taluk. *IAR*, 1974-75, p. 29.

(d) During explorations, remains of three temples of the Paramāra period noticed at Depalpur, Gautampura, Dangwada and Gajnikhedi. *IAR*, 1979-80, p. 53.

Umardha (Hoshangabad) :

Sati stone with illegible inscription. *Hiralal List*, No. 68.

Umaria-Pan (Jabalpur) :

Images of Brahmanical gods and goddesses found. *IAR*, 1962-63, p. 68.

Undasa (Ujjain) :

A memorial pillar of about 11th-12th century AD with an illegible inscription mentioning probably the Paramāras. *GAR*, 1935-36, p. 39.

Valipur (Dhar) :

A group of eight memorial pillars, two with inscriptions, one of them dated in

V.S. 1324 (1267 AD) referring to Paramāra ruler Jayasiṁha of Maṇḍapadurga. *GAR*, 1916-17.

Vasavi (Dhar) :

(a) A temple of 10th-11th cent. AD as well as a rock-cut temple discovered. *IAR*, 1985-86, p. 110.

(b) Ruins of a medieval Brahmanical temple and a rock-cut temple located. *IAR*, 1987-88, p. 138.

Vidisha (Vidisha) :

(a) An abacus crowned by an inverted lotus of about 2nd century BC discovered. *IAR*, 1964-65, p. 74.

(b) Image of Yakṣī datable to c. 2nd century BC. *Vikram Smṛti Granth*, p. 69.

(c) Images of Kubera and Kuberī datable to c. 2nd cent. BC. *MBI*, p. 323.

(d) Colossal images of Yakṣa and Yakṣī of Śuṅga period. *JMPIP*, II, p. 20.

(e) Broken image of Gaṇgā datable to Gupta period. *JMPIP*, II, p. 20.

(f) An image of Gaṅgā similar to above in Boston collection. *HIIA*, pl. XLVIII, No. 177.

(g) Image of Nāga - Nāgī datable to c. 1st-2nd cent, AD. *JMPIP*, II, p. 20.

(h) Medieval images of Brahmā, Sūrya, Śiva, Kārttikeya, Saptamātṛkā, Mahiṣāsuramardinī and Tīrthaṅkara. *JMPIP*, II, p. 20.

Vyas Badaura (Chhatarpur) :

Sixteen temples datable to c. 9th-11th cent. AD discovered near village Vyas Badaura in tehsil Lundi. *IAR*, 1988-89, p. 39.

VII
Literature

Ancient Indian literary accounts are a major source of information for reconstructing the history and culture of Central India from the Vedic times to 13th century AD. The following picture justifies the statement.

Vedic Literature

The Vedic literature seems to exhibit a knowledge of the territory presently occupied by Madhya Pradesh. Though the *Ṛgveda* does not mention the river Narmadā, Revā is the only river of Madhya Pradesh that finds mention in the Vedic literature.[1] It has been identified with the Narmadā in the post-Vedic literature.[2] Similarly the Vindhyas find mention in the *Kauṣītakī Upaniṣad*[3] and subsequently in *Aitareya Brāhmaṇa*[4] and *Vasiṣṭhadharmasūtra*.[5] The Chedis are a very ancient tribe, a part of which settled in M.P. In the Vedic literature they are found mentioned in the *Ṛgveda*. In the *Dānastuti* occurring at the end of one hymn,[6] their king Kasu Chaidya is praised. Rapson identifies him with Vasu of the Epics.[7] References to some non-Aryan tribes are also found in the Vedic literature. Thus, the *Aitareya Brāhmaṇa* mentions Pulindas along with other non-Āryan tribes and terms them as Dasyus. The name of the Pulindas does not appear in the parallel list given in the *Śāṅkhāyana Śrauta Sūtra*. At the time of Aśoka they are found along with the Andhras. Their capital, according to the *Mahābhārata* probably lay to the south-east of the Bhilsa region. Similarly, the Niṣādas mentioned in the later *Saṁhitās* and *Brāhmaṇas* appear to have their settlement in the Vindhya and Satpura ranges.[8]

The Rāmāyaṇa

The *Rāmāyaṇa* provides ample references pertaining to the past history and culture of M.P. As for geographical knowledge of this part of the country, the *Rāmāyaṇa* refers to the river Narmadā as coming out of the Ṛkṣa mountain.[9] The river Śoṇa is very often mentioned by the *Rāmāyaṇa*.[10] Similarly the river Tamasā is referred to by it.[11] It is the same river that rises in the Kaimur range from Tamasā Kuṇḍa in the former Maihar State of M.P. Meandering through Satna and Rewa districts, it enters Uttar Pradesh and falls into the Ganges near Allahabad. References to Mandākinī, Mālinī and Paisuni rivers also occur in the *Rāmāyaṇa* along with Chitrakūṭa and Prasravaṇa.[12] According to the *Rāmāyana* the hermitage of Atri on the Ṛkṣa was not far from Chitrakūṭa.[13] The *Rāmāyaṇa* places Chitrakūṭa at about 2½ yojanas in an uninhabited forest from the hermitage of Bharadwāja which was situated near the confluence of the Gaṅgā and the Yamunā.[14]

The *Rāmāyaṇa* recounts the names of the rivers, mountains and countries in the east, south, west and north, both within and outside India in Chapters 40-43 of the Kiṣkindā-Kāṇḍa. In the list supplied by it, the names of Mount Vindhya, Narmadā Nadī, Mahānadī, Mekala, Daśārṇa Nagara, Avanti and Daṇḍakāraṇya, all located within the territorial jurisdiction of M.P. appear.[15] Vindhyāṭavi and its products and animals have been discussed in detail.[16] The Vindhyas have been referred to several times by the *Rāmāyaṇa*.[17] Of the territories, the *Rāmāyaṇa* mentions one Daśārṇa region and associates it with the Mekalas and utkalas where Sugrīva sent his monkey hosts in quest of Sītā.[18] About Avanti, it may be mentioned that this country was divided into two parts, Ākara and Avanti with its capital at Ujjayinī. This is confirmed by later epigraphical references. From the Uttarakāṇḍa of the *Rāmāyaṇa*,[19] it appears that Rāma gave Vaidiśa to Śatrughna's son Śatrughātin. Vaidiśā in this verse probably refers to the country of which Vidiśā was the capital.

Of the other territories referred to by the *Rāmāyaṇa*, mention may be made of Kośala, Śrīpura and Karuṣa. Kośala is Dakṣiṇa Kośala over which Kuśa ruled. Uttara Kośala with its capital at Śrāvastī was ruled by Lava.[20] It may be mentioned that Daśaratha, father of Rāma had married Kausalyā, the daughter of the King of Dakṣiṇa Kosala. This points to the antiquity of the country. Śrī-pura became the capital of this country subsequently. According to Cunningham, the ancient name of Śrī-pura was Śavaripura, which was named after Śavari, the female mendicant mentioned in the *Rāmāyaṇa*.[21] About the Janapada of Karuṣa, the *Rāmāyāṇa* mentions an interesting story about its origin.[22] This Janapada had extended its territorial jurisdiction over a part of Bundelkhand and Baghelkhand.

The route of Rāma's journey to Laṅkā is a subject matter of keen controversy amongst scholars but there is no doubt that leaving Chitrakūṭa, Rāma passed through the M.P. districts of Satna, Shahdol, Ambikapur, Bilaspur, Raipur and Bastar to reach Daṇḍakāraṇya. Rāma, before proceeding to the dense Daṇḍaka forest stayed for sometime at Rāmagiri (present Ramgarh in the Sarguja district of M.P.).[23] Kālidāsa in the beginning of his *Meghadūta* pays homage to Rāmagiri which was recognised as a holy place in the Gupta period on account of its association with Śrī Rāma.

The Mahābhārata

In the *Mahābhārata* also numerous references are available which are useful as source material for the ancient history and culture of M.P. The *Mahābhārata* is well acquianted with the hills, mountains, rivers and territories existing within Madhya Pradesh. Kāntāra referred to by the *Mahābhārata*[24] is the same as the wild forest tract existing in Bastar to which the Allahabad Pillar inscription of Samudragupta refers as Mahākāntāra. The Nalopākhyāna of the *Mahābhārata*[25] locates Ṛkṣa mountain between Avanti and Dakṣiṇāpatha, while it expressly associates the Vindhya with Payoṣṇī, a river of the Tāptī group.[26] There is reference to Pāriyātra as the abode of the tribe of the Niṣāda,[27] possibly in the Niṣādabhūmi, i.e., Narwar region between Gwalior and Jhansi. The Gośṛṅga hill close to the Niṣādabhūmi is located nearby.[28] According to the *Mahābhārata*[29] the hermitages of the sages Chyavana and Kakṣasena were on the Asita mountain which, on the basis of a literary evidence,[30] is sometimes placed near Ujjayinī. About the Chitrakūṭa hill, the *Mahābhārata* refers to it as situated on the bank of the river Mandākinī and associates it with Kālañjara.[31] In the Chedi country is placed the Kolāhala hill[32] and this range is associated with Śuktimatī (Ken).[33]

There are frequent references in the *Mahābhārata* to the river systems of M.P. Thus the Narmadā has been associated with the Ṛkṣa mountain.[34] The Bhīṣmaparvan[35] mentions the river Vedasmṛti, modern Besula in Malwa which is tributary of the Sindhu[36]. However, Ali and Dey identify it differently. The river Sindhu is generally believed to be identified with the river Kalisindh, a tributary of the Chambal. The *Mahābhārata* possibly refers to it as the Dakṣiṇa Sindhu.[37] The Chambal is termed as Charmaṇavatī in the *Mahābhārata*.[38] According to it, the name was originated from the skin (*charman*) of the sacrificed cows, i.e. from the blood oozing out of the skins of the cows. A large number of cows are said to have been slaughtered at the yajña of Ratnideva. As per the Epic, this river formed the southern boundary of the Pāñchāla country.[39] The name of the river Kuntī appears in the *Mahābhārata*.[40] It has been identified with a small stream joining the Chambal called Aśvanadī or Aśvarathanadī in the *Mahābhārata*.[41]

The *Mahābhārata* refers to Śoṇa and Mahāśoṇa among the rivers crossed by the Pāṇḍavas and Kṛṣṇa on their way to Rājagṛha.[42] Jyotīrathā is said to be a tributary of this river.[43] It has been identified by Pargiter with Johilla, the southern of the two sources of the Śoṇa.

As noted above, the Narmadā, which rises from the Amarkantak hills and falls in the Arabian Sea is also called Revā in the *Śatapatha Brāhamaṇa*.[44] The *Mahābhārata* mentions it as coming out of the Ṛkṣa mountain.[45] The river Daśārṇā which is the same as modern Dhasan flowing past Sagar between the Betwa and the Ken, was named after the country of Daśārṇa mentioned in the *Mahābhārata*.[46] The Bhīṣma Parvan of the *Mahābhārata* makes a reference to the river Chitrotpalā[47] which is identified with the Mahānadī in South Kosala, below its junction with Pyri (ancient Pretoddhāriṇī).

The Mahābhārata connects the river Śuktimatī (Ken) with the Kolāhala range.[48] The river flows through the ancient kingdom of Chedi. The Kolāhala range is placed between Panna and Bijawar in the Rewa division. That on the bank of the river stood the city of Śuktimatī is referred to by the *Mahābhārata*.[49]

The river Veṇvā which is identified with modern Waingaṅgā is connected by the *Mahābhārata* with Godāvarī.[50] It rises near the village Partabpur or Mundara, 16 km. from Seoni on the Satpura plateau, flows through Seoni and Balaghat districts, then enters Maharashtra and falls in the Godāvarī.

Some other rivers of M.P. referred to in the *Mahābhārata* are Hastisomā[51] (Bhīṣma-parvan), modern Hasdeo, a tributary of the Mahānadī in Dakṣiṇa Kosala; Madhuvāhinī[52] (Bhīṣma-parvan), modern Mahawar in Gwalior district; Mālinī, which flows by the side of the Chitrakūṭa range and the hermitage of Kaṇva;[53] Pāṭalavatī[54] (Bhīṣma-parvan), a branch of the Chambal; and Śivā[55] (Bhīṣma-parvan) which flows by the present Durg, district headquarter in Chhattisgarh.

In the *Mahābhārata* there is mention of several territories of ancient India which at present fall within the jurisdiction of M.P. The *Mahābhārata* distinguishes between the kingdoms of Avanti and Māhiṣmatī but seems to refer to two Avanti princes ruling in the Narmadā valley.[56] According to Sircar, the name Avanti was derived from the Avanti branch of the Haihaya class of the famous Yadu or Yādava tribe.[57] Avanti was a vast country in ancient times with sometimes Ujjaynī and at other times Māhiṣmatī as its capital.

The *Mahābhārata* also supplies us some important geographical information about the realm of the Chedis which was one of the countries encircling the Kurus.[58] It places Chedi along with the Matsyas by the Charmaṇavatī (Chambal), the Kāśis of Vārāṇasī (Benaras) and the Kārūṣas in the Śoṇa (Son) valley,[59] but distinguishes it from the Daśārṇas.

Anūpa was an ancient Janapada, the people of which, according to the Purāṇas resided in the Vindhya region. The *Mahābhārata* places the Anūpa region close to the territory of the Ṛṣikas[60] and regards it as an area of the coastal land.[61]

The territory of Daśārṇa is also referred to by the *Mahābhārata* twice in the Sabhāparvan in connection with the victorious marches of Bhīmsena and Nakula and once in the Anugītaparvan, wherein it is stated that Chitrāṅgada, the ruler of Daśārṇa was vanquished by Arjuna.[62] Some more references to this country appear in the *Mahābhārata*.[63]

The *Mahābhārata* makes references to the country of South Kośala connecting it with other South Indian states.[64] The capital of South Kośala was sometimes called Kośalā.[65] The Vanaparvan mentions two routes leading to the countries of Vidarbha and Kośala.[66] Cunningham thinks that Ptolemy's Sageda, the capital of Mahakoshal, may possibly be identified with Chitrāṅgadapura or Maṇipura of the *Mahābhārata*.[67] A few more references to capital cities and towns are available in the *Mahābhārata*. The capital city of Māhiṣmatī finds occurrence in several ancient Indian literary works. In the Mahābhārata the Sabhāparvan mentions the conquest of Māhiṣmatī by Sahadeva by defeating its king Nīla.[68] In the Anuśāsanaparvan,[69] Daśāśva, one of the hundred sons of Ikṣvāku of the solar race, is mentioned as a king of Māhiṣmatī. The same parvan states that the thousand armed Kārtavīrya, the Haihaya, reigned over the whole earth from Māhiṣmatī. Māhiṣmatī was the capital of Mahiṣamaṇḍala, the territory of the Mahiṣas or Mahiṣakas.[70] The Bhīṣmaparvan refers to the people of the Māhiṣakas[71] and classes them as "*Janapada dakṣiṇāḥ*. The second capital mentioned by the *Mahābhārata* is Nalapura (modern Narwar in Gwalior district). It was the capital of Nala, the ruler of the Niṣāda country and is referred to in the Vana Parvan.[72] Ratnapura (modern Ratanpur, Bilaspur district), known in ancient times as Maṇipura and Māṇikapura, is said to have been the scene of some of the stories related in the *Mahābhārata*.[73] Though Cunningham is not ready to accept the traditional account, Dey[74] attempts to show on the basis of an evidence from *Jaimini Bhārata*[75] that Ratnapura was the capital of Mayūradhvaja and his son Tāmradhvaja who fought with Arjuna and Kṛṣṇa while advancing along with the sacrificial horse of king Yudhiṣṭhira.

The third capital city referred to by the *Mahābhārata* is Śuktimatī or Śuktisahvaya.[76] It was supposed to be the capital of Rājā Uparichara of the Chedi-Viṣaya. It was named after the river Śuktimatī (modern Ken, flowing through Bundelkhand) on the bank of which it was situated.

Next, the *Mahābhārata* makes reference to the capital city of Tripurī along with Kośala[77]. The Tripuras and the people of Kośala are referred to together with the Makalas and Kurubindas.[78]

About Vidisha, the capital of Daṣārṇa country, the *Mahābhārata* does not specify the position though Daṣārṇa is referred to by it.[79]

In the *Mahābhārata*, Sahadeva is said to have conquered a place known as Bhojakaṭaka.[80] At another place in the Epic, it is stated that Rukmi, the brother of Rukmiṇī, the consort of Kṛṣṇa, after his defeat at the hands of Kṛṣṇa established his second capital at Bhojakaṭaka.[81] Scholars have identified Bhojakaṭaka with modern Bhojpur situated in Goharganj tahsil of Raisen district of M.P. and is 29 km to the south-east of Bhopal.

Several events of the traditional history of M.P. find reference in the *Mahābhārata*. The legendary Yayāti mentioned in the *Mahābhārata* as a Samrāṭa is said to have divided his vast territories among his five sons, among whom Yadu, the eldest is said to have been given territories towards the south-west embracing the country watered by the river Charmaṇavatī (Chambal), Vetravatī (Betwa) and Śuktimatī. Turvasu got the south-east territory around Rewa.[82] Later on the Haihayas (of the Yādava branch of the Lunar dynasty) continued to prosper in the region south of Malwa and Mahiṣmant, one of their kings founded the city of Māhiṣmatī. The Haihaya power was raised to a great eminence under the leadership of Kārtavīrya Sahasrārjuna who is said to have fought with the Karkoṭaka Nāgas, occupied Anūpa (territories on the Narmadā), captured Māhiṣmatī and made it his capital.

In the Bhārata war, the Epic gives a long list of princes on each side. From Madhyadeśa, the rulers of Vatsa, Kāśi, Chedi, Karūṣa, Daśārṇa and Pañchāla figured among the supporters of the Pāṇḍavas. The Nīla of Māhiṣmatī, Vinda and Anuvinda of Avanti, Niṣāda and Śālva supported the Kaurava forces.

The Purāṇas

The Purāṇas, in their present form, are usually placed, not earlier than the Gupta period. Thus they received their final form more than 2,000 years after the earliest events related by them. Some scholars believe that the original Purāṇa was composed more or less about the same time when the Vedic texts received their final form. Though this theory is questioned, the existence of a Purāṇa text at a very early date is generally accepted. In subsequent ages this Puranic text was vitiated by exaggerations, mythological details, pronounced religious bias and divergences in the texts of the different Purāṇas. They were subjected to various modifications, revisions etc. at different periods.

Various Purāṇas contain accounts related to the past history and culture of M.P. and these are good source material for reconstructing the past of this part of the country. The following account exhibits it.

According to the Purāṇas, the first Nanda ruler is said to have overthrown most of the ruling dynasties of his time. Among them were the Haihayas and the

Vītihotras. The Haihayas occupied a part of Malwa. The Vītihotra sovereignty was terminated before the rise of the Pradyotas of Avanti. According to the Purāṇas, Pulika (Puṇika) had killed his master and placed his own son Pradyota (Chaṇḍa Pradyota) on the throne of Avanti.[83] Pradyota was a very powerful king and contemporary of the Buddha. He was in rivalry with the neighbouring kingdoms of Vatsa, Magadha and Kośala. Many interesting legends centre round his rivalry with Udayana, the king of Kauśāmbī. One of the legends forms the plot for Bhāsa's drama *Svapna-vāsavadattā*. According to the Purāṇas, Chaṇḍa Pradyota Mahāsena ruled for twenty-three years and was followed by four kings, Pālaka, Viśākhayūpa, Ajaka and Nandivardhana who ruled respectively for 24, 50, 21 and 20 years. The last ruler was defeated by Śiśunāga, and Avanti was incorporated with the growing kingdom of Magadha.[84]

The Purāṇas represent the Śuṅga as well as the Kāṇvas and Andhra-Sātavāhanas as the rulers of Magadha. But Magadha lay outside the Andhra – Sātavāhana empire. Sircar has attempted to prove that the later Śuṅga rulers had lost Magadha and were ruling in Central India with Vidiśā as their capital. According to him, king Bhāgbhadra of the Besnagar Garuda Pillar inscription may be identified with Bhadraka, the fifth Śuṅga king according to the Bhāgavata Purāṇa.[85] It is therefore likely that the Śuṅgas were overthrown by the Kāṇvas and the latter by the Sātavāhanas in that region. It appears from the historical section of the Purāṇas[86] that Simuka, originally a feudatory of the Kāṇvas, overthrew his overlord Suśarman who was probably ruling over Malwa and the adjoining regions about the third quarter of the first century BC. The Puranic passage states that Simuka "of the Andhra race will obtain the earth after having violently extirpated the Kāṇvāyana Suśarman and having also destroyed the remnants of the power of the Śuṅgas". The region which Simuka conquered from the Śuṅgas and Kāṇvas may have included the district round Vidisha, which was probably the capital of the later Śuṅgas.

The Puranic chroniclers also provide some details about the Nāga kings who flourished in 3rd-4th century AD after the decline of the Kuṣāṇas at Vidiśā, Kāntipurī, Mathurā and Padmāvatī. The *Viṣṇu Purāṇa* discloses the existence of nine (nava) Nāga kings who reigned at Padmāvatī, Kāntipurī and Mathurā[87] and this account is corroborated by the Vāyu Purāṇa which mentions two houses of the Nāgas — one at Padmāvatī and the other at Mathurā.[88] Mention is also made of the powerful rulers of Vidiśā named Śeśa, Bhogin and Sadāchandra surnamed Chandrāṁśa, who is described as the second Nākhavat (i.e., Nahapāna) and may have been associated with the Śakas.[89] Numismatic evidences prove the existence of the Nāga rulers of Central India.

The Purāṇas also provide considerable evidence for the rule of the Vākāṭakas who held sway over a large part of Central India after the fall of the Sātavāhanas and before the rise of the Chālukyas. According to *Vāyu Purāṇa*, the founder of the dynasty, Vindhyaśakti ruled for 96 years and his son Pravīra 60 years. About the ancestry and original house of Vindhyaśakti, there is a lot of difference of opinion amongst scholars. As per one opinion Vākāṭakas hailed from the village Bijnaur - Bagat in Bundelkhand after which they were named. Also the Puranic Kilakilas, with which Vindhyaśakti is said to have association had something to do with the modern Kilakila river in Panna district of M.P. It is difficult to determine the precise meaning or authenticity of most of the Puranic details about the Vākāṭakas.

The Purāṇas are well acquinted with the geography of Central India. Not only the mountain and river systems are stated but also account of the Janapadas is provided. In the *Bhuvanakośa* or geographical section of the Purāṇas, a list of *Kulaparvata* or *Kulāchala* is given.[90] Some of these like the Śuktimat, the Vindhya, the Ṛkṣa and the Pāriyātra may be located in M.P. Of these, the Śuktimat is "a ring of ranges that encircle the Mahānadī basin which very nearly coincides with the present Mahākoshal and the Puranic Dakṣiṇa Kosala. The Northern and the North-western portion of this divide coincides with the Southern Maikal range, the Southern and Eastern with the hills of Kanker and Sambalpur."[91]

The Vindhya is the chain of mountains along the Narmadā that separates Northern India from the Deccan. About the Ṛkṣa, confusion prevails regarding its identification on account of association of Ṛkṣa with the Narmadā and of the Vindhya with the Revā. The *Bhāgavata*[92] and the *Vāmana Purāṇa*[93] make distinction between the two rivers, while *Revākhaṇḍa* regards them as identical. The *Harivaṁśa* mentions that Māhiṣmatī, the capital of the Narmadānūpa was situated on the feet of Ṛkṣavat.[94] The *Bhāgavata Purāṇa* places the hermitage of Atri on the Ṛkṣa.[95] The location of Amarkantak hills is a problem. Though Ptolemy takes it as a part of the Vindhya (Ovindon), the *Revākhaṇḍa* of the *Skandapurāṇa* describes it as a part of Ṛkṣa.[96]

The Pāriyātra or Pāripatra is the western part of the Vindhyas together with the Aravalli.

In addition to these *Kulaparvatas*, smaller ranges and hillocks abound in M.P. Some of these referred to in the Purāṇas are: Vaidūrya in the *Skanda Purāṇa, Revā Khaṇḍa,*[97] Vindhya-pāda in the *Varāha Purāṇa,*[98] Devaparvata in the *Śiva Purāṇa,*[99] Chitrakūṭa hills in the *Bṛhat-Śiva Purāṇa*[100] and Mekala in the *Padma Purāṇa.*[101]

The systems of rivers issuing from the different mountain ranges often find place in the Purāṇas. The Pāriyātra is mentioned as the source of rivers viz. Sindhu (Kalisindh, a tributary of the Chambal) in the *Varāha Purāṇa*,[102] the *Viṣṇu Purāṇa*[103] and the *Devī Purāṇa*[104]; Mahī (modern Mahī in Malwa) described as Mahatī in *Vāyu Purāṇa*;[105] Pārā[106] (modern Pārvatī, a tributary of the Chambal); Vidiśā (modern Bes or Besali, a tributary of the Betwa) in the *Matsya Purāṇa*;[107] Vetrāvatī (modern Betwa) in the *Matsya* and *Vāmana Purāṇas*;[108] Kṣiprā (modern Śiprā, flowing past Ujjain) in the *Mārkaṇḍeya Purāṇa*;[109] Avarṇī (same as Avanti rising in Mhow near Indore) in the *Mārkaṇḍeya Purāṇa*[110] and Kuntī a tributary of the Chambal in the *Matsya Purāṇa*.[111]

From the Ṛkṣavat are mentioned the river systems of Śoṇa (modern Son rising from the Amarkantak hill) in the *Bhāgavata Purāṇa*;[112] Narmadā mentioned as Revā in the *Mārkaṇḍeya Purāṇa*,[113] as Narmadā in the *Kūrma, Matsya, Brahmāṇḍa, Vāmana* and *Vāyu Purāṇas*[114] and as Dakṣiṇa Gaṅgā in the *Skanda Purāṇa*;[115] Daśārṇā (modern Dhasan, flowing past Sagar between the Betwa and the Ken) in the *Kūrma, Matsya, Brahmāṇḍa, Vāmana, Vāyu*[116] and *Mārkaṇḍeya Purāṇas*;[117] Tamasā (modern Tons) on the bank of which Vālmikī dwelt; Pippalaśroṇī (modern Paisuni or Parsaroni) in the *Vāyu* and *Matsya Purāṇas*;[118] Karamodā (modern Karamnāsā rising from the Vindhya) in the *Vāyu Purāṇa*;[119] Bāluvāhinī (modern Baghain in Bundelkhand) in the *Skanda Purāṇa, Avantya Khaṇḍa (Revā Khaṇḍa*, ch. 4)[120] and Śuktimatī (modern Ken in Bundelkhand) mentioned as Śyenī in the *Matsya Purāṇa*.[121]

The *Purāṇas* mention that from the Vindhyas issue the river systems of Nirvindhyā (modern Newuj, a tributary of the Chambal) also called Nirvandhyā in the *Vāyu Purāṇa*; Veṇvā (modern Wainganga) referred to as Veṇīgaṅgā in *Bṛhat-Śiva Purāṇa*[122] and Veṇā in the *Padma Purāṇa*.[123]

The rivers mentioned in the *Mārkaṇḍya Purāṇa* as issued from the Śuktimat Parvat are: Ṛṣikulyā of *Mārkaṇḍeya Purāṇa*,[124] Kumārī,[125] Mandagā,[126] Mandavāhinī,[127] Kṛpā,[128] Palāśinī,[129] Suni (modern Seonath)[130] and Sandur (modern Sudāmā).[131]

The following rivers mentioned in the Purāṇas as coming out of the Ṛkṣa mountain have not been satisfactorily identified or remain unindentified.

1. Surasā, Sumahā, Surahā (*Vāyu*); Surathā (*Mārkaṇḍeya*), Sukṛśā (*Matsya*); Suvahā (*Brahmāṇḍa*);
2. Kriyā, Kirvā, Drumā (*Vāyu*); Adrijā (*Mārkaṇḍeya*); Kṣamā (*Matsya*); Śivā (*Garuḍa*);
3. Piśālikā or Piśābikā (*Vāyu*);

4. Vipāśā (*Vāyu and Brahmāṇḍa*); Viśālā *(Kūrma)*; Mahāvegā (*Vāyu)*;
5. Mañjulā (*Kūrma*); Jambulā, Vañjulā (*Vāyu*);
6. Śunī - Lajjā (*Matsya*); Sumerujā (*Mārkaṇḍeya*); Siterajā (*Vāyu*); Satsantajā (*Vāmana*);
7. Tridivā, Hṛadikā, Hrādikā (*Matsya*);
8. Kramu, Krama (*Mārkaṇḍeya*); Kramā (*Vāyu*); Vāu (*Vāmana*).

Among the rivers originating from the Vindhyas the following have not been identified properly:

1. Niṣadhāvatī; Niṣadhānadī (*Vāyu*); Mahānadī (*Kūrma*); Ṛṣabhānadī (*Matsya*);
2. Sinibāhu (*Vāyu*); Sinībāli or Sinīvālī (*Mārkaṇḍeya*); Śitibāhu (*Brahmāṇḍa*); Valāka (*Kūrma*); Viśvamātā (*Matsya*); Sinībāhu (*Vāmana*);
3. Kumudvatī;
4. Mahāgaurī
5. Durgā and
6. Antaḥśilā.

Some other rivers mentioned by the Purāṇas are: Hastisomā (modern Hasdeo, a tributary of the Mahānadī),[132] Kāverī (northern Kāverī, i.e. the Narmadā),[133] and Śivā (modern Śivā, flowing close to Durg, the district headquarter in Chhattisgarh region of M.P.).[134]

The Purāṇas also throw some light on the ancient Janapadas of M.P., their capitals, cities, towns and people inhabiting them. The Janapadas mentioned are: Avanti, Chedi, Anūpa, Daśārṇa, Mekala and Jajāhūti. Avanti was a vast country and the *Skanda Purāṇa*[135] calls Ujjayinī 'The city of the Avantis' (*Avantipura*). According to the *Bṛhaddharma Purāṇa* (Madhya-Khaṇḍa, Ch. 24) Avanti is one of the *Sapta-Mokṣadāpurī* (i.e., seven holy cities). It is interesting to note that in the Puranic list of the Janapadas, the Avanti Janapada has been located in the Madhyadeśa, instead of the Western Division. The Janapada of Chedi has found reference in the *Skanda Purāṇa,* Revā-Khaṇḍa[136], where Maṇḍala is said to be another name for Chedi. Similarly Anūpa was an ancient Janapada and the people of Anūpa are mentioned in the Purāṇas along with the people residing in the Vindhya region.[137] There is also mention of the people inhabiting the Daśārṇa

Janapada in the list of the people of the Purāṇas.[138] The people of the Janapada of Mekala, situated around the present Amarkantak hills, are similarly referred to in the Puranic list of peoples.[139] Jajāhūti (Jejākabhukti) with 42,000 villages is referred to in the *Skanda Purāṇa*.[140] It is ancient name of Bundelkhand.

The capital cities referred to in the Purāṇas are : Kośalā, Māhiṣmatī, Mekalā, Tripurī, Tummāṇa, Ujjayinī and Vidiśā. The capital of South Kosala has also been called Kośalā and we get a few references to some kings of Kośala in certain passages of the Purāṇas.[141] Māhiṣmatī was the capital of ancient Mahiṣakamaṇḍala. The *Mārkaṇḍeya Purāṇa*[142] calls the Mahiṣakas as *dakṣiṇāpatha-vāsinaḥ*. The Purāṇas also refer to the kings of Mekalā which was possibly the city of the Mekala country.[143] Tripurī, the capital of the later Kalachuris and the city of legendary fame situated on the bank of the Narmadā is mentioned in the *Skanda Purāṇa,*[144] *Liṅga Purāṇa,*[145] and *Matsya Purāṇa*.[146] According to Sircar[147] there is no reference to the city of Tummāṇa, capital of the Ratanpur branch of the Kalachuris of South Kosala in the Puranic list of people. About Ujjayinī, reference has already been made above to state that it was also called Avantipura, the capital of Avanti in the Āvantya Khaṇḍa of *Skanda Purāṇa*. The *Skanda Purāṇa* also informs us that the great city of Ujjaynī had six earlier names in six different *kalpas* viz. Suvarṇasṛṅgāra, Kuśasthalī, Avantikā, Amarāvatī, Chūḍāmaṇi and Padmāvatī.[148] About Vidiśā, the capital of Daśārṇa, the Purāṇas confirm it as inhabited by the Vaidiśas[149] and that the river also known as Vidiśā (modern Bes or Besali), emerging out of the Pāriyātra and flowing past it, fell into Vetravatī (modern Betwa) near Vidiśānagarī (modern Besnagar).[150] The city (Vidiśā) thus seems to have been situated in the fork between the two rivers, Vetravatī (Betwa) and Vidiśā (Bes).

The Purāṇas also make reference to a few cities and towns of M.P. viz. Devapura, Padmāvatī, Purikā, Tulajāpura and Tumbavana. According to the *Padma Purāṇa,*[151] Rāma visited Devapura in order to save his brother Śatrughna from death. It is generally identified with Rājim on the confluence of the Mahānadī and Pairi in Raipur district of M.P. Reference to Padmāvatī occurs in the *Bhagavata Purāṇa* which mentions the city as situated on the river Sindhu.[152] It is identified with modern Padma Pawaya, 37 km north-east of Narwar on the confluence of Sindhu (Kali Sindh) and Pārā. The city of Purikā is mentioned in the *Mārkaṇḍeya Purāṇa*.[153] It is generally located to the south of Māhiṣmatī. Tulajāpura is referred to in the *Devībhāgavata Purāṇa*.[154] It is identified with Tuljapur, 6 km from Khandwa in East Nimar district of M.P. The people of Tumbavana are referred to in the Puranic list of people.[155] It is identified with Tumain in Guna district of M.P.

Buddhist, Jaina and other Pāli-Prakrit Texts

The Buddhist and Jaina texts and other works of miscellaneous nature in Pali and Prakrit are no less important source material for reconstructing the political and cultural history of ancient Madhya Pradesh.

Sutta Nipāta[156] which is one of the oldest works of Pali Buddhist literature speaks of a Brāhmaṇa Bāvari and his disciples who went to the Buddha in a mission at Śrāvasti and passed through among other places Māhissati (Māhiṣmatī), Ujjenī (Ujjayinī), Gonaddha (Gonarda), Vedisā (Vaidiśa — Vidiśā) and Vana-Savhaya (Tumbavana), all of which may be located in present M.P. The *Aṅguttaranikāya*[157] mentions the stereotyped list of the *solasa-Mahājapadas* and the same is repeated in the *Mahāvastu*,[158] *Vinaya*[159] and *Niddesa*.[160] They refer to two Janapadas of ancient M.P. viz. Chedi and Avanti. The Chedis were an ancient tribe of India. In 6th century BC they occupied the region roughly corresponding to modern Rewa division in Bundelkhand. The *Janavasabha Sutta* leads to infer that the Buddha visited Ceti (Chedi) country several times.[161] The *Chetiya Jātaka* informs us that the capital of the Chedi country was the city of Shotthivatī (Śuktimatī).[162] About Avanti, *Mahāgovindasuttanta* tells us[163] that Mahā-Govinda, the Brahmin chaplin of king Renu divided his empire into seven separate kingdoms. Of these Avanti was one with its capital at Māhiṣmatī. According to *Dīghanikāya*[164] Avanti fell to the share of Vessabahu, one of the seven contemporary kings of the line of Bharata. Bhandarkar is of opinion[165] that Avanti, corresponding roughly to modern western Malwa, had two capitals, one at Ujjayinī and the other at Māhiṣmatī. This is supported by the Buddhist works.[166] But later on Māhiṣmatī seems to become independent country as is confirmed by *Dīpavaṁśa* which calls it as Mahisaraṭṭha (Mahiṣarāṣṭra),[167] Mahāvaṁsa which calls it as Mahiṣamaṇḍala[168] and Buddhaghoṣa who calls the region as *raṭṭham Mahiṣaṁ*.[169] *Dīpavaṁsa* states that Ujjayinī, the capital of Avanti was built by Achchutagāmī.[170] Avanti was an important centre of Buddhism. Some *theras* and *theris* were either born or resided there. From the *Jātakas* it appears that there was an old trade route from Ujjain to Varanasi.[171]

The *Mahāvastu* offers a new name i.e., Daśārṇa in its list of the sixteen Great States of India.[172] It was the old name of Eastern Malwa with Vidiśā (modern Besnagar) as its capital. The *Jātakas* mention that during the time of the Buddha, Daśārṇa was famous for manufacturing swords.[173] Vidiśā, the capital of Daśārṇa has been placed by the *Pārāyaṇa Suttanipāta* on the route running from Pratiṣṭhāna[174] to Śrāvastī. *Mahāvaṁsa* records that Vidiśā was 50 *yojanas* from Pāṭaliputra and was founded by Śakyans who fled from Viḍuḍhabha's massacre.[175]

Buddhaghoṣa indicates[176] that Aśoka stayed at Vessanagara (Besnagar) and married Devī here and by her he had twin sons Ujjenia and Mahinda and a daughter Saṅghamitrā. The *Mahāvaṁsa*,[177] however, relating the same story, calls the place as Chetiyagiri (modern Sanchi). On the basis of a tradition recorded in *Stūpāvadāna* in Kṣemendra's *Bodhisattvāvadānakalpalatā*, Sircar has presumed that owing to a second invasion of the Yavanas, the capital of the Śungas was transferred from Pāṭaliputra to Vidiśā about the close of the second century BC.[178]

The Jaina *Pariśiṣṭaparvan* speaks[179] of inclusion of large parts of East Malwa including Tumbavana in the ancient state of Avanti. About the beginning of 5th century AD Avanti became a powerful state under the rule of the Pradyotas. Early traditions suggest Pradyota's protracted warfare with Udayana, the king of Vatsa. However, Pradyota had good relations with Bimbisāra of Magadha as is stated in the *Vinaya Piṭaka,*[180] Bimbisāra had sent his famous physician Jīvaka to Avanti to cure Pradyota when he fell ill. However, relations between Ajātaśatru, son and successor of Bimbisāra and Pradyota were not good. According to *Majjhimanikāya*,[181] Ajātaśatru once fortified Rājagṛha in anticipation of invasion by Pradyota. *Mahāvagga* states that Pradyota was a cruel king and hence his epithets *Chaṇḍa* and *Mahāsena*. However, he was converted to the Buddhist faith by Kaccāna[182] who is said to have spent a good deal of time in Avanti.[183]

After Pradyota, his son Pālaka came to the throne of Ujjayinī probably after supplanting his elder brother, Gopāla. The Nepalese *Bṛhatkathā* suggests[184] that Gopāla succeeded Pradyota but he abdicated in favour of his brother Pālaka. The Jaina *Āvaśyakakathānaka* (IV) reproduced by Bhadeśvara in his *Kahāvali* states that Pradyota had two great grandsons viz. Avantisena and Maṇiprabha. The former was ruling over Ujjayinī and the latter over Kauśāmbī. The exact date of conquest of Kauśāmbī by Avanti cannot be determined in the existing state of knowledge.

In the meantime Magadha had become a great power. The Jaina *Sthavirāvalicharita* states[185] that relation between king Udāyin of Magadha and the king of Avanti was hostile. Śiśunāga who supplanted the Baimbaka family and became the king of Magadha, is said to have exterminated the power of Avanti and possibly annexed it with the empire of Magadha. Śiśunāga's son Kālāśoka is known to have called the second Buddhist council at Vaiśālī.

The Śaiśunāga line was overthrown by the Nandas and the latter by the Mauryas. According to Buddhist traditions,[186] Avantirāṣṭra with its headquarter at Ujjayinī was one of the provinces of Maurya empire under Bindusāra and Aśoka. Aśoka himself was for a time his father's Viceroy at Ujjayinī.[187] A later

Buddhist work *Mañjuśrīmūlakalpa*[188] speaks of the rule of Maitraka Śilāditya I Dharmāditya (605-09 AD) at Ujjain.

Later Jaina works like *Kuvalayamālā* (778 AD) and *Harivaṁśa Purāṇa* (8th cent. AD) throw light on the political history of the Pratihāras. They prove that Pratihāra Vatasarāja's kingdom comprised both Malwa and eastern Rajasthan.[189]

Some references to the geography of Central India are found in the Buddhist, Jaina and other Pali-Prakrit texts. Malalasekera points out that Papāta hill (*pabbata*) referred to in various Buddhist texts was situated in the Avanti country.[190] The famous city of Kuraraghara which is mentioned by the Buddhist and Jaina writers[191] has also been placed on this hill. It is said that Mahākachchhāna, the reputed disciple of the Buddha, spent a good deal of time in Avanti, dwelling in Kuraraghara city on the Papāta hill.[192] The *Jātaka* refers to another hill, Ghanasela (Ghanaśaila) as situated in the kingdom of Avanti.[193] Its location is yet unidentified. N.L. Dey points out that the *Dīpavaṁśa* identifies Vedisagiri with Vessanagara (Besnagar) in East Malwa.[194] Accordingly Vedisagiri has been equated with Chetiyagiri, Chetiya or Chetiyanagara of the *Mahāvaṁsa*.[195]

The Jaina text *Āvaśyaka Chūrṇi* refers to a hill called Basaṇṇakuṇḍa which is said to have been hallowed by the memory of Mahavīra who visited it.[196] It was stated to have been situated to the north-east of Dasaṇṇapura (i.e., Daśārṇa in E. Malwa).[197] Its identification is yet uncertain. *Āvaśyaka Chūrṇi* also refers to Chitrakūṭa as an isolated hill on the river Paisuni (Payasvinī).[198] Chitrakūṭa also finds mention in Prākṛt literature along with the mountain Gopālagiri.[199] One Kuñjarāvarta Parvata near Vidiśā finds reference in Jaina texts. According to *Maraṇasamādhi*,[200] Vajrasvāmī had attained *Nirvāṇa* on this hill. He had arrived there along with 500 disciples from Rathāvarta hill.[201]

References to some river systems of M.P. appear in the Buddhist literary works. Thus, Buddhaghosa refers to Besnagara by the name of Vessanagara. The name of river Bes or Besali on which Besnagar is situated is evidently derived from Vessanagara. Similarly reference to the river Śuktimatī (Ken) in Bundelkhand occurs in the *Chetiya Jātaka* wherein it is stated that the city of the same name which was the capital of the Chedi people, stood on the bank of this river.

The Jaina literary traditions provide a few more references worth considering. According to the Jaina *Jambūdvīpa-Prajñapati* Kuśavati was the capital of Dakṣiṇa Kośala.[202] *Āvaśyakachūrṇi*[203] refers to the city of Daśapura (modern Mandsaur). In the early Jaina texts Mṛttikāvatī appears to be the capital of Dasanna (Daśārṇa).[204] The *Sthavirāvalīcharita* mentions that the temple of Mahākāla at Ujjayinī was built by Avanti Sukumāra's son[205] and that in the courtyard of the temple there was a small reservoir called Koṭi-tīrtha.[206]

Pāṇini

The *Aṣṭādhyāyī* of Pāṇini is a limited source material which throws light on the Janapadas and people of ancient Madhya Pradesh. In the list of countries of the South mentioned by Panini,[207] we come across the names of Avanti and Kośala (South Kośala). It also refers to the Mālavas (people of Malwa) as war-like people.[208] Reference to the Chedi country also appears in *Aṣṭādhyāyī*.[209] Pāṇini also mentions the Karuṣas[210] people of the Karuṣa country located in the Vindhya region. A stray reference to the river Charmaṇavatī (Chambal)[211] also appears in the *Aṣṭādhyāyī*.

Kauṭilya

In the *Arthaśāstra* of Kauṭilya, some references to the Janapadas of M.P. occur. The *Arthaśāstra* states[212] that the Janapada of Chedi is known for its good breed of elephants. Daśārṇa on the other hand can supply only middle class of elephants.[213] Reference to Karuṣas[214] (people of Karuṣa country) also appears in the *Arthaśāstra*. Some scholars believe that the village Chanak, 37 km to the south-east of Panna is the birthplace of Chāṇakya, the author of *Arthaśāstra*.[215]

Patañjali

The *Mahābhāṣya* of Patañjali (c. 2nd cent. BC) is a major source material for reconstructing the past history and culture of Malwa. The traditional birthplace of Patañjali was Gonarda, which, according to *Suttanipāta* was situated midway between Ujjain and Besnagar (Vidiśā). The *Mahābhāśya* is a commentary on the *Aṣṭādhyāyī* of Pāṇini. The aim of Patañjali was to discuss grammatical problems, but incidentally he gives information of the social and cultural life prevalent in second century BC. He throws light on the contemporary and early political history, administrative organisation, religion, education and literature, society, marriage and position of women, pastimes and recreations, food and drinks, dress and ornaments and economic conditions of the times. He makes repeated references to the personality of Puṣyamitra Śuṅga, to the invasion of the Yavanas who besieged Sāketa and Madhyamikā and to the yajñas performed by the Śuṅga monarch. Patañjali makes a reference to the cities of Māhiṣmatī and Ujjayinī in his comments on *Vārttikas* 10 and 15 under Pāṇini. He states that the distance between the two cities was appreciable, but could as a special feat, be covered between sunset and sunrise.[216]

Bharata

The *Nāṭyaśāstra* of Bharata, a work of 3rd century AD along with some other works mentions Avanti and Mālva as separate countries. This helps us to conclude that the name Mālava for both Daśārna (Ākara) and Avanti became prevalent much later. To this extent the *Nāṭyasastra* of Bharata is a helpful source of information.

Vātsyāyana

The *Kāmasūtra* of Vātsyāyana, a work of about 3rd century AD mentions Avanti and Mālava as separate countries. The commentary on the *Kāmasūtra* (VI, 5, 22 and 24) identifies Mālava with Pūrva - Mālva and gives the name of Avanti to Ujjain region.[217] This helps us to conclude that the name of Mālva for both Daśārṇa (Ākara) and Avanti became prevalent much later. To this extent Vātsyāyana's *Kāmasūtra* is a helpful source of information. P.C. Bagchi holds the view that Vātsyāyana most probably lived in Ujjain.

Śūdraka

The *Mṛchchhakaṭika* of king Śūdraka (c. 4th-5th cent. AD) is helpful in some way to throw light on the early history of Avanti. It is known that after Pradyota, his son Pālaka came to the throne of Ujjayinī probably after supplanting his elder brother Gopāla. According to *Mṛchchhakaṭika*, Pālaka, who was not a popular ruler, was ousted by Āryaka, who was probably the son of Gopāla. The work depicts a clear picture of the social life at Ujjayinī under the Gupta rule.[218]

Kālidāsa

Kālidāsa, "The most delicate and fragrant flower of the age-long nourished and enriched plant of Indian culture"[219] spent major part of his creative life in Madhya Pradesh, particularly Ujjayinī. He lived in the first half of the 5th cent. AD during the reign of the Gupta emperor Chandragupta II and Kumāragupta I, though this point is disputed by some scholars who place him in 1st cent. BC as court poet of king Vikramāditya of Ujjayinī, the founder of Vikram Saṁvat in 57 BC. As per a recently propounded theory,[220] Kālidāsa was the court-poet of Chaṣṭana, the founder of the Saka Era in 78 AD. He was the author of several famous works, of which two are *khaṇḍakāvyas* viz. *Ṛtusaṁhāra* and *Meghadūta*; two epics viz. *Kumārasambhava* and *Raghuvaṁsa;* and three dramas namely *Mālavikāgnimitra*, *Vikramorvasıyam* and *Abhijnana Sakuntalam.* It is said that he had edited and improved the Prakrit *Kāvya Setubandha* written by Vākāṭaka king Pravarasena II. His works are veritable source of information for reconstructing the past glory of M.P.

Kālidāsa has a love for the geographical conditions of Madhya Pradesh which he describes incidentally. In his works he has often referred to the mountains and hills, river systems, Janapadas and countries and the cities of M.P. Apart from the seasons, flora and fauna, the mountains and hills referred to by him are: Vindhya Pādāparvata (Vindhyan ranges) in *Meghadūta*,[221] Āmrakūṭa (Amarkantak hills) in *Meghadūta*,[222] Chitrakūṭa hills situated within Daṇḍakāraṇya in *Raghuvaṁśa*,[223] Rāmagiri (Ramgarh hills in Sarguja district) where the exiled Yakṣa of *Meghadūta* resided,[224] Nīchaiḥgiri of Daśārṇa (Udaigiri hills in Vidisha) in Meghadūta,[225] and Devagiri (which has been placed just after crossing the river Gambhir between Ujjain and Mandsaur near Chambal river) in *Meghadūta*.[226]

The river systems of M.P. referred to by Kālidāsa are : Śoṇa (Son rising in Amarkantaka hills) in *Raghuvaṁśa*,[227] Mandākinī (a tributory of Paisuni in Bundelkhand) in *Raghuvaṁśa*,[228] Tamasā (Tons) in *Raghuvaṁśa*,[229] Vetravatī (Betwa) in *Meghadūta*,[230] Sindhu (Kalisindh) a tributary of Chambal in *Meghadūtā*[231] and *Mālavikāgnimitra*,[232] Nirvindhyā (Nevuz, a tributary of Chambal flowing between Betwa and Kalisindh) in *Meghadūta*,[233] Gambhīrā in *Meghadūta*,[234] Śiprā in *Meghadūta*,[235] also known as Viśālā on the bank of which the celebrated city of Ujjayinī stood, Narmadā in Raghuvaṁśa[236] and *Meghadūta*,[237] Surbhi Tanayā (Chambal, another name of ancient Charmaṇavatī) in *Meghadūta*,[238] Daśarṇā (Dhasan) in *Meghadūta*[239] and Vidiśā (Bes or Besali near Besnagar) in *Mālavikāginimitra*.[240]

The Janapadas mentioned by Kālidāsa in his works are: Anūpa with Māhiṣmatī on the Revā as its capital in *Raghuvaṁśa*,[241] Daśārṇa (E. Malwa) with Vidiśā situated on the Vetravatī as its capital in *Meghadūta*[242] and Mālakṣetra or Mālabhūmi (Malda in the vicinity of Ratanpur in Bilaspur district) in *Meghadūta*.[243] Mention is also made, in passing, of a few cities like Vidiśā,[244] Daśapura,[245] Ujjayinī[246] and Māhiṣmatī.[247] The prosperity of the city of Ujjayinī that was situated on the bank of the river Śiprā, a tributary of the Charmaṇavatī (Chambal) has been narrated at length by Kālidāsa in his *Meghadūta*.[248] The sanctity of the temple of Mahākalā is also referred to by Kālidāsa.[249]

Apart from his love of geography, Kālidāsa had a fascination for historical events. In his works he has immortalised the protohistoric themes of Urvaśī and Śakuntalā. He was well aware of the romantic episode of Vāsavadattā of Ujjayinī with Udayana of Kauśāmbī. His drama *Mālavikāgnimitra* narrates a historical event. It states that crown prince Agnimitra, son and successor of Śuṅga ruler Puṣyamitra served as his father's viceroy at Vidiśā. Agnimitra's brother-in-law (his wife's brother) named Vīrasena was placed in charge of a fortress on the frontier on the banks of the Narmadā.[250] The *Mālavikāgnimitra* also refers to an independent kingdom recently established in Vidarbha. Yajñasena, the king of Vidarbha was natural enemy of the Śuṅgas as he was relation (sister's husband) of the *Sachīva* (minister) of the Mauryan emperor. Thus the relations between

Vidarbha and Vidiśā became strained. The poet narrates how Agnimitra's friend, Mādhavasena, who was a cousin of Yagñasena, was arrested by an *Antapāla* (governor of the frontier) of Yajñasena on his way to Vidiśā. Agnimitra at once called upon Yagñasena for his release failing which orders were given to Vīrasena to invade Vidiśā. In the fight, Yajñasena was defeated and his territory of Vidarbha was divided between Yajñasena and Mādhavasena under Puṣyamitra as their suzerain.

There was also a conflict between the Śuṅgas and the Indo-Greeks, reflections of which appear in *Mālavikāgnimitra*. According to Kālidāsa, the conflict took place in connection with the horse sacrifice of Puṣyamitra when his troops, escorting the horse under Vasumitra, his grandson, were stopped by the Yavanas on the south bank of the river 'Sindhu'. Some scholars are inclined to identify this river with Kalisindh (a tributary of the Chambal) in Malwa area. The Yavanas were defeated and the horse brought back safely home.

The cultural life depicted in the works of Kālidāsa is a great source material to reconstruct the cultural history of contemporary Madhya Pradesh.

Varāhamihira

Varāhamihara who lived towards the close of the 5th century AD has given us no less than six works. Of these, his *Bṛhat-Saṁhitā* is a useful source of reference for providing data pertaining to ancient historical geography of Madhya Pradesh.

The mountain systems of Madhya Pradesh referred to by *Bṛhat-Saṁhitā* are Vindhya and Chitrakūṭa hill. He places the inhabitants of the recesses of Vindhyas in the south-eastern division[250a] and refers to the forests of the Vindhya.[251] Chitrakūṭa is placed by him in the southern division.[252]

The river system of M.P. referred to in the work are: Mahānadī,[253] Mandākinī,[254] Narmadā[255] (also called Revā),[256] Payoṣnī,[257] Śiprā,[258], Śoṇa,[259] Vedasmṛti[260] (Besula, a tributary of Kalisindh in Malwa), Pārā[261] (Pārvatī in Malwa), Vetravatī[262] (Betwa), Tāpī[263] (Tapti) and Nirvindhyā[264] (Kalisindh in Malwa).

Among the Janapadas, towns, cities and inhabitants of the regions concerned referred to in the work, mention may be made of the following: Avanti[265] and Avantikā[266] (king or other inhabitants of Avanti); Chaidya[267] (people of Chedi country), Chedi[268] and Chedikā[269] (people of Chedi), Chedi-pa[270] (the ruler of Chedi); Chitrakūṭa in the southern division;[271] Daṇḍaka[272] (a country or people) and Daṇḍākavana in the southern division;[273] Daśapura in the southern division;[274] Daśārṇa[275] and Dāśārṇa[276] (people of Daśārṇa in the south-east division); Gonarda, a people in the southern division[277] (birthplace of Patañjali in Malwa); Haihaya, a people in the western division;[278] Kośala (South Kosala), a country and the people of it in the south-east division[279] and Kauśalaka[280] and Kauśala,[281] the people of Kośala; Mālva, a country and the people of it in the northern division;[282] Niśāda, a people in the south-east division;[283] Pulinda, a people[284] and the Pulinda tribe (Gaṇa),[285] Purika, a people in the south-east division,[286] Tripurī (Tewar-Jabalpur district), a city in the south-east division,[287] and Tripura, the city;[288] Tumbavana (Tumain), a forest in the southern division;[289] Udayagiri, 'the mountain of sunrise', in the eastern division;[290] Ujjayinī (Ujjain) the city[291] and Vidiśā (the capital and river in Malwa).[292]

Viśākhadatta

The drama *Devīchandragupta* of Viśākhadatta (6th cent. AD), now lost but a few passages from which are quoted in other books, has led some scholars to think the possibility of a short reign of Rāmagupta before Chandragupta II. Evidence of copper coins bearing the legend 'Rāma' and discovery of three inscriptions on Jaina images from Vidisha naming Rāmagupta as 'Mahārājadhirāja', has led serious thought to the existence of Rāmagupta as a regular Gupta ruler, predecessor of Chandragupta II, though it is still awaiting conclusive evidence. As such Viśākhadatta's work is an important literary source material for M.P. His other work *Mudrārākṣasa* is useful to the extent only that it mentions river Śoṇa (Son) only as a passing reference.[293]

Daṇḍin

The *Daśakumāracharita* of Daṇḍin (c. 6th cent. AD) supplies us the information that the famous temple of Vindyavāsini Devī was situated on the bank of the Narmadā.[294]

Harṣa

Śrī Harṣa or Harṣa Vardhana (606-674 AD), the king of Kanauj was author of three plays viz. *Ratnāvalī, Priyadarśikā* and *Nāgānanda*. Of these *Ratnāvalī* provides the historical data that Dakṣiṇa Kośala was invaded and conquered by Udayana, the king of Vatsa.[295]

Bāṇa

Among five works ascribed to Bāṇa who was court-poet of Harṣa (606-647 AD), *Harṣacharita*, a historical *Kāvya*, and *Kādambrī*, a prose romance provide data related to ancient M.P. The historical data supplied by *Harṣacharita* are : (i) Reference to Nāgārjuna (who was living in South Kosala) and his ruler-friend of Sātavāhana dynasty.[296] Rule of the Sātavāhanas over South Kosala is confirmed by a number of archaeological evidences. (ii) Reference to the presence of two later

Gupta rulers Kumāragupta and Mādhavagupta, the sons of king Mahāsengupta of East Malwa before Harṣa.[297] The term 'Mālava' refers only to East Malwa as compared to 'Avanti' referred to in *Kādambarī* representing West Malwa. It may be mentioned that Avanti as Malwa was not popular before the Paramāra occupation of that region in the second half of the 10th cent. AD. (iii) Reference to Nāgasena, the Nāga ruler of Padmāvatī.[298]

Bāṇa was most probably born and brought up near Chandreh in the present Sidhi district of M.P.[299] He has left to us an enchanting account of the area located in the valley of the Son river. The description of the forest life by Bāṇa remains an unsurpassed account on the subject in the entire Sanskrit literature. He has also given fine descriptions of the rivers Son (Śoṇa) which he also calls as Hiraṇyavāha,[300] Vetravatī (Betwa) surrounding Vidiśā and the Mālava ladies,[301] the Vindhyas and its rich forest products[302] and the city of Ujjayinī.

Amara

Amara (before 8th cent. AD) in his *Nāmaliṅgānuśāsana*, usually called *Amarakośa*, has provided some geographical data related to M.P. He has referred to the Vindhyas along with Himavān, Mālyavan and Pāriyātraka mountains,[303] the river Narmadā which he has termed as 'Mekala-Kanyā'[304] and the river Son, which has been termed as Hiraṇyavāha.[305]

Bhavabhūti

The noted Sanskrit dramatist Bhavabhūti (middle of 8th cent. AD) was associated with Padmāvatī. The city of Padmāvatī has been immortalised by Bhavabhūti who made this flourishing city the scene of his drama *Mālatī-Mādhava*. It was situated 60 km to the south of Gwalior on the banks of the Sindhu[306] (modern Sind) and the other rivers in the vicinity were Pārā[307] (modern Pārā or Pārvatī), Lavanā[308] (modern Luna), Madhumatī[309] (modern Madhuwar) and Pāṭalavatī,[310] to all of which Bhavabhūti refers in his *Mālatī-Mādhava*. An elaborate description of Padmāvatī appears in *Mālatī-Mādhava*.[311] It is stated to be a rich town with magnificent buildings and was a great centre of Vedic learning. One of Bhavabhūti's predecessors was a great poet and had performed Vājapeya sacrifice. His father Gopāla Bhaṭṭa was also a poet. Bhavabhūti had an affection for Padmāvatī, wherein he lived for sometime to complete his drama *Mālatī-Mādhava*. He had a good knowledge of Vindhyāṭavī and Daṇḍaka forests to which he has made reference in his *Uttararāma-Charita*.[312]

Murāri

In the drama *Anargharāghava* of Murāri (c. 8th-9th cent. AD) there is a reference to Māhiṣmatī as *agra-mahiṣī* in Act VII. From this Konow infers that Murāri was a protege of a Kalachuri prince at Māhiṣmatī.[313] That Māhiṣmatī was the capital of Chedi-maṇḍala at the time of the Kalachuris is confirmed on independent evidences.

Literature under the Kalachuris of Tripurī and Dakṣiṇa Kosala

Māyurāja

Author of the Sanskrit play *Udāttarāghava*, he is the first Kalachuri poet known to us. Reference to him occurs in one of the analogic verses of Rājaśekhara given in *Sūkti-muktāvali* of Jalhaṇa[314] which speaks of Māyurāja as a Kalachuri poet. The play is not available now, but the work is cited five times in the *Daśarūpaka*[315] and is known earlier to Abhinavagupta[316] and Kuntaka.[317] It has been suggested that he was a Kalachuri king[318] who flourished sometimes between Bhavabhūti and Rājaśekhara, i.e. between 750-880 AD.

Bhīmaṭa

Bhīmaṭa was another Kalachuri poet. Rājaśekhara calls him *Kālañjarapati*[319] which suggests that he was a Kalchuri king. According to Rājaśekhara, he was the author of five plays. A *Manoramā-Vatasarāja* by Bhīmaṭa is cited in *Nāṭyadarpaṇa* (p. 144). Another of his work entitled *Svapnadaśānana* is mentioned by Bhoja and Rājaśekhara.

Rājasekhara

Rājaśekhara, the court poet of the Kalachuri king Yuvarājadeva I (915-945 AD) was the most celebrated author of the period. He had spent his earlier career at Kanauj as court poet of Pratihāra king Mahendrapāla who regarded him as his guru. During the reign of Mahipāla, the power of the Pratihāras declined and Rājaśekhara then came to Tripurī where he was greatly honoured by Yuvarājadeva I.

The extant works of Rājaśekhara available today are his two dramas *Karpūramañjarī* and *Viddhaśālabhañjikā* based on two fictitious plots, and two other dramas viz. *Bālarāmāyaṇa* and *Bālabhārata* (incomplete) based on the *Rāmāyaṇa* and the *Mahābhārata*. Added to these is his work *Kāyamīmāṁsā*, a work on poetics, which, to be accurate, is its first *adhikaraṇa* styled by him as *Kavirahasya*. His non-extant works include six *Prabandhas* written in six different languages, a *mahākāvya* named *Harivilāsa* and another greater work named *Bhuvanakośa* of eighteen *adhyāyas*, of which the extant *Kāvyamīmāṁsā* formed the first *adhyāya*. Rājaśekhara is also credited with a *nāṭikā* having the title *Ratnamañjari* by Renou. According to him another work *Asṭa-patra-dala-kamala* is mentioned by Bhoja as that of Rājaśekhara.

The problem of chronology of Rājaśekhara's works has engaged the attention of scholars for sometime in the past. Various theories have been propounded to provide a chronology of his works. The chronological order of his extant and non-extant works usually accepted is as follows:

1. The six *Prabhandhas*
2. *Bālarāmāyaṇa*
3. *Bālabhārata*
4. *Karpūramañjarī*
5. *Viddhaśālabhañjikā*
6. *Bhuvanakośa*
7. *Kāvyamīmāṁsā*

Of these, the first four were written during his stay at Kanauj and the last three during his stay at Tripurī. Rājaśekhara's works continued to be studied in the Chedi century and considerably influenced the compositions of the later poets of the Chedi country. His last three works written at Tripurī truly reflect the life and culture of contemporary Madhya Pradesh.

Rājaśekhara seems to have been very fond of and much acquainted with the geography of India. His *Kāvyamīmāṁsā* is full of such geographical data some of which are related to M.P. also.[320] He refers to the Vindhya ranges and points to the river systems of M.P. viz. Narmadā (also called Mekalasutā in *Karpūramañjarī*)[321] supposed to form boundaries between the Āryāvarta and Dakṣiṇāpatha,[322] Śiprā, Śoṇa, Payoṣṇī and Tāpī. References to a few countries and cities of ancient Madhya Pradesh also appear in his works. These are: Avanti (of which an exaggerated territorial jurisdiction is stated in *Kāvyamīmāṁsā*),[323] Tosala (Dakṣiṇa Kosala), Daśapura (Mandsaur), Dāśeraka (Malwa), Devasabhā (Dewas), Māhiṣmatī, Mālava (Malwa or Avanti), Vidiśā, Ujjayinī and Chedi.[324]

Rājaśekhara had a fascination for historical events also as he had love for geography. His contributions to solve many knotty problems of the political history of ancient India are many. While illustrating different topics in his *Kāvyamīmāṁsā*, Rājaśekhara cites examples of verses from earlier works, which throw a floodlight on the problems of political history. For example in Chapter IX (*Arthavyāpti*) in *Kāvyamīmāṁsā*, he narrates some important historical event connected with king Śri Śarmagupta, his queen Dhruvasvāminī and one Khaśādhipati. Śrī Śarmagupta is stated to have offered his wife to Khaśādhipati having been defeated by him. This incident narrated by Rājaśekhara having compared with information collected from drama *Devīchandragupta* of Viśākhadatta, the Sanjan Plates of Amoghavarṣa I, Bāṇa's *Harṣacharita, Sṛṅgāraprakāśa* of Bhoja, the Cambay plates of Govinda IV and *Nāṭyadarpaṇa* of Rāmachandra and Guṇachandra has gone a long way to prove the existence of a Gupta ruler Rāmagupta whose coins and inscriptions have been found at Vidisha.

Two more verses quoted by Rājaśekhara in Chapter XI (*Kavirahasya*) have thrown a floodlight on the vexed problem of the date of Kālidāsa. Also, while mentioning the four boundaries of the city of Kanauj, the capital of his patron Mahandrapāla and Mahipāla, Rājaśekhara clears up several topographical problems connected with the city and helps us in identifying certain well-known names of places, the identifications of which were open to doubt for a long time.

The *Viddhaśālabhañjikā* of Rājaśekhara similarly contains a chain of historical events pertaining to the achievements of his patron king Yuvarājadeva I. This play was staged at Tripurī and Yuvarādeva I himself was the hero of this play. The play contains the following historical events:

(1) Yuvarājadeva married the daughter of Chandravarman, the king of Lāṭa, and his matrimonial alliance apparently strengthened his position.

(2) He espoused the cause of Vīrapāla, alias Chandravarman, the king of Kuntala, who had been dethroned by his kinsmen and sent an army which fought with a confederacy of kings on the bank of Payoṣnī, defeated it and placed Vīrapāla on the throne of Kuntala.

It is not possible to say definitely if the first of these incidents was a historical event, for it is difficult to determine to which royal family Chandravarman of Lāṭa belonged. The second event, however, seems to be a fact as the date supplied therein has been corroborated on independent evidences. V.V. Mirashi, Altekar and Dasaratha Sharma have identified Vīrapāla of *Viddhaśālabhañjikā* with Baddiga Amoghavarṣa III, the Rāṣṭrakūta ruler who was son-in-law of Yuvarājadeva I.

Similarly the contributions of the works of Rājaśekhara to the elucidation of the cultural history of India in general and M.P. in particular are many and varied.

Vidyāpati

According to a well-known *Subhāṣita*,[325] Vidyāpati was the court poet of Kalachuri Karṇa (1041-1073 AD). Several Sanskrit verses of this poet in some of which he praises Karṇa in a clever manner are cited in Sanskrit anthologies.

Gaṅgādhara

His name is known from *Vikramāṅkadevacharita* from which we learn that he was challenged and defeated, evidently in a poetic contest, by Bilhaṇa, the celebrated Kashmirian poet who visited Karṇa's court at Varanasi.[326] While at Varanasi, Bilhana delighted Karna with his sweet poetry.[327]

Vallana

He was also a court poet of Kalachuri Karṇa. Several *Subhāṣitas* composed by him are found in old anthologies like *Kavīndravachana-samuchchaya* and *Saduktikarṇāmṛta*. In one of these he praises Karṇa.[328]

Karpūra and Nāchirāja

They are known from Merutuṅg's *Prabandhachintāmaṇi*[329] as court poets of Kalachuri Karṇa. Both Karpūra[330] and Nāchirāja[331] have left beautiful verses in praise of Karṇa.

Kanakamāra

He is the author of *Apabhraṁśa* work *Karakaṇḍachariu*,[332] wherein it is stated that he delighated the mind of king Karṇa, who was probably no other than Kalachuri Karṇa.

Prākṛata Paiṅgala[333] quotes a few verses in praise of Kalachuri Karṇa. The authorship of these verses is not assigned in the commentaries.

Nārāyaṇa

He was patronised by the Kalachuri kings of South Kosala. In his Pujāripāli stone inscription which he composed, he states that he was the author of a *kāvya* named *Rāmābhyudaya*. Several works of this name are known but he seems to be different from them.

The inscriptions of the Kalachuris refer to a number of poets who composed the *praśastis*. Some of the authors of these *prasaśtis* were poets of no mean order and their contributions have served a long way to glorify the cultural history of the times of the Kalachuris.

Literature under the Parāmāras of Malwa

There were remarkable literary activities during the rule of the Paramāras over Malwa. Ample literature was produced in different branches of learning in Sanskrit, Prakrit and *Apabhraṁśa*. The beginning was from the time of Vākpati Muñja ending with Arjunavarman, reaching its zenith during the reign of illustrious Bhojadeva. Some of the kings themselves were poets of high rank. Ujjayinī and Dhārā were the chief centres of literary activities. The literary contribution of this age has gone a long way to serve as source material to political and cultural history of Malwa and its relations with the rest of the country. The major landmarks of the literary activities may be summarised as under:

Vākpati (Muñja)

Vākpati Muñja, the ruler of Malwa was a talented poet himself. The Udaigiri praśasti and Padmagupta, the court poet of Sindhurāja have praised him as a poet of high order. None of his complete works has so far been available though he is said to have written *Muñjapratidēśavyavasthā* which possibly provided a geographical description of India.[334] Several stanzas composed by this princely poet have been quoted by Jalhaṇa, Kṣemendra, Vallabhadeva, Dhanika, Merutuṅga and Bhoja in their respective works.

Vākpati was not only a poet; he patronised scholars who made remarkable contributions to different branches of letters. His court poets included Dhanañjaya, the writer of *Daśarūpaka* (a work on *Nāṭyaśāstra*), his brother Dhanika who wrote *Kāvyanirṇaya* and a commentary on *Daśarūpaka* and *Halāyudha*, the commentator on Piṅgala's work on metrics. Dhanapāla, the author of *Pāiyalachchī* and *Tilakamañjarī* who was contemporary of three Paramāra rulers, Siyaka II, Muñja and Bhoja, earned his favour and was awarded the title of '*Sarasvati*'. Amitagati completed his *Subhāśitaratnasandoha* during his reign.

Sindhurāja

In the reign of Sindhurāja, the successor of Vākapatirāja, Padmagupta alias Parimala composed the Sanskrit *Mahākāvya Navasāhasāṅkacharita*. This work in 18 cantos is based on historical event viz. Sindhurāja's aid to Śaṅkhapāla, the Nāga ruler of Chakrakoṭya (Bastar) who sought it to defeat some of his enemies, and consequently, the wedding of the former's daughter with the Parmāra king.[335]

Padmagupta makes a veiled reference to Sītā, a poetess who composed songs eulogising Upendra, the founder of the Paramāra dynasty. Merutuṅga has described her as contemporary of Bhojadeva. She seems to be living before Sindhurāja closed his reign and for some of the initial years of Bhoja's reign. However, none of her works are available.

Bhoja

Bhojadeva was Sindhurāja's successor and credit is given to him as author of over forty standard works on a variety of subjects including literature, poetics, grammar, lexicography, philosophy, Dharmaśāstra, medicine, astrology, astronomy, architecture and engineering.[336] The Udaipur *prasaśti* calls him '*Kavirāja*' and Panaheda inscription gives him the epithet '*Vidyānidhi*'.

In the field of *Kāvya*, Bhoja composed the *Avanikumārasataka*, the *Khadgaśataka* and the *Kodaṇḍakāvya*, all inscribed on stone presently fixed in the Bhojaśālā at Dhar. Also, he composed the *Sṛngāramañjarikathā* and *Champū-Rāmāyaṇa*, also known as *Bhoja-Champū*.

In the field of grammar, Bhoja is known to have written a grammar to which reference is made by Bhaṭṭojī Dīkshita and Jaina grammarian Vardhamāna. He also composed a grammar of Prakrit referred to by Jinavijayasūri.

In the field of poetics and dramaturgy, Bhoja composed a voluminous work entitled *Sarasvatīkaṇṭhābharaṇa* and another, *Śṛṅgāraprakāśa*. He also wrote a work on lexicography to which reference is made by Kṣīrasvamin in his commentary on Amarakośa wherein Bhoja is often quoted as a lexicographer, grammarian and commentator. Another work of Bhoja entitled *Nāmamālikā* has been edited from a manuscript found at Mysore.

Bhoja is author of four books in Jyotiṣa viz. *Rājamārtaṇḍa*, *Rājamṛgāṅka*, *Ādityapratāpasiddhānta* and *Vidvajjanavallabha*. In the last mentioned work he takes to himself the credit of vanquishing Karṇa, the king of Ḍāhala who was his contemporary.

In the domain of philosophy and religion, a number of works were written by Bhoja. His *Rājavārtika* on the Sānkhya system of philosophy is not available but is cited by Vāchaspati Miśra. His *Nyāyavārtika* is a work on logic and *Rājamārtaṇḍa* is an excellent commentary on Patañjali's *Yogasūtra*. *Pūrtāmārtaṇḍa*, his work on *Dharmaśāstra* is not available but has been quoted by Vijñāneśvara and Jimutavāhana. Aufrecht refers to Bhoja's *Chārucharyā* and *Vyavahārasamuchchaya* but these have not come down to us. *Vyavahāramañjarī* which is a book on *Dharmaśāstra* is also ascribed to Bhoja and referred to by Vimalabodha. His two works viz. *Tatvaprakāśa* and *Siddhāntasangraha* are related to Śaivism. These are referred to by Mādhava, Vidyāraṇya and Yatīndra.

Bhoja's famous work on *Vāstuśāstra*, i.e. architecture and art-craftmanship is *Samarāṅgaṇasūtradhāra*. Three works on medicine are also ascribed to him. These are: *Rājamṛgāṅka*, *Āyurvedasarvasva* and *Rājamārtaṇḍa*. Śāraṅgavadeva refers to Bhoja as a writer on music. In the field of administration he wrote *Chāṇakyanītiśāstra* and *Yuktikalpataru*. His *Śālihotra* is a work on testing horses and curing their diseases. The composition of a work entitled *Vidvajjanavallabha* dealing with questions related to diverse topics is also ascribed to Bhoja. *Prabhāvakacharita* mentions that Bhoja was author of works on *aṅka*, *svapna* and *sāmudrika*. However, these have not come down to us. Despite this, he was regarded as an authority on many subjects and he is quoted or referred to by many later writers and poets in their works on different subjects.

Bhoja had made Dhārā a seat of learning and held his literary court in the *Sarasvati Mandira,* also known as *Bhāratī-Bhavana* and *Śāradā-Sadana*, popularly known as *Bhojaśālā*, wherein he consecrated an image of Sarasvatī. His court was adorned with learned men and poets who were authors of remarkable works. One of the members of his court was Sūrāchārya, as mentioned in *Prabandhachintāmaṇi.* Another member was Uvaṭa, a Vedic scholar and author of *Mantrabhāṣya*, a commentary on *Vājasaneya Saṁhitā*. Another learned scholar was Chittapa, disciple of Kardamarāja, quotations of whose unknown work are found in later Sanskrit anthologies and some other works. Dhanapāla, son of Sarvadeva was another scholar of renown in the court of Bhoja. His prose romance *Tilakamañjarī* throws light on the contemporary socio-political conditions prevailing during the time of Bhoja. Daśabala, another Buddhist scholar from Valabhī who composed a work on astronomy entitled *Chintāmaṇisāraṇikā* was also a contemporary of Bhoja.

Naravarman

The next princely poet was Naravarman, the nephew of Bhoja. He was composer of the highly ornate Nagpur Museum stone inscription and the Sarpabandha inscriptions found at Dhar, Ujjain and Un. Poet Chittapa, referred to above continued to live during his reign.

Vindhyavarman

After Naravarman closed his reign, the Paramāra supremacy was temporarily eclipsed till the time of Vindhyavarman who succeeded in recovering it in the closing years of the 12th century AD. Literary activities were resumed. Bilhaṇa, the Minister of War and Peace under Vindhyavarman composed the fragmentary Mandu inscription which pays homage to Sarasvatī. Another contemporary scholar patronised by Vindhyavarman was Sulhaṇa, the author of Kedāra's *Vṛttaratnākara* in V.E. 1246, i.e., 1190 AD. Paṇḍita Āśādhara, who was also a contemporary of Vindhyavarman, Subhaṭavarman, Arjunavarman, Devapāla and Jaitugideva wrote a commentary on Rudraṭa's *Kāvyālaṅkāra, Aṣṭāṅgahṛdayodyota* which is a commentary on the Vāgbhaṭa *saṁhitā* and some other works of sectarian interest.

Arjunavarman

The reign of Arjunavarman, the grandson of Vindhyavarman witnessed a revival of poetic activities. The king himself composed *Rasikasañjivanī*, which is a commentary on *Amaruśataka*, and the royal preceptor, Madana, who was highly honoured by him by the title of *Bālasarasvatī*, composed a *nāṭikā*, a play in four acts, two of which have come down to us. This work entitled *Pārijātamañjarī* alias *Vijayaśrī* was staged in the temple of goddess Śāradā at Dhārā, to celebrate the victory of Arjunavarman over Jayasiṁha, the Chaulukya contemporary of Gujarat, which is doubtless a historical reference. His second work entitled *Bālasarasvatīya* or *Bālasarasvatīkāvya* has not come down to us. Some of his verses from this work are quoted in *Rasikasañjīvanī* and Jalhana's *Sūktimuktāvalī*.

Jaina Literary Works

A good number of Jaina literary works were also composed during the rule of various rulers of the Paramāra dynasty of Malwa. Chronologically the first of these scholars was Devasena who composed *Darṁsaṇasāra*, a treatise on philosophy composed at Dhārā in V.E. 990 (933-34 AD). His two other works were *Tattvasāra* and *Ārādhanāsāra*.

Of the reign of Vākpati Muñja, we have at least three Jaina writers viz. Hariṣeṇa, author of *Dharmaparīkṣā*, Mahāsena composer of *Pradyumnacharita* and Amitagati who composed *Subhāśitaratnasandoha*. Amitagati is also known to have composed works viz. *Upāsakāchāra, Dharmaparīkṣā* (V.E. 1070) and *Pañchasaṁgraha* (V.E. 1073) and a few other works. Dhanapāla was another renowned Jaina author who was contemporary of Sīyaka, Vākpatī Muñja and Bhoja. Besides his works noted above he wrote a lexicon of Prakrit entitled *Pāiyalachchhīnāmamālā* in V.E. 1029 (972 AD), *Satyapurīya-Māhātmya, Mahāvīrastuti, Ṛṣabhapañchaśikā* and a commentary on *Chaturviṁśatikā*.

Jaina scholars who were contemporary of Bhoja were : Vīra and Śrīchandra who had composed some Sanskrit poems; Nemichandra — the Jaina philosopher; Prabhāchandra, a Jaina scholar and author of *Prameyakamalamārtaṇḍa*; Nayanandin who composed *Sudarśanacharita, Sakalavihivihāna* and *Ārāhaṇā*. Jinavallabha, a contemporary of Naravarman wrote *Mahāvīrastotra*.

Paṇḍita Āśādhara was the most important Jaina scholar of 13th century AD living at Nalakachchhapura (modern Nālchhā, 25 km South East of Dhar). A large number of works dealing with Jainism have been attributed to him. These consist of devotional poems, commentaries and the doctrine of Jainism. His most popular work is *Dharmāmṛta* divided into two parts, on both of which he wrote independent commentaries. His other important works were *Jinayajñakalpa* (V.E. 1285) and *Trisastismrtisastra* (V.E. 1292). Some of these works are historically useful. Dāmodara, a friend of Āśādhara had composed a poem *Nemināthachariu* in the reign of Devapāla.

Most of the above-mentioned Jaina works are of sectarian value and of much little use for historians.

The *Dvayāśraya-Kāvya* of Hemachandra,[337] the *Pārthaparākrama Vyāyoga* of Prahlādana[338] and *Surathotsava* of Somesvara[339] are useful as indirect source material for reconstructing the past of Madhya Pradesh.

Literature under the Chandellas of Jejākabhukti

One of the few literary compositions of the period of the Chandella rule over Bundelkhand is *Prabodhachandrodaya*, a drama in six acts written by Kṛṣṇa Miśra. The indirect theme of the drama is to commemorate the victory of Gopāla, either a feudatory or a military general of the Chandellas over the Kalachuri king Karṇadeva who had routed the Chandella army during the reign of Devavarman, capturing a large part of his kingdom. The drama gives Gopāla the entire credit of saving the Chandella sovereignty in this catastrophy and reinstating Kīrtivarman on the throne. The victory was glorious and we learn from the drama that it was staged before Kīrtivarman.

About literary activities of the later period we find that Paramardin, who was on the Chandella throne from 1116 to 1202 AD was himself a poet. He composed a long inscription paying homage to Śiva. His minister Vatsarāja was prolific writer. His six dramas were composed to illustrate six out of ten types of Sanskrit dramas. These were : *Karpūracharita,* a *bhāṇa* or comic monologue; *Hāsyachūḍāmaṇi*, a *prahasana* or farce in one act; *Rukmiṇīharaṇa*, an *īhāmṛga* in four acts; *Tripuradāha Dima* in four acts; *Samudramanthana*, a *Śamvakāra* in three acts and *Kirātārjunīya-Vyāyoga*, a heroic play composed during the reign of Trailokyavarman, representing king's success over his enemies. Some of these were staged on the occasions of the *Yātrāmahotsavas* of Nīlakaṇṭha and Chakrasvamin at Kālañjara. Another notable scholar at the court of Chandellas was the Sāndhivigrahika Gadādhara who has been styled as *'Kavi-Chakravarti'*. Jaganika, the reputed author of *Ālhākhaṇḍa* was also living at the court of this ruler. A Jaina work composed during the reign of Paramardin is surmised from a verse in the *Dhanyakumāracharita*, written by a Jaina scholar Guṇabhadra.

The epigraphic literature of the time embellished with flight of fancy and imagination is also specimen of the literary activities of the period concerned. The entire literature taken together is a rich source material for reconstructing the history and culture of the times of the Chandellas of Jejākabhukti.

Folk Literature

Under this category may be placed works like *Bṛhatkathā* of Guṇāḍhya and *Kathāsaritasāgara*, romantic tales, didactic tales, fables and literature related to local or regional folks. A selected few of such literary pieces are useful as a source material for reconstructing the past glory of Madhya Pradesh. Thus, the traditions about king Vikramāditya of Ujjayinī, the reputed founder of Vikram Saṁvat are preserved in legends of the *Vetāla Pañchaviṁśati* (c. 12th cent. AD), *Dvatriṁśat Puttalikā* (c. 11th-13th cent. AD) and *Kālakāchāraya Kathā*. The last mentioned work provides details of the Śaka conquest of Ujjayinī and their final defeat at the hands of Vikramāditya in fuller details. Some scholars have attempted to prove the historical character of these tales. However, others do not agree. In any case these are very useful in solving mystery regarding the founder of Vikram Saṁvat which is yet awaiting final solution.

There are some works of similar nature based on bardic accounts still current in Central India which are useful in throwing light on the early medieval dynasties of M.P. One of them is *Mahobā Khaṇḍa* (also known as *Parmāla Rāso*)[340] generally taken to be part of *Pṛthīvīrāja Rāso* of Chanda Bardāī. However, the question of date of the authorship of this work is a matter of controversy and many believe it to be an independent work of an unknown author of a later date. Local traditions have been preserved in this work in the form of curious stories in Puranic style to describe the origin and growth of the Chandella dynasty. The story related in this work has been rejected by V.A. Smith as a 'silly legend'. But a critical examination of the legend may reveal, in spite of its apparent absurdities, a substratum of fact.

Pṛthvīrāja Rāso of Chanda Bardāī[341] and *Ālhā Khaṇḍa* of Jaganika Rao[342] are two other similar works which provide accounts related to the serious hostilities between Pṛthvīrāja Chauhan and Paramardi. The *Ālhā Khaṇḍa* specially focuses the heroism displayed by the two Banāphar chiefs Ālhā and his brother Udal. Much of these bardic accounts which are works of a very late period are full of unhistorical material which was added in course of time either to glorify Pṛthvīrāja or Paramardi. However, it cannot be denied that these accounts contain some historical truth as is evidenced by contemporary inscriptions and other literary sources.

A folk legend of similar nature exists at Vārāṇāsī which extols the munificent activities of king Karan Ḍahāriā.[343] It has been proved beyond doubt that the legend is related to the historical figure Karṇa of the Kaḷachuri dynasty of Tripurī.

In the field of art and architecture, folk legends are often found connected with famous monuments, sacred places of strategic importance, rivers and mountains. A good many of these have been recorded by A. Cunningham and J.D. Beglar in their *Archaeological Survey of India Reports* in twenty-three volumes. The story of Madhavānal Kāmakandalā associated with village Bilaharī in Jabalpur district, formerly known as Puśpāvatī and monuments existing therein[344] or the local chronicles related to the genealogies of the Kalachuri kings of Ratanpur till their final defeat at the hands of the Marathas in the middle of the 18th century AD[345] are instances of this kind. The editors of the District Gazetteers of M.P. and other Reports have also recorded such folk legends and local chronicles. For reconstruction of unbiased local and regional history, a careful examination of the folk literature of the concerned area is a necessity and therefore the importance of folk literature as a source material providing supporting evidence in reconstructing and revealing historical truth need never be underestimated.

Muslim Literary Sources

Contemporary and later Muslim literary sources have often come to our aid to corroborate evidence or supplement our information relating to the early medieval dynasties of M.P. The noteworthy works are:[346] *Aīn-i-Akbarī* of Abūl Fazal, *Kitāb-ul-Hind* of Al-Bīrūnī, *Kitāb Zain-ul Akhbār* of Mahmud Gardizi, *Muntakāb-ut-Tawarikh* of Abd-ul-Qādir Badauni, *Tabaqāt-i-Akbarī* of Nizāmuddin-Ahmad, *Tabaquat-i-Nāsirī* of Minhāj-ud-dīn, *Tāj-ul-Ma'asir* of Hasan-un-Nizāmī, *Tarīkh-i-Firishtā* of Muhammad Qasim, *Tarīkh-i-Fīrūz Shāhī* of Ziā-ud-dīn Barnī, *Tazjiyatu-l-Amsār* of Abd-u-lah Wassāf and *Ta'rīkh-i-'Alāī* of Amir Khusrav. *The History of India as told by its own Historians* edited by Sir H.M. Elliot and John Dowson and published in eight volumes[347] serves as a useful source book of reference pertaining to Muslim literary source material.

References

1. *Śatapatha Brāhmaṇa*, xii, 8. 1, 17; 9. 3, 1; cf. *IA*, Vol. XXX, p. 239 n.
2. Sircar, D.C., *Cosmography and Geography in Early Indian Literature*, Calcutta, 1967, p. 17.
3. II, 13; also *Vedic Index*, Vol. I, pp. 336-37.
4. VII, 18.
5. 5, 1, 9.
6. *Ṛgveda*, VIII, 5, 37-39.
7. Raychaudhuri, H.C., *Political History of Ancient India*, 6th ed., 1953, p. 130.
8. Majumdar, R.C. (ed.), *The Vedic Age*, 5th ed., Bombay, 1988, p. 265.
9. *Rām.*, Laṅkā. 27, 9.
10. *Imperial Gazetteer of India*, Vol. XXIII, p. 76.
11. *Ram.*, II, ch. 46.
12. Bhattacharya, P.K., *Historical Geography of Madhya Pradesh*, Delhi, 1976, pp. 101-02.
13. *Rām.*, II, 117, 5.

14. *Ibid.*, 54, 28-30.
15. Sircar, D.C., *op. cit.*, pp. 62-63.
16. *Rām.*, II, 94.9-10.
17. *Ibid.*, IV: 36, 2; 49.1; 52.12; 52.16; etc.
18. *Ibid.*, IV.41, 10.
19. *Ibid.*, VIII.121.
20. *Ibid.*, VII.120, 7.
21. Cunningham, *Archaeological Survey of India Reports*, Vol. VII, p. 168.
22. *Rām.*, 1.23.
23. Several theories regarding the location of Rāmagiri have been propounded till date.
24. *Mbh.*, II, 31, 12-13.
25. *Ibid.*, III.61, 21.
26. *Ibid.*, 61, 22.
27. *Ibid.*, XII.135, 3-5.
28. *Ibid.*, II.31.
29. *Ibid.*, III.89, 11-12.
30. Bajpai, K.D. (ed.), *The Geographical Encyclopaedia of Ancient and Medieval India*, pt. I, Varanasi, 1967, p. 35.
31. *Mbh.*, III.85, 86.
32. *Ibid.*, I, 63.
33. *Ibid.*
34. *Ibid.*, XII, 52, 32.
35. *Ibid.*, VI. 9.
36. Sircar, D.C., *Studies in the Geography of Ancient and Medieval India*, Delhi, 1960, p. 45 n.
37. *Mbh.*, III, ch. 82.
38. *Ibid.*, VII, ch. 67.
39. *Ibid.*, I, ch. 140.
40. *Ibid.*, VI, ch. 9; IV, ch. I.
41. *Ibid.*, III, ch. 306.
42. *Ibid.*, II.20, 27-29.
43. *Ibid.*, III, ch. 85.
44. *Śat. Br.*, XII.8, 1; 9, 3, 1.
45. *Mbh.*, XII. 52, 32.
46. *Ibid.*, ch. 32.
47. Sorensen, S., *Index to the Mahābhārata*, London, 1904, p. 178.

48. *Mbh.*, I, ch. 63.
49. *Ibid.*, III, ch. 22.
50. *Ibid.*, III, ch. 85.
51. Sorensen, S., *op. cit.*, p. 320.
52. *Ibid.*, p. 450.
53. *Ibid.*, p. 461.
54. *Ibid.*, p. 545.
55. *Ibid.*, p. 214.
56. *Mbh.*, II.31, 10.
57. Sircar, D.C., *op. cit.*, p. 35 n.
58. *Mbh.*, IV, I, II.
59. *Ibid.*, V. 22, 25; 74, 16; 198, 2; VI, 47, 4; 54, 8.
60. *Ibid.*, V, 4, 18.
61. *Ibid.*, II.30, 27; III.51, 23.
62. Sorensen, S., *op. cit.*, p. 225.
63. *Mbh.*, III, 19; 1, 105; 8; 2, 26, 4-5; 2, 29, 4-6; 36, 66, 12-13, 14, 85, 5-6; 5, 190, 10.
64. *Mbh.*, II. 31, 12.
65. Majumdar, R.C. (ed.), *The Classical Age*, Fourth ed., Bombay, 1988, p. 218.
66. *Mbh.*, III.61.
67. *CASIR*, XVII, p. 68.
68. *Mbh.*, II, 31.
69. *Ibid.*, XIII. 2, 6.
70. *Ibid.*, 152, 3.
71. *Ibid.*, VI, 9.
72. *Ibid.*, III, ch. 53.
73. *CASIR*, VII, p. 216.
74. Dey, N.L., *op. cit.*, p. 168, s.v. Ratnapura.
75. *Jaimini*, ch. 41.
76. *Mbh.*, III, 20, 50; XIV, 83, 2.
77. *Ibid.*, III.253, 10.
78. *Ibid.*, VI.87, 9.
79. Sorensen, S. *op. cit.*, p. 225.
80. *Mbh.*, II. 31, 11-12.
81. *Ibid.*, V. 158, 14-15
82. Majumdar, R.C. (ed.), *The Vedic Age*, p. 278.
83. Majumdar, R.C. (ed.), *The Age of Imperial Unity* (6th ed.), Bombay, 1990, p. 14.

84. *Ibid.*
85. Sircar, D.C., *Select Inscriptions*, p. 90, fn. 4.
86. Pargiter, *The Purana Text of the Dyansties of the Kali Age*, 1962, p. 16.
87. Trivedi, H.V., *Catalogue of the Coins of the Nāga Kings at Padmāvatī*, Gwalior, 1957, p. i.
88. *Ibid.*
89. Pargiter, *op. cit.*, p. 49.
90. *Mark*. 57, 10-11.
91. Ali, S.M., *Geography of the Purāṇas*, New Delhi, 1983, p. 113.
92. *Bhāgavata*, V. 19, 17.
93. *Vāmana*, XIII.25, 30.
94. *Harivaṁsá* (Viṣṇu-Parva), ch. XXXVIII.
95. *Bhāgavata*, IV.i, 14-15.
96. *Revā Khaṇḍa*, V. 51.
97. Dey, N.L., *GDAMI*, p. 16.
98. *Varāha*. ch. 85.
99. *Śiva Purāṇa*, I. 58.
100. *Bṛhat-Śiva Purāṇa*, I. 83.
101. *Padma, Svargaloka (Ādi)*, ch. 6.
102. *Varāha*. ch. 85.
103. *Imperial Gazetteer of India*, Vol. XXII, p. 432.
104. *Devī Purāṇa*, ch. 39, 5.
105. Sircar, D.C., *Studies in the Geography of Ancient and Medieval India*, Delhi, 1960, p. 450.
106. *Ibid.*, p. 46 n.
107. *Ibid.*
108. *Ibid.*
109. *Ibid.*
110. *Ibid.*
111. *Ibid.*
112. *Imperial Gagetteer of India*, Vol. XXIII, p. 76.
113. *Mārk*. IV. 22.
114. Raychaudhuri, H.C., *Studies in Indian Antiquities*, 1958, p. 109.
115. *Skanda P.*, *Revā Khaṇḍa*, ch. 4.
116. Raychaudhuri, H.C., *op. cit.*, p. 109.
117. *Mārk*. ch. 54.
118. Sircar, D.C., *SGAMI.*, p. 47 n.

119. *Vāyu.*, pp. 88, 113.
120. Dey, N.L., *GDAMI*, p. 21.
121. *Matsya.*, ch. 113, v.25.
122. *Bṛhat-Śiva P., Uttara*, ch. 20.
123. *Padma P., Ādi*, ch. 3.
124. *Ṛṣīkā* of *Vāyu P., Kāśikā* of *Matsya P., Ṛṣikā* of *Brahmāṇḍa P.* is *Ṛṣikulyā* of modern times, vide Ali, S.M., *op. cit.*, p. 125.
125. Sukumārī of *Vāyu, Matsya* and *Brahmāṇḍa P.* is Suktel of modern times, which joins the Mahānadī at Sonpur. Ali, S.M., *op. cit.*
126. *Ibid.* It is modern Mand. Ali, S.M., *op. cit.*
127. *Ibid.* It is modern Mahānadī proper. Ali, S.M., *op. cit.*
128. Kūpā of *Vāyu P.* is modern Arpā, a tributary of the Mahānadī. Ali, S.M., *op. cit.*
129. Pasini of *Matsya P.* is modern Jonk in Raipur dist. of M.P. Ali. S.M., *op. cit.*
130. Tributary of the Mahānadī. Ali, S.M., *op. cit.*
131. It meets the Mahānadī at Rājim. Ali, S.M., *op. cit.*
132. *Padma P., Ādi*, ch. 3.
133. *Matsya P.*, 22, 46, 64 and *Kūrma P.*, ii, 37, 16, 22.
134. *Garuḍa P.*, I.55, 8.
135. *Skanda P.*, ch. 43.
136. *Skanda P.*, Revā Khaṇḍa, ch. 56.
137. Sircar, D.C., *SGAMI*, p. 36.
138. *Ibid.*
139. *Ibid.*, pp. 33, 34, note.
140. *Skanda P.*, Maheśvara - Khaṇḍa, 39, 142.
141. Majumdar, R.C. (ed), *The Classical Age*, 4th ed., Bombay, 1988, p. 218.
142. *Mārk.*, ch. 57, v. 46.
143. Majumdar R.C., *op. cit.*, p. 222.
144. *Āvantya Khaṇḍa.*
145. *Liṅga Purāṇa*, pt. I, ch. 71.
146. *Matsya*, ch. 116.
147. Sircar, D.C., *SGAMI*, p. 35 and note 1.
148. *Skanda P.*, ch. 43.
149. Sircar, D.C., *SGAMI*, pp. 34 n.
150. *Ibid.*
151. *Padma P., Pātāla*, ch. 27, vs. 58-59.
152. *Bhāg. P.*, Book XII, ch. I.
153. *Mārkaṇḍeya P.*, ch. 57.

154. *Devī Bhāgavata P.*, VII, 38.
155. Sircar, D.C., *SGAMI*, pp. 32, 35 and notes.
156. *Suttanipāta*, vs. 976-77 and 1011-13.
157. *Aṅguttara*, I, 213; IV, 252, 256, 260.
158. *Mahāvastu*, I, 34; II, 3.
159. *Vinaya* Texts, II, 146 n.
160. *Niddesa*, II, 37.
161. cf. *Dīghanikāya*, PTS, II, 200 and passim. See Malalasekera, *op. cit.*, p. 911.
162. *Chetiya*, No. 422.
163. *Dīgha*, II, 235.
164. *Dīgha*, II, 236.
165. Bhandarkar, D.R., *Carmichael Lectures*, p. 54.
166. *Jātaka*, IV, p. 390; *Sacred Books of the Buddhists*, III, 270.
167. *Dīpa*, VIII, 1, 2.
168. *Mahāvaṁsa*, XII, 3, 29.
169. *Vinayapiṭaka* (ed. Oldenberg, III), p. 314 ff.
170. *Dīpavaṁsa* (ed. Oldenberg), p. 57.
171. *Jātaka*, II, pp. 248 ff.
172. *Mahāvastu*, I, 34.
173. *Jātaka*, III, 338; VI, 238.
174. Sircar, D.C., *SGAMI*, pp. 206 ff.
175. Puri, B.N., *Cities of Ancient India*, Delhi, 1966, p. 127.
176. Turnour, *Pali Annals*, in JASB, VII, 930. Also *CASIR*, X, p. 37.
177. *Mahāvaṁsa* (tr. by Turnour), p. 76.
178. Sircar, D.C., *JRAS*, 1963, p. 20.
179. *Pariśiṣṭaparvan*, XII, 2-3.
180. Malalasekera, G.P., *Dictionary of Pāli Proper Names*, Vol. I, London, 1960, p. 838.
181. *Majjhimanikāya*, III, 7.
182. *Theragāthā*, Pāli Text Society (PTS), I, 485; Malalasekera, *op. cit.*, pp. 192-95.
183. *Saṁyuttanikāya*, PTS, III, 9, 12; IV, 15-16; Udana Commentary, PTS, 307; *Aṅguttaranikāya*, PTS, V, 46.
184. Lacote, F., *Essay on Gunadhya and the Brhatkathā* (Eng. tr. by Tabard), Bangalore, 1923, p. 176.
185. VI, 189-90; Pradhan, *Chronology of Ancient India*, p. 217.
186. Raychaudhuri, H.C., *op. cit.*, pp. 287-88.
187. *Mahāvamsa* (ed. Turnour), ch. XIII, 8.

188. Jayswal, *Imperial History of India*, text, p. 43.
189. Majumdar, R.C. (ed.), *The Age of Imperial Kanauj*, 3rd ed., Bombay, 1984, p. 21.
190. *Malalasekera, op. cit.*, Vol. I, pp. 192-95.
191. Raychaudhuri, H.C., *PHAI*, p. 145.
192. cf. *Saṁyuttanikāya*, PTS, Vol. III, pp. 12 and IV, pp. 15-16; Udana Commentary, PTS, p. 307; *Aṅguttaranikāya*, PTS, Vol. V, p. 46.
193. *Jātaka*, Vol. V, No. 133.
194. Dey, N.L., *GDAMI*, p. 28.
195. *Ibid.*, p. 29.
196. *Āvasyaka Chūrṇi*, Jinadasagani, 1928, p. 476.
197. *Ibid.*
198. *Ibid.*, p. 461.
199. *Bhagavatī Ṭīkā*, 7, 6.
200. *Maraṇasamādhi*, 472, p. 128-A. Vāsudevahimḍī, p. 122.
201. *Ibid.*, 470, p. 472; Malayagiri, *Āvaśyakaṭīkā*, p. 395-A.
202. Law, B.C., *Historical Geography of Ancient India*, Paris, 2nd. ed., 1968, p. 199.
203. *Āvasyaka Chūrṇī*, Jinadasagani, Ratlam, 1928, pp. 400 ff.
204. Kirfel, *Die Kosmorgraphie der Inder,* Leipzig (1920), pp. 225-26.
205. *Sthavirāvalīcharita*, XI, v. 177.
206. *Ibid.*, XXII.
207. *Aṣṭādhyāyī*, IV, I, 176; I, 171.
208. *Ibid.*, V, 3, 114.
209. *Ibid.*, 4, 2, 116.
210. *Ibid.*, 4, 1, 78.
211. *Ibid.*, VIII, 2, 12.
212. *Arthaśāstra*, 2, 2, 15.
213. *Ibid.*
214. *Ibid.*, 2, 2.
215. *Journal of the M.P. Itihasa Parishad*, Bhopal, No. 8, 1970, p.33.
216. Fleet, *JRAS*, 1910, pp. 440-41.
217. Sircar, D.C., *SGAMI*, p. 91.
218. See "*Ujjayini in Mṛchchhakaṭika*" by S. Mukherjee in B.C. Law Volume (ed. Bhandarkar), pt. I.
219. Agnihotri, P.D., in *Journal of M.P.I.P.*, No. 8, 1970, p. 37.
220. Jain, B.C., *Kalidasa and his Times*, Delhi, 1990.
221. *Megha Pū*, 19.
222. *Ibid.*, 17-18. There is difference of opinion among scholars regarding the

identification of this hill.

223. *Raghu.*, XII, 9 (Daṇḍakāranya), 15 (Chitrakūṭa).

224. There is controversy about the location of this hill.

225. *Megha. Pū*, 27.

226. *Ibid.*, 42, 46, 47, 48.

227. *Raghu*, VII, 36.

228. *Ibid.*, XIII, 48. The river of the same name mentioned in *Kumārasambhava, Vikramorvaśīya, Mālavikāgnimitra* and *Meghadūta* is different.

229. *Ibid.*, IX, 20, 27; XIV, 76.

230. *Megha, Pū,* 24.

231. *Ibid.*, 24.

232. p. 102.

233. *Megha.*, Pū, 28-29.

234. *Ibid.*, 42. It also speaks of another branch of the Śiprā viz. the *Gandhavatī* on which stood the famous temple of Mahākāla at Ujjain.

235. *Ibid.*, 27, 29.

236. *Raghu.*, V, 39, 42, 43; VI, 43; VII, 2, 3, 20.

237. *Megha., Pū,* 19. It calls the river as 'Revā'.

238. *Ibid.*, 49.

239. *Ibid.*, 23.

240. *Māl.*, 5, 1.

241. *Raghu.*, VI, 37-44.

242. *Megha.*, *Pū*, 24-25.

243. *Ibid.*, 16.

244. *Ibid.*, 24-25. Also *Mālavikāgnimitra*, Act V (ed. Vidyanidhi), p. 370.

245. *Ibid.*, 49.

246. *Ibid.*, 32-43.

247. *Raghu.*, VI, 37-44.

248. *Megha., Pū.,* 30-34.

249. *Ibid.*, 36.

250. *Mālavikāgimitra*, Act I.

250a. XIV.9.

251. XVI.3.

252. XVI.17.

253. XVI.10.

254. XVI.10.

255. V.64; XVI, 1, 9.

256. XII, 6.
257. XVI, 10.
258. XVI. 9.
259. V.65; XVI.1, 9.
260. XVI.32.
261. XVI.10.
262. XVI.9.
263. XVI.12.
264. XVI.9.
265. V. 40; IX.17, 18, 21.
266. V. 64; LXXXVI.2.
267. XI. 59.
268. XVI.3; XXXII.2.
269. XIV.8.
270. XLIII.8.
271. XIV.13; XVI.17.
272. XVI.11.
273. XIV.16.
274. XIV.12.
275. V.40; X.15; XXXII.11.
276. XIV.10; XVI.26.
277. XIV.12; IX.13; XXXII.22.
278. XIV.20.
279. XIV.8.
280. XIV.7.
281. X.14.
282. XIV.27; IV.24; XVI.26; XXXII.19; LXIX.11.
283. XIV.10, V.76.
284. IV.22; V. 77, 78; IX.17, 29, 40; XVI.2, 33.
285. V. 39.
286. XIV.10.
287. XIV. 9.
288. V.39.
289. XIV.15.
290. XIV.7.
291. X.15; XII.14; LXIX.30.
292. XVI.32.

293. *Mudrārākṣasa*, 4.2.16.
294. *Daśakumāracharita* (ed. Agashe, Bombay 1919), p. 197.
295. *Ratnāvalī*, Act IV.
296. Agrawala, V.S., *Harṣacharita — Eka Sānskritika Adhyayana,* Patna, 1953, p. 197.
297. *Ibid.*, pp. 68-69.
298. *Ibid.*, p. 132.
299. Bajpai, K.D., *Sources of the History of India*, Vol. VI, Calcutta, 1989, p. 252.
300. *Harṣacharita* (K.P. Parab, ed.), Bombay, 1925, p. 19.
301. *Kādambarī* (ed. Siddhanta Vagisa), pp. 19, 183.
302. Agarwala, V.S., *op. cit.*, p. 193:
303. 2, 3, 3.
304. 1.2-3, 32.
305. *Amarakośa* (Nirnaya Sagar ed.), p. 534.
306. *Mālatimādhava*, Act IV, IX.
307. *CASIR*, VII, p. 308.
308. *Mālatimādhava*, *op. cit.*
309. *Ibid.*
310. *Ibid.*, Act IX.
311. *Ibid.*, Act IV.
312. *Uttararāma-Charita* (Allahabad ed.), pp. 53 and 421.
313. Konow, S., *Das indische Drama*, Berlin, 1920, p. 83.
314. *Sūkti-muktāvali,* IV, 82.
315. *Daśarūpaka*, ii, 58; iii, 3, 24; iv. 13, 28.
316. Abhinavagupta in his commentary on *Bharata*, ch. XIX.
317. S.K. De, ed. Calcutta, 1928, pp. 225, 244.
318. *IA*, XLI, pp. 139 ff.
319. *Sūktimuktāvali*, p. 46.
320. Dalal, C.D., *Kāvyamīmāṁsā* (G.O.S. No. 1), 1934, pp. 281-314.
321. Konow, S., *Karpūramañjarī*, p. 182.
322. cf. Rājaśekhara's *Bālarāmāyaṇa*, Act IV; see Apte, *Rājaśekhara — His Life and Times*, 9.21.
323. *Kāvyamīmāṁsā, op. cit.*, ch. 3, p. 9.
324. Konow, *op. cit.*
325. Vallabhadeva, *Subhāṣitāvalī* (Bombay), v. 186. Also, Merutuṅga, *Prabandhachintāmaṇi* (ed. Jinavijaya Muni), p. 50.
326. Bilhaṇa, *Vikramāṅkadevacharita* (ed. Buhlar), XVIII, 95.

327. *Ibid.*, v. 93.
328. Śrīdharadāsa, *Saduktikarṇāmṛta,* ed. by H.D. Sharma, III, 10, 2.
329. *Prabandhachintāmaṇi, op. cit.*, 5.50.
330. *op. cit.*, p. 50.
331. Khare, *Sources of the Mediaeval History of the Deccan* (Marathi), Intrd., p. 39.
332. *Collected Works of Bhandarkar*, Vol. II, p. cii.
333. *Prakarta Paingala* (Bibliotheca Indica Series), I, 69, 96, 126, 185.
334. *Asiatic Researches*, Vol. IX, p. 176.
335. For details, see *CII*, IV, pp. cxviii, and *IA*, LXII, pp. 101 ff.
336. For a list of Bhoja's works, see Aufrecht, Th., *Catalogus Catalogorum*, I. 418; II, 95; III.90; *HAL*, XCVII f; *HSP.*, 249 ff; *HD.* I, 276 ff; *Bhojarāja*, 69 f; *EI.*, I, 231 f; *PCM.*, p. 50. Also see Madras University Publication No. 11 given in the beginning of *Sarasvatī Kaṇṭhābharaṇa*, ed. Raghavan. Also see *PBP*, p. 316, where Bhoja is stated to have written 84 works.
337. *IA*, IV, pp. 72 ff.
338. GOS, Baroda, 1917.
339. Bombay, 1902.
340. Ed. by S.S. Das, Benaras, 1920.
341. Ed. by M.V. Pandia and S.S. Das, Benaras, 1913.
342. *Lays of Ālhā*, translated by Waterfield.
343. This legend has been published by Grierson in *IA*, Vol. XVI (Jan. 1887), pp. 46-48.
344. *CASIR*, Vol. XXI, pp. 93 ff. Also see *Mādhavanal Kāmakandalā Prabhandha,* Vol. I (GOS), Baroda, 1981.
345. *Ibid.*, Vol. XVII, pp. 68 ff.
346. For details of publications of these works, see Bibliography in the following pages.
347. *Ibid.*

VIII
Foreign Travellers and Writers

Indica of Megasthenes

The *Indica* of Megasthenes has made reference to two rivers of Central India viz. Prinas and Kenas which flow into the Ganges.[1] Mc Crindle has identified Prinas with Tamasā (modern Tons), a river of Bundelkhand region, which is the same as Parṇāśā of the Purāṇas.[2] Megasthenes also tells us that Pāṭaliputra was on the banks of the Ganges and 'the Erannoboas would be third of the Indian rivers'.[3] Scholars regard Erannoboas as corruption of Hiraṇyavāha, i.e. Son. It may be mentioned here that though the ancient city of Pāṭaliputra stood at the junction of the Son and the Ganges, Son afterwards gradually changed its lower course and at present it drains itself into the Ganges about 25 miles to the west of Patna, i.e. ancient Pāṭaliputra.

The Periplus of the Erythrean Sea

This is an anonymous Greek work entitled *Periplus Maris Erythraei*, composed about the eighth decade of the first century AD when Ujjayinī was not a capital city, i.e. sometime before the Kārdamakas. Śakas made Ujjayinī (Ozéné) their capital in the second quarter of the second century AD. Ptolemy mentions Ozéné (Ujjayinī) as the capital of Śaka Chaṣṭana.[4] The work states that from Ozéné (i.e. Ujjayinī) "are brought down all things needed for the welfare of the country around Barygaza (Broach) and many things for our trade".[5] The work is acquainted with some geographical locations of Madhya Pradesh viz. river Narmadā mentioned as Naomados[6] etc.

Ptolemy's Geography

This work composed in about the middle of second century AD provides some geographical data pertaining to ancient Madhya Pradesh. The Ouïndion[7] ranges referred to in the Ptolemy's geography have been identified with Vindhyas. Ptolemy describes the Ouxtenton (Ṛkṣavant) as the source of the Toundis, the Dosaron and the Adams.[8] Raychaudhuri takes the Dosaron as Daśārṇā (Dhasān near Sagar) which occurs in the list of rivers issuing from the Ṛkṣa as given in the Purāṇas. Ptolemy again represents the Ouïndion (Vindhya) as the source of both the

Namados (Narmadā) and the Nanagouna (Tapti).[9] Ptolemy refers to the rivers Mahānadī as Manada[10] and Son as Soa.[11] The territory of Mandalai referred to by Ptolemy has been identified with the highland where Son and Narmadā have their sources.[12] Cunningham thinks that Ptolemy mentions Chhattisgarh or Mahakoshal as the country of Adisathri, bounded on the south by Adisathron range of mountains, and having its capital at Sageda (possibly Chitrāṅgadapura or Maṇipura of the *Mahābhārata* or modern Sirpur) with a part in the north-east called Balantipurgaon (possibly the famous stronghold of Bandogarh in Rewa).[13] Ptolemy also makes Ozéné (Ujjain) as the capital of Tiastanes (the Kārdamaka-Śaka Satrap Chaṣṭana).[14]

Hiuen-Tsang's Si-yu-ki[15]

The *Si-yu-ki* of Hiuen-Tsang who made extensive tours in different parts of India during 629-645 AD has provided many interesting details about the history and culture of Central India. The following account is evident:

"The Pilgrim's description next proceeds to relate that from Kalinga he went north-west by hill and wood for above 1800 *li* to Kosala. This country, more than 6000 *li* in circuit, was surrounded by mountains and was a succession of woods and marshes, its capital being above 40 *li* in circuit. The soil of the country was rich and fertile, the towns and villages were close together; the people were prosperous, tall of stature and black in colour; the king was a kshatriya by birth, a Buddhist in religion, and of noted benevolence. There were above 100 Buddhist monasteries, and about 10,000 Brethren, all Mahayanists. Near the south of the city (that is apparently, the capital) was an old monastery with an Asoka tope where Buddha had vanquished Tirthikas by the exhibition of supernormal powers, and in which Nāgārjuna P'uśa had afterwards lodged. Contemporary with this P'usa was the king styled *Sha-to-p'o-ha* or "Leading-right" (yin-chêng) who treated Nāgārjuna with ceremonious respect, and kept a guard at his residence. The record then tells of the visit made by Deva P'usa from Sengkala to this monastery in order to have a discussion with Nāgārjuna".[16]

The country of Kosala (*Kiao-sa-lo)* referred to by Hiuen-Tsang was Southern Kosala (modern Chhattisgarh region of M.P.). As per the tradition recorded by Hiuen-Tsang when Nāgārjuna (c. second century AD) lived in the monastery built by Aśoka to the south of the capital city of Dakṣiṇa Kosala, the king of the land was *Sha-to-p'o-ha,* i.e. Sātavahanas. On several numismatic evidences the rule of the Sātavāhanas over Dakṣiṇa Kosala has been proved beyond doubt. The concerned ruler was possibly Yajña Sātakarṇi. It may also be mentioned that the archaeological excavations conducted during 1954-55 at Sirpur, the ancient capital of South Kosala, has brought to light remains of stupas, monasteries, sculptures, Chinese coins, seals, sealings and numerous antiquities related to Buddhism in support of the statement of Hiuen-Tsang.

The account of Hiuen-Tsang has also made a reference to the Malava (*Mo-la-po*) country which was situated on the south-east side of the Mo-ha or Mahi river in Gujarat.[17] It may be mentioned that about the beginning of the 7th century AD there were at least two Mālava territories, one in the Māhi valley in Gujarat and the second in East Malwa in Madhya Pradesh. Hiuen-Tsang recognises a separate country with *U-she-yen-na* (Ujjain) as capital, to the east of Mālava (*Mo-la-po*) country.[18] "This country he describes as being above 6000 *li*, and its capital as being above 30 *li*, in circuit; in its products and in the ways of the people it resembled Surath; it had a rich and flourishing population. There were some tens of Buddhist Monasteries, of which the majority were in ruins, and only three or four were in a state of preservation; the Brethren, who were students of both 'Vehicles', were above 300 in number; there were some tens of Deva-Temples, and the non-Buddhists lived pell-mell. The King was of the brahmin caste; he was well learned in heterodox lore, but was not a Buddhist. Not far from the capital was a tope at the place where Asoka had made a Hell (that is, a jail like a hell, as before)".[19]

One more country in Madhya Pradesh visited by Hiuen-Tsang was *Chih-chi-to* or *Chi-ki-to* (according to Beal) which has been identified by Cunningham and Beal with Jajhoti or Jajhaoti which had its capital at Khajuraho in Bundelkhand.[20] In words of Watters: "Going on with his narrative the pilgrim relates that he went north-east from Ujayana above 1000 *li* to *Chih-chi-to* (Julien's *Chi-ki-t'o*). This country was above 4000 *li*, and its capital about 15 *li*, in circuit; the soil was rich, the crops were abundant, and pulse and wheat were products. The majority of the people were not Buddhists, but there were some tens of monasteries with a few Brethren; there were above ten Deva-temples and 1000 professed adherents of the other systems. The king, who was a brahmin, was a firm believer in Buddhism, and encouraged men of merit, and learned scholars of other lands collected here in numbers".[21]

Some scholars prefer to identify *Chi-chi-to* with Chitor in Rajasthan[22] while others identify it with Chitrakūṭa in Bundelkhand.[23]

Maheśvarapura (*Mo-hi-ssu-fa-lo-pu-lo*) was the last place in M.P. visited by Hiuen-Tsang. According to Watters: "The narrative proceeds to relate that from *Chih-chi-t'o* the pilgrim went north above 900 *li* to *Mo-hi-ssu-fa-lo-pu-lo* (Maheśvarapura). This country was above 3000 *li*, and its capital was above 30 *li*, in circuit. In its products and the ways of the people it resembled Ujayana; the people were not Buddhists; there were a few score Deva-temples, and the majority belonged to the Pāśupatas. The king was a brahmin, and was not a believer in Buddhism."[24]

Cunningham has identified Maheśvarapura with Mandla.[25] However, most of the scholars prefer to equate it with Gwalior region.

Al-Bīrūnī's Kitāb-ul-Hind[26]

The *Kitāb-ul-Hind* of Al-Bīrūnī provides interesting geographical data as well as information related to history and culture of Madhya Pradesh. The following extract evinces it:

"Marching from Kanoj towards the south-east, on the western side of the Ganges, you come to the realm of Jajāhūtī (Jejākabhukti, Jajhotī in Bundelkhand), 30 *farsakh* from Kanoj. The capital of the country is Kajūrāha (Kharjūravāhaka, Khajurāho). Between this town and Kanoj there are two of the most famous fortresses of India, Gwaliyar (Gopagiri, Gwalior) and Kālanjar (Kālañjara in the Banda District). Dahāla (Dāhala), . . . a country the capital of which is Tiaurī (Tripurī in the Jabalpur District), and the ruler of which is now Gangeya (Kalachuri Gāṅgeya)"[27]

The extract quoted below supplies important data about Malwa.

"The distance between Māhūra and Kanoj is the same as that between Kanoj and Bazāna, viz. 28 *farsakh*.[28] If a man travels from Māhūra to Ujjain (Ujjayinī), he passes through villages which are only five *farsakh* and less distant from each other. At the end of a march of a 35 *farsakh*, he comes to a large village called Dūdahī (near Lalitpur in the Jhansi District); thence to Bāmahūr, 17 *farsakh* from Dūdahī; Bhāilsāh (Bhāyillasvāmin, Bhilsa), 5 *farsakh*, a place most famous among the Hindus. The name of the town is identical with that of the idol worshipped there. Thence to Ardīn (Ujjayinī), 9 *farsakh*. The idol worshipped there is called Mahākāla; Dhār (Dhārā), 7 *farsakh*".[29]

"Marching from Bazāna southward, you come to Maiwār (Mevāḍa), 25 *farsakh* from Bazāna. This is a kingdom the capital of which is Jattaraur (Citrakūṭa, Cittaūḍa, Citoḍ). From this town to Mālavā and its capital, Dhār, the distance is 20 *farsakh*. The city of Ūjain lies 7 *farasakh* to the east of Dhār. From Ūjain to Bhāilasān, which likewise belongs to Mālavā, the distance is 10 *farsakh*".

"Marching from Dhār southward, you come to Bhūmihara, 20 *farsakh* from Dhār; Kand, 20 *farsakh*; Namāvur (Nimāḍ) on the banks of the Narmadā (Narbadā), 10 *farsakh*; Alīspūr (Ellichpur), 20 *farsakh*; Mandagir (Nāndeḍ), on the banks of the river Godāvar (Godāvarī), 60 *farsakh*."

"Again marching from Dhār southward, you come to the valley of Namiyya, 7 *farsakh* from Dhār; Mahratta-desh (Mahārāṣṭra-deśa), 18 *farsakh*; the province of Kunkan (the North Konkan), and its capital Tāna (Sthānaka, Thānā) on the sea-coast, 25 *farsakh*".[30]

Al-Bīrūnī also makes reference to king Vikramāditya of Ujjain and Bhojadeva of Dhār regarding whose activities he has narrated several interesting tales.[31]

References

1. Mc Crindle, *Megasthenes and Arrian*, p. 135.
2. *Ibid.*
3. Majumdar, R.C. (ed.), *The Classical Accounts of India*, Calcutta, 1960, pp. 221-22.
4. Sircar, D.C., *Cosmography and Geography in Indian Literature*, Calcutta, 1967, p. 111.
5. Schoff, W.H., (tr.) *Periplus Maris Erythraci*, ed. by Fabricius, London, 1912, Sec. 48, 49.
6. *Ibid.*, p. 175.
7. *Ptolemy* (ed. Majumdar-Sastri), pp. 76-81, 224-27.
8. *Ibid.*, VII, i, 39-41.
9. *Ibid.*, VII, i, 31-32; Sircar, D.C., *op. cit.*, pp. 125-27.
10. *Ibid.*
11. *Ibid.*, p. 126.
12. Mc Crindle's *Ptolemy*, p. 168.
13. *CASIR*, VII, p. 68.
14. Sircar, D.C., *op. cit.*, pp. 131 and 114.
15. See Beal's translation (Calcutta reprint, 1957). Also T. Watters, *On Yuan Chwang's Travels in India* (AD 629-45), ed. by T.W. Rhys Davids and S.W. Bushell, London, 1904. First Indian edition, Delhi, 1961.
16. Watters, *op. cit.*, Vol. II, p. 200.
17. *Ibid.*, p. 242.
18. Cunningham, *The Ancient Geography of India*, rep. ed. Varanasi, 1963, p. 412.
19. Watters, *op. cit.*, Vol. II, p. 250.
20. Cunningham, *op. cit.*, p. 405.
21. Watters, *op. cit.*, Vol. II, p. 251.
22. *Ibid.*; Ray, H.C., *DHNI*, Vol. II, p. 670.
23. Ganguly, D.C., *JUPHS*, XIX, pp. 90-100.
24. Watters, T., *op. cit.*, Vol. II, p. 251.
25. Cunningham, *op. cit.*

26. Sachau, E.C., *Alberuni's India*, Vol. I, Chapter VIII, pp. 198ff. The vowel *wāw* has been transliterated as long *o*, the same as *ū*.
27. Sircar, D.C., *op. cit.*, p. 156.
28. Sachau has shown that 1 *farsakh* or *kuroh* (*krośa*) = 4 Arabian miles (2186 yards each) = about 3 3/4 English geographical miles (2025 yds. each).
29. Sircar, D.C., *op. cit.*, p. 156.
30. *Ibid.*, pp. 156-57.
31. Sachau, *op. cit.*, pp. 189-92.

Appendices

Appendix I

Radiocarbon Dates from M.P.

(After Possehl - 1988)

Site	*No*	*5568 BP*	*5730 BC*	*Calibration*	*Cultural Assn*	*Date list*
Adamgarh	TF-120	7240 ± 125 BP	5505±129 BC	NA	Microliths	TATA V
Adamgarh	TF -116	2765 ± 105 BP	900±108 BC	1105-805	Middle Palaeolithic	TATA V
Baghor	SUA-1422	5305±90 BP	3514±90 BC	4110-3795	Microliths	
Baghor	BETA-4793	25485±420 BP	24300±430 BC		Upper Palaeolithic	
Baghor	PRL -711	12450±220 BP	10875±227 BC	NA	Upper Palaeolithic	PRL V
Baghor	BETA-4792	11525±120 BP	9921±125 BC		Upper Palaeolithic	
Baghor	SUA-1420	10415±140 BP	8777±145 BC		Upper Palaeolithic	
Baghor II	PRL-715	8090±220 BP	6385±227BC	NA	Microliths	PRL V
Baghor III	PRL-714	6460±180 BP	4705±185BC	5565-5205 BC	Upper Palaeolithic	PRL V
Barkhera	PRL-113	7250±135 BP	5520±139 BC	N.A.	Chalcolithic?	PRL I
Barkhera	PRL-111	3170±105 BP	1315±108 BC	1660-1360 BC	Malwa	PRL I
Besnagar	TF-387	2350±100 BP	470±103 BC	600-385BC	NBP	TATA V
Besnagar	PRL-283	2200±130 BP	315-134BC	415-130 BC	NBP	PRL III
Besnagar	TF-254	2180±105 BP	295±108 BC	400-150 BC	Not Given	TATA IV
Bhimbetka	PRL-49	Modern	N.A	N.A	Microliths, Burial I	PRL I
Bhimbetka	PRL-536	950±110 BP	970±113 AD	915-1220 AD	Microliths	PRL V
Bhimbetka	PRL-17	7570±210 BP	5845±216 BC	N.A.	Microliths	PRL I
Bhimbetka	PRL-314	630±100 BP	1300±103 AD	N.A.	Burial	PRL III
Bhimbetka	PRL-50	5860±110 BP	4085±113 BC	4950-4560 BC	Microliths, Burial 3	PRL I
Bhimbetka	PRL-321	370±130 BP	1570±134 AD	NA	Microliths	PRL III
Bhimbetka	PRL 318	3560±100BP	1715±103BC	2135-1755BC	Microliths	PRL III
Bhimbetka	PRL-306	2820±110 BP	955±113 BC	1125-825 BC	Microliths	PRL III

Appendix I (Contd.)

Site	*No*	*5568 BP*	*5730 BC*	*Calibration*	*Cultural Assn*	*Date list*
Bhimbetka	PRL-534	2780±150 BP	915±155 BC	1125-795 BC	Microliths	PRL V
Bhimbetka	PRL-18	2650±125 BP	780±129 BC	890-770 BC	Microliths	PRL I
Bhimbetka	PRL-317	2490±100 BP	615±103 BC	795-420 BC	Microliths	PRL III
Bhimbetka	PRL-310	2320±100 BP	440±103 BC	445-375 BC	Microliths	PRL III
Bhimbetka	PRL-51	2050±110 BP	160±113 BC	185 BC-35 AD	Microliths, Burial 2	PRL I
Bhimbetka	PRL-316	1930±100 BP	40±103 BC	35 BC-95 AD	Microliths	PRL III
Bhimbetka	PRL-789	17670±490 BP	16250±505 BC	N.A.	Middle Palaeolithic	PRL V
Bhimbetka	PRL-315	1760±180 BP	135±185 AD	10-465 AD	Microliths, Burial	PRL III
Bhimbetka	PRL-788	17230±480 BP	15795±494 BC	N.A.	Middle Palaeolithic	PRL V
Bhimbetka	PRL-787	15370±570 BP	13880±587 BC	N.A.	Middle Palaeolithic	PRL V
Bhimbetka	PRL-535	1160±150 BP	755±155 AD	790-1175 AD	Microliths	PRL V
Bhimbetka	PRL-311	1060±80 BP	860±82 AD	870-1050 AD	Microliths	PRL III
Dangwada	PRL-690	3400±150 BP	1550±155 BC	1935-1560 BC	Malwa Period	PRL V
Dangwada	PRL-693	3280±100 BP	1430±103 BC	1720-1430 BC	Malwa Period	PRL V
Dangwada	PRL-691	3200±120 BP	1345±124 BC	1670-1380 BC	Malwa Period	PRL V
Dangwada	PRL-686	3110±140 BP	1255±144 BC	1645-1235 BC	Malwa Period	PRLV
Dangwada	PRL-692	2900±140 BP	1035±144 BC	1365-860 BC	Malwa Period	PRLV
Eran	P-529	3868±72 BP	2035±74 BC	2425-2295 BC	Period II, Iron ?	PENN VI
Eran	TF-331	3355±90 BP	1505±93 BC	1865-1565 BC	Period I, Malwa	TATA V
Eran	TF-329	3300±105 BP	1450±108 BC	1745-1520 BC	Period I, Malwa	TATA V
Eran	TF-327	3280±100 BP	1430±103 BC	1720-1430 BC	Period I, Malwa	TATA V
Eran	TF-330	3220±100 BP	1365±103 BC	1680-1395 BC	Period I, Malwa	TATA V
Eran	P-525	3193±69 BP	1340±71 BC	1645-1400 BC	Period I, Malwa	PENN VI

Appendix I (Contd.)

Site	*No*	*5568 BP*	*5730 BC*	*Calibration*	*Cultural Assn*	*Date list*
Eran	P-526	3136 ± 68 BP	1280 ± 70 BC	1555-1355 BC	Period I, Malwa	Penn VI
Eran	P-324	3130 ± 105 BP	1275 ± 108 BC	1575-1280 BC	Period I, Malwa	TATA V
Eran	TF-326	2905 ± 105 BP	1040 ± 108 BC	1335-1015 BC	Period I, Malwa	TATA V
Eran	P-528	2878 ± 65 BP	1015 ± 67 BC	1130-1020 BC	Period I, Malwa	PENN VI
Eran	P-527	2515 ± 58 BP	640 ± 60 BC	795-585 BC	Period II, Iron ?	PENN VI
Gerwa Well	PRL-710	26090 ± 800 BP	24925 ± 824 BC	N.A.	Middle Palaeoloithic	PRL V
Kayatha	TF-680	3850 ± 95 BP	2015 ± 98 BC	2430-2165 BC	Period I, Kayatha	TATA VI
Kayatha	TF-400	3800 ± 105 BP	1965 ± 108 BC	2415-2130 BC	Period ?	TATA V
Kayatha	TF-781	3720 ± 105 BP	1880 ± 108 BC	2325-1965 BC	Period I, Kayatha	TATA VII
Kayatha	TF-779	3685 ± 105 BP	1845 ± 108 BC	2310-1925 BC	Period I, Kayatha	TATA VII
Kayatha	TF-780	3680 ± 95 BP	1840 ± 98 BC	2305-1905 BC	Period I, Kayatha	TATA VII
Kayatha	TF-777	3625 ± 95 BP	1785 ± 98 BC	2185-1875 BC	Period II, Banas	TATA VII
Kayatha	TF-396	3575 ± 105 BP	1730 ± 108 BC	2150-1770 BC	Period ?	TATA V
Kayatha	TF-778	3550 ± 95 BP	1705 ± 98 BC	2125-1745 BC	Period I/II Kayatha/ Banas	TATA VII
Kayatha	TF-678	3530 ± 100 BP	1685 ± 103 BC	2100-1720 BC	Period II, Banas	TATA VI
Kayatha	TF-399	3525 ± 100 BP	1680 ± 103 BC	2100-1720 BC	Period II, Banas	TATA V
Kayatha	TF-398	3520 ± 100 BP	1675 ± 103 BC	2015-1710 BC	Period III, Malwa	TATA VI
Kayatha	TF-974	3485 ± 95 BP	1640 ± 98 BC	1980-1690 BC	Period I, Kayatha	TATA IX
Kayatha	TF-776	3455 ± 110 BP	1610 ± 113 BC	1955-1680 BC	Period II, Banas	TATA VII
Kayatha	TF-397	3350 ± 100 BP	1500 ± 103 BC	1785-1560 BC	Period III, Malwa	TATA V
Kayatha	TF-405	3320 ± 100 BP	1470 ± 103 BC	1760-1540 BC	Period I, Kayatha	TATA VI
Kayatha	TF-402	3240 ± 100 BP	1385 ± 103 BC	1690-1405 BC	Period ?	TATA V
Kayatha	TF-401	3190 ± 105 BP	1335 ± 108 BC	1670-1375 BC	Period II, Banas	TATA V

Appendix I (Contd.)

Site	*No*	*5568 BP*	*5730 BC*	*Calibration*	*Cultural Assn*	*Date list*
Kayatha	TF-676	3160 ± 105 BP	1305 ± 108 BC	1650-1350 BC	Period III, Malwa	TATA VI
Kayatha	TF-679	3155 ± 130 BP	1300 ± 134 BC	1675-1260 BC	Period II, Banas	TATA VI
Kayatha	TF-394	2380 ± 95 BP	500 ± 98 BC	620-395 BC	Period ?	TATA V
Kayatha	TF-674	2350 ± 95 BP	470 ± 98 BC	600-385 BC	Period?	TATA VI
Navdatoli	P-476	4125 ± 69 BP	2300 ± 71 BC	2890-2640 BC	Phase II, Malwa, Little Jorwe,.Bichrome	PENN VI
Navdatoli	P-202	3503 ± 128 BP	1660 ± 132 BC	2120-1675 BC	Phase II, Malwa, Little Jorwe, Bichrome	PENN III
Navdatoli	P-201	3492 ± 128 BP	1645 ± 132 BC	2105-1670 BC	Phase I, Malwa, Bichrome, Ahar	PENN III
Navdatoli	P-200	3457 ± 127 BP	1610 ± 131 BC	1990-1660 BC	Phase I, Malwa, Bichrome, Ahar	PENN III
Navdatoli	P-475	3455 ± 70 BP	1610 ± 72 BC	1905-1695 BC	Phase I, Malwa, Bichrome, Ahar	PENN VI
Navdatoli	P-204	3449 ± 127 BP	1600 ± 131 BC	1980-1650 BC	Phase III, Malwa, Jorwe, Cream Slipped	PENN III
Navdatoli	TF-59	3380 ± 105 BP	1530 ± 108 BC	1875-1580 BC	Phase I, Malwa, Bichrome, Ahar	TATA I
Navdatoli	P-205	3294 ± 125 BP	1445 ± 129 BC	1770-1410 BC	Phase IV, Malwa, Jorwe, Coarse Red	PENN III
Ratikarar	TF-967	32750 ± 1770 BP	31783 ± 1825 BC	N.A.	Middle Palaeolithic	
Tripuri	TF-681	2155 ± 100 BP	270 ± 103 BC	395-135 BC	Early Historic Pottery	TATA VI
Ujjain	TF-409	2335 ± 95 BP	455 ± 98 BC	595-385 BC	NBP	TATA VI
Ujjain	TF-407	1990 ± 100 BP	100 ± 103 BC	165 BC-60 AD	Black and Red Ware	TATA VI

Appendix II

Ostrich Egg Shell Sites In M.P.

(After Giriraj Kumar *et al* - 1990)

Main River Valley	*River or Nala*	*Site*	*District and State*	*Geo-Coordinates*	*Discoverer(s)*
Betwa	A nala joining Kalisindh	Ravi Shanker Nagar, Bhopal	Bhopal (M.P.)	23^0 15.0'N, 77^0 25.0' E	Wakankar, V.S. (1973)
Betwa	Choti-Jamunajhiri	Bhimbetka	Raisen (M.P.)	22^0 57.0'N, 77^0 36.0' E	Wakankar, V.S. (1973)
Narmada	Narmada	Hoshangabad	Hoshangabad (M.P.)	22^0 47.0' N, 77^0 42.0' E	Wakankar, V.S. (1982)
Narmade	Narmada	Chote Barda	Khargaon (M.P.)	22^0 16.0' N, 75^0 05.0' E	Wakankar, V.S. (1984)
Narmade	Narmada	Ratikheda	Khargaon (M.P.)	22^0 17.0' N, 75^0 05.0' E	Wakankar, V.S. (1984)
Chambal	Chambal	Nagda	Ujjain (M.P.)	23^0 27.0' N, 75^0 35.0' E	Kumar, G. *et al.* (1980)
Chambal	Chambal	Dangawada	Ujjain (M.P.)	23^0 25.0' N, 75^0 35.0' E	Kumar, G. *et al.* (1980)
Chambal	A small nala joining Chambal	Rajota	Ujjain (M.P.)	23^0 10.0' N, 75^0 29.0' E	Wakankar, V.S. (1980)
Chambal	Chamala	Badanagar	Ujjain (M.P.)	23^0 03.0' N, 75^0 23.0' E	Wakankar, V.S. (1980)
Chambal	Utavali ka Nala	Near Badanagar (M.P.)	Ujjain (M.P.)	23^0 06.2' N, 75^0 20.0' E	Wakankar, V.S. and G. Kumar (1981)
Chambal	A nala joining Chamala	Bheru-Pachlana	Ujjain (M.P.)	23^0 13.0' N, 75^0 20.2' E	Wakankar, V.S. and Hemant Jain (1981)
Chambal	A nala joining Chamala	Runija	Ujjain (M.P.)	23^0.09.0' N, 75^0 16.2' E	Kumar, G. and Hemant Jain (1981)
Chambal	Saun	Pahadgadh	Morena (M.P.)	26^0 12.3' N, 77^0 40'. 0' E	Kumar, G. *et al.* (1980)
Gambhira	A nala joining Gambhiri	Banykheri (Aslaoda)	Ujjain (M.P.)	23^0.13.3' N, 75^0 37.2' E	Kumar, G. (1982)
Kalisindh	A nala joining Ahu	Osarna	Mandasaur (M.P.)	24^0.31.8' N, 75^0 51.0' E	Pancholi, R. (1986)

Appendix II (Contd.)

Main River Valley	*River or Nala*	*Site*	*District and State*	*Geo-Coordinates*	*Discoverer(s)*
Kalisindh	Rewa	Bhanpura	Mandasaur (M.P.)	24^{0}31.0' N, 75^{0} 45.0' E	Pancholi, R. (1982)
Kalisindh	Garoth nala	Garoth	Mandasaur (M.P.)	24^{0}17.71' N, 75^{0} 40.5' E	Wakankar, V.S. and R. Pancholi (1981)
Kalisindh	A nala joining Rewa	Bhansoda	Mandasaur (M.P.)	24^{0}27.1' N, 75^{0} 47.3' E	Pancholi, R. and G. Kumar (1981)
Kalisindh	A nala joining Rewa	Ramnagar	Mandasaur (M.P.)	24^{0}27.4' N, 75^{0} 46.8' E	Pancholi, R. and G. Kumar (1981)
Kalisindh	A nala joining Rewa	Kherkhedi	Mandasaur (M.P.)	24^{0}28.0' N, 75^{0} 45.8' E	Pancholi, R. and G. Kumar (1981)
Parvati	Janjalinala	Janjali Naka	Guna (M.P.)	24^{0}22.0' N, 77^{0} 08.0' E	Kumar, G. (1982)
Parvati	Chepot	Ruthiai	Guna (M.P.)	24^{0}32.78' N, 77^{0} 11' E	Kumar, G. and Hridyashri (1986)
Kalisindh	A nala joining Rewa	Lotkhedi	Mandsaur (M.P.)	24^{0}30.0' N, 75^{0} 45.0' E	Pancholi, A. and R. Pancholi (1989)

Select Bibliography

Chapters I-II

Agrawal, D.P. & Ghosh, A., Eds. : *Radiocarbon and Indian Archaeology,* Bombay, 1973.

Agrawal, D.P., & Kusumgar, S. : *Prehistoric Chronology and Radiocarbon Dating in India*, Delhi, 1974.

Ahmed, N. : *The Stone Age Cultures of the Upper Son Valley*, Delhi, 1977.

Allchin, B. & R. : *Birth of Indian Civilization,* Harmondsworth, 1968.

Ansari, Z.D. & Dhavalikar, M.K. : *Excavation at Kayatha*, Poona, 1975.

Bajpai, K.D. : *Sagar Through the Ages*, Sagar, 1964.

——— : *Cultural Heritage of India*, Vol. 1, Delhi, 1985.

Bajpai, K.D. & Pandey, S.K. : *Excavation at Tumain,* Bhopal, M.P., 1985.

——— : *Malhar* 1975-78, Sagar, 1978.

Banerjee, N.R. : Nagda: 1955-57, New Delhi, 1986.

Brown, J.C. : *Catalogue of Prehistoric Antiquities in the Indian Museum at Calcutta*, Simla, 1917.

Chakravarty, K.K., (Ed.) : *Rock Art of India*, Delhi, 1984.

Chakravarty, K.K. *et al.*, (Eds.) : *Dangwada Excavations*, Bhopal, 1989.

——— : *Vidisha Through the Ages*, Delhi, 1990.

Cunningham, A. : *Archaeological Survey of India Reports.*

De Terra, H., & Paterson, T.T. : *Studies on the Ice Age in India and Associated Human Cultures*, Washington, 1939.

Dixit, M.G. : *Madhya Pradesh Ke Puratattva Ki Ruprekha*, 1954.

——— : *Tripuri-1952*, Nagpur, 1955.

Dixit, S.K. : *Ujjayini, Itihas Tatha Puratattva*, 1968.

Foote, R.B. : *Indian Prehistoric and Protohistoric Antiquities,* Madras, 1916.

Ghosh, A., (Ed.) : *An Encyclopaedia of Indian Archaeology*, Vols. I-II, Delhi, 1989.

Gordon, D.H. : *Prehistoric Background of Indian Culture*, Bombay, 1958.

Gupta, J. : *Pragaitihasik Bharatiya Chitrakala,* Allahabad, 1965.

Jayaswal, V. : *Palaeohistory of India*, Delhi, 1978.

Jorge, Armand : *Excavations of Durkadi Nullah*, Delhi, 1984.

Kanoongo, S. : *Ujjayini Ka Sanskritik Itihasa*, Indore, 1972.

Khare, M.D. : *Painted Rock - Shelters*, Bhopal, 1981.

——— : *Malwa Through the Ages*, Bhopal, 1981.

——— : *Vidisha*, Bhopal, 1985.

Khatri, A.P. : "Stone Age Cultures of Malwa", Unpublished thesis, Poona.

Lal, B.B. : *Indian Archaeology Since Independence,* Delhi, 1964.

Masih, P. : *Madhya Pradesh Ki Pragaitihasik Chitrakala,* Bhopal, 1996.

Mathpal, Y. : *Prehistoric Rock Paintings of Bhimbetka*, Delhi, 1984.

Misra, V.N. & Mate, M.S., (Eds.) : *Indian Prehistory — 1964*, Poona, 1965.

Misra, V.N., Mathpal, Y. and Nagar, M. : *Bhimbetka : Prehistoric Man and His Art in Central India*, Poona, 1977.

Neumayer, Erwin : *Prehistoric Indian Rock Paintings*, Delhi, 1983.

Pandey, R.P. : *Prehistoric Archaeology of Madhya Pradesh*, Delhi, 1987.

Pandey, S.K. : *Indian Rock Art*, Delhi, 1993.

Patil, D.R. : *The Cultural Heritage of Madhya Bharat*, Gwalior, 1952.

Sankalia, H.D., Subbarao, B., & Deo, S.B. : *Excavations at Maheshwar and Navdatoli, 1952-53*, Poona – Baroda, 1958.

Sankalia, H.D. : *Tripuri Excavation — 1966 : Short Report*, 1966.

Sankalia, H.D., Deo, S.B., & Ansari, Z.D. : *Chalcolithic Navdatoli : The Excavation at Navdatoli : 1957-59,* Poona – Baroda, 1971.

Sankalia, H.D. : *Prehistory and Protohistory of India and Pakistan*, Poona, 1974.

Sharma, R.K. : *Madhya Pradesh Ke Puratattva ka Sandarbha Grantha*, Bhopal, 1974.

Sharma, R.K. & Ali, R. : *Archaeology of Bhopal Region*, Delhi, 1980.

Sharma, R.K. & Tripathi, K.K. (Eds.) : *Prehistoric Art in India,* Delhi, 1956.

Sharma, R.K. (Eds.) : *Indian Archaeology, New Perspectives*, Delhi, 1982.

Sharma, R.K. & Mishra, S.N. : *Excavations at Kakrehta*, Delhi, 1993.

Shastri, A.M. : *Tripuri*, Bhopal, 1971.

Shastri, A.M., Sharma, R.K., & Prasad, A., (Eds.) : *Vajapeya*, Vols. I-II, Delhi, 1987.

Singh, R. : "Palaeolithic Industries of North Bundelkhand", Unpublished thesis, Poona, 1965.

Subbarao, B. : *Personality of India*, Baroda, 1958.

Supekar, S.G. : "Pleistocene Stratigraphy and Prehistoric Archaeology of the Central Narmada Basin", Unpublished thesis, Poona, 1968.

Wainright, G.V. : *Pleistocene Deposits of the Lower Narmada Valley and Early Stone Age Industry from the River Chambal*, Baroda, 1964.

Wakankar, V.S. & Brooks, R.R.R. : *Stone Age Paintings in India,* Bombay, 1976.

Wakankar, V.S. : *Kasrawad Utkhanan*, Ujjain.

Chapter III

A. Inscriptions

Barua, B.M. : *Asoka and his Inscriptions*, Calcutta, 1944.

Barua, B.M. and Sinha, G. (Eds.) : *Barhut Inscriptions*, Calcutta, 1926.

Bhandarkar, D.R. (Ed.) : List of Inscriptions of Northern India, Appendix to *Epigraphia Indica*, Vols. XIX-XXIII.

Bhandarkar, D.R. (Ed.) : *Inscriptions of Asoka*, Calcutta, 1920.

Bhandarkar, D.R., Chhabra, B.Ch, & Gai, G.S. (Eds.) : *Inscriptions of the Early Gupta Kings*, Delhi, 1981.

Chaudhury, S. : *Bibliography of Studies in Indian Epigraphy* (1926-50), Baroda, 1966.

Dwivedi, H.N. (Ed.) : *Gwalior Rajya ke Abhilekh*, Gwalior, 1947.

Fleet, J.F. (Ed.) : Inscriptions of the Early Gupta Kings and their Successors, *CII*, Vol. III, Calcutta, 1888.

Hiralal, R.B. (Ed.) : *Inscriptions in the Central Provinces and Berar,* 2nd Edition, Nagpur, 1932.

Hultzsch, E. (Ed.) : *Inscription of Asoka*, *CII*, Vol. I, London, 1925.

Lele, C.B. (Ed.) : *Paramara Inscriptions in the Dhar State* (875-1310 AD), Dhar State Historical Series.

Luders, (Ed.) : *List of Brahmi Inscriptions up to 400 AD, Epigraphia Indica*, Vol. X.

Mirashi, V.V. (Ed.) : Inscriptions of the Kalachuri Chedi Era, *CII*, Vol. IV, Pt. I and II, Ootacumund, 1965.

——— : Inscriptions of the Vakatakas, *CII*, Vol. V, 1963.

Pandeya, L.P. : 'Mahakoshal in Inscriptions', *MHSP*, 19.

Ramesh, K.V. and Tewari, S.P. (Eds.) : *A Copper Plate Hoard of the Gupta Period from Bagh, M.P.*, Delhi, 1990.

Shastri, A.M. (Ed.) : *Inscriptions of the Sarabhapuriyas, Panduvamsis and Somavamsis,* pt. I-II, Delhi, 1995.

Sircar, D.C. (Ed.) : *Select Inscriptions bearing on Indian History and Civilization*, Vol. I, Calcutta, 1942.

Trivedi, H.V. (Ed.) : *Inscriptions of the Paramaras, Chandellas, Kachchhapaghatas etc.,* Pt. I, II and III, Delhi, 1978, 1987, 1991.

B. Modern Books

Bajpai, K.D. (Ed.) : *Cultural Heritage of India*, Vol. I, Delhi, 1985.

Banerji, R.D. : *The Age of Imperial Guptas,* Varanasi, 1933.

Beohar, R.S. : *Tripuri Ka Itihasa*, Jabalpur, 1939.

Bhandarkar, R.D. : *Asoka*, Calcutta, 1932.

Bhatia, P. : *The Paramaras*, Delhi, 1970.

Bose, N.S. : *The History of the Candellas*, Calcutta, 1956.

Chahal, I.M. (Ed.) : *Approaches to the Art and Archaeology of M.P.*, Bhopal, 1994.

Chakaravarty, K.K. (Ed.) : *Vidisha Through the Ages*, Bhopal, 1990.

Cousens, H. : *List of Antiquarian Remains in C.P. and Berar,* Nagpur, 1901.

Dandekar, R.N. : *A History of the Guptas*, Pune, 1941.

Dikshit, M.G. : *Tripuri 1952*, Nagpur, 1955.

Dikshit, R.K. : *The Candellas of Jejakabhukti,* Delhi, 1977.

Dikshit, S.K. : *Ujjayini Ka Itihasa*, Indore, 1968.

Dwivedi, C. : *Eran Ka Rajnaitik Tatha Sanskritik Itihas*, Delhi, 1984.

Dwivedi, H.N. : *Madhya Bharat Ka Itihas*, Pt. I, Gwalior, 1956.

Ganguly, D.C. : *History of the Paramara Dynasty,* Decca, 1933.

Gupta, P.L. : *Prachin Chhattisgarh*, Raipur, 1973.

Jain, K.C. : *Malwa Through the Ages*, Delhi, 1972.

Khare, M.D. (Ed.) : *Vidisha*, Bhopal, 1985.

——— (Ed.) : *Malwa Through the Ages*, Bhopal, 1981.

Majumdar, R.C. & Altekar, A.S. (Eds.) : *A New History of the Indian People, Vol. VI., The Vakataka Gupta Age*, Lahore, 1946.

Majumdar, R.C. and Pusalkar, A.D. (Eds.) : *The History and Culture of the Indian People*, Bombay, Vol. 1-5, 1951-57.

Majumdar, R.C. and Dasgupta, K.K. (Eds.) : *A Comprehensive History of India*, Vol. III, Pt. I & II, Delhi, 1981-82.

Mirashi, V.V. : *Studies in Indology*, Vol. I-IV, Nagpur.

——— : *Kalachuri Nripati Ani Tyancha Kal,* Nagpur.

Mishra, R.N. : *Bharhut,* Bhopal, 1971.

Mitra, S.K. : *Early Rulers of Khajuraho,* Calcutta, 1958.

Nema, S.R. : *The Political History of the Somavamsi Kings of South Kosala and Orissa*, Delhi, 1978.

Nigam, M.L. : *Cultural History of Bundelkhand*, Delhi, 1983.

Pandey, C.B. : *Andhra Satavahana Samrajya Ka Itihas*, Delhi, 1963.

Patil, D.R. : *The Cultural Heritage of Madhya Bharat*, Delhi, 1963.

Puri, B.N. : *The History of the Gurjara Pratiharas,* Bombay, 1957.

Raizada, A. (Ed.) : *Heritage of Shajapur*, Bhopal, 1992.

——— : *Art, Archaeology and History of Ratlam*, Bhopal, 1992.

Ray, H.C. : *The Dynastic History of Northern India*, Vol. I, II, Calcutta, 1931-36.

Raychaudhuri, H.C. : *The Political History of Ancient India*, 5th Ed., Calcutta, 1950.

Seth, K.N. : *Growth of the Paramara Power in Malwa,* Bhopal, 1965.

Shah, K.K. : *Ancient Bundlekhand*, Delhi, 1988.

Shastri, A.M. : *Tripuri*, Bhopal, 1971.

Shastri, K.A.N. (Ed.) : *A Comprehensive History of India, Vol. II — The Mauryas and Satavahanas*, Delhi, 1987.

Sharma, M.L. : *Padmavati*, Bhopal, 1971.

Sharma, R.K. : *The Kalachuris and Their Times*, Delhi, 1980.

——— : *Madhya Pradesh Ke Puratattva Ka Sandarbha Grantha,* Bhopal, 1974.

——— : *Studies in Shell Script,* Delhi, 1990.

Sharma, R.S. (Ed.) : *A Comprehensive History of India,* Vol. IV, Pt. I, Delhi, 1992.

Thakur, V.S. : *Rajim*, Bhopal, 1972.

Thapar, R. : *Asoka and the Decline of the Mauryas*, Oxford, 1953.

Trivedi, C.B. : *Dasapura*, Bhopal, 1979.

Trivedi, S.D. : *Bundelkhand Ka Puratattva*, Jhansi, 1984.

Yazdani, G. : *The Early History of the Deccan*, Oxford, 1960.

Chapter IV

Ahmad, N. : *'The bearing of archeaological evidence from Maheshwar on the chronology of Madhya Pradesh coins', SPC PC*, pp. 48-50. 'On the local coins of Maheshwar and Navdatoli Excavation', *SPLC*, pp. 89-94.

Allan, J. : *Catalogue of Coins of Ancient India in the British Museum*, London, 1936.

Altekar, A.S. : *Coinage of Gupta Empire* (Hindi translation also).

——— : *Catalogue of the Gupta Gold Coins in the Bayana Hoard.*

Bajpai, K.D. (Ed.) : *Malhar 1975-78*, Sagar, 1978.

——— : *Excavation at Tumain*, Bhopal, 1985.

——— : *Sagar Through the Ages*, Sagar.

——— : *Indian Numismatic Studies*, New Delhi, 1976.

Bhandarkar, D.R. : *Carmichael Lectures on Ancient Indian Numismatics,* Calcutta, 1921.

Bidyabinod, B.B. : *Supplementary Catalogue of the Coins in the Indian Museum, Non-Muhammadan Series,* Calcutta, 1923.

·Brown, C.J. : *Catalogue of the coins of the Guptas, the Maukharis etc. in the Provincial Museum, Lucknow*, Allahabad, 1920.

Chakaravarty, K.K. : *Dangwada Excavations,* Bhopal, 1989.

Chakaravarty, S.K. : *A Study of Ancient Indian Numismatics*, Calcutta, 1931.

Chhattopadhyaya, B. : *The Age of the Kushanas — A Numismatic Study*, Calcutta, 1967.

Cunningham, A. : *Coins of Ancient India from the Earliest Times down to the Seventh Century AD*, London 1891 (Reprinted, 1963).

——— : *Coins of Medieval India from the Seventh Century down to the Muhammadan Conquest*, London 1894 (Reprinted, 1967).

——— : *Coins of Alexander's Successors in the East.*

——— : *The Greeks and Indo-Scythians, Part I*, London, 1869 (Reprinted, 1969).

——— : *Coins of the Indo-Scythians*. Rep. *Num. Chron.*, London, 1888-92 (Reprinted, 1962).

——— : *Later Indo-Scythians*. Rep. *Num. Chron,* London, 1893-95.

Dikshit, M.G. : *Tripuri — 1952*, Nagpur, 1955.

Gairola, T.R. : *'Weights of Punch-Marked Coins from Barwni (M.B.),'* AI, No. 7, pp. 79-85.

Gardner, Percy : *'The Coins of the Greek and Scythian Kings of Bactria and India'*, London, 1886.

Ghosh, A. (Ed.) : *An Encyclopaedia of Indian Archaeology,* Delhi, 1989.

Gupta, P. L. : *A Survey of Indian Numismatography,* Varanasi, 1964.

——— : *Bibliography of Indian Numismatics*, Pt. I & II, Varanasi, 1977.

——— : *Ancient Indian Silver Punch-Marked Coins*, Nasik, 1985.

Herzfeld, E. : *Kushano-Sassanian Coins,* MASI, Calcutta, 1930. Also MASI, Nos. 59, 62.

Jain, B.C. : *Inventory of the Hoards and Finds of Coins and Seals from Madhya Pradesh, Numismatic Notes and Monographs*, No. 5, Varanasi, 1957.

Khare, M.D. : *'A Note on the Punch-Marked Coins from the Recent Excavations at Eran', SPCPC.*

Mahalingam, T.V. : *'The Bearing of Local Coins on the Religious Condition of Central India', SPLC*, pp. 54-58.

Maity, S.K. : *Early Indian Coin and Currency System*, New Delhi, 1971.

Mirashi, V.V. : *Studies in Indology*, Vols. 1-4, Nagpur.

Narain, A.K. : *Coin Types of Indo-Greek Kings.*

Narain, A.K. and Jenkins, G.K. : *Coins Types of the Saka Pahlava Kings of India*.

Nath, B.B. : '*Kalachuri Coins from Sonpur*', *OHRS*, Vol. I, pp. 36-40.

Pandey, D.B. : '*Minting Techniaue of Central Indian Local Coins*', *SPLC*, pp. 87-88.

Paruck, F.D.J. : *Sassanian Coins*, Bombay, 1924.

Rajguru, S.N. : '*New Hoard of Gold Coins of the Nagvamsi Kings of Chakrakotya*', *OHRS*, Vol. 8, pp. 75-82.

Rapson, E.J. : *Indian Coins,* Strassburg, 1897 (Reprinted, 1969).

——— : *Catalogue of Coins of the Andhra Dynasty, the Western Kshatrapas, the Traikutaka Dynasty and the Bodhi Dynasty* (Catalogue of India Coins in the British Museum, Vol. IV), London, 1908.

Roy, P.C. : *The Coinage of Northern India*, Delhi, 1980.

Roy, T.N. : '*The Bearing of Maheswar Navdatoli Excavation on the chronology of local coins*'. *SPLC*.

Sankalia, H.D. : *Excavations at Maheshwar and Navdatoli*, Pune, 1958.

Sarma, I.K. : *Coinage of the Satavahana Empire*, Delhi, 1980.

Satya Shrava : *The Kusana Numismatics,* Delhi, 1985.

Sharma, R.K. : *Excavation at Kakrehta,* Delhi, 1992.

——— : *Madhya Pradesh Ke Puratattva Ka Sandarbha Grantha*, Bhopal, 1974.

Shastri, A.M. : '*Religious Study of the Symbols on the Local Coins of Central India*', *SPLC*, pp. 70-86.

——— : *Tripuri*, Bhopal, 1971.

——— : *Kausambi Hoard of Magha Coins*, Nagpur, 1979.

Singhal, C.R. : *Bibliography of Indian Coins,* Bombay, 1950.

Smith, V.A. : *Catalogue of Coins in the Indian Museum, Calcutta, including the Cabinet of the Asiatic Society of Bengal, Vol. I,* Oxford, 1906.

Trivedi, H.V. : *Catalogue of the Coins of the Naga Dynasty of Padmavati,* Gwalior, 1957.

Whitehead, R.B. : *Catalogue of Coins in the Punjab Museum*, Lahore, Vol. I, *Indo-Greek Coins*, Oxford, 1914.

Wright, H.N. : *Catalogue of Coins in the Indian Museum, Calcutta, including the Cabinet of the Asiatic Society of Bengal,* Vol. II, Oxford, 1907.

——— : *'A Study of the Metrology of the Local Coins in Central India', SPLC*, pp. 120-32.

——— : The *Religious Study of a Symbol on an Avanti Coin', SPLC*, pp. 133-36.

——— : *'The Bearing of Excavations on the Chronology of the Local Coins of Central India', SPLC*, pp. 157-60.

Chapter V

A. Books in English

Agrawal, Urmila : *Khajuraho Sculptures and their Significance,* New Delhi, 1964.

Agarwala, V.S. : *Gupta Art*, Lucknow, 1948.

——— : *Indian Art,* Varanasi, 1965.

——— : *Studies in Indian Art*, Varanasi, 1965.

Ali, R. : *Art and Architecture of the Kalachuris*, Delhi, 1980.

——— : *Pratihara Art in India*, Delhi, 1987.

Anand, Mulk Raj and Kramarisch, S. : *Homage to Khajuraho,* Marg Publication, Bombay, 1957.

Bajpai, K.D. : *Five Phases of Indian Art*, Jodhpur, 1994.

Banerjea, J.N. : *Development of Hindu Iconography*, Calcutta, 1956.

Banerji, R.D. : *The Haihayas of Tripuri and Their Monuments*, Calcutta, 1931.

Barenes E : *Dhar and Mandu*, Bombay, 1902.

Baura, B.M. : *Barhut*, Pt. I-III, Calcutta, 1934.

Bhattacharya, B.C. : *Indian Images*, Pt. I, Calcutta, Simla, 1921.

——— : *The Jaina Iconography*, Lahore, 1939.

Brown, P. : *Indian Architecture* (Buddhist and Hindu Periods), 3rd. Ed., Bombay, 1956.

Burgess, James : *Buddhist Cave Temples and Their Inscriptions,* 2nd Ed., 1964.

Chakravarty, K.K. and Sharma, R.K. (Ed.) : *Art of the Kalachuris,* Bhopal, 1991.

Chahal, I.M. (Ed.) : *Approaches to the Art and Archaeology of M.P.*, Bhopal, 1994.

Coomaraswamy, A.K. : *History of Indian and Indonesian Art,* London, 1927, Dover Edition, New York, 1965.

Cousens, H. : *Lists of Antiquarian Remains in C.P. and Berar.*

Cunningham, A. : *Bhilsa Topes*, London, 1854.

——— : *The Stupa of Bharhut* (Reprinted), Varanasi, 1962.

Day, M.C. : *My Pilgrimage to Ajanta and Bagh*, London, 1925.

Dhama, B.L. : *A Guide to Khajuraho*, Bombay, 1927.

Dhavalikar, M.K. : *Sanchi — A Cultural Study*, Pune, 1965.

Dwivedi, S.K. : *Temple Sculptures of India*, Delhi, 1991.

Fergusson, J. : *History of Indian and Eastern Architecture,* London, 1910.

Fergusson, J. and Burgess : *Cave Temples of India,* 2nd Ed., 1969.

Foucher, A. : *The Beginnings of Buddhist Art,* London, 1918.

Ganguli, O.C., Goswami, A. and Tarafdar, A. : *The Art of the Chandellas*, Calcutta, 1957.

Garde, M.B. : *Archaeology in Gwalior*, 1934.

——— : *A Hand Book of Gwalior*, 1936.

——— : *Directory of Forts in Gwalior State.*

——— : *Padmavati*, Gwalior, 1952.

——— : *Guide to Surwaya.*

——— : *Guide to Chanderi*, 1978.

Government of Madhya Bharat : *Descriptive and Classified List of Archaeological Monuments in Madhya Bharat*, Gwalior, 1952.

Haldar, A.K. : *Buddhist Caves of Bagh,* Burlington Magazine, 1910-11.

——— : *'The Paintings of the Bagh Caves'*, Rupam No. 8, 1921.

Havel, E.B. : *Indian Sculpture and Painting,* London, 1908.

——— : *The Ideals of Indian Art,* London, 1911.

Kramrisch, S. : *Indian Sculpture*, Calcutta, 1933.

——— : *The Hindu Temple*, 2 Vols., Calcutta, 1946.

Krishna, Deva : *Temples of Khajuraho*, 2 Vols., New Delhi, 1990.

——— : *Temples of India,* Delhi, 1995.

Kanwar Lal : *Immortal Khajuraho*, Delhi, 1965.

Luard, C.E. : *Dhar and Mandu*, Allahabad, 1912.

Luard, C.E. and Lele, K.K. : *Paramaras of Dhar and Malwa,* Bomabay, 1908.

Maisey, F.C. : *Sanchi and its Remains*, London, 1892.

Manwani, S.N. : *Evolution of Art and Architecture in Central India*, Delhi, 1988.

Marshall, Sir John : *Guide to Sanchi*, 2nd Ed., Delhi, 1956.

——— : *The Bagh Caves* (Reprinted), Delhi, 1982.

Marshall, and Foucher : *Monuments of Sanchi*, 3 Vols., Delhi, 1940.

Mishra, R.N. : *Sculptures of Dahala and Dakshina Kosala and their Background — Kalachuri Phase*, Delhi, 1987.

——— : *Yaksha Cult and Iconography*, Delhi, 1981.

Mishra, O.P. : *Mother Goddess in Central India*, Delhi, 1985.

Mishra, S.N. : *Gupta Art and Architecture*, Delhi, 1992.

Mitra, D. : *Sanchi*, 2nd Ed., New Delhi, 1965.

Nagraju, S. : *Buddhist Architecture of Western India*, Delhi, 1981.

Patil, D.R. : *Monuments of Udayagiri Hills.*

——— : *The Cultural Heritage of Madhya Bharat*, Gwalior, 1952.

Raizada, A., Upadhayaya, M.A. and Mishra, O.P. (Eds.) : *Art, Archaeology and History of Ratlam*, Delhi, 1992.

Rao, T.A.G. : *Elements of Hindu Iconography*, 2 Vols., Madras, 1914, 1916 (Reprinted, 1968).

Ray, Nihar Ranjan : *Maurya and Sunga Art*, Calcutta, 1945.

Rowland, B. : *The Art and Architecture of India*, London, 1953.

Saraswai, S.K. : *A Survey of Indian Sculpture*, Calcutta, 1957.

Sharma, R.K. : *The Temple of Chausatha Yogini at Bheraghat*, Delhi, 1978.

——— : *Art of the Paramaras of Malwa (Ed.)*, Delhi, 1979.

——— : *Krishna Smriti — Studies in Indian Art and Archaeology* (Ed.), Delhi, 1995.

Singh, A.P. : *Forts and Fortifications in India*, Delhi, 1987.

——— : *Monuments of Mandu*, Delhi, 1994.

Smith, V.A. : *History of Fine Art in India and Ceylon*, 3rd ed., Bombay.

Trivedi, H.V. : *The Bibliography of Madhya Bharat Archaeology*, Gwalior, 1953.

Trivedi, R.D. : *Temples of Pratihara Period in Central India*, Delhi, 1990.

Vidya Prakash : *Khajuraho*, Bombay, 1967.

Wauchope, R.S. : *Buddhist Cave Temples of India*, Calcutta, 1933.

William, J.G. : *The Art of Gupta India, Empire and Province,* Delhi, 1983.

Yazdani G. : *Mandu — The City of Joy,* Oxford, 1929.

Zennas, E. and Auboyer, J. : *Khajuraho*, The Hague, 1960.

B. Books in Hindi

कंवल, रामलाल : **प्राचीन मालवा में मंदिर वास्तुकला**, दिल्ली, १९८४।

खरे, महेश्वीदयाल : **बाघ की गुफायें**, भोपाल, १९७१,
विदिशा, भोपाल, १९८५।

गर्ग, आर० एस० : **केन्द्रीय संग्रहालय इंदौर, मूर्तिकला**, भाग-१ **शैव प्रतिमायें**, भाग-२, **शाक्त प्रतिमायें**, भोपाल, १९८०।

झा, विवेकदत्त : **बस्तर का मूर्तिशिल्प**, भोपाल, १९८९।

ठाकुर विष्णुसिंह : **राजिम**, भोपाल, १९७२।

त्रिवेदी, सी० बी० : **दशपुर**, भोपाल, १९७८।

द्विवेदी, हरिहर निवास : **त्रिपुरी (विदिशा, पद्मावती और बाघ)**, ग्वालियर, १९५४।

दीक्षित, मो० ग० : **मध्यप्रदेश के पुरातत्त्व की रूपरेखा**, सागर, १९५४।

दीक्षित, स० का० : **उज्जयिनी – इतिहास तथा पुरातत्त्व**, इंदौर, १९६८।

बाजपेयी, माधुरी : **मध्यप्रदेश की जैनकला**, दिल्ली, १९९३।

मिश्र, आर० एन० : **भरहुत**, भोपाल, १९७१।

मिश्र भास्करनाथ : **साँची**, भोपाल, १९८२।

मुनि कान्तिसागर : **खण्डहरों का वैभव**, काशी, १९५६।

शर्मा, सीताराम : **भोरमदेव**, भोपाल, १९८९।

शास्त्री, अजयमित्र : **त्रिपुरी**, भोपाल, १९७१।

सुल्लेरे, एस० के० : **अजयगढ़ और कालंजर की देव प्रतिमायें**, दिल्ली, १९८७।

Chapters VI-VII

A. Original Texts and Translations

Abhijñāna Śākuntalam of Kālidāsa : Devanagari Rec. Ed. M. Williams, 2nd Ed., Oxford, 1876.

Agni Purāṇa : Ed. by R. Mitra, B.I., Calcutta, 1873-79. Ed. *ASS*. Poona, 1900.

Ain-i-Akbarī of Abul Fazl : Eng. tr. by H. Blochmann, Vol. I and H.S. Jarrett (Vols.

II-III), BI, Calcutta, 1868-94.

Aitareya Brāhmana : Ed. K.S. Agashe, Poona, 1896. Tr. by Keith. H.O. S. Vol. XXV, Cambridge, Mass, 1920.

Ālhā Khaṇda of Jagnaik Rao : Tr. by Waterfield.

Amarakośa of Amarasiṁha : Ed. by T. Ganapati Sastri, 4 Pts., Trivandrum, 1914-17.

Anargharāghava of Murārī : Ed. by Premchandra Tarkavagis, Calcutta, 1860.

Aṅguttara Nikāya : Eng. tr. (The book of Gradual Sayings), Vol. I, II and V by F.L. Woodward and Vol. III and IV by E. M. Hare, PTS, London, 1932-36.

Arthaśāstra of Kauṭilya : Ed. & by Shama Sastry, Mysore, 1919.

Ārya Mañjuśrī Mūlakalpa : Ed. by T. G. Sastri, Trivandrum, 1925.

Aṣṭādhyāyī of Pāṇini : Ed by S. C. Vasu, Allahabad, 1891.

Auchityavichāra of Kṣemendra : Ed. KM. I. 115 ff. Extracts, JBBRAS , XVI, 167-69 (Peterson).

Bālabhārata of Rājaśekhara : Ed. by C. Cappeller, Strassburg, 1885.

Bālabhārata of Rājaśekhara : Ed. by J. Vidyasagar, Calcutta, 1884.

Bhāgavata Purāṇa : Eng. tr. by J.M. Sanyal, Calcutta, 1930-39.

Bhaviṣya Purāṇa : Pub. by Venkatesvara Press, Bombay, 1910.

Brahmāṇḍa Purāṇa : ASS, Poona, 1895.

Bṛhatkathāmañjarī of Kṣemendra : Ed. by Sivadatta and Parade, NSP, Bombay, 1931. Eng. tr. by S. Levi, JA, 1886.

Bṛhatkathāślokasaṁgraha of Buddhasvāmin : Ed. by Lacote, 28 Vols, Paris, 1908-1929.

Bṛhatsaṁhitā by Varāhamihira : Ed. by H. Kern, BI, Calcutta, 1865. Eng. tr. by Shastri and Bhat, 2 Vols., Bangalore, 1947.

Chāṇakyanītisāra of Bhoja : Ed. by N. N. Law, Calcutta, 1917.

Daṁśanasāra of Devasena : Pub. by Jaina Digambar Granthmala, Bombay, V, 1974.

Daśakumāra-Charita of Daṇḍin : Ed. by G. Buhlar and P. Peterson. Eng. Tr. by M.R. Kale, 3rd Ed., Bombay, 1928.

Daśarūpaka of Dhanañjaya : Ed. by F. E. Hall, BI, Calcutta, 1865. Eng. tr. GCO. Hass, New York, 1912.

Dhammapada : Eng. tr. by F. Max Muller, SBE, Oxford, 1898.

Dīgha Nikāya : Eng. tr. by T. W. Rhys Davids, 3 Vols, SBE, London, 1899, 1910, 1921.

Dīpavaṁsa : Ed. and tr. by H. Oldenberg, London, 1879.

Dvāśraya Mahākāvya of Hemachandra : Ed. A.V. Kathavate, Bombay, 1915.

Garuḍa Purāṇa : Eng. tr. M N. Dutt, Calcutta, 1908.

Harivaṁśa Purāṇa : Ed. by R. Kinjawadekar, Poona, 1936.

Harṣa-Charita of Bāṇa : Ed. by A. A. Furher, Bombay, 1909. Eng. tr. by E.B. Cowell and F.W. Thomas, London, 1897.

Hiuen-Tsang : Tr. by S. Julien, Paris, 1857-68. Also by S. Beal (Buddhist Records of the Western World), London, 1884.

Indica : Fragments of Megasthenes : Ed. by E.A. Schwanbeck, Bonn, 1846.

Jātaka : Ed. by V. Fausböll, 7 vols., London, 1877-97.

Kādambarī of Bāṇa : Ed. P. Peterson, Bombay, 1900. Eng. tr. by C. M. Ridding, London, 1896.

Kāmasūtra of Vātsyāyana with the commentary by Jayamangala. Ed. by Sahityacharya D. L. Goswami, Benaras, 1929. Eng. tr. by B. N. Basu and revised by R.L. Ghosh, 5th ed., Calcutta, 1944.

Karakaṇḍa – Chariu of Kanakamāra : Ed. with tr. by H.L. Jain, Karanja, 1934.

Karpūramañjarī of Rājaśekhara : Ed. by Manmohan Ghosh, Calcutta, 1939. Eng. tr. by C. R. Lanman, HOS, Cambridge, Mass, 1901.

Kathāsaritasāgara of Somadeva : English tr. by C. H. Tawney, 2 vols., Calcutta, 1880, 1887.

Kāvyamīmāṁsā of Rājaśekhara : Ed. by C.D. Dalal and R. A. Sastri, GOS, 3rd Ed., Baroda, 1934.

Kitāb-ul-Hind and Āthārāl -Bāquia of al -Bīrūnī : Eng. tr. (Alberuni's India) by E.C. Sachau, London, 1914.

Kumārasaṁbhava of Kālidāsa : Eng. tr. by R. T. H. Criffith, 2nd Ed., London, 1879.

Kūrma Purāṇa : Ed. by N. Mukhopadhaya, BI, Calcutta, 1890.

Liṅga Purāṇa : Ed. by J. Vidyasagar, BI, Calcutta, 1885.

Mādhavānal-Kāmakandalā Prabandha : Ed. by M. R. Majumdar, GOS, No. 93,

Baroda, 1981.

Mahābhāṣya of Patañjali : Ed. by Kielhorn, Bombay, 1892-1909.

Mahāvaṁsa : Eng. tr. by W. Geiger and M. H. Bode, London, 1912.

Mahābhārata : Critical Edition by Bhandarkar Oriental Res. Instt., Pune, Eds. V.S. Sukthankar and others. Eng. tr. by M.N. Dutt, Calcutta, 1895-1905.

Mahāvastu : Ed. by E. Senart, Paris, 1882-97.

Mahobā Khaṇḍa (Parmāla Rāso) of Chand Bardāyī : Ed. by S. S. Das, Benaras, 1920.

Majjhima Nikāya : Eng. tr. by Lord Chalmers, 2 Vols., SBB, London, 1926-27.

Mālatīmādhava of Bhavabhūti with the comm. of Jagaddhara. Critically edited by R.G. Bhandarkar, BSS, Bombay, 1876.

Mālavikāgnimitra of Kālidāsa : Eng. tr. by C. H. Tawney, London, 1891.

Mārkaṇḍeya Purāṇa : Eng. tr. by F. E. Pargiter, Calcutta, 1904.

Matsya Purāṇa : Eng. tr. by A. Taluqdar of Oudh, SBH, 2 vols., Allahabad, 1916-17.

Meghadūta of Kālidāsa : Ed. with metrical Eng. tr. by H.H. Wilson, Calcutta, 1813. Eng. tr. by C. King, London, 1930.

Mṛcchakaṭika of Śūdraka : Tr. by Ryder, A.W., Cambridge, 1905.

Mudrārākṣasa of Viśākhadatta : Ed. with Eng. tr. by K. H. Dhruva, 2nd Ed., Poona, 1923.

Nāmamālikā of Bhoja : Ed. by E.D. Kulkarni and V.D. Gokhle, Poona, 1955.

Navasāhasāṅkacharita of Padmagupta : Ed. by V.S. Islampurkar, BSS, Bombay, 1895. Eng tr. JBBBRAS, XXVI, 153 ff.

Niddesa : *Mahāniddesa*. Ed. by L. De la Vallee Poussin and E.J. Thomas, PTS, London, 1916-17.

Nyāyavārtika of Bhoja : Pub. Bengal Asiatic Society, Calcutta, 1922.

Padma Purāṇa : Pub. Ventakeshwar Press, Bombay, 1895.

Paiyalachchīnāmamālā of Dhanapāla : Ed. by G. Buhler, Gottingen, 1879.

Pārthaparākrama of Prahlādanadeva : Ed. by C. D. Dalal, GOS, Baroda, 1917.

Pārijātamañjarii (or Vijayaśrī) of Madana : Ed. by E. Hultzsch, Leipzig, 1906.

Periplus Maris Erythraei : Eng. tr. by J. W. Mc Crindle, Calcutta, Bombay,

London, 1879.

Prabandhachintāmaṇi of Merutuṅga : Ed. by Muni Jinavijaya, SJS, Shantiniketan, 1933. Eng. tr. by C. H. Tawney, BI, Calcutta, 1901.

Prabandha Kośa of Rājaśekhara : Ed. Jinavijaya Muni, Santiniketan, 1935.

Prabodha-chandrodaya of Kṛṣṇa Miśra : Ed. by H. Brockhaus, Leipzig, 1845. Eng. tr. J. Taylor, London, 1862.

Prākṛata Paiṅgala : Bibliotheca Indica Series, Calcutta.

Prameyakamalamārtaṇḍa of Prabhāchandra. Ed. by M. Shastri, Bombay, 1941.

Pṛthvīrāja Vijaya of Jayānaka : Ed. by S.K. Belvalkar, Calcutta, 1914-22.

Pṛthvīrāja Rāso of Chand Bardāyī : Ed. by M. V. Pandia and S.S. Das, Benaras, 1913.

Raghuvaṁśa of Kālidāsa : Ed. with Eng. tr. by G. Naudargikar, 3rd Ed., Bombay, 1897.

Rājamārtaṇḍa of Bhoja : Ed. & tr. by R. Mitra, B. I., Calcutta, 1883.

Rāmāyaṇa : Eng tr. by M.N. Dutt, Calcutta, 1895-1905.

Rāmāyaṇa-Champū of Bhoja : Ed. by K.P. Parab, Bombay, 1898.

Ratnāvalī of Harṣa : Ed. by K.P. Parab, NSP, Bombay, 1895.

Rasikasañjivanī of Arjunavarman : Ed. by Durgaprasad and Parab, Bombay, 1916, Kavyamala No. 18.

Ṛgveda : Saṁhitā and Pāda text with Sāyana's comm. Ed. by. F. Max Muller (Second Ed.), 1890-92. Also critical ed. by Vaidika Samsodhana Mandala, Pune, 4 Vols., 1933.

Ṛtusaṁhāra of Kālidāsa : Eng. tr. by E.P. Mathers, London, 1929.

Rūpakaśataka of Vatsarāja : Ed. by C.D. Dalal, GOS, Baroda, 1918.

Saduktikarṇāmṛta of Śrīdharadāsa : Ed. by H.D. Sharma, Lahore, 1933.

Śālihotra of Bhoja : Ed. by E.D. Kulkarni, Poona, 1953.

Samarāṅgaṇa Sūtradhāra of Bhoja : Ed. by T. Ganapati Sastri, GOS, 2 Vols., Baroda, 1924-25.

Saṁyutta Nikāya : Eng. tr. by Mrs. Davids and F. L. Woodward, PTS, London, 1917-30.

Śāṅkhāyana Śrautasūtra : Ed. with Comm. of Varadatta Suta Anartiya and

Govinda by A. Hillebrandt, Calcutta, 1886-89.

Sarasvatī-Kaṇṭhābharaṇa of Bhoja : Ed. by A. Barooah, Calcutta, 1883-84.

Śatapatha Brāhmaṇa : Ed. by A. Waber, London, 1885. Eng. trans. by J. Eggeling. SBE., XII, XXVI, XLI, XLIII, XIV, Oxford, 1882-1900.

Śiva Purāṇa : Pub. Venkateshwar Press, Bombay.

Sṛṅgāra-Prakāśa of Bhoja : Ed. by G. R. Josyer, Mysore, 1955.

Sthavirāvalicharita : Ed. by H. Jacobi, BI, Calcutta, 1883-91, 2nd Ed., 1932.

Subhāṣitāvalī of Vallabhadeva : Ed. by P. Peterson and Durga Prasad, BSS, Bombay, 1886.

Subhāśitaratnasandoha of Amitgati : Ed. by Bhavadatta and W.L. Panshikar, NSP, 2nd Ed., Bombay, 1909.

Surathotsava of Someśvara : Ed. by Sivadatta and Parab, NSP, Bombay, 1902.

Sutta Nipāta : Eng. tr. by V. Fausböll, SBE, Oxford, 1898.

Tabaqāt-i-Akbarī of Nizammuddin : Eng. tr. by B.Dey, BI, Calcutta, 1931.

Tabaqāt-i-Nāsirī of Minhāj-ud dīn : Eng. by H. G. Raverty, London, 1881.

Tāj-ul-Ma'āsir of Hasan-un-Nizāmī : Extracts trans, HIED, II, 204-43.

Tárīkh-i-'Alāī of Amir Khusrav : Eng. tr. by M. Habib, Bombay, 1931.

Ta'rikh-i-Firishta : Eng.tr. (Rise of the Mahomedan Power in India) by J. Briggs, Vols. I- IV, London, 1829.

Ta'rikh-i-Firuz Shahi of Zia-ud-din Barni : Ed. by W.N. Lees etc., BI, Calcutta, 1860-62.

Ta'rikh -i-Yaminī of Al-Utbī : Ed. by Ali, Lahore, Eng. tr. by J. Reynolds, London, 1858.

Tazjiyatu-l-Amsār of Abd-u-lah Wassaf : Extr. trans, HIED, III, 24.

Therigāthā Commentary : Ed. by E. Muller, PTS, London, 1893.

Tilakamañjarī of Dhanapāla : Nirnaya Sagar Press, Bombay, 1903.

Uttararāma-Charita of Bhavabhāti : Edited with Eng. tr. by S. K. Belvalkar, HOS, Text, Poona, 1921. Tr. by C. H. Tawney, Calcutta, 1871.

Varāha Purāṇa : Ed. by H. Sastri, BI, Calcutta, 1893.

Vasiṣṭha Dharmasūtra : Ed. by A. A. Fuhrer, Bombay, 1916.

Vāyu Purāṇa : Ed. by R. Mitra, 2 Vols., BI, Calcutta, 1880-88.

Viddhaśālabhañjkā of Rājaśekhara : Ed. by B. R. Arte, Poona, 1886, tr. by L. H. Gray in JAOS, XXVII, 1-71

Vikramorvaśīyam of Kālidāsa : Eng. tr. by E.B. Cowel, Hertford, 1851.

Vikramāṅkadevacharita of Bilhaṇa : Ed. by G. Buhler, Bombay, Sanskrit Series. No. XIV, 1875.

Vinaya Piṭaka : Eng. tr. by T.W. Rhys Davids and H. Oldenberg, SBE, Oxford, 1881-85.

Viṣṇu Purāṇa : Eng. tr. by H.H. Wilson, 5 Vols., London, 1864-70.

Vṛttaratnākara of Kedāra : Ed. C.A.S. M. Sthavira, 3rd. Ed., Bombay, 1926.

Yoga-sūtras of Bhoja with Rājamārtaṇḍa and other comm., Ed. by D. Shastri, Kashi S. S. Benaras, 1930.

Yuan Chwang : Tr. by T. Watters (On Yuan Chwang's Travels in India), Ed. by T. W. Rhys Davids and S.W. Bushell, 2 Vols., London, 1904-05.

Yuga Purāṇa : Ed. and tr. by K.P. Jayaswal, JBORS, XIV, 397-421.

Yukti- Kalpataru of Bhoja : Ed. by Isvara Chandra Sastri, COS, Calcutta, 1917.

Zain-ul-Akbār of Mahmūd Gardīzī : Ed. by A. Nazim, Berlin, 1928.

B. Modern Works

Agrawal, K.L. : *Vindhya Kshetra ka Aitihasik Bhugol,* Satna, 1987.

Agrawala, V.S. : *Harsacharita Ek Sanskritika Adhyanana,* Patna, 1953.

——— : *India as Known to Panini,* Allahabad, 1953.

Ali, S.M. : *Geography of the Puranas,* New Delhi, 1983.

Aufrecht, S.T. : *Catalogus Catalogorum,* 3 parts, Leipzig, 1895-1903.

Ayyangar, P.T.S. : *Bhojaraja,* Madras, 1931.

Bajpai, K.D. : *The Geographical Encyclopaedia of Ancient and Mediaeval India,* Pt. I, Varanasi, 1967.

——— : *Cultural History of India,* Vol. I (Madhya Pradesh), New Delhi, 1985.

——— : *Sagar through the Ages*, Sagar, 1964.

Banerji, R.D. : *The Haihayas of Tripuri and Their Monuments,* MASI, Calcutta, 1931.

Beal, S. : *Si-yu-ki Buddhist Records of the Western World.* Tr. from the Chinese of Hiuen Tsang, 2 Vols., London, 1906.

Bhandarkar, D.R. : *Carmichael Lectures on the Ancient History of India,* 1918, Calcutta, 1921.

Bhandarkar, D.R and others (Eds.) : *B.C. Law Volume,* Pt. I-II, Poona, 1946.

Bhatia, P. : *The Paramara,* New Delhi, 1970.

Bhattacharya, P.K : *Historical Geography of Madhya Pradesh,* Delhi, 1976.

Bose, N.S. : *History of the Candellas,* Calcutta, 1956.

Chakladar, H.C. : *Social Life in Ancient India,* Calcutta, 1954.

Chakravarty, K. K. (Ed.) : *Vidisha Through the Ages,* Delhi, 1990.

Cunningham, A. : *The Ancient Geography of India,* Varanasi, 1963.

——— : *Bhilsa Topes.* Reprint Ed. Delhi, 1968.

——— : *Archaeological Survey of India Reports,* Vol. I to XXIII. Rep. Ed. Delhi, 1994.

Das, N.C. : *Ancient Geography of Asia Compiled from Valmiki Ramayana,* Krishnanagar, 1896, Rep. 1971.

Dasgupta and De : *History of Sanskrit Literature,*Vol. I, Calcutta University, Calcutta.

Day, U.N. : *Medieval Malwa,* Delhi, 1965.

Deo, J.P.S : *Cultural Profile of South Kosala,* Delhi, 1987.

Dey, N.L. : *Geographical Dictionary of Ancient and Medieval India,* London, 1927.

Dwivedi, H.N. : *Madhya Bharat Ka Itihas,* Gwalior, 1956.

Edgerton, F. (ed. & tr.) : *Vikramacharita* (Vikrama's adventures or thirty-two tales of the throne), Pts. I–II, 1926.

Elliot and Dowson : *History of India as told by its Own Historians,* 8 Vols., London, 1866-77.

Farquhar, J.N. : *An Outline of the Religious Literature of India,* Oxford, 1920.

Fleet, J.F. : *Corpus Inscriptionum Indicarum,* Vol. III, Calcutta, 1889.

Ganguly, D.C. : *History of the Paramara Dynasty,* Dacca, 1933.

Gupta, H.G. : *Betawa,* Bhopal, 1989.

Gupta, P.L. : *Prachin Chhattisgarh,* Raipur, 1973.

Guru, S.D. : *Madhya Pradesh, Videshi Yatriyon Ki Nigah Men,* Bhopal, 1980.

Hultzsch : *Corpus Inscriptionum Indicarum,* Vol. I, Oxford, 1925.

Jain, J.C. : *Life in Ancient India as depicted in the Jain Canons,* Bombay, 1947.

Jain, K.C. : *Malwa Through the Ages,* Delhi, 1972.

——— : *Kalidasa and his times,* Delhi, 1990.

Kane, P.V. : *History of the Dharmasastras,* 4 Vols., Poona, 1930-53.

Keith, A.B. : *History of Sanskrit Literature,*Oxford, 1928.

Khare, M.D. : *Vidisha*, Bhopal, 1985.

Konow, S. : *Corpus Inscriptionum Indicarum,* Vol. II, Calcutta, 1929.

Law, B.C. : *Historical Geography of Ancient India,* Paris, 1954, 2nd ed., 1968.

——— : *Kshatriya Tribes in Ancient India,* Calcutta and Simla, 1923.

——— : *Ancient Mid-Indian Kshatriya Tribes,* Calcutta and Simla, 1924.

——— : *Geographical Aspects of Kalidasa's Works,* Calcutta, 1954.

——— : *Mountains of India,* Calcutta, 1944.

——— : *Rivers of India*, Calcutta, 1944.

——— : *Ujjayini in Ancient Literature,* Gwalior, 1944.

Luard, C.E., and Lele, K.K. : *Paramaras of Dhar and Malwa,* Bombay, 1908.

Macdonell, A.A. : *History of Sanskrit Literature,* London, 1980.

Macdonell, A.A. and Keith, A.B. : *Vedic Index, 2 Vols.,* London, 1912.

Majumdar, R.C. (Ed.) : *The History and Culture of the Indian People:*

Vol. I, *The Vedic Age,* 5th ed., Bombay, 1988.

Vol. II, *The Age of Imperial Unity,* 6th ed., Bombay, 1990.

Vol. III, *The Classical Age,* 4th ed., Bombay, 1988.

Vol. IV, *The Age of Imperial Kanauj,* 3rd. ed., Bombay, 1984.

Vol. V, *The Struggle for Empire,* 4th ed., Bombay, 1989.

The Classical Accounts of India, Calcutta, 1960.

Majumdar, R.C. and Altekar, A.S. (Eds.) : *The Vakataka Gupta Age,* Vol. VI, Lahore, 1946.

Majumdar, S.N. : *Mc Crindle's Ancient India as described by Ptolemy,* 1927.

Malalasekera, G.P. : *Dictionary of Pali Proper Names,* Vol. I, London, 1960.

Mark, Collins : *The Geographical Data of the Raghuvaṁsa and Daśakumāra-Carita,* Leipzig, 1907.

Mc Crindle, J.W. : *Ancient India as described in Classical Literature,* Westminster, 1901.

——— : *Ancient India as described by Ptolemy*. Ed. by S.N. Majumdar, Calcutta, 1927.

——— : *Ancient India as described by Megasthenes and Arrian,* Calcutta, Bombay, London,1877.

Mehta, M.L. : *Dasapura Janpada Sanskriti,* Mandsaur, 1962.

Mirashi, V.V. (Ed.) : *Corpus Inscriptionum Indicarum, Vols.* IV-V, Ootacumund, 1955, 1963.

——— : *Kalachuri Naresh Aur Unka Kal,* Bhopal, Samvat 2022.

Mishra, B.N. : *Sanchi,* Bhopal, 1982.

Mishra, D.P. : *The Search for Lanka,* Delhi, 1985.

Mishra, K.C. : *Chandel Aur Unka Rajatva Kal,* Varanasi, Samvat 2011.

Mishra, R.N. : *Bharhut,* Bhopal, 1971.

Mitra, S.K. : *The Early Rulers of Khajuraho,* Calcutta, 1958.

Mittal, A.C. : *The Inscriptions of the Paramaras,* Ahmedabad, 1979.

Motichandra : *Sarthavaha,* Patna, 1953.

——— : *Geographical and Economic Studies of the Mahabharata,* Lucknow, 1945.

Narain, A.K. : *The Indo-Greeks,* Oxford, 1957.

Nema, S.R. : *Political History of the Somavamsi Kings of South Kosala and Orissa,* New Delhi, 1978.

Pandey, R.B. : *Vikramaditya of Ujjayini,* Banaras, 1951.

Pargiter, F.E. : *The Purana Text of the Dynasties of the Kali Age,* Indian Reprint, 1962.

——— : *Ancient Indian Historical Traditions,* London, 1922.

Pradhan, S.N. : *Chronology of Ancient India.*

Puri, B.N. : *India in the time of Patanjali,* Bombay, 1957.

——— : *The Gurjara Pratiharas,* Bombay, 1957.

——— : *Cities of Ancient India,* Delhi, 1966.

Raghavan, P. : *Sagar Virasat Aur Vikas,* Delhi, 1992.

Raizada, A. (Ed). : *Art, Archaeology and History of Ratlam,* Bhopal, 1992.

Ray, H.C. : *Dynastic History of Northern India,* 2 Vols., Calcutta, 1931 and 1936.

Raychaudhury, H.C. : *Political History of Ancient India,* 6th ed., Calcutta, 1953.

——— : *Studies in Indian Antiquities,* Calcutta, 1958.

Ray, N.R. (Ed.) : *Sources of the History of India,* Vol. VI, Calcutta, 1989.

Reu, B.N. : *Raja Bhoja,* Prayaga, 1932.

Saran, P. : *Descriptive Catalogue of Non-Persian Sources of Medieval Indian History,* Bombay, 1965.

Sastri, K.A.N. : *A Comprehensive History of India,* Vol. II, Calcutta, 1957.

——— : *The Cholas,* Madras, 1935, 1963.

——— : *The Age of the Nandas and Mauryas,* Delhi, 1967.

Sen, B.C. : *Studies in the Jatakas,* Calcutta, 1930.

Shah, K.K. : *Ancient Bundelkhand,* Delhi, 1988.

Sharma, S.R. : *Bhoramdeo,* Bhopal, 1989.

Shastri, A.M. : *India as seen in the Brhatsamhita of Varahamihira,* Delhi, 1969.

——— : *Tripuri,* Bhopal, 1971.

Shukla, Hiralal : *Lanka ki Khoj,* Allahabad, 1977.

Singh, M.R. : *Geographical data in the early Puranas—A Critical study,* 1972.

Singh, Rajendra : *Tripuri Ka Itihasa,* Jabalpur, 1939.

Sinha, B.C. : *History of the Sunga Dynasty,* Delhi, 1977.

Sircar, D.C. : *Cosmography and Geography in Early Indian Literature,* Calcutta, 1967.

——— : *Studies in the Geography of Ancient and Mediaeval India,* Delhi, 1990.

——— : *Select Inscriptions,* Calcutta, 1942.

——— : *Ancient Malwa and the Vikramaditya Tradition,* Delhi, 1969.

Sörensen, S. : *Index to the Mahabharata,* London, 1904.

Thakur, V.S. : *Rajim,* Bhopal, 1972.

Tiwari, G.L. : *Bundelkhand Ka Itihasa,* Kasi, V.S. 1990.

Tod, J. : *Annals and Antiquities of Rajasthan,* Ed. by W. Crooke, Oxford, 1920.

Tripathi, B.P. : *Bundelkhand ki Prachinata,* Varanasi, 1965.

Tripathi, R.S. : *History of Kanauj,* Banaras, 1937.

Trivedi, C. B. : *Dasapura,* Bhopal, 1979.

Trivedi H.V. : *Corpus Inscriptionum Indicarum, Vol. VII, Inscriptions of the Paramaras, Chandellas, Kachchhapaghatas and Two Minor Dynasties,* Vol. I-III, Delhi, 1991.

——— : *Catalogue of the Coins of the Naga Kings of Padmavati,* Gwalior, 1957.

Upadhyaya, B.S. : *India in Kalidasa,* Delhi, 1967-68.

Vaidya, C.V. : *Epic India,* Bombay, 1907.

Watters, T. : *On Yuan Chwang's Travels in India,* Ed. by T.W. Rhys Davids and S.W. Bushell, 2 Vols., London, 1904-05.

Winternitz, M. : *A History of Indian Literature,* 3 Vols., 2nd ed., Delhi, 1972.

Reports, Journals and Gazetteers (Relevant Volumes)

Ancient India

Archaeological Survey of India Reports by Cunningham

Annual Reports of Indian Archaeology

Annual Reports of Indian Epigraphy

Annual Administration Report, Archaeological Dept., Gwalior State

Artibus Asiae

Bulletin of the Deccan College Post-Graduate and Research Institute

Bulletin of Ancient Indian History, Culture and Archaeology Department, Sagar University, Sagar

Epigraphia Indica

Indian Archaeology—A Review

Indian Art and Letters

Indian Historical Quarterly

Indian Antiquary

Journal of Indian Museum

Journal of the Bihar & Orissa Research Society

Journal of the Banaras Hindu University

Journal of the M. S. University of Baroda

Journal of the American Oriental Society

Journal of Indian History
Journal of the Epigraphical Society of India
Journal of M.P. Itihasa Parishad
Journal of the Numismatic Society of India
Journal of the Numismatic Society of Madhya Pradesh
Journal of the Academy of Indian Numismatics and Sigilliography
Journal of the Royal Asiatic Society
Journal of the Asiatic Society of Bengal
Journal of the Andhra Historical Society
Journal of the Bombay Br. of the Royal Asiatic Society
Man and Environment
Marg
Memoirs of the Archaeological Survey of India
Nagpur Museum Bulletin
Numismatic Digest
Numismatic Supplent
Puratan
Puratattva
Prachya Pratibha
Science and Culture.

Index

D

Pl.61. Ramban Museum : Gupta coins

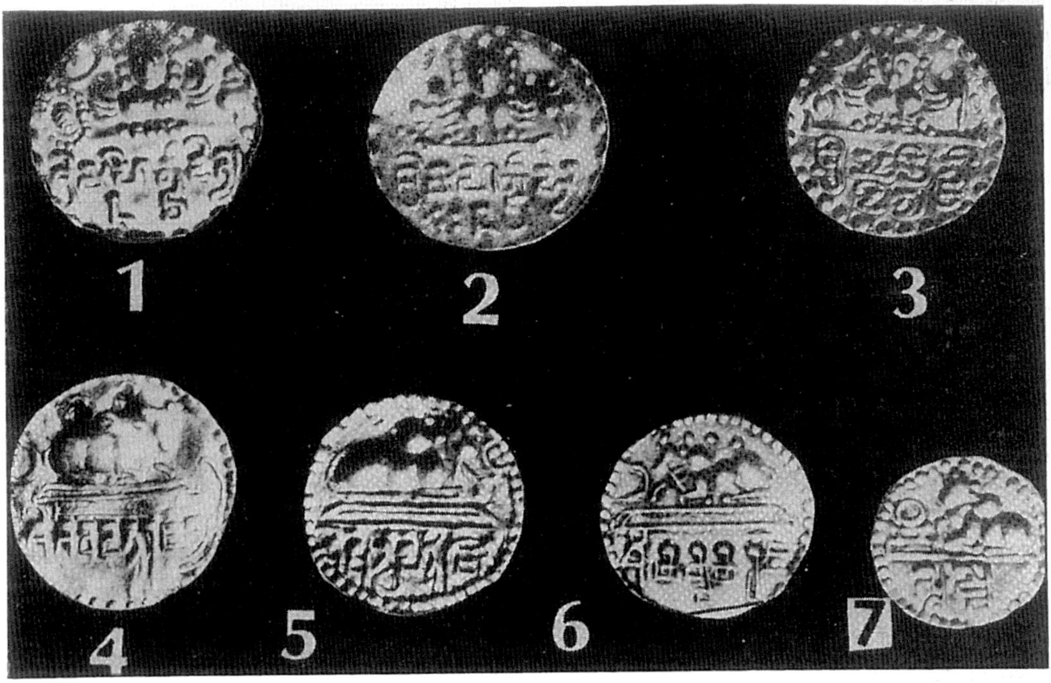

Pl.62. Kulia : Repousse coins of Mahendraditya, Bhavadatta, Arthapati, Nandanaraja and Stambha

1 2 3

Pl.63. Repousse coins of Prasannamatra

Pl.64. Sanchi : General view of Stupa I

Pl.65. Sanchi : General view of Stupa No. 3

Pl.66. Satdhara : Remains of a Stupa

Pl.67. Rajim : Rajiv Lochan temple-
General view from south-west

Pl.68. Sirpur : Lakshman temple

Pl.69. Naresar : Krakotakesvara temple (c. 8th cent. A.D.)

Pl.70. Gwalior : Teli-ka-Mandir

Pl.71. Indor : (Guna) : Siva temple (Gopadri style) (c.8th cent. A.D.)

Pl.72. Batesar : Bhutesvara Mahadeva temple (Kachchhapaghata style Sikhara)

Pl.73. Khajuraho : Javari temple-General view

Pl.74. Khajuraho : Lakshman temple-View from east

Pl.75. Khajuraho : Ghantai temple

Pl.76. Khajuraho : Kandariya Mahadeva temple

Pl.77. Khajuraho : Parsvanatha temple

Pl.78. Khajuraho : Adinatha temple

Pl.79. Khajuraho : Waman temple-General view

Pl.80. Khajuraho : Vishwanath temple

Pl.81. Khajuraho : Varaha and Devi temple from south-west

Pl.82. Khajuraho Devi Jagadamba temple

Pl.83. Chandrehe : Siva temple : Details from south

Pl.84. Bheraghat : Circular cloister of Chaunsatha Yogini temple

Pl.85. Bheraghat : General view of Siva temple

Pl.86. Rannod : Monastery-General view from north (c.10th-11th cent. A.D.)

Pl.87. Kadwaha : Saiva monastery

Pl.88. Pali (Bilaspur) : Siva temple-General view

Pl.89. Janjgir : Vishnu temple

Pl.90. Deo Baloda : Mahadeva temple

Pl.91. Arang : Temple of Bhand Deval-
General view

Pl.92. Chhapari : Bhoram Deo temple

Pl.93. Gyaraspur : Ath-Khamba

Pl.94. Padhaoli : Siva temple-General view

Pl.95. Suhania : Kakanmadh-View from south-east

Pl.96. Gwalior : Sas-Bahu temple

Pl.97. Udaipur : Udayeshwara temple-General view

Pl.98. Vidisha : Bijamandal

Pl.99. Un:Chaubara Dera No. 2-view from south-west

Pl.100. Sanchi : Stupa I, Northern Gate, left side

Pl.101. Sanchi : Stupa I, Details of Northern Gateway

Pl.102. Sanchi : Stupa I, Details of Eastern Gateway

Pl.103. Sanchi : Details of carvings

Pl.104. Besnagar : Heliodoros pillar

Pl.105. Nachna : Chaturmukha Linga

Pl.106. Tala : Image of Siva

Pl.107. Mandsaur : Siva with two lingas

Pl.108. Sirpur : Bronze image of Tara

Pl.109. Deepadih : Salabhanjika

Pl.110. Gyaraspur : Surasundari

Pl.111. Badoh Pathari : Indra

Pl.112. Khajuraho : Harihara (Jardine Museum collection)

Pl.113. Khajuraho : Jaina images from Santinatha temple

Pl.114. Khajuraho : Varaha Avatara (Jardine Museum collection)

Pl.115. Gwalior Museum : Varaha

Pl.116. Shivpuri Museum : Jaina Tirthankara

Pl.117. Bhopal Museum : Siva

Pl.118. Gwalior Museum : Woman in graceful pose

Pl.119. Gwalior Museum : Skanda

Pl.120. Gwalior Museum : Saraswati

Pl.121. Gwalior Museum : Bust of Siva and Parvati from Tumain

Pl.122. Bhanpura : Nandi

Pl.123. Dhubela Museum : Army on march

Pl.124. Bhopal Museum : Tripurantaka Siva

Pl.125. M.G.M. Museum, Raipur : Narasimha from Karitalai

Pl.126. Bheraghat : Yogini Sri Audara in the temple of Chaunsatha Yogini

Pl.127. Arang : Jaina deities in Bhand Deval temple